JAPANESE PRIVATE INTERNATIONAL LAW

This is the leading reference on Japanese private international law in English. The chapters systematically cover the whole of Japanese private international law, not just questions likely to arise in commercial matters, but also in family, succession, cross-border insolvency, intellectual property, competition (antitrust) and environmental disputes. The chapters do not merely cover the traditional conflict of law areas of jurisdiction, applicable law (choice of law) and enforcement. They also look into conflict of law questions arising in arbitration and assess Japanese involvement in the global harmonisation of private international law. In addition to summarising relevant principles and scholarly views, the authors discuss case law whenever possible, identify deficiencies and anticipate difficulties in the existing law. The book thus presents the Japanese conflict of laws through a combination of common and civil law analytical techniques and perspectives, providing readers worldwide with a more profound and comprehensive understanding of the subject.

Volume 5 in the series Studies in Private International Law – Asia

Studies in Private International Law – Asia

Editor: Anselmo Reyes
Advisory Editor: Paul Beaumont

Much has been written about private international law in the EU and the US. Less is known about the conflict of laws in Asia. Thus, little attention has been paid so far to the modernisation of private international law codes and rules that has been taking place over the last decade all over Asia. That trend continues. Now is the time to take stock of those reforms that have already taken place and suggest further improvements for the future.

Published under the celebrated series *Studies in Private International Law*, this monograph sub-series provides a forum for discussion and analysis of private international law in Asia. The series is not solely a survey of jurisdictions for practitioners. Comprising in-depth thematic and country-specific studies, each volume considers the private international law of Asian countries from a variety of perspectives. An underlying assumption is that private international law in different jurisdictions follow broad discernible patterns. Each volume in this sub-series highlights those patterns and discusses how rules in different Asian jurisdictions are either converging with, or diverging from, the patterns identified. Such an analytical framework will assist academics, judges, lawyers and legislators to envisage ways in which laws affecting cross-border relationships can be harmonised across jurisdictions and be made more responsive to the needs of citizens in Asia and elsewhere.

Volume 1: Recognition and Enforcement of Judgments in Civil and Commercial Matters
Edited by Anselmo Reyes

Volume 2: Indonesian Private International Law
Afifah Kusumadara

Volume 3: Chinese Private International Law
Edited by Xiaohong Liu and Zhengyi Zhang

Volume 4: Direct Jurisdiction: Asian Perspectives
Edited by Anselmo Reyes and Wilson Lui

Volume 5: Japanese Private International Law
Kazuaki Nishioka and Yuko Nishitani

Japanese Private International Law

Kazuaki Nishioka
and
Yuko Nishitani

•HART•
OXFORD • LONDON • NEW YORK • NEW DELHI • SYDNEY

HART PUBLISHING

Bloomsbury Publishing Plc

Kemp House, Chawley Park, Cumnor Hill, Oxford, OX2 9PH, UK

1385 Broadway, New York, NY 10018, USA

29 Earlsfort Terrace, Dublin 2, Ireland

HART PUBLISHING, the Hart/Stag logo, BLOOMSBURY and the Diana logo are trademarks of Bloomsbury Publishing Plc

First published in Great Britain 2021

A catalogue record for this book is available from the British Library.

Library of Congress Cataloging-in-Publication data

Names: Nishioka, Kazuaki, author. | Nishitani, Yuko, author.

Title: Japanese private international law / Kazuaki Nishioka and Yuko Nishitani.

Description: Oxford, UK ; New York, NY : Hart Publishing, an imprint of Bloomsbury Publishing, 2021. | Series: Studies in private international law - Asia ; volume 5 | Includes bibliographical references and index.

Identifiers: LCCN 2021033863 (print) | LCCN 2021033864 (ebook) | ISBN 9781509924295 (hardback) | ISBN 9781509924301 (pdf) | ISBN 9781509924318 (Epub)

Subjects: LCSH: Conflict of laws—Japan.

Classification: LCC KNX480 .N57 2021 (print) | LCC KNX480 (ebook) | DDC 340.90952—dc23

LC record available at https://lccn.loc.gov/2021033863

LC ebook record available at https://lccn.loc.gov/2021033864

ISBN: HB: 978-1-50992-429-5
ePDF: 978-1-50992-430-1
ePub: 978-1-50992-431-8

Typeset by Compuscript Ltd, Shannon
Printed and bound in Great Britain by TJ Books Ltd, Padstow, Cornwall

To find out more about our authors and books visit www.hartpublishing.co.uk. Here you will find extracts, author information, details of forthcoming events and the option to sign up for our newsletters.

FOREWORD

This is the third volume in Hart's *Studies in Private International Law: Asia* country series. The previous two books surveyed modern Indonesian and Chinese conflict of law systems. The authors of those books observed that the latter systems are relatively recent developments and so many unanswered questions remain. In contrast, Japan's modern private international law system has been codified since the *Horei* (法例) was enacted by the Meiji government in 1898. It will be apparent from this book that, from then on, Japanese legislators and legal scholars have strived to develop a system that comprehensively and scientifically addresses just about every conceivable situation involving foreign elements likely to come up before the Japanese courts. Even then, in the case of gaps or unforeseen situations, Japanese judges are afforded a degree of discretion in the handling of such matters by means of statutory escape clauses or through resort to natural reason (*jori* 条理). It will also be plain from this book that, despite the passage of over 120 years, there remains a vigorous debate among Japanese scholars as to how numerous private international law questions should be approached, with some commentators strongly espousing one view and others equally forcefully advocating another, often diametrically opposed, opinion. This book has not shied away from diving into controversies and expressing its own view after summarising the differing camps on a particular issue. Thus, this book will likely have the distinction that just about every reader who delves into it will find something (perhaps many things) with which to disagree. If that should transpire, then this book will have fulfilled its task. Private international law norms are not a static body of immutable rules. They constantly evolve as the needs of communities change. That evolution is driven by debate as to how questions of jurisdiction, choice of law, recognition, enforcement and harmonisation should be handled in light of current circumstances. There are few doctrinal answers, only seemingly endless questions.

I hope that I will be forgiven for concluding this Foreword on a personal note. That is because this book has been written by two close friends and I would like to pay tribute to them both. This book is a cooperative effort between Dr Kazuaki Nishioka and Professor Yuko Nishitani. Because of Professor Nishitani's busy schedule, the text was first drafted in its entirety by Dr Nishioka and then passed to Professor Nishitani for comment and revision. Dr Nishioka's involvement in the book is particularly poignant for me as, six years ago, he was the only student who registered for my Doshisha course covering private international law in common law jurisdictions. I have over the succeeding years learned much from him about private international law in Japan and other civil law jurisdictions. *Homines dum docent discunt.* As editor of the series, it fell upon me to be the 'bad cop' and repeatedly urge the authors to stick to agreed deadlines. Nonetheless, as Professor Nishitani wrote in response to one of my emails, while she understood my concern, it was her belief that 'we should deliver a text which accurately reflects the current state of Japanese law'. I think that the book has benefited from the extra time taken and I am grateful to Professor Nishitani for standing up to my editorial pressures.

Anselmo Reyes
Kyoto, 29 April 2021

CONTENTS

LIST OF ABBREVIATIONS

Law Reports

HJ	Hanrei Jiho (Law Cases Reports)
HT	Hanrei Taimuzu (Law Times Reports)
Kagetsu	Katei Saiban Geppo (Monthly Bulletin on Family Courts)
Kaminshu	Kakyu Saibansho Minji Hanreishu (Lower Courts Reports (Civil Cases))
Kinho	Kinyu Homu Jijo (Banking Law Journal)
Kinsho	Kinyu Shoji Hanrei (Financial and Business Law Precedents)
Kominshu	Koto Saibansho Minji Hanreishu (High Courts Reports (Civil Cases))
Minshu	Saiko Saibansho Minji Hanreishu (Supreme Court Reports (Civil Cases))
Rohan	Rodo Hanrei (Labour Law Precedents)
Saiji	Saibansho Jiho (Journal of Courts)
Shinbun	Horitsu Shinbun (Newsletter for Lawyers)
Shumin	Saiko Saibansho Saibanshu Minji (Supreme Court Cases (Civil))

Primary Legal Sources and Abbreviations

AA	Arbitration Act (Act No 138 of 1 August 2003)
ACJJ	Act on Civil Jurisdiction of Japan with respect to a Foreign State, etc (Act No 24 of 24 April 2009)
ACUIC	Act on Currency Units and Issuance of Coins (Act No 42 of 1 June 1987)
AICGS	Act on International Carriage of Goods by Sea (Act No 172 of 1957)
AABC	Act on Assistance Based on Commission by Foreign Courts (Act No 63 of 13 March 1905)
AGRAL	Act on General Rules for Application of Laws (Act No 78 of 21 June 2006)
AIHCAC	Act for Implementation of the Convention on the Civil Aspects of International Child Abduction (Act No 48 of 19 June 2013)

ALAFW	Act on the Law Applicable to the Form of Wills (Act No 100 of 10 June 1964)
ALAOS	Act on the Law Applicable to the Obligation of Support (Act No 84 of 12 June 1986)
ALOPD	Act on Liability for Oil Pollution Damage (Act No 95 of 27 December 1975)
ALSL	Act on Limitation of Shipowner Liability (Act No 94 of 27 December 1975)
APPIL	Asian Principles of Private International Law
ARAFIP	Act on Recognition and Assistance for Foreign Insolvency Proceedings (Act No 129 of 29 November 2000)
ASPCP	Act on Special Provisions Concerning Civil Procedure Attendant upon Implementation of the Convention on Civil Procedure and Another Convention (Act No 115 of 5 June 1970)
AVGC	Act on Voluntary Guardianship Contract (Act No 150 of 8 December 1999)
BA	Bankruptcy Act (Act No 75 of 2 June 2004)
BC	Berne Convention for the Protection of Literary and Artistic Works (Treaty No 4 of 6 March 1975)
BEA	Bills of Exchange Act (Act No 20 of 15 July 1932)
Brussels I	Council Regulation (EC) No 44/2001 of 22 December 2000 on jurisdiction and the recognition and enforcement of judgments in civil and commercial matters [2001] OJ L12/1
Brussels I Recast	Regulation (EU) No 1215/2012 of the European Parliament and of the Council of 12 December 2012 on jurisdiction and the recognition and enforcement of judgments in civil and commercial matters (recast) [2012] OJ L351/1
BIT	Bilateral Investment Treaty
CA	Company Act (Act No 86 of 26 July 2005)
CC	Civil Code (Act No 89 of 27 April 1896)
CCP	Code of Civil Procedure (Act No 109 of 26 June 1996)
CEA	Civil Execution Act (Act No 4 of 30 March 1979)
CHA	Cheques Act (Act No 57 of 29 July 1933)
CIRA	Civil Rehabilitation Act (Act No 225 of 22 December 1999)
CISG	United Nations Convention on Contracts for the International Sales of Goods of 11 April 1980 (Treaty No 8 of 7 July 2008)

CLC	International Convention on Civil Liability for Oil Pollution Damage of 27 November 1992 (Treaty No 18 of 19 September 1995)
CMA	Civil Mediation Act (Act No 222 of 9 June 1951)
CORA	Corporate Reorganisation Act (Act No 154 of 13 December 2002)
CPA	Copyright Law (Act No 48 of 6 May 1970)
CPIUN	Convention on the Privileges and Immunities of the United Nations (Treaty No 12 of 18 April 1963)
CPRA	Civil Provisional Remedies Act (Act No 91 of 22 December 1989)
CPTPP	Comprehensive and Progressive Agreement for Trans-Pacific Partnership
CSC	Convention on Supplementary Compensation for Nuclear Damage of 12 September 1997 (Treaty No 1 of 16 January 2015)
DHC-1999	Preliminary Draft Convention on Jurisdiction and Foreign Judgments in Civil and Commercial Matters adopted by the Special Commission on 30 October 1999
DRCPA	Domestic Relations Case Procedure Act (Act No 52 of 25 May 2011)
EPA	Economic Partnership Agreement
FRA	Family Register Act (Act No 224 of 22 December 1947)
FTA	Free Trade Agreement
FUND 1971	International Convention on the Establishment of an International Fund for Compensation for Oil Pollution Damage of 18 December 1971
FUND 1976	Protocol to the International Convention on the Establishment of an International Fund for Compensation for Oil Pollution Damage
FUND 1992	Protocol of 1992 to the International Convention on the Establishment of an International Fund for Compensation for Oil Pollution Damage of 27 November 1992 (Treaty No 19 of 19 September 1995)
FUND 2003	Protocol of 2003 to the International Convention on the Establishment of an International Fund for Compensation for Oil Pollution Damage (Treaty No 5 of 18 February 2005)
GC	Convention on the Execution of Foreign Arbitral Awards of 26 September 1927 (Treaty No 11 of 18 August 1952) (Geneva Convention)
GP	Protocol on Arbitration Clauses (Treaty No 3 of 3 July 1928) (Geneva Protocol)
HCA	Convention of 5 October 1961 Abolishing the Requirement of Legalisation for Foreign Public Documents (Treaty No 8 of 5 June 1970)
HCAC	Convention of 25 October 1980 on the Civil Aspects of International Child Abduction (Treaty No 2 of 29 January 2014)

HCC	Convention of 30 June 2005 on Choice of Court Agreements (Hague Choice of Court Convention)
HCCH	Hague Conference on Private International Law
HCPC	Convention of 1 March 1954 on Civil Procedure (Treaty No 6 of 5 June 1969)
HCTE	Convention of 18 March 1970 on the Taking of Evidence Abroad in Civil or Commercial Matters
HFTDC	Convention of 5 October 1961 on the Conflicts of Laws Relating to the Form of Testamentary Dispositions (Treaty No 9 of 10 June 1964)
HIRC	Convention of 23 November 2007 on the International Recovery of Child Support and Other Forms of Family Maintenance
HJC	Convention of 2 July 2019 on the Recognition and Enforcement of Foreign Judgments in Civil or Commercial Matters (Hague Judgments Convention)
HMCC	Convention of 24 October 1956 on the Law Applicable to Maintenance Obligations towards Children (Treaty No 8 of 17 August 1977)
HMOC	Convention of 2 October 1973 on the Law Applicable to Maintenance Obligations (Treaty No 3 of 12 June 1986)
Horei	Act on General Rules for Application of Laws (Act No 97 of 7 May 1898)
HPRC	Convention of 19 October 1996 on Jurisdiction, Applicable Law, Recognition, Enforcement and Co-operation in Respect of Parental Responsibility and Measures for the Protection of Children
HREC	Convention of 1 February 1971 on the Recognition and Enforcement of Foreign Judgments in Civil and Commercial Matters
HSC	Convention of 15 November 1965 on the Service Abroad of Judicial and Extrajudicial Documents in Civil or Commercial Matters (Treaty No 7 of 5 June 1970) (Hague Service Convention)
HSEC	Convention of 5 July 2006 on the Law Applicable to Certain Rights in Respect of Securities held with an Intermediary (Hague Securities Convention)
ICSID	Convention on the Settlement of Investment Disputes between States and Nationals of Other States of 18 March 1965 (Treaty No 10 of 25 August 1967) (ICSID Convention)
IPBA	Intellectual Property Basic Act (Act No 122 of 4 December 2002)
IPR	Intellectual property right
ISDS	Investor–State dispute settlement
JC	The Constitution of Japan (Constitution of 3 November 1946)

JCA	Central Authority of Japan
JCAA	Japanese Commercial Arbitration Association
JIDRC	Japan International Dispute Resolution Centre
LLMC-1976	Convention on Limitation of Liability for Maritime Claims of 19 November 1976 (Treaty No 4 of 8 May 2006)
LLMC-1996	Protocol of 1996 to amend the Convention on Limitation of Liability for Maritime claims, 1996
Lugano-1988	Convention on jurisdiction and the enforcement of judgments in civil and commercial matters done at Lugano on 16 September 1988 [1988] OJ L319/9
Lugano-2007	Convention on jurisdiction and the recognition and enforcement of judgments in civil and commercial matters of 30 October 2007 [2007] OJ L339/3
MC	Convention for the Unification of Certain Rules for International Carriage by Air of 28 May 1999 (Montreal Convention)
METI	Ministry of Economy, Trade and Industry
MIT	Multilateral Investment Treaty
MOFA	Ministry of Foreign Affairs
NYC	Convention on the Recognition and Enforcement of Foreign Arbitral Awards of 10 June 1958 (Treaty No 10 of 14 July 1961) (New York Convention)
NIA	Negotiable Instrument Act (Act No 20 of 15 July 1932)
PA	Patent Act (Act No 121 of 13 April 1959)
PC	Paris Convention for the Protection of Industrial Property (Treaty No 2 of 6 March 1975)
PLA	Product Liability Act (Act No 85 of July 1 1994)
PRC	People's Republic of China
PSLA	Personal Status Litigation Act (Act No 109 of 16 July 2003)
RSPCP	Rules on Special Provisions Concerning Civil Procedure Attendant upon Implementation of the Convention on Civil Procedure and Another Convention (Supreme Court Rules No 6 of 7 July 1970)
Rome Convention	Convention on the Law Applicable to Contractual Obligations of 19 June 1980
Rome I	Regulation (EC) No 593/2008 of the European Parliament and of the Council of 17 June 2008 on the law applicable to contractual obligations (Rome I) [2008] OJ L177/6

Rome II	Regulation (EC) No 864/2007 of the European Parliament and of the Council of 11 July 2007 on the law applicable to non-contractual obligations (Rome II) [2007] OJ L199/40
SPIL	Swiss Private International Law (Bundesgesetz über das Internationale Privatrecht, SR 291)
TA	Trust Act (Act No 108 of 15 December 2006)
UCP	Uniform Customs and Practice for Documentary Credits
UCPA	Unfair Competition Prevention Act (No 47 of 19 May 1933)
UNCJI	United Nations Convention on Jurisdictional Immunities of States and Their Property of 2 December 2004
UNCITRAL	United Nations Commission on International Trade Law
UNIDROIT	International Institution for the Unification of Private Law
VCCR	Vienna Convention on Consular Relations of 24 April 1963 (Treaty No 14 of 11 October 1983)
VCDR	Vienna Convention on Diplomatic Relations of 18 April 1961 (Treaty No 14 of 26 June 1964)
WC	Convention for the unification of Certain rules Relating to International Carriage by Air of 12 October 1929 (Warsaw Convention) (Treaty No 17 of 18 August 1953)

Journals

IPRax	Praxis des Internationalen Private- und Verfahrensrechts
JAIL	Japanese Annual of International Law
JJL	Journal of Japanese Law/Zeitschrift für Japanisches Recht
JPIL	Journal of Private International Law
JYIL	Japanese Yearbook of International Law
NBL	New Business Law
RIW	Recht der Internationalen Wirtschaftsrecht
YJPIL	Yearbook of Japanese Private International Law
YPIL	Yearbook of Private International Law

TABLE OF CASES

Supreme Court and Great Court of Cassation

High Courts

District Courts

Family Courts

TABLE OF PRIMARY JAPANESE PIL LEGAL SOURCES

National PIL Rules

International Arrangements

1

Introduction

I. The Subject Matter of Japanese Private International Law

Private international law in Japan (*Kokusai Shiho*国際私法)[1] is understood to deal with cross-border private legal relationships, typically covering three matters: (a) international (adjudicative) jurisdiction (whether a court can hear and determine the merits of a case), (b) applicable law or governing law (what law the court should apply to determine the merits of a case), and (c) recognition and enforcement of foreign judgments (whether and under what conditions a foreign judgment can be recognised and enforced in another state, here in Japan). However, nowadays most private international law textbooks and materials in Japan also cover (d) international commercial arbitration. It can thus be said that it is now generally accepted that the subject matters of private international law in Japan cover these four areas.[2] This book will accordingly consider these four topics.

II. Sources of Private International Law

There are four sources of Japanese private international law: (a) national legislation; (b) international agreements or conventions; (c) case law or court decisions; (d) *jori* and scholarly writings.

A. Major National Legislation

Choice of law issues are mainly dealt with in the Act on General Rules for Application of Laws (AGRAL), the Act on the Law Applicable to Maintenance Obligation (ALAOS), the Act on the Law Applicable to the Forms of Wills (ALAFW), the Negotiable Instrument Act (NIA) articles 88–94, and the Cheques Act (CHA) articles 76–81. International jurisdiction is principally covered by three statutes. For civil and commercial matters, the Code of Civil Procedure (CCP) applies, and for personal status and family matters, the Personal Status Litigation Act (PSLA) and the Domestic Relations Case Procedure Act (DRCPA) apply. Recognition and enforcement of foreign judgments is regulated as to recognition

[1] In contrast to 'private international law in a broad sense', choice of law rules are sometimes referred to as 'private international in a narrow sense'. To be clear, the expression 'private international law in a narrow sense' will be used here to mean 'choice of law rules' or 'conflicts rules'.

[2] Matters (b), (c) and (d) are part of 'international civil procedure law' which also covers the service of documents overseas, international rules of evidence and cross-border insolvency.

by CCP, PSLA and DRCPA and as to enforcement by the Civil Execution Act (CEA). International arbitration is regulated by the Arbitration Act (AA).

B. International Agreements or Conventions

Japan has so far ratified seven conventions adopted by the Hague Conference on Private International Law (HCCH): (a) the Convention of 1 March 1954 on Civil Procedure (HCPC) (implemented domestically by the Act on Special Provisions Concerning Civil Procedure Attendant upon Implementation of the Convention on Civil Procedure and Another Convention: ASPCP); (b) the Convention of 24 October 1956 on the Law Applicable to Maintenance Obligations towards Children (HMCC); (c) the Convention of 5 October 1961 on the Conflicts of Laws Relating to the Form of Testamentary Dispositions (HFTDC) (implemented domestically by the Act on the Law Applicable to the Form of Wills: ALAFW); (d) the Convention of 5 October 1961 Abolishing the Requirement of Legalisation for Foreign Public Documents (HAC); (e) the Convention of 15 November 1965 on the Service Abroad of Judicial and Extrajudicial Documents in Civil or Commercial Matters (HSC) (implemented domestically by the Act on Special Provisions Concerning Civil Procedure Attendant upon Implementation of the Convention on Civil Procedure and Another Convention: ASPCP); (f) Convention of 2 October 1973 of the Law Applicable to Maintenance Obligations (HMOC); and (g) the Convention of 25 October 1980 on the Civil Aspects of International Child Abduction (HCAC) (implemented domestically by the Act on Implementation of Convention on the Civil Aspects of International Child Abduction: AIHCAC).

In addition, Japan has joined several international arrangements or conventions in specific areas that touch upon choice of law, international jurisdiction, or recognition and enforcement of foreign judgments. In particular, Japan is party to the Convention for the Unification of Certain Rules Relating to International Carriage by Air of 12 October 1929 and its protocols (the Warsaw Convention: WC) (international jurisdiction); the Convention Relating to the Status of Refugees of 28 July 1951 (CRSR) (choice of law); the Convention on Supplementary Compensation for Nuclear Damage of 12 September 1997 (CSC) (choice of law, international jurisdiction, and recognition and enforcement); the Convention for the Unification of Certain Rules for International Carriage by Air of 28 May 1999 (the Montreal Convention: MC) (international jurisdiction); the UN Convention on Jurisdictional Immunities of States and Their Property of 2 December 2004 (UNCJI) (international jurisdiction); the International Convention on Civil Liability for Oil Pollution Damage of 29 November 1969 (CLC) (international jurisdiction and recognition and enforcement); and the International Convention on the Establishment of an International Fund for Compensation for Oil Pollution Damage of 18 December 1971, superseded by the Protocol of 27 November 1992 and supplemented by the Protocol of 16 May 2003 (FUND 1992 and FUND 2003) (international jurisdiction and recognition and enforcement).

In respect of international arbitration, Japan is party to the Convention on the Execution of Foreign Arbitral Awards of 26 September 1927 (the Geneva Convention: GC);[3] the Convention on the Recognition and Enforcement of Foreign Arbitral Awards of

[3] By NYC article 7(2), the GC ceased to have effect as between Japan and contracting states to the GC upon the latter joining NYC.

10 June 1958 (the New York Convention: NYC); and the Convention on the Settlement of Investment Disputes between States and Nationals of Other States of 18 March 1965 (the ICSID Convention: ICSID). There are also bilateral treaties that regulate the recognition and enforcement of arbitral awards with a number of countries, including the US, the UK, the PRC, Pakistan, Peru, El Salvador, Argentina, Romania, Poland, Bulgaria, and Hungary (see chapter five, section E).

C. Case Law or Court Decisions

The Japanese legal system is a unique mixture of Western elements and East-Asian ethics and customs. From the second half of the nineteenth century, following the Meiji Restoration in 1868, the Japanese legal system has drawn heavily from French and German models. After the Second World War, however, many fundamental reforms were made under the strong influence of the US. That being said, Japan is generally regarded as belonging to the civil law family, statutes being the main source of law. Although court decisions are not regarded as law per se in Japan, they play an important role in providing non-binding, but persuasive guidelines on how future similar cases should be decided.

D. *Jori* and Scholarly Writing

When there exists no explicit rule or previous court decision on an issue, the court seised has to rely on *jori* to determine a case.[4] *Jori* can be defined as 'general principles of law', 'principles of reason', *naturalis ratio*, 'reasonableness', or the 'rule of reason'.[5] For instance, AGRAL does not contain provisions on agency, debt assumption and set-off. To deal with legal issues relating to those matters, a court needs to apply *jori*. In other words, *jori* has the function of filling lacunae in Japanese law. In actuality, scholarly writing often cites cases and theories from foreign jurisdictions such as the UK, the US, the EU, Germany, France, Italy and Switzerland and are considered within the framework of *jori* to be applied in a given case. Thus, scholarly writing (doctrine) can function as normative sources for the resolution of legal issues. Judges, however, do not usually cite doctrinal works in their decisions or judgments.

III. History of Private International Law in Japan

The history of Japanese private international law dates back to the mid-nineteenth century.[6] After the Meiji Restoration, an early priority of the new government was to abolish the

[4] Yoshiaki Sakurada, *Kokusai Shiho* (*Private International Law*), 7th edn (Yuhikaku, 2020) 25 (Sakurada); Takao Sawaki and Masato Dogauchi, *Kokusai Shiho Nyumon* (*Introduction to Private International Law*), 8th edn (Yuhikaku, 2018) 11 (Sawaki=Dogauchi).

[5] *Jori* is regarded as secondary law in Japan. On *jori* generally, see Yoshiyuki Noda, *Introduction to Japanese Law* (University of Tokyo Press, 1976) 222.

[6] See Masato Dogauchi, 'Historical Development of Japanese Private International Law' in Jürgen Basedow et al (eds), *Japanese and European Private International Law in Comparative Perspective* (Mohr Siebeck, 2008) 23; Yoshiaki Sakurada, 'The Origin and Evolution of Private International Law in Japan' (2013) 56 *JYIL* 164.

unequal treaties that Japan had been forced to conclude with a number of foreign countries since 1858 (such as the US, the UK, France and Russia). One purpose of those treaties had been to provide foreigners in Japan with legal protection by establishing consular jurisdictions. This was done because the Japanese legal system in those days was feudal in character and deemed to be underdeveloped by the US and European countries. To show its capability to handle cross-border cases pursuant to the rule of law, Japan modernised its legal system by modelling reforms of the same after the systems in leading states of that time. As part of this endeavour, the codification of private international law (choice of law rules) was deemed necessary, much as the codification of civil law and civil procedure. This can be regarded as the starting point of Japanese private international law.

In 1898, Japan enacted its first Private International Law (*Horei*) and thereby caught up with Western states in terms of developing the infrastructure of its legal system. The *Horei* had originally been drafted in 1890 based on French, Italian and Belgian laws at the time (the Former *Horei*). This law, however, never came into force. Eight years later, Japan enacted a revised Private International Law, largely modelled after the original drafts of the German Private International Law (EGBGB) prepared by Professor Albert Gebhard.

After its enactment, the *Horei* was significantly modernised and modified by two major amendments in 1989 and 2006.[7] In the latter amendment, Japan changed the name of the statute from *Horei* to *Ho no tekiyou ni kansuru tsuu soku hou* (Act on General Rules for Application of Laws (AGRAL)). Since then, AGRAL has been the primary source of private international law (choice of law rules) in Japan.

With regard to civil procedure, there were no provisions dealing with international (direct) jurisdiction before 2012 except for international conventions limited to particular issues. In the absence of written rules, Japanese courts decided jurisdictional issues for a long time based on the notion of *jori*. In 2011, CCP was eventually amended and black-letter rules for international (direct) jurisdiction in civil and commercial matters were introduced for the first time (articles 3.2–3.11). The new rules entered into force in 2012. As for international jurisdiction in matters of civil status and family, new provisions were adopted and promulgated on 25 April 2018.

Prior to their amendment in 1979, rules on recognition and enforcement of civil judgments were set out together in CCP (articles 200, 514 and 515). In 1979 the rules were separated with the transfer of enforcement rules from CCP to CEA. Today, rules on recognition are found in CCP article 118, subject to minor amendments on recognition as part of the complete revision of CCP in 1996, while rules on enforcement are in CEA article 24.

International arbitration in Japan goes back at least to the nineteenth century. The arbitration system was first established by the CCP of 1890. Since then, Japan has developed special laws dealing with arbitration. In 2003, the Arbitration Act was enacted, grounded primarily on the 1985 UNCITRAL Model Law. International arbitration in Japan is

[7] On the 2006 amendment, see Hironori Wanami, 'Background and Outline of the Modernization of Japanese Private International Law' in Jürgen Basedow et al (eds), *Japanese and European Private International Law in Comparative Perspective* (Mohr Siebeck, 2008) 61; see also Yuko Nishitani, 'Die Reform des internationalen Privatrechts in Japan' (2007) *IPRax* 552; Koji Takahashi, 'A Major Reform of Japanese Private International Law' (2006) 2 *JPIL* 311; Yasuhiro Okuda, 'Reform of Japan's Private International Law: Act on the General Rules of the Application of Laws' (2006) 8 *YPIL* 145; Yoshiaki Sakurada and Ewa Schwittek, 'Die Reform des japanischen internationalen Privatrechts' (2012) 76 *Rabels Zeitschrift für ausländisches und internationales Privatrecht* 86.

thus similar with the regimes in other countries which have adopted the UNCITRAL Model Law. In January 2020, the Japanese government set up a research group to assess whether it was necessary to amend or update the Japanese arbitration and mediation system in light of the 2006 Amendments of the UNCITRAL Model Law and the 2018 Singapore Convention on Mediation. The Legislative Sub-Committee on Arbitration Law was established in October 2020 and statutory amendments are expected to be completed soon.

IV. Preliminary Matters

A. Uniform Substantive Laws

With regard to the application of Japanese private international law in a narrow sense or choice of law rules, the first question to be considered is whether areas governed by uniform substantive law exist, because such law would eliminate the possibility of conflicts of laws. That is, uniform substantive law would render reference to choice of law rules superfluous. Unlike other jurisdictions (such as Germany), however, Japan has acceded to relatively few international treaties for the unification of private law.[8] Consequently, choice of law rules remain highly relevant and are often applied to resolve conflict of laws. The most important uniform law is the UN Convention on Contracts for the International Sale of Goods (CISG) of 11 April 1980. Japan only acceded to CISG as the seventy-first Member State on 1 July 2008. CISG applies directly in Japan, without the need for incorporation into domestic law, for sale of goods contracts that fall within its scope (CISG article 1(1)(a) and (b)). The majority of the sales contracts that Japanese companies conclude with foreign business partners will be subject to CISG in principle, because the most important trading partners of Japanese companies in sales contracts are companies from the PRC (Mainland China), the US, the Republic of Korea, Taiwan, Hong Kong, Thailand, Singapore, Germany and Australia. These jurisdictions (with the exception of Taiwan and Hong Kong) are all CISG states. Nevertheless, most contracting parties in Japan have so far generally excluded the application of CISG pursuant to CISG article 6.[9]

The legal issues relating to bills of exchange and cheques are subject to the 1930 Geneva Uniform Bill of Exchange Convention and the 1930 Cheque Convention. Japan implemented both instruments into the Negotiable Instrument Act (NIA) and the Cheques Act (CHA) respectively. The two statutes contain their own choice of law rules for cross-border bill of exchange and cheque transactions (NIA articles 88–94 and CHA articles 76–81).

In the area of maritime transport law, Japan has ratified the International Convention for the Unification of Certain Rules of Law Relating to Bills of Lading (the Hague Rules)

[8] For an analysis of Japan's attitude and strategy on uniform substantive law, see Hiroo Sono, 'Going Forward with Uniform Private Law Treaties: A Study in Japan's Behavioral Pattern' (2017) 60 *JYIL* 10; Tomotaka Fujita, 'When Does Japan Not Conclude Uniform Private Law Conventions?' (2017) 60 *JYIL* 59.

[9] There are only a few cases in which Japanese courts have applied or mentioned CISG. For instance, Judgment of Tokyo District Court, 18 July 2012, HJ 2198, 73; Judgment of Tokyo High Court, 29 March 2017, 2017WLJPCA03296012; Judgment of Tokyo District Court, 3 June 2019, 2019WLJPCA06038003.

and implemented the same domestically by the Act on International Carriage of Goods by Sea of 1957 (AICGS). AICGS was amended in 1992 through the ratification of the 1979 Protocol (the Hague–Visby Rules). Japan has also ratified the two Brussels Conventions, that is, the International Convention for the Unification of Certain Rules of Law with Respect to Collisions between Vessels and the International Convention for the Unification of Certain Rules of Law Respecting Assistance and Salvage at Sea.[10] Japan has also acceded to the International Convention on Civil Liability for Oil Pollution Damage of 1969[11] and its 1976 Protocol and 1992 Protocol of Amendment. Finally, Japan has ratified the International Convention relating to the Limitation of the Liability of Owners of Sea-Going Ships[12] and acceded to the Convention on Limitation of Liability for Maritime Claims[13] and its 1996 Protocol (the Protocol of 1996 to Amend the Convention on Limitation of Liability for Maritime Claims). On air transportation, Japan has acceded to the 1929 Convention for the unification of Certain rules Relating to International Carriage by Air of 12 October 1929 (the Warsaw Convention: WC), along with the Hague Protocol of 1955 (Protocol to Amend the Convention for the Unification of Certain Rules Relating to International Carriage by Air) and the Montreal Additional Protocol No 4 (Additional Protocol No 4 to Amend the Convention for the Unification of Certain Rules Relating to International Carriage by Air). The 1999 Convention for the Unification of Certain Rules for International Carriage by Air (the Montreal Convention: MC) has also been adopted.

The requirements for applying these conventions differ from one to another. AICGS is, according to the prevailing view, not directly applicable, but only applicable if the matter in question is subject to Japanese law and falls within the scope of AICGS article 1.[14] In contrast, WC and MC are directly applicable if the matter falls within their scope of application.[15] However, both WC and MC only standardise the law on certain issues (such as those relating to international jurisdiction, the liability requirements for the air carrier and the maximum amount of compensation) and leave open other issues (such as the scope and content of compensation and who is entitled to claim the same). The gaps in the law are, according to the prevailing view, to be filled by the law called for under the choice of law rules of the forum state.[16]

[10] Japan also ratified the 1957 International Convention on the Limitation of the Liability of Owners of Ships on 1 March 1976, but it denounced the instrument on 19 May 1983.

[11] This Convention, together with the International Convention on the Establishment of an International Fund for Compensation for Oil Pollution Damage of 18 December 1971 (FUND 1971) has been implemented by the Act on Liability for Oil Pollution Damage (ALOPD). FUND 1971 was amended by the London Protocol of 19 November 1976 (which entered into force on 22 November 1994 and to which Japan acceded on 24 August 1994) and by the 1976 Protocol to the International Convention on the Establishment of an International Fund for Compensation for Oil Pollution Damage (FUND 1976), the 1992 Protocol to the International Convention on the Establishment of an International Fund for Compensation for Oil Pollution Damage (FUND 1992), and the 2003 Protocol to the International Convention on the Establishment of an International Fund for Compensation for Oil pollution Damage (FUND 2003).

[12] This Convention was implemented by the Act on Limitation of Shipowner Liability (ALSL).

[13] This Convention was implemented by ALSL.

[14] Akira Takakuwa, *Shinban – Kokusai Shotorihiki Ho* (*Law of Cross-border Business Transactions [New Edition]*) (Toshindo, 2019) 115–16. Also Judgment of Tokyo District Court, 20 June 1964, HJ 382, 42; Judgment of Tokyo High Court, 24 February 1969, *Kominshu* 22(1), 80.

[15] Takakuwa (n 14) 155–56.

[16] Yuko Nishitani, 'Das Warschauer Abkommen und die Bestimmung des anwendbaren Rechts – Urteil des DG Tokyo vom 25.9.2000' (2002) 13 *JJL* 269.

B. Basics of Japanese Choice of Law Rules

The task of choice of law rules is to determine the law applicable to a cross-border private law relationship. The basic principle of Japanese choice of law rules is the reference to the law of the state that is most closely connected with the legal relationship concerned. Geared towards the closest connection to find the most appropriate law to govern the legal relationship in question, the Japanese choice of law rules aim to realise international harmony of decisions. For this purpose, AGRAL assumes the equality of domestic law and foreign law and defines connecting factors according to the respective type of legal relationship (for connecting factors, see section V). For example, the law applicable to a contract is primarily based on the intent of the contracting parties ('party autonomy', AGRAL article 7) and the law applicable to a tort is based on the place of the tort (*lex loci delicti*, AGRAL article 17).

If a country consists of several territorial units which constitute separate legal systems (such as the US, the UK and the PRC), the applicable choice of law rule refers to the legal system of a particular state or province within the country, insofar as the connecting factor indicates a specific place. For instance, when it comes to determining the validity of a purported transfer of the ownership of a property located in San Francisco, AGRAL article 13(2) as the operative choice of law rule stipulates that the law of the place in which the property is situates (*lex situs*) should be applied. The rule means that the question of validity of the transfer should be decided by reference to the law of the state of California and not to US federal law. Only when the law of nationality of a person belonging to such a multi-unit state is designated in family matters, will AGRAL provide fallback rules to specify which state law or province law ought to apply to the case at hand.

As a matter of principle, the law governing an issue is solely determined by the connecting factor specified in the relevant choice of law rule, without prior reference to the content of the substantive body of law. In principle, Japanese choice of law rules follow the traditional method of conflict of laws which originates from Savigny and which is likewise characteristic of most civil law jurisdictions. The influence of US 'revolutionary' conflict of laws theories, which orient the application of law according to governmental interests and determine applicable law flexibly from case to case, is partly also noticeable under Japanese choice of law rules, but only in the form of alternative connecting factors (AGRAL articles 28 and 20 and ALAFW article 2), the closest connection test (AGRAL article 8) and an escape clause (AGRAL articles 15 and 20).

Although there seems to be a consensus on the subject matter of private international law (see section I), there is still debate concerning under what circumstances the court should apply choice of law rules to determine the law applicable to the merits of the case at hand. In other words, what is the nature of choice of law rules? According to the prevailing view, a choice of law rule must be applied only to cases that have at least one cross-border element (such as a transaction between a Japanese and a Swiss company or a marriage between a Japanese and a Swiss national).[17] On the other hand, the minority opinion is that choice of law rules are general rules for the application of laws and should therefore apply in all situations.[18] According to this latter view, choice of law rules apply even in a purely

[17] Sakurada, *Kokusai Shiho* (*Private International Law*) (n 4) 27.
[18] Sawaki=Dogauchi (n 4) 6–7.

domestic case and Japanese law is, of course, designated as the applicable law by an operative choice of law rule.

C. Characterisation

To designate the law applicable to a case, one must first clarify what kind of legal relationship (eg, contract, tort, marriage) is involved. For instance, when the issue concerns the material validity of a contract, the legal relationship in question is 'characterised' as contract, so AGRAL articles 7–9 will apply. When, on the other hand, the formal validity of a contract is at issue, the legal relationship in question is 'characterised' as formality of a juridical act, so AGRAL article 10 will apply. 'Characterisation' is thus a prerequisite for determining the applicable choice of law rules.

Although there exists no provision regulating how characterisation must be carried out, it is now generally recognised that its criteria should exclusively be inferred from Japanese private international law, not from Japanese or foreign substantive law.[19] While, for instance, product liability is, at the substantive level, governed by the Product Liability Act (PLA) and the concept of a 'product' under PLA article 2 only extends to a 'movable which is manufactured or processed', the term 'product' in AGRAL article 18 covers not only such movables, but also unprocessed natural products.[20]

As to the controversial question of whether concurrent tortious claims for damages arising out of contractual obligations should be treated separately at the choice of law level, the legislature has expressed its position in favour of an independent characterisation as tort.[21] Nonetheless, while the operative choice of law rule would generally designate the *lex loci delicti* for tort (AGRAL article 17), a tortious claim arising out of contractual obligations may be subject to an ancillary reference to the law governing the contract (AGRAL article 20), with a view to regulating the concurrent tortious and contractual claims by one and the same law.

Insofar as no clear criteria for characterisation can be discerned from the text of AGRAL, resort may be made to a teleological interpretation. This means that the legislative reasoning and purpose of the potentially relevant conflicts rules, the competing interests involved and the AGRAL system as a whole must be taken into account. Additionally, comparative studies as to how characterisation is carried out in other jurisdictions may offer helpful and much needed guidance, as well as lead to a harmony of approaches across borders.[22]

D. Types of Japanese Choice of Law Rules

Once characterised, the legal issue at hand is referred to the governing law through a preordained connecting factor in a choice of law rule. Typically, two types of choice of law rules

[19] Sakurada, *Kokusai Shiho* (*Private International Law*) (n 4) 77; Sawaki=Dogauchi (n 4) 20.
[20] *Hosoku Setsumei* (AGRAL) 197.
[21] *Hosoku Setsumei* (AGRAL) 187.
[22] Sakurada, *Kokusai Shiho* (*Private International Law*) (n 4) 79.

are employed in Japanese private international law: bilateral (or all-sided) or unilateral (or one-sided) choice of law rules.

If a choice of law rule is supposed to designate both Japanese law and foreign law, such rule is called bilateral or all-sided. Examples are AGRAL article 13 (rights *in rem*), article 17 (tort), article 24 (celebration of marriage) and article 36 (inheritance). In contrast, a unilateral or one-sided choice of law rule only provides for the application of domestic law (here, Japanese law). Examples are AGRAL article 5 (ruling for the commencement of adult guardianship, etc) and article 6 (adjudication of disappearance). Given the spirit of private international law (ie, the equality of domestic law and foreign law), bilateral choice of law rules certainly conform better with the expectations of justice at the choice of law level. Most Japanese choice of law rules under AGRAL and other statutes, therefore, are grounded on such rules. Unilateral rules are the exception. These unilateral rules are normally used where the Japanese legislator intends to carry through legal values of Japanese laws or where the legislator has decided to spare domestic (Japanese) authorities from the burden of having to determine and apply foreign law.

E. Types of Reference

The most basic form of choice of law rules contains just one connecting factor and refers a case to the whole legal order of the state to which that connecting factor indicates. AGRAL article 36 is a typical example. According to that provision, 'inheritance shall be governed by the national law of the deceased'. The connecting factor in respect of all issues of inheritance (eg, commencement, eligibility, acceptance or waiver of inheritance, rights and obligations arising out of inheritance, administration of assets etc) is the nationality of the deceased, so that the entire questions about inheritance from the deceased will be determined in accordance with that law.

Choice of law rules in Japan have also adopted five other types of reference. The first is 'alternative reference'. A choice of law rule may set out several possible connecting factors. The selection of the appropriate connecting factor from among the options will depend on the issue in question. For instance, AGRAL article 10(1) provides that 'the formalities for a juridical act shall be governed by the law applicable to the formation of the act' and article 10(2) further stipulates that 'notwithstanding the preceding paragraph, formalities that comply with the law of the place where an act was done shall be valid'. Article 10(2) provides an alternative connecting factor to promote a particular outcome, ie, the formal validity of a juridical act (*lex validitatis*). Article 10(2) increases the likelihood that a juristic act will be found formally valid by setting forth several eligible laws to be selected to validate the juristic act. The Act on the Law Applicable to the Form of Wills (ALAFW) article 2 is a similar type of reference. It stipulates that:

> A will shall be valid in terms of form if its form complies with any of the following laws: (i) the law of the place where the act was undertaken; (ii) the law of the country of which the testator had nationality, either at the time he/she made the will or at the time of his/her death; (iii) the law of the place where the testator had domicile, either at the time he/she made the will or at the time of his/her death; (iv) the law of the place where the testator had habitual residence, either at the time he/she made the will or at the time of his/her death; or (v) in the case of a will concerning real property, the law of the place where the real property is located.

This choice of law rule with the five alternative connecting factors is intended to ensure that, as much as possible, the will is found to be formally valid (*favor testamenti*). So long as the will is formally valid under at least one of the five options stipulated, then it will be treated as formally valid.

The second is the 'cumulative reference'. A choice of law rule provides for multiple connecting factors that apply cumulatively and not alternatively. As a result, it is necessary that the requirements of all of the laws identified are satisfied. For instance, according to AGRAL article 22(1):

> [i]n the case where a tort shall be governed by foreign law, if facts to which the foreign law should be applied do not constitute a tort under Japanese law, no claim under the foreign law may be made for damages or any other remedies.

Thus, the question whether an act constitutes an actionable tort must be assessed by reference to both the applicable foreign law and Japanese law. In other words, unless the act is tortious in nature under both the applicable foreign law and Japanese law, it will not be actionable (the 'double actionability rule').

The third is a 'cascading reference'. A choice of law rule may contain several connecting factors in a cascading system, examining a series of connecting factors shared by several persons step by step. For instance, AGRAL article 25 on the effect of marriage provides:

> The effect of a marriage shall be governed by the national law of the husband and wife if their national law is the same or, where that is not the case, by the law of the habitual residence of the husband and wife if their law of habitual residence is the same or, where neither of these is the case, by the law of the place most closely connected with the husband and wife.

This cascade of options is intended to achieve the equality of spouses and, at the same time, preserve the fundamental principle of Japanese choice of law rules, that is, reference to the law of the state most closely connected with the legal relationship at hand. One must apply the listed connecting factors in the stipulated sequence. If the first factor is not possible, then one proceeds to the second and so forth in the order set out in the choice of law rule until one finds a factor that is applicable.

The fourth is 'accessory reference'. A choice of law rule may refer a case to the law that is applicable to a related legal relationship. For instance, AGRAL article 20 on tort adopts an accessory reference approach, where a tortious claim arises by breaching contractual obligations between the parties. In such a case, the law applicable to the tort is determined in principle by referring to the law governing the underlying contract. The choice of law rule in AGRAL article 20 operates within the framework of an escape clause. The provision states:

> Notwithstanding the preceding three articles, the existence and effect of a claim arising from a tort shall be governed by the law of the place with which the tort is clearly more closely connected, instead of the law of the place indicated in the preceding three articles, where the parties had their habitual residence in the places governed by the same law at the time of the occurrence of the tort, where *the tort was committed in breach of an obligation under a contract between the parties*, or where other circumstances so require.[23]

The accessory reference subjects, where appropriate, related issues to one and the same law, instead of designating a different law by mechanically applying usual choice of law rules.

[23] Emphasis added.

It ensures that the entire dispute is treated in a unified manner by avoiding problems of characterisation and conflicting law applications.

The fifth is 'distributive reference'. For example, AGRAL article 24(1) stipulates: 'The formation [substantive validity] of a marriage shall be governed by the national law of each party'. Accordingly, in a marriage between a German and a Japanese national, the German must be eligible to enter into marriage under German law, while the Japanese must have capacity to celebrate marriage under Japanese law (for details, see chapter three, section V.A.i). It might be argued that this type of reference is identical in effect to the cumulative application of laws. Some authors, therefore, have argued that a distributive refence is merely an aspect of cumulative reference. There are, however, exceptions to these ordinary modes of reference (see section VIII).

With regard to 'special reference' to overriding mandatory rules (*Sonderanknüpfung der Eingriffsnormen*), Japanese choice of law rules do not have any explicit provision to such effect (see section VIII.A).

F. Incidental Question

To determine a legal issue, courts sometimes need to decide a preliminary question. For instance, before a court decides whether a Japanese widow can inherit her deceased English husband's property overseas, the court will need to consider whether the couple's marriage was valid. Such question is referred to as an 'incidental question' (or 'preliminary question'). According to the prevailing view and court practice, the law applicable to an incidental question is determined by the choice of law rules of the forum.[24] Incidental questions will not be referred in an accessory manner to the choice of law rules of the *lex causae*. There is no presumption that the law governing the main question or its choice of law rules (in the example above, whether the widow will inherit all, some or none of her husband's property in (say) the UK as a matter of English law) must also be or determine the law governing the incidental question (in the example, whether the widow and deceased contracted a valid marriage in Japan). Instead, the law governing the incidental question will be determined by independently applying the Japanese choice of law for the celebration of the marriage.

There is, however, a minority view among scholars that, exceptionally, the incidental question may be determined by reference to the choice of law rules of the *lex causae* (ie, the law governing the main question) if and only if:

- (a) there is no close connection between the legal relationship in question and the Japanese courts as the forum (in the example above, the relationship between the spouses in their lifetime and the Japanese courts); and,
- (b) applying the choice of law rules of the *lex causae*:
  - (i) would guarantee harmony between the decision of the Japanese court (as the forum) and the likely outcome before the foreign court of the closest connection to the relationship; or
  - (ii) would give effect to the parties' best interests and mutual expectations.[25]

[24] Judgment of Supreme Court, 27 January 2000, *Minshu* 54(1), 1; Sakurada, *Kokusai Shiho* (*Private International Law*) (n 4) 151; Sawaki=Dogauchi (n 4) 24.

[25] Ryoichi Yamada, *Kokusai Shiho* (*Private International Law*), 3rd edn (Yuhikaku, 2014) 163 (Yamada).

Nonetheless, it is submitted that such a *lex causae* approach should be rejected, even on an exceptional basis. It would unnecessarily complicate and cause uncertainty in the determination of governing law, running counter to the parties' foreseeability and legal certainty.

G. Adaptation

Since applicable law is determined depending on the type of legal relationship, the application of two laws can lead to contradictory results in individual cases. The technique to deal with such a problem is called 'adaptation' or 'adjustment'.

For instance, when a female minor marries an adult male, the effect of the marriage as between her husband and herself is subject to AGRAL article 25 and the relationship between her parents and herself is subject to AGRAL article 32. In that case, she may be subject to her parents' custody right to determine her residence even after her marriage pursuant to the law governing the parental relationship. At the same time, she may be subject to her spouse's right to request her to live together according to the law applicable to the marital relationship. The question would then be which law takes precedence.

Such contradiction or gap between the applicable laws ought to be resolved through the adaptation or adjustment of (a) the scope of the relevant choice of law rules (at the choice of law level) or (b) the contents of applicable substantive law (at the substantive law level). In this regard, there exists no explicit provision under Japanese law on how to approach conflicts of this nature. Nonetheless, there should be little or no adaptation question under well-structured and coordinated choice of law rules. It is submitted that an adaptation at the choice of law level should first be attempted (for instance, by restricting the scope of the choice of law rule on parental authority to relationships between parents and an unmarried minor), and then move to an adaptation at the substantive law level as a last resort (for instance, by construing parental authority as only capable of being exercised over an unmarried minor).[26]

H. *Dépeçage*

Depeçage is the technique of applying different laws to different issues in a single legal relationship, typically a contractual relationship. Under Japanese private international law, there is no explicit provision on *depeçage*. However, this does not mean *depeçage* is not possible under Japanese law. There is a judgment in which the Tokyo District Court denied *depeçage* in principle (albeit under *Horei*).[27] But typically for insurance contracts, there are lower court judgments that have applied English law 'as to liability for and settlement of any and all claims' based on the parties' express choice, while at the same time applying Japanese law to the validity of the same insurance contract and the notification obligation of the insured.[28] Among Japanese commentators, *depeçage* seems to be generally accepted.

[26] Sakurada, *Kokusai Shiho* (*Private International Law*) (n 4) 154.

[27] Judgment of Tokyo District Court, 28 May 2001, HT 1093, 174.

[28] Judgment of Tokyo District Court, 30 May 1977, HJ 880, 79; Judgment of Tokyo High Court, 9 February 2000, HJ 1749, 157; Judgment of Tokyo District Court, 26 February 2002, 2002WLJPCA02260015.

It has been argued that *depeçage* is not necessarily excluded, even where the parties have not chosen the law applicable to their contract.[29] Insofar as issues are separable, there is no good reason to deny *depeçage*.

I. *Renvoi* and Transmission

AGRAL article 41, first sentence permits and regulates *renvoi*.[30] The scope of that provision is nevertheless limited because it permits only a reference to Japanese law (namely, the *lex fori*), and *renvoi* is granted if and only if the relevant Japanese choice of law rule refers to the personal law of the person in question. As a result, transmission (ie, a reference to the law of a third state) is not allowed. The cases of *renvoi* under AGRAL article 41 are limited to legal capacity (age of majority), substantive and formal validity of marriage, legal parentage, adoption and specific personal status, as well as succession,[31] and substantive validity and effects of a will.[32] Furthermore, according to prevailing opinion, an indirect referral back to Japanese law (for instance, where the Japanese choice of law rule refers to the law of state A, the conflicts rule of state A then refers to the law of state B, and the choice of law rule of state B refers back to Japanese law) is also not permissible.[33] However, a minority opinion among scholars contends that indirect referral should be permitted, insofar as the choice of law rule of state A 'indirectly' refers to Japanese law, because the requirement of AGRAL article 41 ('if Japanese law shall govern in accordance with the law of the country of the national law') will then be met.[34] On the other hand, according to prevailing opinion, a double reference (ie, double *renvoi*) is held inadmissible, and there has so far been only one decision admitting a double reference.[35] Note that the Bills of Exchange Act article 88(1)(2) and CHA article 76(1)(2) on legal capacity not only permit references back to Japanese law, but also allow further reference to the law of a third country (transmission).[36]

V. Connecting Factors

There is no connecting factor that is only used in Japanese choice of law rules. Nevertheless, there are some points to bear in mind as set out in the sections below.

[29] Sawaki=Dogauchi (n 4) 189; Jun Yokoyama, *Kokusai Shiho* (*Private International Law*) (Sanseido, 2012) 28.

[30] Nevertheless, the prevailing view in Japan is that *renvoi* lacks a theoretical ground. Sakurada, *Kokusai Shiho* (*Private International Law*) (n 4) 116; Sawaki=Dogauchi (n 4) 44–46.

[31] For instance, Judgment of Supreme Court, 8 March 1994, *Shumin* 172, 1 ((1995) 38 *JAIL* 142); Decision of Kobe Family Court, 27 July 1994, *Kagetsu* 47(5), 60 ((1995) 39 *JAIL* 277); Decision of Tokyo Family Court, 15 October 1999, *Kagetsu* 52(3), 60; Judgment of Tokyo District Court, 16 January 2018, 2018WLJPCA01168015.

[32] Judgment of Tokyo District Court, 20 December 1991, HT 792, 207.

[33] Sakurada, *Kokusai Shiho* (*Private International Law*) (n 4) 122; Sawaki=Dogauchi (n 4) 44.

[34] Aki Kitazawa, 'Article 41 (Hanchi)' in Yoshiaki Sakurada and Masato Dogauchi (eds), *Chushaku Kokusai Shiho: Dai 2 kan (Commentary on Private International Law: Volume 2)* (Yuhikaku, 2011) 328 (Sakurada/Dogauchi (2)); Yoshio Tameike, *Kokusai Shiho Kogi* (*Private International Law Course*), 3rd edn (Yuhikaku, 2005) 164 (Tameike); Yamada (n 25) 71.

[35] Judgment of Tokyo High Court, 3 July 1979, *Komishu* 32(2), 126.

[36] Sakurada, *Kokusai Shiho* (*Private International Law*) (n 4) 124.

A. Nationality

(1) Since the enactment of Japanese choice of law rules, nationality has been the principal connecting factor on questions of legal capacity, family and succession. This means that the 'personal law', which is proper to each natural person and governs the personal status and family relationship, has been determined by the principle of nationality. From a theoretical viewpoint, the principle of nationality has been justified by arguing that nationality reflects the customs, traditions, religion and cultural background of each individual. From a practical viewpoint, the reference to nationality has the advantages of being stable (in the sense that it cannot easily be changed) and, compared with domicile or habitual residence, resistant to manipulation. In addition, nationality can be easily identified by an ID, passport or entry in the Japanese family and personal register. This is an important consideration for Japanese local offices which maintain family registers and have only formal control powers.[37]

(2) The determination of personal law requires particular rules in cases of multiple nationalities, statelessness and refugees, and in relation to states that comprise more than one private law system. If a person has multiple nationalities and one of them is Japanese, Japan is deemed to be his or her home country for the purpose of choice of law rules (AGRAL article 38(1), second sentence). If the person has several foreign nationalities to the exclusion of Japanese, the nationality of the country where the person habitually resides determines his or her personal law (AGRAL article 38(1), first case). If the person is not habitually resident in any of the states of which he or she is a national, the law of the state which he or she holds the closest connection with is considered as his or her personal law (article 38(1) first sentence, second case).

If the person concerned is stateless, the law of his or her habitual residence becomes his or her personal law (AGRAL article 38(2)), except for family matters covered by AGRAL article 25–27 and 32. For refugees, the Refugee Convention article 12(1) provides that the law of their domicile, and in its absence, the law of their residence governs their personal statute. Since the notion of domicile is held to be determined by individual contracting states, this rule is generally understood as referring to the law of habitual residence for the purpose of Japanese choice of law rules.

When a natural person has nationality of a multi-unit state where different legal systems coexist among different regions or provinces within the state, AGRAL article 38(3) refers to the interstate (or interregional) law of the foreign state to determine his or her personal law (indirect reference), and in its absence, to the law of the territorial unit that has the closest connection with him or her in the eyes of the Japanese judge (direct reference). This approach of indirect reference aims to achieve international harmony of decisions with the state concerned. Notably, in the case of the US, it has been disputed whether such an interstate law is available. While Japanese court decisions traditionally affirmed it, on the grounds that domicile of the person

[37] On the development of the nationality principle in Japan, Yuko Nishitani, 'Mancini and the Principle of Nationality in Japanese Private International Law' in Heinz-Peter Mansel et al (eds), *Festschrift für Erik Jayme* vol 1 (Sellier, 2004).

generally serves as the connecting factor in the US,[38] recent court decisions and the majority of commentators deny it, considering that the notion of domicile differs among states in the absence of uniform conflicts rules in the US.[39]

When a person belongs to a state (such as Indonesia, Malaysia or India, as well as most Maghreb and Middle Eastern countries), where personal laws are divided according to the religion or ethnic group, the Japanese judge needs to determine which personal law applies. AGRAL article 40(1) follows the same approach as article 38(3), referring to the interpersonal law of that state to determine the applicable personal law (indirect reference), and in its absence, to the law which he or she is most closely linked to in the eyes of the Japanese judge (direct reference).[40]

In all these settings, the 'cascading reference' (AGRAL articles 25–27 and 32) requires in general that the applicable personal law of each person be first specified, prior to ascertaining whether there is a common national law between the parties. For example, in determining the law applicable to divorce of a US couple, of whom the husband is domiciled in the State of New York and the wife in California, the Japanese judge will have to deny the existence of common national law, since the husband's personal law is New York law and the wife's personal law California law. When the party is stateless, he or she cannot have a national law, whereas in the case of a refugee, the prevailing opinion seems to accept that the law of his or her habitual residence be applied in the capacity of his or her own national law. Thus, there could be a common national law between the spouses when, for example, a German husband and a Syrian wife having the status of refugee and habitually residing in Germany seek divorce before the Japanese courts.

As an exception, interreligious or interethnic marriages in light of AGRAL article 40(1) require a different approach according to the prevailing opinion. States, whose personal laws are divided depending on the religion or ethnic group, usually provide specific interreligious or interethnic rules internally, which ought to be followed by the Japanese judge. Suppose an Egyptian couple living in Japan, of which the husband is Muslim and the wife Catholic, seek divorce before the Japanese courts. The judge should not decide as if the personal law of the husband were the Islamic law of Egypt and that of the wife the Canonic law of Egypt, so there would be no common national law under AGRAL articles 27 and 38(3). Rather, since Islamic law is given precedence and governs such an interreligious marriage and divorce in Egypt, the judge should simply apply the Islamic law of Egypt as the common national law of the spouses.

(3) As for corporations or legal persons, it is widely accepted among court practices and commentators that the incorporation theory should be followed and the *lex societatis* (the law of the place of incorporation) should be applied. The notion 'nationality of corporations', however, is no longer used (see chapter two, section V.B).

[38] Judgment of Tokyo District Court, 3 April 1958, *Kaminshu* 9(4), 576; Judgment of Urawa District Court, 14 May 1982, *Kagetsu* 36(2), 112; Judgment of Yokohama District Court, 19 October 1982, *Kagetsu* 36(2), 101.

[39] Judgment of Yokohama District Court, 29 May 1998, HT 1992, 249; Judgment of Yokohama District Court, 31 October 1991, *Kagetsu* 44(12), 105 ((1993) 36 *JAIL* 221); Sakurada, *Kokusai Shiho* (*Private International Law*) (n 4) 102; Sawaki=Dogauchi (n 4) 39.

[40] Decision of Utsunomiya Family Court, 20 July 2007, *Kagetsu* 59(12), 106.

B. Domicile

Japanese private international law is familiar with the notion of domicile (*Jusho:* 住所)[41] but, as a matter of choice of law, only one provision still employs this connecting factor to determine the applicable law (ALAFW article 2(3)). On the other hand, in international civil procedure law, the notion of the defendant's domicile plays an important role as the primary ground for assuming international adjudicatory jurisdiction to hear a cross-border case. Under Japanese private international law, domicile is generally held to be determined in accordance with the Civil Code (CC) article 22.[42] Thus, domicile is defined as the place in which the person establishes his or her centre of life, as is manifested by the fact of actually living there.

C. Habitual Residence

With its reform of 1989, *Horei* adopted the connecting factor of habitual residence, which had already been introduced into the Japanese legal system by ratifying the HCCH Conventions. The 2006 AGRAL upheld the conflicts rules reformed in 1989.

In contrast to other countries, the Japanese legislature assumed that every person could have only one habitual residence. Thus, AGRAL article 39 solely addresses cases in which a person's habitual residence is unknown and principally refer to his or her temporary residence instead. Since AGRAL came into force in 2007, habitual residence also serves as a connecting factor for contractual and non-contractual matters (AGRAL articles 8, 11, 15, 18, 19 and 20), in addition to family matters (marriage and parental relationship under AGRAL articles 25–27 and 32) as under *Horei*.

Although habitual residence is used as a connecting factor in a wide range of matters in Japan, there exists no provision defining it. This is because the notion comes from (and is associated with) the HCCH Conventions, which have so far refrained from defining habitual residence. Nor has the Japanese Supreme Court had an opportunity to clarify how to establish habitual residence. It is at least widely recognised that habitual residence attaches less importance to the person's intention than domicile. Habitual residence rather relies on various objective parameters, such as the purpose, length, duration and stability of the person's residence in a certain place.[43]

Notably, the Ministry of Justice issued a circular notice in 1989 to clarify the standards of determining habitual residence in the family registry practice, with a view to facilitating the task of family registrars that only have formal control powers.[44] According to the circular notice, the family registrar can certify the habitual residence of a Japanese national when the

[41] *Jusho* is different from (and should not be confused with) the notion of domicile in common law jurisdictions. For instance, a person's *jusho* is situated in a certain locality within a country (such as Tokyo or Kyoto), not in a country or state such as Japan, Germany or Massachusetts.

[42] CC article 22 reads as follows: '[t]he principal place wherein a person lives shall be his/her domicile'.

[43] Decision of Mito Family Court, 4 March 1991, *Kagetsu* 45(12), 57; Sakurada, *Kokusai Shiho* (*Private International Law*) (n 4) 91.

[44] The Circular Notice of Director General of the Civil Affairs Bureau (No.3900 of the Civil Affairs Second Division on 2 October 1989).

latter submits a residence certificate within one year of issue. Even if a Japanese national has emigrated from Japan and had his or her residence registration deleted, he or she is deemed to continue habitually residing in Japan for five years after his or her departure in principle, and for one year in exceptional circumstances under proviso 2(1) of the circular notice.[45] The Japanese national acquires habitual residence in a foreign country after five years or one year of residence there accordingly. As for foreign nationals coming to Japan, their habitual residence in Japan is established when they have stayed there for at least five years in principle, which is reduced to one year pursuant to proviso 2(2) of the circular notice, depending on his or her residential status under the Immigration Control and Refugee Recognition Act. Until the foreign national obtains his or her habitual residence in Japan, it remains in the foreign state.

While these standards are clear and simple, they could diminish flexibility and run counter to the purpose and objective of habitual residence, which is supposed to indicate the actual connection of the person with the state. Since the circular notice is only binding upon family registrars, judges are free to ascertain the habitual residence of a person by taking various factors into consideration. It is submitted that a flexible approach tailored to the case at hand is desirable in determining habitual residence for the purpose of AGRAL.[46]

D. Other Connecting Factors

In addition to nationality, domicile and habitual residence, Japanese choice of law rules adopt, as indicators showing the closest connection to a specific legal issue, various connecting factors, including the place of a juristic act (AGRAL articles 4, 10(2) and 34(2)), the parties' intention as an expression of party autonomy (AGRAL articles 7, 9, 16, 21 and 26(2)), the situs of property (AGRAL article 13), the place of unjust enrichment and *negotiorum gestio* (AGRAL article 14) and the place of tort (AGRAL article 17).

VI. Substance and Procedure

While the substance of a case is subject to the law designated under relevant choice of law rules in AGRAL (*lex causae*), procedure is governed by the law of the place where a court is situated (*lex fori*). Although the Former *Horei* article 13(1) of 1890 provided that the matters of procedure should be governed by the law of the country where legal proceedings were taking place, it no longer entered into force. The *Horei* enacted in 1898 did not adopt this provision. Since then, there has been no explicit provision regulating the matter, except for MC article 33(4).[47]

[45] Proviso 2(1)(2) of the circular notice reduces the required duration of residence from five years to one year, when the person has nationality or permanent residence permit of that state, or has residence permit in the capacity of a spouse or adopted child of a national of that state.

[46] Sakurada, *Kokusai Shiho* (*Private International Law*) (n 4) 92. In fact, there has been one judgment in which an inferior court certified the habitual residence of the parties concerned in accordance with a different standard from that in the notice in foot note 44. See Decision of Yokohama District Court, 31 October 1991, *Kagetsu* 44(12), 105 ((1993) 36 *JAIL* 221).

[47] MC article 33(4) explicitly states '[q]uestions of procedure shall be governed by the law of the court of the case'.

Normally, a state enacts procedural rules with a view to implementing the state's substantive law. As a result, while there is no discrepancy between the forum's procedural law and substantive law when the case is governed by the *lex fori*, applying foreign substantive law instead may be difficult and even incompatible with the forum's procedural law, which will require an adaptation. For instance, a will may require probate (ie, to be certified before coming into effect) under its governing law, but Japanese law does not provide corresponding procedural rules. How should the Japanese courts rule on the validity of the will? In such a case, it is submitted that the Japanese courts should follow the procedural requirements of the law governing the will and, if necessary, adjust the procedural rules of Japan to carry out probate in as close a manner as possible as provided by foreign law. Because some procedural rules are closely linked to the substantive law institutions, it is not always easy to draw a clear line between substance and procedure.

VII. Proof, Ascertainment and Application of Foreign Law

Under Japanese private international law, the ascertainment of the internationality of the case and the application of choice of law rules is not subject to the pleading/invocation or disposition of the parties, but is held to be the judge's obligation. Thus, the judge conducts *ex officio* investigation to find out international elements of the case at hand and which law applies to it.[48] Once the law applicable to the merits of the case is determined, the content of that law must further be identified. While Japanese judges can readily apply Japanese law,[49] they may encounter considerable difficulties in applying unfamiliar foreign law.[50] In particular, the content of the governing foreign law must be scrutinised and identified.

According to the prevailing view, the Japanese judge is obliged to ascertain and apply foreign law *ex officio*.[51] In this sense, the application of foreign law is regarded as a matter of law, not as a matter of fact. Thus, the *iura novit curia* principle (ie, the principle that the judge is supposed to know all the law) applies to both domestic law and foreign law.

Notably, there is a minority view among scholars, according to which, in light of procedural justice, the parties should be required to inform the judge of the content of the applicable foreign law and to prove the same, while the judge retains authority to

[48] Yuko Nishitani, 'Treatment of and Access to Foreign Law in Japan' (2018) 46 *JJL* 69, 71 ff (Nishitani/Foreign Law); for a comparative study, see also Yuko Nishitani, 'General Report' in Yuko Nishitani (ed), *Treatment of Foreign Law: Dynamics towards Convergence?* (Springer, 2017) 3 ff; Yuko Nishitani, 'Foreign Law in Domestic Courts: Challenges and Future Developments' in Franco Ferrari and Diego Fernández Arroyo (eds), *Private International Law: Contemporary Challenges and Continuing Relevance* (Edward Elgar Publishing, 2019).

[49] Due to international elements in cross-border cases, special consideration may be needed to apply Japanese law. In one case, despite CC article 986 requiring the use of a seal (*hanko*) on a holograph will, an inferior court held that such seal was not required for those who recently became naturalised citizens of Japan. (Judgment of the Supreme Court, 24 December 1974, *Minshu* 28(10), 2152).

[50] According to the case, the laws of states that have not been recognised by Japan (such as North Korea and Chinese Taiwan) can nonetheless be designated as applicable law. See Judgment of Supreme Court, 22 December 1959, *Shumin* 38, 583; Judgment of Kyoto District Court, 7 July 1956, *Kagetsu* 8(7), 59; Judgment of Tokyo District Court, 29 November 2010, 2010WLJPCA11298007.

[51] Shun'ichiro Nakano, 'Japan: Proof of and Information About Foreign Law in Japan' in Yuko Nishitani (ed), *Treatment of Foreign Law: Dynamics towards Convergence?* (Springer, 2017) 531; Nishitani/Foreign Law (n 48) 74 ff; Sawaki=Dogauchi (n 4) 52; Sakurada, *Kokusai Shiho* (*Private International Law*) (n 4) 127.

conduct his or her own investigation on foreign law.[52] Some other authors go even further and contend that foreign law ought to be treated as 'fact' in adversarial proceedings in civil and commercial matters, with the parties thus incurring the obligation to plead and prove foreign law as in common law jurisdictions. The latter authors accept the *ex officio* application and ascertainment of foreign law solely in proceedings dominated by the principle of *ex officio* investigation, such as disputes over personal status or family relations.[53]

These scholarly opinions, however, have largely been criticised, on the grounds that domestic law and foreign law ought to be treated as equivalent and therefore, once designated by choice of law rules, be ascertained and applied *ex officio*. Despite that, the judge is entitled to ask the parties to assist and submit documents for an improved access to foreign law. In fact, particularly in high-profile cross-border commercial disputes, parties are interested in actively adducing materials, documents or expert opinion on foreign law.[54] In this case, once both parties agree on the content of foreign law, the judge may *de facto* proceed to apply it as such.[55] The judge is, however, held to examine foreign law more thoroughly and carefully in status and family matters, which are governed by the principle of *ex officio* investigation. It is generally submitted that the judge ought to apply foreign law as it is interpreted and applied in the relevant legal system.

As other means for ascertaining foreign law *ex officio*, the judge can call for support on the civil or family department of the Supreme Court, which is better equipped with materials and information for this purpose. Judicial assistance via diplomatic channels is also available but usually not sought, because it is time consuming and the result is often unsatisfactory. Submission of expert opinion is occasionally mandated by the court, provided both parties agree to use it. The judge cannot request experts or legal institutions *ex officio* to provide information on foreign law. With these limited means, Japanese judges ought to make their best efforts to ascertain and apply foreign law *ex officio*.

Despite the judge's attempt, the content of foreign law may remain unclear. How should the judge then proceed? For the sake of fairness and justice, it is not permissible for the judge to dismiss the case, on the ground that the applicable foreign law is unascertainable. Nor should the judge simply proceed to apply the *lex fori* (Japanese law), as it would undermine the objective of private international law. In Japan, it is generally acknowledged that the court should, based on *jori*, assume how the question would be resolved pursuant to the applicable foreign law, taking into account its statutory provisions and decided cases. Some lower courts inferred the likely outcome of the case in light of the characteristics and fundamental principles of the entire foreign legal system (including its social

[52] Akira Mikaduki, 'Gaikoku Ho no Tekiyo to Saibansho' in Takao Sawaki and Yoshimitsu Aoyama (eds), *Kokusai Minjisosho Ho no Riron* (Yuhikaku, 1987) 250. Nevertheless, this view actually lies between the adversarial system whereby the court is presented with information by the parties and the inquisitorial system which considers it permissible for the judge to apply *ex officio* the relevant foreign law if he or she has the necessary means to do so. A few commentators argue that foreign law should be treated as a fact and the adversarial principle should be used in ordinary civil and commercial proceedings. Yasunori Honma, Shun'ichiro Nakano and Hajime Sakai, *Kokusai Minji Tetsuzuki-ho* (*International Procedure Law*), 2nd edn (Yuhikaku, 2012) 166 (Honma/Nakano/Sakai).

[53] Honma/Nakano/Sakai (n 52) 165.

[54] It is well known that the parties, especially in commercial disputes with a high value between large companies, submit sufficient evidence of the contents of relevant foreign laws in order to speed up the procedure and possibly achieve a more favourable result.

[55] Sawaki=Dogauchi (n 4) 52.

and cultural background).[56] Some other lower courts took a similar approach by referring to the related, sister legal systems (particularly socialist regimes).[57] While some commentators suggest pointing to the 'second-closest' connection to achieve the goal of private international law,[58] this solution is arguably of scarce use and contradicts the choice of law rules by substituting the originally designated foreign law. In any event, judges should make all efforts to ascertain foreign law and limit a fallback to the *lex fori* (Japanese law) as the last resort in cases where they cannot find out the content of foreign law within a reasonable time frame and costs.[59]

According to established case law and the prevailing view of scholars, an incorrect application of foreign law is subject to judicial review.[60] The Supreme Court is supposed to ensure that foreign law is correctly and uniformly interpreted and applied by Japanese courts. Notably, since the reform of CCP in 1996, judicial review is limited to 'important matters relating to the interpretation of the law' and subject to a certiorari of the Supreme Court.

VIII. Mandatory Rules, *ordre public*, Escape Clause and Evasion of Law

A. Mandatory Rules

When the parties choose the law of state A as the law governing their contract, the court of state B (before which a dispute arising from the parties' contract has been brought) will typically apply the law of state A (as the law agreed by the parties), including its mandatory rules, to determine the merits of the relevant dispute.

Notably, mandatory rules are classified into two categories. First, mandatory rules may be 'relative' in the sense that they will only apply when the law of the state to which those rules belong has been designated as the governing law. In the above example, only the mandatory rules of State A are applied to invalidate conflicting terms of the parties' agreement within the framework of the applicable law, whereas the relative mandatory rules of other states, including Japan, do not come into play. Second, mandatory rules may be 'absolute'

[56] Decision of Nagano Family Court, 12 March 1982, *Kagetsu* 35(1), 105; Decision of Osaka District Court, 27 September 1985, HJ 1179, 94.

[57] In order to ascertain the contents of North Korean family law, several lower courts have referred to the law of South Korea (Decision of Fukuoka District Court, 14 January 1958, *Kaminshu* 9(1), 15; Decision of Osaka Family Court, 22 August 1962, *Kagetsu* 15(2), 163) or the law of the socialist states such as the former Soviet Union (Decision of Tokyo Family Court, 13 June 1963, *Kagetsu* 15(10), 153; Judgment of Tokyo District Court, 19 March 1976, *Kaminshu* 27(1-4), 125).

[58] Tadashi Kanzaki, '*Junkyo Gaikokuho no Fumei o megutte*' 107 (6) *Hogaku Kyokai Zasshi* (1990) 1039; Yamamoto/Sakurada/Dogauchi (2) 362.

[59] Decision of Nagano Family Court, 12 March 1982, *Kagetsu* 35(1), 105; Decision of Osaka District Court, 27 September 1985, HJ 1179, 94; Decision of Kyoto District Court, 30 September 1987, HJ 1275, 107; Sakurada, *Kokusai Shiho* (*Private International Law*) (n 4) 132; Sawaki=Dogauchi (n 4) 55–56.

[60] Judgment of Supreme Court, 2 July 1981, *Minshu* 35(5), 881; Judgment of Supreme Court, 25 February 1997, *Kagetsu* 49(7), 56 (41 *JAIL* 111); Judgment of Supreme Court, 18 March 2008, *Shumin* 227, 571; Tameike (n 34) 251; Yamada (n 25) 139.

in the sense that they override the applicable foreign law which may otherwise be applicable. Each state normally has statutory provisions, which are enacted to preserve the state's fundamental principles and cater for its social, economic or political interests. Because such statutory provisions – absolute mandatory rules – take precedence over the applicable foreign law, they are called 'overriding mandatory rules', 'internationally mandatory rules', '*Eingriffsnormen*' or '*lois de police*'. Overriding mandatory rules typically encompass antitrust law, import or export regulation, foreign exchange law, labour law and possibly also consumer law.[61]

In the example above, overriding mandatory rules of the *lex fori* will always intervene to uphold the fundamental principles of the forum state, to the exclusion of conflicting norms of the law of State A. This is the principle of absolute, unilateral application of overriding mandatory rules of the forum state, which is presupposed in Japan and generally granted worldwide.

A similar scenario may arise in relation to the law of a third State C.[62] Suppose that the parties choose the law of State A as the law governing their contract, and that one party did not perform his or her contractual obligation, on the ground that such performance would be prohibited and be regarded as a crime under overriding regulatory rules of State C (such as embargo). When such a case is pending before the court of State B, how should the judge deal with this situation?

Under *Horei*, there was scarcely doubt that the overriding mandatory rules of Japanese law should always apply regardless of the applicable foreign law. Some court decisions applied Japanese labour law provisions as overriding mandatory rules.[63] Notably, AGRAL refrained from introducing an explicit provision on the application of overriding mandatory rules of Japanese law due to difficulties of clearly defining overriding mandatory rules and identifying the requirements for their application.[64] It was also pointed out that a provision dealing solely with the applicability of overriding mandatory rules of Japanese law could unduly be understood *a contrario* as excluding any reference to overriding mandatory rules of a third state, whereas there was no consensus over the applicability of or reference to overriding mandatory rules of a third state.[65] Thus, in the absence of clear provisions in AGRAL, it is up to future case law and academic discussions to define the scope of overriding mandatory rules and the extent of their application.

Notably, since overriding mandatory rules of Japanese law always take precedence over the law governing the contract, they can also play a role in consumer and

[61] See Rome Convention article 7; Rome I article 9; SPIL article 18.

[62] See SPIL article 19.

[63] Judgment of Tokyo District Court, 24 February 2004, HJ 1853, 38 ((2005) 48 *JAIL* 191). There is a judgment in which the Tokyo District Court, regardless of the parties' choice of California law and US federal law, applied Japanese labour law rules as part of Japanese public policy of Japan and as having effect only in Japan (Decision of Tokyo District Court, 26 April 1965, HJ 408, 14).

[64] Kunio Koide (ed), *Chikujo Kaisetsu Ho no Tekiyo ni kansuru Tsusokuho* (*Commentary on the Act on General Rules for Application of Law*), expanded edn (Shojihomu, 2015) 88.

[65] *Hosoku Setsumei* (AGRAL) 235; 3rd Meeting (AGRAL). Under Japanese law, overriding mandatory rules may be found in the following laws: Anti-monopoly Act, Foreign Exchange Law, Labour Standards Act, Labour Union Act, Minimum Wage Act, Industrial Accident Compensation Insurance Act, Interest Rate Restriction Act, and Consumer Protection Act. See Yuko Nishintai, 'Party Autonomy and its Restrictions by Mandatory Rules in Japanese Private International Law' in Jürgen Basedow, Harald Baum and Yuko Nishitani (eds), *Japanese and European Private International Law in Comparative Perspective* (Mohr Siebeck, 2008) 101.

employee protection. To combat an abusive or improper choice of applicable law, AGRAL articles 11(1) and 12(1) require that the consumer or employee themselves invoke specific mandatory rules of the law of the consumer's habitual residence or the law of the state most closely connected with the employment contract. These unfortunate provisions may not suffice to protect weaker parties, since it is left to the initiative of the consumer or employee to make a declaration accordingly (see chapter three, sections I.A and I.B). This drawback can partly be countered by overriding mandatory rules of Japanese law, since the judge is obliged to apply them *ex officio* even in the absence of such a declaration by the consumer or employee.

B. *Ordre public* or Public Policy

Since Japanese choice of law rules point to foreign law regardless of its content in principle, one must still examine under AGRAL article 42 whether the result of applying the relevant foreign law to the case at hand will be compatible with public policy or *ordre public*[66] of Japan and whether the fundamental values of Japanese law are preserved (as to public policy at the stage of the recognition and enforcement of foreign judgments, see chapter five, section I.D; for public policy at the stage of recognition and enforcement of foreign arbitral awards, see chapter five, section I.E). In this sense, *ordre public* is an exceptional, but necessary, device to avoid or prevent unacceptable results from a Japanese perspective, as well as serve as a corrective tool to the application of foreign law.

It must be borne in mind that the concept of *ordre public* under AGRAL article 42 (at the choice of law level) considerably differs from the concept of public policy under CC article 90 (at the substantive law level).[67] Otherwise, all foreign laws that run counter to mandatory rules of Japanese law would be excluded as being contrary to *ordre public* under AGRAL article 42. As for the objectives inhering the two concepts, while *ordre public* under AGRAL article 42 is geared towards the result of applying foreign law, public policy under CC article 90 constitutes a general principle to control the validity of legal acts. Thus, the former *ordre public* solely intervenes when the result of applying foreign law would be so serious as violating common decency or fundamental legal principles of Japan.[68]

For the purpose of the *ordre public* control, though not evident from the text of AGRAL article 42, it is also required that the facts of the case demonstrate a sufficiently close connection with Japan (namely, proximity to Japan). A close link between the case and the forum

[66] As evident from the words 'policy' and '*ordre*', *ordre public* and public policy are not equivalent. Whilst the term 'policy' suggests that 'the principles concerned are enshrined in wider societal and political ideas', the term '*ordre*' is 'closer to the English expression 'law and order' and has fewer political connotations when compared with policy.Ioanna Thoma, *Encyclopaedia of Private International Law* (Edward Elgar Publishing, 2017) 1454. It seems however that *ordre public* and public policy are, in general, used interchangeably in Japan as *Kojo* (公序)'. See Toshiyuki Kono, 'Japan', in Jürgen Basedow, Giesela Rühl, Franco Ferrari and Pedro De Miguel Asensio (eds), *Encyclopedia of Private International Law* (Edward Elgar Publishing, 2017) 2226; Sawaki=Dogauchi (n 4) 56; Kent Anderson and Yasuhiro Okuda, 'Japan's Private International Law: Act on the General Rules of Application of Laws [*Ho no Tekiyo ni Kansuru Tsusokuho*], Law No 10 of 1898 (as newly titled and amended 21 June 2006)]' (2006) 8(1) *Asian-Pacific Law & Policy Journal* 160.

[67] Sakurada, *Kokusai Shiho* (*Private International Law*) (n 4) 136; Sawaki=Dogauchi (n 4) 58.

[68] Judgment of Supreme Court, 12 March 1998, *Minshu* 52(2), 342 ((1999) 42 *JAIL* 152).

state serves to justify internationally that the Japanese judge intervenes to exclude the application of the governing foreign law. The mere fact that Japan has international jurisdiction in a case is generally not sufficient to meet this proximity requirement.

As a result, the reference to *ordre public* presupposes, first, that the result of applying foreign law runs counter to fundamental principles of Japanese law and, second, that the case has sufficient proximity to Japan. Typically, these two requirements are in an inverse relationship. The more closely the case is related to Japan, the lower the threshold is for *ordre public* to intervene.

A violation of *ordre public* is determined in light of the result of applying foreign law in the individual case. It is, however, not clear whether the relevant time ought to be (a) when the parties entered into and effectuated a legal relationship, or (b) when the court is applying foreign law. Since the *ordre public* control is meant to preserve current Japanese fundamental values, incompatibility with *ordre public* should be gauged at the present time. Nothing could be gained by evaluating *ordre public* as at some point in the past.[69] If a fundamental legal value has changed over time, there is no need to protect the previously valid value.

When the *ordre public* control functions, the application of foreign law is excluded due to incompatibility with the *ordre public* of Japan. The next question is how and under which law the legal issue in question should be handled. Most court decisions suggest that the *lex fori* (ie, Japanese law) applies to fill in the legal lacunae.[70] Notably, the recent majority view denies such lacunae, considering that the judge already has given an answer to the legal issue by excluding foreign law on *ordre public* grounds.[71] This would be the case when, for example, Philippine law that solely grants legal separation and not divorce is excluded in a Filipino–Japanese divorce case on *ordre public* grounds. In such a case, the prevailing view opines that the judge has already given an answer that the marriage ought to be dissolved. Yet, in some other cases, there are indeed legal lacunae that need to be filled by certain law. When, for example, the application of foreign law that provides for a prescription period of 50 years for usual claims is excluded, the judge needs to find a solution on when the claims are time-barred. For the sake of fairness and justice, a 'substantive law solution at the level of conflict of laws' could possibly be sought (eg, prescription period of 20 years), instead of simply referring to the *lex fori* (eg, prescription period of five years under CC article 166(1) No 1).

There have so far been numerous judgments in which the courts have denied the application of foreign law due to incompatibility with *ordre public* in a wide range of areas (particularly, family law areas).[72] The Supreme Court has itself so far denied, or considered denying, the application of foreign law in a number of situations, including cases involving: (a) former Korean law designating father by definition as the sole custodian at divorce;[73]

[69] Sawaki=Dogauchi (n 4) 59.

[70] For instance, Judgment of Supreme Court, 20 July 1984, *Minshu* 38(8), 1051 ((1985) 28 *JAIL* 221). Furthermore, there are some lower court judgments which applied the second most closely connected law to decide the merits of a case (Judgment of Tokyo District Court, 28 November 1990, HJ 1384, 71 ((1991) 35 *JAIL* 167)). This approach should not be taken simply because the *ordre public* control is not to designate another applicable law.

[71] Sawaki=Dogauchi (n 4) 59–60.

[72] For details, see Toshiyuki Kono, 'Article 42 (Kojo)' in Yoshiaki Sakurada and Masato Dogauchi (eds), *Chushaku Kokusai Shiho: Dai 2 kan* (*Commentary on Private International Law: Volume 2*) (Yuhikaku, 2011) 332–42; Sakurada, *Kokusai Shiho* (*Private International Law*) (n 4) 141–47.

[73] Judgment of Supreme Court, 31 March 1977, *Minshu* 31(2), 365.

(b) former Korean law denying the spouse's compensatory claims at divorce;[74] and (c) US patent law requiring an extraterritorial application to the infringing conduct undertaken in Japan.[75] On the other hand, the Supreme Court held the application of Korean law to be compatible with *ordre public*, despite its shorter statute of limitation (one year since taking note of the person's death) than that of Japanese law (three years since the person's death) in bringing a claim against a deceased person for the establishment of legal parentage.[76]

In addition to the general provision on *ordre public* in AGRAL article 42, there are special corrective rules in respect of the law applicable to tort in AGRAL article 22 (see chapter three, section II.C.i.e).

C. Escape Clause

Japanese choice of law rules designate, in an abstract manner, the law which allegedly has the closest connection to the legal relationship concerned. The conflicts rules are by their nature general and abstract. The issues at hand are mechanically referred to a particular law through a preordained connecting factor, which is supposed to realise the closest connection. This approach is conducive to predictability and certainty. But it does not necessarily secure the application of the law of the state that has the closest connection to the case at hand. In dealing with the latter situations, Japanese law has been influenced by US revolutionary conflict of laws theories, geared towards governmental interests, closest connection or better law approach based on a flexible case-by-case analysis. Thus, AGRAL has an 'escape clause' in articles 15 and 20 to 'correct' an overly mechanical determination of the applicable law. These provisions with limited scope and function ought to be applied in a restrictive way. Correction is available if, and only if, the circumstances of an individual case indicate that there is some other place that is 'obviously more closely connected with' the legal relationship concerned. The escape clause seeks justice at choice of law level, not at substantive law level.

D. Evasion of Law (*fraus legis*)

It has long been discussed whether a person is allowed to deliberately alter his or her situation so as to procure that a specific connecting factor and choice of law rule is applied. For example, by changing nationality, habitual residence, or the place where movable property is located, the party may attempt to manipulate matters so that a more favourable law is applied. A well-known example is the establishment of a company, without conducting any business there, in a jurisdiction which is favourable to corporate activities and tax payment. There are many well-known jurisdictions of this kind, such as Delaware in the US, the British Virgin Islands, Bermuda and Liechtenstein. Unlike in some other countries like France or Belgium, such an evasion of the law that might otherwise be applicable (*Gesetzesumgehung*, *fraude*

[74] Judgment of Supreme Court, 20 July 1984, *Minshu* 38(8), 1051 ((1985) 28 *JAIL* 221).
[75] Judgment of Supreme Court, 26 September 2002, *Minshu* 56(7), 1551 ((2002) 45 *JAIL* 175).
[76] Judgment of Supreme Court, 27 June 1975, *Shumin* 115, 161.

à la loi or *fraus legis*) is not regulated in Japan and the applicable law is determined solely on the basis of objective criteria.[77] This is justified by the fact that the change of connecting factors is followed in the absence of the party's intent to manipulate, which is in any case difficult to prove. It was felt that focusing on good faith or bad faith at choice of law level would unnecessarily protract proceedings and cause legal uncertainty.[78]

[77] Former Horei article 10 regulated the evasion of Japanese law.
[78] Sakurada, *Kokusai Shiho* (*Private International Law*) (n 4) 98; Tameike (n 34) 198–99; Yamada (n 25) 157–58.

2

Jurisdiction

I. General Principles

A. Overview/Legal Sources

With regard to international adjudicatory jurisdiction to determine the merits of a case (often referred to as 'direct jurisdiction') in civil and commercial matters as well as family law and succession law matters, Japan has concluded a small number of international conventions limited to specific areas. It has not ratified any conventions of the Hague Conference on Private International Law (HCCH) in this regard. Thus, international jurisdiction of the Japanese courts is mainly governed by domestic laws. The main legal sources are the Code of Civil Procedure (CCP), the Civil Provisional Remedies Act (CPRA), the Personal Status Litigation Act (PSLA) and the Domestic Relations Case Procedure Act (DRCPA). Among the limited number of international instruments Japan is party to, the Warsaw Convention (WC); the Convention on Limitation of Liability for Maritime Claims of 19 November 1976 (LLMC-1976); the Convention on Supplementary Compensation for Nuclear Damage of 12 September 1997(CSC); the Montreal Convention (MC); the International Convention on Civil Liability for Oil Pollution Damage of 29 November 1969 (CLC); the Protocol of 1992 to the International Convention on the Establishment of an International Fund for Compensation for Oil Pollution Damage of 27 November 1992 (FUND 1992); and the Protocol of 2003 to the International Convention on the Establishment of an International Fund for Compensation for Oil Pollution Damage (FUND) 2003 provide for jurisdiction rules. When any of these conventions applies, therefore, Japanese courts may take jurisdiction in accordance with their relevant provisions (WC article 28; LLMC articles 10 and 11; CSC article 13; MC articles 33 and 46; CLC article 9; FUND 1992 article 7; and FUND 2003 article 7). In the following, we will chiefly discuss domestic rules on international jurisdiction provided by CCP, CPRA, PSLA and DRCPA.

B. General Principles and Framework

Prior to 2011, there were no provisions dealing with international jurisdiction except for those in the specific international conventions mentioned above. Hence, jurisdiction rules have been principally established by case law since the 1981 *Malaysia Airlines* case,[1] referring

[1] Judgment of Supreme Court, 16 October 1981, *Minshu* 35(7), 1224 ((1983) 26 *JAIL* 122) (*Malaysia Airlines* case). Goto, a Japanese national domiciled in Japan, purchased a flight ticket in Malaysia and boarded a domestic

to *jori* (*naturalis ratio*)[2] based on the ideas of fairness between the parties and the sound and prompt administration of justice.[3] In the concrete application of *jori*, courts assumed international jurisdiction insofar as a specific court in Japan, such as the Tokyo District Court, had local jurisdiction pursuant to the local jurisdictional rules in CCP, which are geared towards determining the competent courts within Japan. The local jurisdiction of a particular court in Japan was considered to presuppose the existence of international jurisdiction of the entire Japanese courts in the international arena (the 'reverse presumption theory').[4] After this principle became case law, lower courts later introduced a corrective rule that authorised the judge to decline international jurisdiction under 'exceptional circumstances', where the exercise of jurisdiction would run counter to fairness between the parties and the sound and prompt administration of justice. This corrective rule aiming to deter an exorbitant jurisdiction was confirmed by the Supreme Court in 1997.[5] However, by examining relevant factors and weighing interests of the parties on a case-by-case basis, Japanese case law at that time failed to guarantee legal certainty and foreseeability for the parties.[6]

Apparently, Japan needed clear-cut statutory rules to determine international jurisdiction. The legislature, however, refrained from taking action during a thorough reform of CCP in 1996 because detailed rules could not be developed within a limited time frame. In addition, negotiations over the text of a double convention dealing with international jurisdiction as well as the enforcement of judgments were still ongoing within the Hague Conference's Judgments Project and a final outcome of those discussions was being awaited. It was not until a convention limited to choice of court agreements was adopted by the Hague Conference in 2005 that Japan proceeded with its domestic legislation on international jurisdiction.[7] After the preparatory work was completed in 2008,[8] the Ministry of Justice established a Division on International Jurisdiction within the Legislative Council on 3 September 2008. Consultations took place in the Division from October 2008 to January 2010.[9] With respect to its Interim Draft dated 28 July 2009, academics, practitioners, industry and other stakeholders were given an opportunity to submit their opinions.[10]

flight operated by Malaysia Airlines in Penang heading for Kuala Lumpur. Following a hijacking, Goto was killed along with all the other passengers and crew members. His wife and two children, all Japanese nationals domiciled in Japan, filed a claim for damages against Malaysia Airlines before the Nagoya District Court. The Supreme Court granted 'general' jurisdiction to the Japanese courts following ex-Article 4(3) CCP, which conferred local jurisdiction on the basis of a foreign company's office within Japan (the 'reverse presumption theory').

[2] *Jori* is regarded as secondary law in Japan. On *jori* generally, see Yoshiyuki Noda, *Introduction to Japanese Law* (University of Tokyo Press, 1976) 222.

[3] For the history and court practice on jurisdiction prior to the 2011 amendment, see Masato Dogauchi, 'New Japanese Rules on International Jurisdiction: General Observation' (2011) 54 *JYIL* 260, 261–68 (Dogauchi/Jurisdiction).

[4] In contrast to German case law, the double functionality of the domestic jurisdiction rules of CCP was not assumed. See Sueo Ikehara, *Kokusai Shiho: Soron* (*Private International Law: General Part*) (Yuhikaku, 1973) 14–19 (Ikehara/*Kokusai Shiho*).

[5] Judgment of Supreme Court, 11 November 1997, *Minshu* 51(10), 4055 ((1998) 41 *JAIL* 117).

[6] Yuko Nishitani, '§ 26: Internationales Privat- und Zivilverfahrensrecht' in Harald Baum and Moritz Bälz (eds), *Handbuch Japanisches Handels- und Wirtschaftsrecht* (*Handbook on Japanese Commercial law and Economic law*) (Carl Heymanns Verlag, 2011) [113]–[115]).

[7] Minutes of 1st Meeting (CCP). See Dogauchi/Jurisdiction (n 3) 268; Motoko Yoshida, 'Neue Regelungen zur internationalen Zuständigkeit der Gerichte in Japan' (2012) 58 *RIW* 118, 119–20.

[8] For details, see *Hokokusho* (CCP), available at: www.moj.go.jp/content/000012193.pdf.

[9] For details, see minutes of meetings (CCP).

[10] See Interim Draft on the Legislation on International Jurisdiction of 28 July 2009 (Interim Draft (CCP)); and *Hosoku Setsumei* (CCP), available at: www.e-gov.go.jp/.

The Division's proposal of 15 January 2010 was approved by the Legislative Council on 5 February 2010[11] and elaborated into a bill.[12] Due to a political impasse, however, it was not until 28 April 2011 that the National Diet adopted the bill. With this amendment of CCP and CPRA, black-letter rules for jurisdiction in civil and commercial matters were introduced for the first time (CCP articles 3-2–3-11 and CPRA article 11). The new rules entered into force on 1 April 2012.

Legislative work largely relied on existing case law and academic opinion in Japan, aiming primarily at adopting rules parallel to local jurisdiction rules (CCP articles 4–22). From a comparative law perspective, the legislature took into consideration Council Regulation (EC) No 44/2001 of 22 December 2000 on jurisdiction and the recognition and enforcement of judgments in civil and commercial matters (Brussels I); the Convention on jurisdiction and the enforcement of judgments in civil and commercial matters done at Lugano on 16 September 1988 (Lugano-1988); the Convention on jurisdiction and the recognition and enforcement of judgments in civil and commercial matters of 30 October 2007 (Lugano-2007); Preliminary Draft Convention on Jurisdiction and Foreign Judgments in Civil and Commercial Matters adopted by the Special Commission on 30 October 1999 (DHC-1999); and Convention of 30 June 2005 on Choice of Court Agreements (Hague Choice of Court Convention) (HCC) as well as German and several other foreign domestic legislations.[13] Furthermore, the legislature always examined whether a corresponding exercise of jurisdiction by the courts of a foreign state would be acceptable such that judgments by the latter courts based on the relevant jurisdictional ground would in turn be recognised in Japan pursuant to CCP article 118.[14] This is because the indirect jurisdiction of foreign courts under article 118(1) principally follows the rules on direct jurisdiction of the Japanese courts (see chapter four, section I.C.ii).[15]

In respect of family law (or domestic relation) matters,[16] new statutory rules have recently been introduced in PSLA and DRCPA.[17] These rules came into force on 1 April 2019. Although both PSLA and DRCPA cover family law matters, they offer different dispute resolution methods (namely, open-court proceedings in principle and closed proceedings).[18] PSLA covers contentious matters such as divorce and establishment of parentage and provides for open-court proceedings with exceptions for closed hearings of

[11] An English translation is available at Toshiyuki Kono, Ruben Pauwels and Paulius Jurčys, 'MOJ Proposal on International Jurisdiction (February 2010)' (2010) 30 *JJL* 147, 156–61.

[12] Bill No 34 of the Cabinet (submitted to the House of Councillors in the National Diet on 2 March 2010).

[13] *Hokokusho* (CCP) 3, available at: www.moj.go.jp/content/000012193.pdf; Dogauchi/Jurisdiction (n 3) 269–76.

[14] *Hosoku Setsumei* (CCP) 2–3, available at: www.e-gov.go.jp/.

[15] *cf* Judgment of Supreme Court, 28 April 1998, *Minshu* 52(3), 853 ((1999) 42 *JAIL* 155); Judgment of Supreme Court, 24 April 2014, *Minshu* 68(4), 329 ((2015) 58 *JYIL* 463), For the recognition and enforcement of foreign judgments in Japan, see ch 4 below.

[16] Exceptionally, some pecuniary matters in succession are subject to the jurisdictional rules of CCP.

[17] For an overview of the new rules of PSLA and DRCPA, see Yuko Nishitani, 'New International Civil Procedure Law of Japan in Status and Family Matters' (2019) 62 *JYIL* 119.

[18] This is because, as family law disputes often revolve around the parties' complex feelings towards each other, the handling of such disputes by a court requires not only the determination of legal issues, but also the resolution of emotional conflicts between the parties. For this purpose, it is not usually appropriate to deal with such disputes in open court proceedings. For proceedings under PSLA and DRCPA respectively, see, Supreme Court of Japan, 'Guide to the Family Court of Japan (2018)', available at: www.courts.go.jp/english/vc-files/courts-en/file/Guide_to_the_Family_Court_of_Japan2018.pdf.

the parties or witnesses, that is, litigation (*Jinji Sosho Jiken*). DRCPA mainly covers non-contentious matters such as the administration of an absentee's property, the annulment of disappearance adjudication, the permission to adopt and the establishment of special adoption. DRCPA provides for closed proceedings, that is, adjudication by the court (*Kaji Shinpan Jiken*). In addition, DRCPA provides, as an alternative dispute resolution method, conciliation by the court in contentious and non-contentious matters (*Kaji Chotei Jiken*).[19] Furthermore, pursuant to DRCPA article 257(1),[20] insofar as matters of personal status and other family affairs (except for matters in Appended Table 1)[21] are concerned, a person first must refer a dispute to conciliation by the family courts. Therefore, for instance, where a wife seeks divorce, she must first refer her case to conciliation by the relevant family court. The aforementioned statutes provide various jurisdictional grounds based on the principles of 'fairness between the parties' and 'the sound and prompt administration of justice' (justice at the procedural law level), which Japanese courts had adopted prior to the 2011 CCP amendment.[22] There are some other principles, for instance, the respect for national sovereignty. Aiming to pursue its national interests, Japan has subjected certain matters to the exclusive jurisdiction of the Japanese courts (see section II.A.viii). In the area of family law, PSLA and DRCPA are based on the ideas just discussed, but in certain matters attach more importance to justice at the substantive law level, such as the best interests of the child and protection of the weaker party (see section III).[23]

When it comes to disputes on the merits, the jurisdiction of a Japanese court is principally determined in accordance with relevant domestic laws, that is, CCP, PSLA or DRCPA. These statutes adopt a two-pronged approach. A Japanese court must first examine whether a jurisdictional ground in a relevant provision empowers it to assume jurisdiction over a case. Second, it must examine whether it should hear and determine the merits of the case, by considering the individual circumstances of such case (CCP article 3-9; PSLA article 3-5; DRCPA article 3-14; see sections II.A.ii, III.A.i and III.A.ii). In other words, there is always a 'safety valve' under these statutes.

Notably, CCP, PSLA and DRPCA adopt different structures for jurisdictional rules. CCP contains two heads of jurisdiction, namely, general and specific jurisdiction. The former general jurisdiction is primarily grounded on the defendant's domicile and applies in all cases, irrespective of whether a claim has arisen out of the defendant's particular contact with the forum state (Japan). It provides a list of all-purpose grounds for establishing jurisdiction (see section II.A). In contrast, the latter specific jurisdiction applies only to specific cases or claims (for details of specific grounds, see section II.B). PSLA has seven general grounds applicable in all personal status matters, while DRCPA sets out a number of special grounds applicable only in particular circumstances (see section III.A).

[19] *Kaji Jiken* sometimes refers to all family law matters and sometimes refers to family law matters other than *Jinji Sosho Jiken* (ie, only to *Kaji Shinpan Jiken* and *Kaji Chotei Jiken*).

[20] Article 257(1) reads: 'A person who intends to file an action on a case where a conciliation may be possible pursuant to the provision of Article 244 must first file a petition for conciliation of domestic relations with a family court'. This is often referred to as *Chotei Zenchi Shugi*（調停前置主義） or 'the priority of conciliation'.

[21] Appended Table 1 refers to 134 matters, for instance, commencement of guardianship and appointment of a guardian of an adult.

[22] Dogauchi/Jurisdiction (n 3) 265.

[23] Takao Sawaki and Masato Dogauchi, *Kokusai Shiho Nyumon* (*Introduction to Private International Law*), 8th edn (Yuhikaku, 2018) 314 (Sawaki=Dogauchi).

C. Service of Process

To initiate court proceedings, it is necessary to serve process on a defendant. Various documents may also have to be served on the parties in the course of or after proceedings. For service of process, international conventions or arrangements are critical. In particular, the Convention of 1 March 1954 on Civil Procedure (HCPC) and the Convention of 15 November 1965 on the Service Abroad of Judicial and Extrajudicial Documents in Civil or Commercial Matters (Hague Service Convention) (HSC) play an important role. To implement certain provisions of these conventions, Japan has enacted a statute, the Act on Special Provisions Concerning Civil Procedure Attendant upon Implementation of the Convention on Civil Procedure and Another Convention (ASPCP) and procedural rules (Rules on Special Provisions Concerning Civil Procedure Attendant upon Implementation of the Convention on Civil Procedure and Another Convention). Similarly, there are bilateral consular conventions with the US[24] and UK[25] respectively and some judicial arrangements.[26] In the absence of international conventions or arrangements, service of process may be conducted in accordance with relevant national laws. Service of process outside Japan (ie, from Japan to overseas) is subject to CCP, while service of process within Japan (namely, from overseas to Japan) is governed by the Act on Assistance Based on Commission by Foreign Courts (AABC).

i. Service of Process Outside Japan

For service of process outside Japan (namely, from Japan to overseas), there are basically five ways, although available methods vary from one instrument to another: (a) service through diplomatic or consular agents of the requesting state in the state addressed; (b) service through a designated authority in the state addressed; (c) service through a Central Authority in the stated addressed; (d) service through diplomatic channels; and (e) service through a competent court of the state addressed.[27] In light of CCP article 108 and ASPCP article 6,[28] service by post is not possible, even where the 1954 Convention applies.[29] To decide which method should be taken, one must first examine whether the relevant foreign state is a party to HSC. If it is, the next question is whether, pursuant to HSC article 8(2), that state has declared that it will not allow service through diplomatic

[24] Consular Convention between Japan and the US (Treaty No 16 of 17 July 1964).

[25] Consular Convention between Japan and the UK (Treaty No 22 of 29 September 1965).

[26] For instance, Switzerland, Denmark, Italy, Sri Lanka, Brazil, Thailand, Germany, the UK, Norway, Australia, Iran, Austria, Kuwait, Iraq and Israel (see Saiko Saibansho Jimu Sokyoku Minjikyoku (ed), *Kokusai Minji Jiken Tetsuzuki Handbook* (*Handbook in International Civil Procedure*) (Hosokai, 2013) 223–25) (*Handbook-ICP*). In addition, some states have served process upon individual agreements without prior arrangement (for instance, Singapore and Peru (see *Handbook-ICP*, ibid, 431–33).

[27] See *Handbook-ICP* (n 26) 30–42.

[28] Article 6(1) on 'Service of Documents' provides: 'Matters pertaining to service of extrajudicial documents in foreign state, which are set forth in Article 1, paragraph (1) of the Civil Procedure Convention, are subject to the jurisdiction of the district court that has jurisdiction over the place where the person requesting the service has a general venue'.

[29] Akira Takakuwa and Yamazaki, 'Gaikoku heno Sotatsu to Gaikoku kara no Sotatsu' in Akira Takakuwa and Masato Dogauchi (eds), *Shin Saiban Jitsumu Taikei (3): Kokusai Minji Soshoho (Zaisanho Kankei)* (*International Civil Litigation Law (Proprietary Matters)*) (Seirinshoin, 2002) 197).

or consular agents of the requesting state within its territory (ie, the state will not permit service by such means upon persons other than Japanese nationals). If it has so declared (as has been done, for instance, by South Korea, the People's Republic of China (PRC), Germany and France),[30] service upon Japanese nationals can be effected through Japanese diplomatic or consular agents or the Central Authority, while service upon non-Japanese nationals can only be effected through the Central Authority. If a state has not made a declaration (as, for instance, in the cases of the US, Canada and the UK), service on a person can be effected through Japanese diplomatic or consular agents or the Central Authority, regardless of the person's nationality. Where the foreign state is not party to HSC, one must check whether the state is party to HCPC.[31] If so, one must ascertain whether the state has opposed service through the requesting state's diplomatic or consular agents pursuant to HCPC article 6(1)(iii). But, as far as service through Japanese diplomatic or consular agents on Japanese citizens in the state addressed is concerned, by HCCP article 6(2), a foreign state cannot oppose such service.[32] Therefore, the question is actually whether the state addressed has opposed such service on non-Japanese nationals. If the state has not done so, service upon persons, regardless of nationality, can be effected through Japanese diplomatic or consular agents in the state addressed or the designated authority of the state addressed. On the other hand, if it has declared its opposition, service on Japanese nationals can be effected through Japanese diplomatic or consular agents in the foreign state or the designated authority of the state addressed, while service upon non-Japanese nationals can only be effected through the designated authority.

Service through Japanese diplomatic or consular agents abroad entails requesting the latter to deliver relevant documents. Such means is available under HCPC article 6(1)(3), HSC article 8(1), US Consular Convention article 17(1)(e)(i), and UK Consular Convention article 25, and individual agreements. The Japanese court before which a claim has been brought forwards the process and other documents to a Japanese diplomatic or consular agent in the state addressed through the Supreme Court and the Ministry of Foreign Affairs (MOFA) which will eventually cause the documents to be served on the person addressed in the foreign state.[33] Service of process is made without going through any foreign authority. Pursuant to HCPC article 6 and HSC article 8(2), a foreign state can object to service of

[30] See: www.hcch.net/en/instruments/conventions/authorities1/?cid=17.

[31] In relation to Contracting States to both HCPC and HSC, the rules under HCPC are replaced by those of HSC (HSC article 22). Accordingly, service through a designated authority will be used where an addressee is situated in a state which is a Contracting State only to HCPC.

[32] HCPC article 6 reads:

> 'The provisions of the foregoing Articles shall not interfere with:
>
> (1) the freedom to send documents, through postal channels, directly to the persons concerned abroad;
> (2) the freedom of the persons concerned to have service effected directly through the judicial officers or competent officials of the country of destination;
> (3) the freedom of each State to have service effected directly by its diplomatic or consular agents of documents intended for persons abroad.
>
> In each of these cases, the freedom mentioned shall only exist if allowed by conventions concluded between the States concerned or if, should there be no convention, the State on the territory of which service must be effected does not object. That State may not object when, in the cases mentioned in sub-paragraph 3 of the above paragraph, the document is to be served without any compulsion on a national of the requesting State'.

[33] *Handbook-ICP* (n 26) 34.

process by such means. But even if a foreign state does so, service of process on a Japanese national in the foreign state through a Japanese consul would still be available. Under the two Consular Conventions which Japan has entered into, the relevant foreign states cannot object to service through Japanese consular offices abroad (US Consular Convention article 17(1)(e); UK Consular Convention article 25). This means of service would be faster than other means and the attachment of a translation is not necessarily required. As a result, it is the most frequently used means in practice.[34] Nevertheless, the addressee may decline to receive documents. In such a case, service of process must be conducted in another way. Service through a designated authority may be possible. This is the principal means under HCPC article 1(1). The court forwards relevant judicial documents to the designated authority in the foreign state through the Supreme Court, MOFA and a consul in the state addressed. The consul will eventually cause the documents to be served on the addressee.[35] Where a foreign state has made a declaration under HCPC article 1(3), service will be effected through diplomatic channels, instead of a designated authority. Service through a Central Authority is available under HSC Article 2. The court seised forwards the relevant judicial documents to the Central Authority of the foreign state. This is done through the Supreme Court.[36] As service will be made without going through a consul or the Ministry of Foreign Affairs in the foreign state, this is a much simplified means when compared with that under HCPC. Service through diplomatic channels is available under HCPC Article 1(3) (in particular, with Russia). In this case, the Japanese court forwards the relevant documents to the relevant authority in the foreign state through the Supreme Court, MOFA, the Japanese ambassador in the foreign state, and the Ministry of Foreign Affairs of the state addressed.[37] Process and other documents can be served through a competent court of the state addressed, upon individual acceptance by the foreign state or a bilateral arrangement (such as with Brazil).[38] The Japanese court forwards the documents to the competent court in the foreign addressed state through the Supreme Court, MOFA, the Japanese embassy in the foreign state, and the Ministry of Foreign Affairs of the foreign state.[39] In the absence of bilateral arrangements, service may be carried out under CCP article 108. This stipulates that '[s]ervice to be effected in a foreign country is served as commissioned by the presiding judge to the competent government agency of that country or the Japanese ambassador, minister, or consul stationed in that country'. In other words, service of process must be done through diplomatic channels (namely, MOFA).[40] Nevertheless, service of process by a Japanese ambassador, minister, or consul would constitute an exercise of national sovereignty. Therefore, such means of service can only be employed if the state address authorises their use by way of a convention or other instrument.

[34] Takakuwa and Yamazaki (n 29) 202.
[35] *Handbook-ICP* (n 26) 38.
[36] ibid 36.
[37] ibid 40.
[38] As Brazil has not allowed service of process through a consul (even where an addressee is Japanese), only service through a competent court is available. See *Handbook-ICP* (n 26) 33 and 41.
[39] *Handbook-ICP* (n 26) 40–41.
[40] ibid 40.

In a case where 'it is impossible to effect service through the means under CCP article 108 or it is found to be impossible to effect service even through such means', or where 'even after six months have elapsed since the competent government agency of a foreign country issued a commission pursuant to the provision of article 108, no paper document that certifies that the agency has effected service is sent' (CCP article 110(1), (3) and (4)), the court clerk may effect service by publication. In addition, where service of process is to be made in a foreign state with which Japan does not have diplomatic relationship (such as Taiwan and North Korea), process may not be forwarded to relevant authorities of such state and there would be no Japanese ambassador or officer stationed in the same. In such case, service by publication may be made.[41]

ii. *Service of Foreign Proceedings in Japan*

For service of process from foreign states to Japan, analogous methods to the five discussed above would be available: (a) service through a foreign diplomatic or consular agents stationed in Japan; (b) service through an authority designated by the Japanese government; (c) service through the Central Authority in Japan; (d) service through diplomatic channels; and (e) service through a competent court in Japan.[42] The Minister of Foreign Affairs is the designated authority under HCPC and the Central Authority under HSC (ASPCP articles 2 and 24). Accordingly, service of foreign proceedings will be forwarded from the designated authority or Central Authority of the requesting state to the Minister of Foreign Affairs. In December 2018, Japan declared its opposition to HSC articles 8 and 10(a),[43] so that service through foreign diplomatic or consular agents in Japan and service by post are not available under the HSC.[44] There is an exception, however, for service through a foreign diplomatic or consular agents within Japan upon a national of the state in which the documents originate. Where HCPC, HSC and consular conventions have no application, service of foreign proceedings in Japan may be carried out through a competent court in accordance with bilateral arrangements or AABC article 1-2. The latter allows documents to be forwarded through diplomatic channels, but sets out specific requirements (such as the attachment of a Japanese translation and the provision of a guarantee that the relevant foreign state will bear the necessary costs of service and will permit the same or similar assistance to the Japanese courts). Where a Japanese translation is not attached, service cannot be effected.[45]

[41] ibid 42.

[42] ibid 52.

[43] See: www.hcch.net/en/instruments/conventions/status-table/notifications/?csid=407&disp=resdn.

[44] Prior to the objection in December 2018, Japan had stated that service by post 'would not be deemed valid service in Japan in circumstances where the rights of the addressee were not respected'. See *Conclusions and Recommendations adopted by the Special Commission on the Practical Operation of the Hague Apostille, Evidence, and Service Conventions* (28 October–4 November 2003) 57. From the government's position, it follows that service by post to a respondent in Japan would be invalid. Indeed, lower courts have held that service by post without a Japanese translation is invalid (Judgment of Tokyo District Court, 21 December 1976, HJ 870, 96. Judgment of Tokyo District Court, 11 November 1988, HJ 1315, 96; Judgment of Tokyo District Court, 26 March 1990, *Kinsho* 857, 39.

[45] *Handbook-ICP* (n 26) 57.

D. Taking Evidence Abroad or in Japan

In the course of cross-border proceedings, it may be necessary to use evidence and/or means of proof located in Japan or a foreign country, such as submission of documents possessed by the party or a third party in a foreign country, or depositions of witnesses residing in a foreign country. As to taking evidence in cross-border settings, the Convention of 18 March 1970 on the Taking of Evidence Abroad in Civil or Commercial Matters plays an important role around the globe, but Japan is not yet party to it. As a result, in order to take evidence abroad for use in Japanese proceedings or take evidence in Japan for use in foreign proceedings, the parties have to rely on other arrangements, like HCPC, or ad hoc agreements between Japan and foreign countries.

i. Taking Evidence Abroad for Use in Japanese Proceedings

To address requests to take evidence abroad for use in Japanese proceedings, there are four avenues available: taking evidence through (a) the consulate (diplomatic officers or consular agents) of the requesting state (ie, Japan); (b) the designated authority of the requested state; (c) the relevant authority of the requested state (via diplomatic channels under HCPC); and (d) the competent court of the requested state.

To decide which method to take, one must first examine whether the foreign state involved is party to HCPC. If the answer is 'yes', (c) is always available, and (b) limited to civil and commercial matters (HCPC article 8). Unless the requested state has made a declaration pursuant to HCPC article 15,[46] (a) can also be used limited to civil and commercial matters (HCPC article 8). If the foreign state is not a party to HCPC, the available methods will depend on the attitude of that state. Generally speaking, (d) can normally be used. Some states may also allow (a), possibly grounded on special agreements with foreign states, such as the Consular Conventions with the US (article 17(1)(e)(ii)) and the UK (article 25) or ad hoc arrangements.[47] The Japanese court seised by the lawsuit forwards the letter of request to the civil section of the administrative department of the Supreme Court, which in turn forwards it to MOFA and its consul in the foreign state. The evidence will then be taken by the consular agent in the foreign state pursuant to CCP.[48] Taking evidence in this manner is a quick route, but its effectiveness is not assured because the witness can refuse to answer questions.[49]

In carrying out method (b), the Japanese court before which a lawsuit is pending sends a letter of request to the Supreme Court which forwards it to MOFA. MOFA will in turn transmit the request to the Japanese embassy in the foreign country. The embassy then forwards

[46] HCPC article 15 reads: 'The provisions of the foregoing articles shall not exclude the right of each State to have Letters of Request executed directly by its diplomatic officers or consular agents, if that is allowed by conventions concluded between the States concerned or if the State on the territory of which the Letter is to be executed does not object'.

[47] *Handbook-ICP* (n 26) 46; Notification No 1722 from Vice-Minister of Justice on 22 September 1953.

[48] *Handbook-ICP* (n 26) 46.

[49] Takeo Kosugi, 'Gaikoku deno Shoko Shirabe' in Akira Takakuwa and Masato Dogauchi (eds), *Shin Saiban Jitsumu Taikei (3): Kokusai Minji Soshoho (Zaisanho Kankei) (International Civil Litigation Law (Proprietary Matters))* (Seirinshoin, 2002) 223.

the letter to the designated authority of the requested state which will take the requisite evidence in accordance with the law of the foreign state.[50] Taking evidence in this manner will require that the letter of request be accompanied by a translation in the language of the foreign state.[51]

In the case of (c) diplomatic channels (which includes taking evidence from witnesses or parties and the examination of documents and objects), HCPC articles 8–14 apply. HCPC article 9(3) provides that '[a]ny Contracting State may declare, by a communication addressed to the other Contracting States, that it intends that Letters of Request to be executed on its territory be transmitted through diplomatic channels'. Russia, Ukraine and Poland have so far made such a declaration. In the case of a request for taking evidence in those countries, method (b) is not available. The letter of request with its translation will be forwarded via the Supreme Court of Japan and MOFA to the ambassador of Japan in the foreign state. The latter will then forward the request to the Ministry of Foreign Affairs of the requested state and from there to the competent office.[52] Taking evidence will be conducted according to the national procedural law of the requested state. This type of taking evidence is effective, but typically time-consuming and costly.

As for method (d) of taking evidence though the competent court of the requested state, it could be based on bilateral agreements or ad hoc arrangements. The letter of request will be forwarded via the Supreme Court of Japan and MOFA to the Japanese embassy in the foreign state. The embassy will forward the request to the Ministry of Foreign Affairs of the requested state and from there the request will be sent to the competent court.[53] A written translation must be attached except in the case of evidence from Brazil.[54] Taking evidence will be conducted according to the national procedural law of the requested state.

According to CCP article 184(2), even if evidence is taken in a foreign country in a manner that contravenes the laws of the foreign country, it will still be considered valid evidence in Japanese proceedings, so long as it does not contravene CCP. In the case of proceedings before the Japanese court, it is possible for the court to order the party to submit relevant documents, whether situated in Japan or elsewhere (under CCP articles 219–23). On the other hand, the Japanese court can order a third party to do so only when he or she or the relevant document is in Japan.[55] When a party fails to follow the order, the court may find the opposite party's allegation concerning the contents and details of the document to be true (CCP article 224).

ii. Taking Evidence in Japan for Use in Foreign Proceedings

As for taking evidence in Japan for use in foreign proceedings, there are two ways to make a request, namely, via (a) the designated authority under HCPC; and (b) the competent

[50] *Handbook-ICP* (n 26) 48.
[51] ibid.
[52] ibid 49.
[53] ibid.
[54] ibid 50–51. The Circular Notice of the Secretary General of the Supreme Court addressed to the presidents of the high courts, district courts and family courts (No 89 of the Civil Affairs Second Division of the Supreme Court on 10 April 1991).
[55] Kosugi (n 49) 218–21.

Japanese court pursuant to bilateral agreements or an ad hoc arrangement. To decide which method to take, one needs to consider whether the foreign state involved is a party to HCPC. If it is, taking evidence through the designated authority is available. If it is not, taking evidence can only be done through the competent Japanese court. In the case of evidence through the designated authority, the latter is the Foreign Minister of Japan (HCPC articles 8–14 and ASPCP article 2). The request letter must be provided together with the list of questions to be put to the witness, a case description and a translation of the case description. These documents are forwarded from a consul in a foreign state, via the MOFA and the civil section of the administrative department of the Supreme Court to the competent district court (ASPCP article 3(2)). Taking evidence will be conducted according to CCP (HCPC articles 11(1) and 14(1), and ASPCP article 5). However, according to HCPC article 14(2), it can be carried out in accordance with a special method or procedure requested by the requesting authority, provided that this is not contrary to Japanese law.[56] Upon bilateral agreements or ad hoc arrangements, taking evidence can be carried out through the competent court. Likewise, the letter of request will be forwarded by the Japanese embassy in a foreign country to the competent district court, via MOFA and the Supreme Court (AABC article 1(2)). In this case, taking evidence is carried out in accordance with the relevant provisions of CCP (AABC article 3). In addition, taking evidence by a foreign consul in Japan is available insofar as it is provided and permitted in a bilateral convention such as the Consular Conventions with the US (article 17(1)(e)(ii)), and the UK (article 25). In this case, taking evidence by foreign counsel can be conducted without the involvement of the Japanese court or other institution. In other words, a consul from the US can take depositions from all witnesses present in Japan within the US consulate in accordance with US law.

Although often used, a US-style discovery, in particular the taking of depositions from witnesses and parties, violates the Consular Convention when carried out by US attorneys outside the US consulate in Japan. It is an unjustified extraterritorial application of the US Federal Rules of Civil Procedure and infringse upon the sovereignty of Japan. According to the prevailing view, however, a judgment given in the US on the basis of such taking of evidence can still be recognised in Japan, unless it obviously runs counter to procedural public policy (CCP article 118(3)).[57] As a matter of fact, a person involved in US proceedings may have little option but to abide by the request for deposition in Japan to avoid adverse consequences in the US proceedings. The person may otherwise have to travel to the US and make a deposition there, which is more cumbersome and inconvenient.[58]

On the other hand, taking evidence in Japan for use in foreign arbitration seems to be acceptable and held not to violate the sovereignty of Japan. Arguably, this is because arbitration is purely based on the parties' agreement and the witnesses concerned would be providing evidence of their own accord.

[56] *Handbook-ICP* (n 26) 60–61.
[57] Kosugi (n 49) 248.
[58] Sawaki=Dogauchi (n 23) 341.

II. Civil and Commercial Matters

A. General Rules

i. Defendant's Domicile

CCP article 3-2 sets out the general rule for jurisdiction of the Japanese courts in civil and commercial matters:

(1) The courts shall have jurisdiction over an action against a natural person:
- when he/she is domiciled in Japan;
- if he/she has no domicile or if his/her domicile is unknown, when he/she is resident in Japan; or
- if he/she has no residence or if his/her residence is unknown, when he/she has ever been domiciled in Japan prior to filing the action (except where he/she was domiciled abroad after he/she was last domiciled in Japan).

(2) Notwithstanding the provision of the preceding paragraph, the courts shall have jurisdiction over an action against an ambassador, minister, or any other Japanese national in a foreign country who enjoys immunity from the jurisdiction of that country.

(3) The courts shall have jurisdiction over an action against a legal person or any other association or foundation:
- when its principal office is located in Japan; or
- if it has no office or if the location of its office is unknown, when its representative or any other principal person in charge of its business is domiciled in Japan.

Where a natural person is concerned, general jurisdiction is first founded on a defendant's domicile (the traditional principle of *actor sequitur forum rei*) (article 3-2(1)); second on the defendant's residence (in the absence of a domicile in Japan or abroad);[59] and third on the defendant's last domicile in Japan unless subsequently domiciled abroad. On the concepts of domicile, residence and principal office, see chapter one, sections V.A and V.C. These rules are meant to secure that at least one state has general jurisdiction over a defendant.[60] They adopt the connecting factor of domicile as a pointer to where a natural person has his or her life centre.

In the case of a legal person or any other association or foundation, general jurisdiction is based on the place of its principal office (article 3-2(3)). If the registered principal office and the factual principal office are in different states, both ground general jurisdiction.[61] If the entity does not have an office in Japan or its location is unknown, the general jurisdiction of the Japanese courts is grounded on the domicile of its representative or any other person in charge of its business in Japan.

With regard to a Japanese ambassador, minister, or other Japanese national in a foreign country who enjoys immunity from the jurisdiction of that country, Japanese courts may

[59] Sawaki=Dogauchi (n 23) 271.
[60] *Hokokusho* (CCP) 7, available at: www.moj.go.jp/content/000012193.pdf.
[61] *Hokokusho* (CCP) 11, available at: www.moj.go.jp/content/000012193.pdf.

assume jurisdiction over them (article 3-2(2)). This rule is to secure that at least one state has general jurisdiction over such persons, whether or not domiciled in Japan.[62]

Japanese courts may assume jurisdiction on the basis of the grounds of specific jurisdiction in CCP articles 3-3–3-8. It should be noted that some jurisdictional grounds such as the place of performance and the place of tort are available only in the circumstances specified (the former in contractual, and the latter in tortious, matters), while other grounds such as the situs of property and the location of an office or business activities are available in a wide spectrum of cases. The latter grounds, in practical terms, frequently play an important role in the determination of direct jurisdiction.

ii. Forum non conveniens

CCP article 3-9 sets out a corrective rule in the form of a 'special circumstances' test that originates from case law.[63] It stipulates as follows:

> Even where the Japanese courts have jurisdiction over an action (except where the action has been brought on the basis of an exclusive jurisdiction agreement in favor of the Japanese courts), the court may dismiss the whole or part of the proceedings if, taking into account the nature of the case, the burden of the defendant to answer the claim, the location of evidence and any other factors, the court finds that there are special circumstances in which hearing and determining the case in Japan would impair fairness between the parties or hinder the proper and efficient conduct of the hearing.[64]

In summary, Japanese courts may wholly or partly dismiss proceedings if hearing and determining the merits of a case in Japan would impair fairness between the parties or hinder the sound and efficient administration of justice.[65] In that case, Japanese courts will not have jurisdiction (ie, technically, it will not merely be a matter of the court declining to exercise jurisdiction). In order to decide this, the court seised must consider the circumstances of individual cases including the nature of the case, the burden of the defendant to answer the claim, and other circumstances. Accordingly, as was decided in the *Ento Koku*

[62] Tatsufumi Sato and Yasuhiko Kobayashi, *Ichimon Itto Heisei 23 Nen Minji Soshoho to Kaisei: Kokusai Saiban Kankatsu Hosei no Seibi* (*Explanatory Note on the 2011 Reform of the Code of Civil Procedure and others: Improvement of the institution on International Adjudicative Jurisdiction*) (Shojihomu, 2012) 25 (Sato=Kobayashi).

[63] Judgment of Supreme Court, 11 November 1997, *Minshu* 51(10), 4055 ((1998) 41 *JAIL* 117). See also Dogauchi/Jurisdiction (n 3) 265–68. The plaintiff X, a Japanese company, signed a contract with the defendant Y, a Japanese national domiciled in Germany. X commissioned Y to purchase automobiles in Europe and engage in market research. X brought an action before the Chiba District Court for the restitution of funds entrusted to Y. As a general framework, the Supreme Court primarily relied on domestic jurisdiction rules (the 'reverse presumption theory'), while introducing a corrective rule to refuse Japan's jurisdiction under 'special circumstances' whereby exercising jurisdiction would run counter to fairness between the parties and an equitable and prompt administration of justice. But the Supreme Court did not ascertain any specific jurisdictional grounds in Japan. Rather, it only referred to the following special circumstances to refuse Japan's jurisdiction: (a) it would be beyond Y's expectation that the claim for restitution be made before a Japanese court, while the parties had not agreed on performance in Japan or the choice of Japanese law; (b) Y's home and principal place of business, as well as the evidence for the defence, were located in Germany; and (c) X imported automobiles from Germany, so it would not be excessively burdensome for X to bring a suit there.

[64] Cited from Koji Takahashi, 'Japan's Newly Enacted Rules on International Jurisdiction: with a Reflection on Some Issues of Interpretation' (2011) 13 *JYPIL* 146, 156.

[65] On the other hand, jurisdiction by necessity (*forum necessitatis*) can be granted *de lege lata* to guarantee the plaintiff's right to be heard. Sato=Kobayashi (n 62) 181.

case in 1986,[66] even if Japan is able to assume jurisdiction under CCP articles 3-3–3-8, a damages claim arising out of an air crash in Taiwan may be dismissed under CCP article 3-9 on the basis that the judge does not have access to the evidence found in Taiwan in the absence of diplomatic relations and available judicial assistance.[67] Jurisdiction may not be refused under CCP article 3-9 if the parties have conferred exclusive jurisdiction on the Japanese court by a choice of court agreement (CCP article 3-9)[68] or if a statute has conferred exclusive jurisdiction on the Japanese court (CCP article 3-10). Consequently, CCP article 3-9 must be taken into account, even where the jurisdiction of the Japanese courts is grounded on articles 3-2 and 3-8, that is, general jurisdiction and the defendant's submission.[69] Accordingly, exceptionally, a judge may dismiss a damages claim against a Japanese company based on product liability if a number of similar actions are already pending before a foreign court and filing further claims there would be more reasonable than commencing a fresh action in Japan.[70]

The corrective rule in article 3-9 is comparable to the doctrine of *forum non conveniens* applied in common law jurisdictions, but not generally used in civil law systems. However, the Japanese corrective rule differs from common law *forum non conveniens*. For instance, the Japanese rule does not mandate the assessment of the relative appropriateness of alternative forums, but restricts itself to an assessment of the appropriateness of hearing and determining a case in Japan.[71] It is unclear and still debatable whether dismissal under CCP article 3-9 is mandatory or discretionary.[72] Some authors take the view, by reference to the wording of the provision, that the Japanese corrective rule merely gives the judge a discretion to dismiss an action.[73] In contrast, others are of opinion that unlike *forum non conveniens*, the rule requires the judge to deny the existence of jurisdiction when specific circumstances are found to exist, instead of refraining from exercising jurisdiction as a matter of discretion on the ground that another court appears to be a better forum. In this latter view, a Japanese judge has the duty to dismiss a claim whenever the requirements of article 3-9 are fulfilled.[74] In any event, it cannot be denied that a wide margin of appreciation (in effect, equivalent to

[66] Judgment of Tokyo District Court, 20 June 1986, HJ 1196, 87.

[67] Sawaki=Dogauchi (n 23) 309; Jun Yokoyama, *Private International Law in Japan*, 2nd edn (Kluwer Law International, 2019).

[68] In view of the corrective rule for domestic jurisdiction that also governs an exclusive choice of court agreement (CCP articles 11 and 17), it was extensively discussed whether and how far CCP article 3-9 should control it as well. For the sake of the parties' intent and foreseeability, an exclusive choice of court agreement was eventually excluded from the scope of article 3-9. Minutes of 13th–15th Meetings (CCP); Sato=Kobayashi (n 62) 162.

[69] In fact, there have been some cases in which Japanese lower courts have declined jurisdiction under CCP article 3-9, even where a defendant was domiciled or had a principal office in Japan. For instance, Judgment of Tokyo District Court, 22 February 2013, 2013WLJPCA02226001; Judgment of Tokyo District Court, 24 January 2018, HT, 1465, 250.

[70] Sato=Kobayashi (n 62) 164.

[71] Koji Takahashi, 'The Jurisdiction of Japanese Courts in A Comparative Context' (2015) 11 *JPIL* 103, 107 (Takahashi/Jurisdiction). Where concurrent proceedings abroad exist, Japanese courts may consider the appropriateness of competing fora but only to the extent necessary to give an answer to that question. See discussion of *lis alibi pendens* in section II.A.ii.

[72] For further discussion, see Dogauchi/Jurisdiction (n 3) 275–76; Takahashi/Jurisdiction (n 71) 160–67.

[73] Yoshimitsu Aoyama, et al, 'Kokusai Saiban Kankatsu: Minjisoshôhô Kaisei wo ukete' ('International Jurisdiction: Following the Reform of the CCP') (2012) 30 *Nomos* (Kansai University) 109, 173–76 Takahashi/Jurisdiction (n 71) 104–10.

[74] Yuko Nishitani, 'International Jurisdiction of Japanese Courts in a Comparative Perspective' (2013) 60 *Netherlands International Law Review* 251, 271 (Nishitani/Jurisdiction); Sawaki=Dogauchi (n 23) 310

a margin of discretion) is left for the judge, when ascertaining whether the requirements of article 3–9 are fulfilled.[75]

There has so far been one case in which the Supreme Court declined jurisdiction by applying the special circumstances test under CCP Article 3-9.[76] The case involved a dispute between a Japanese corporation (X1), its chairperson (X2) and a Nevada corporation (Y). X1 had been engaged in developing, producing and marketing pinball machines as its principal business. Company A, a subsidiary of X1 and a Nevada corporation, held approximately 20 per cent of Y's share capital. Y operated a casino as its principal business and held a gaming licence in Nevada. X2 was a director of Y. According to the laws and regulations of Nevada, the holder of a gaming licence may be deprived of a licence if the regulatory authorities find the holder unfit to hold the licence by reason of involvement in criminal activity. Under its articles of incorporation, Y could mandatorily redeem any shares held by a shareholder where the board of directors finds that the shareholder is likely to pose a threat to the licence. On 18 February 2012, Y's board (with the exception of X2) found that A, X1 and X2 were unfit to be shareholders and adopted a resolution to redeem A's shares in Y. On 19 February 2012, Y posted a notice to that effect on its website. On the same day, Y sued A, X1 and X2 in the Nevada court for a declaration that Y had acted in accordance with its articles. Y also sought damages based on X2's breach of fiduciary duty. On 12 March 2012, A and X1 filed a counterclaim against Y and its directors, alleging that the board resolution was invalid and seeking the suspension of the resolution and the payment of damages. In August 2012, X1 and X2 sued Y before the Tokyo District Court, seeking tortious damages on the basis that their reputation had been affected by the notice posted by Y on its website. The Court held that hearing and determining the case in Japan would impair fairness between the parties and hinder the proper and efficient conduct of the hearing. In so concluding, the Court considered such factors as the progress of the proceedings in the US, the close connection of the parties to the proceedings in the US, the location of the relevant evidence, and the previous communications between the parties with regard to dispute resolution.

iii. Lis alibi pendens

In international transaction, courts of plural states may have jurisdiction over one and the same case ('concurrent jurisdictions'). A party normally tries to bring a case before a court in one's own state to take 'home advantage' and save the costs of proceedings. A party may also attempt to find the most favourable forum for a case in terms of advantages on substantive law level ('forum shopping'). If each party tries to be the first to bring a case in the forum that is most favourable to one's case ('forum running'), simultaneous litigation in different states may arise ('international parallel litigation'). International parallel litigation

[75] Takahashi/Jurisdiction (n 71) 105, fn 9.

[76] Judgment of Supreme Court, 10 March 2016, *Minshu* 70(3), 846 ((2017) 60 *JYIL* 488). Also, there have been at least six reported judgments in which lower courts have declined jurisdiction under the special circumstances test in CCP article 3-9. For instance, Judgment of Tokyo District Court, 22 February 2013, 2013WLJPCA02226001; Judgment of Tokyo District Court, 24 January 2018, HT 1465, 250; Judgment of Tokyo District Court, 31 October 2017, 2017WLJPCA10318017; Judgment of Tokyo District Court, 13 September 2017, 2017WLJPCA09138010; Judgment of Tokyo District Court, 14 July 2016, 2016WLJPCA07148030; Judgment of Yokohama District Court, 6 August 2014, HJ 2264, 62.

can arise, for instance, where a plaintiff seeks a judgment on liability against a defendant in a foreign court and the defendant in the foreign proceedings applies to its home court for a declaration of non-liability. The defendant's intention may be to forestall the recognition and enforcement by the courts in the defendant's home state of any judgment by the foreign court in the plaintiff's favour. Parallel litigation imposes a burden on all parties and are a waste of judicial resources. Moreover, there is a risk that the courts involved will come to conflicting decisions. Consequently, each state will typically regulate this situation to eliminate or minimise its occurrence.[77]

In preparing the 2011 amendments of CCP and CPRA, the Division on International Jurisdiction extensively deliberated whether to adopt a specific rule on the matter. In the 2009 Interim Draft (CCP), it was suggested[78] that, in accordance with the *lis alibi pendens* doctrine, the judge should be authorised to stay proceedings involving the same cause of action between the same parties as in the foreign action, if the latter was instituted first and a judgment capable of recognition under CCP article 118 could be expected. The proposed rule aimed to curtail parallel litigation at a preliminary stage by giving priority to the court first seised of a matter. The rationale was that, once recognised, the effects of a foreign judgment would automatically be equated with those of a Japanese judgment, including for the purposes of *res judicata*.[79] Different stakeholders, however, criticised the proposal on the ground that the probability of a future foreign judgment being recognised can hardly be ascertained. It was argued that the same result could be attained by staying proceedings and postponing a court's hearing of the merits. It was contended that Japanese companies involved in cross-border parallel litigation would be unduly disadvantaged before a foreign court which would not reciprocate by staying proceedings.[80] A revised suggestion that the order to stay proceedings be restricted to a four-month period, which would be renewable but not subject to appeal, was similarly unsuccessful. While judges expressed concern from the standpoint of a sound and prompt administration of justice, lawyers preferred to maintain the option to litigate before the Japanese courts in a strategic manner.[81] Because of a lack of unanimity, the Division eventually did not adopt the provision.

Thus, it remains an open question precisely how Japanese courts will deal with the situation. In academic literature, opinions basically divide into two groups and there seems to be no consensus.[82] The first approach is to give priority to the earlier proceeding, that is, to apply CCP Article 142 by analogy to cross-border parallel proceedings. Foreign judgments, once recognised, enjoy the same effect as Japanese judgments. Therefore, foreign proceedings should be taken into consideration, if a future judgment given by the court first seised is likely to be recognised in Japan. Accordingly, if the subject matter of a dispute is identical to that of the foreign proceedings and if the requirements[83] of CCP article 118 for the recognition of a foreign judgment are likely to be satisfied, then the Japanese court should

[77] For instance, Brussels *Ibis* article 29; SPIL article 9.

[78] Interim Draft (CCP) VIII-1 (A)(B); *Hosoku Setsumei* (CCP) 55–60, available at: www.e-gov.go.jp/.

[79] Yoshihisa Hayakawa, 'Lis Pendens' (2011) 54 *JYIL* 324; Nishitani/Baum/Bälz (n 6) [171–173].

[80] Sato=Kobayashi (n 62) 176–77.

[81] ibid 177.

[82] For details, Masato Dogauchi, 'Kokusai Sosho Kyogo' in Akira Takakuwa and Masato Dogauchi (eds), *Shin Saiban Jitsumu Taikei (3) Kokusai Minji Sosho-ho (Zaisanho Kankei) (International Civil Litigation Law (Proprietary Matters))* (Seirinshoin, 2002) 145.

[83] Namely, indirect jurisdiction, proper service of process, reciprocity and conformity with public policy.

refuse to determine the case. The Japanese court should only examine the case, if and only if a concrete judgment is submitted to it.[84] The second approach is to deal with the issue under the special circumstances test in CCP article 3-9, enabling the Japanese court to deal with the matter flexibly. This second approach can prevent parallel proceedings from occurring. But the difficulty is that it does not provide concrete criteria for determining which court is in a 'proper' position to hear and determine the merits of a case. The approach is also inconsistent with the scheme underlying the CCP for two reasons. First, CCP article 142 prohibits parties from filing another action if an action between the parties is already pending before a court. Second, the requirement of indirect jurisdiction under CCP article 118(1) simply means that the foreign court has indirect jurisdiction. The provision does not require that the foreign court be the 'appropriate' forum for the determination of the parties' dispute.

To resolve the debate, it is expedient to refer to the *Masaki Bussan* case (1991).[85] A Japanese company X produced noodle machines and sold them to Y, a US company. Y sued X before the Californian court for indemnification of the damages that Y might incur in a product liability action filed by a third party. X sued Y before the Tokyo District Court to seek a negative declaration of liability against Y, aiming to hamper the enforcement of any future US judgment. Although the Japanese court was competent as the *locus delicti commissi*, the judge declined international jurisdiction by applying the 'exceptional circumstances' test. The judge opined that California was a more appropriate forum on the grounds that X's claim depended on the outcome of the Californian proceedings that were already at an advanced stage, the evidence was located in the US, and conducting a defence before the Japanese court would result in an excessive burden for Y. Following this reasoning, international parallel litigation can, in effect, be regulated by restricting international jurisdiction pursuant to CCP article 3-9 and by analogy with the *forum non conveniens* approach taken in the US and other common law jurisdictions. In so applying article 3-9, Japanese judges should consider the stage of the foreign proceedings, the connection between the subject matter of the claim and the forum, the location of the evidence, and the probability that a subsequent foreign judgment will be recognised in Japan under CCP article 118.[86] In addition, in a recent case of related proceedings (not parallel proceedings), the Supreme Court adopted a similar approach.[87] The Supreme Court dismissed Japanese proceedings under the special circumstances test in CCP article 3-9, holding that 'hearing and determining the case in Japan would impair fairness between the parties or hinder the proper and efficient conduct of the hearing'. In applying the 'special circumstances' test, the Court considered such factors as the progress of the proceedings in the US, the close connection of the proceedings in the US, the location of the relevant evidence, and the previous communications between the parties in terms of dispute resolution.

iv. Anti-Suit Injunctions

There is no rule of jurisdiction that prohibits a party from bringing or maintaining actions (even a parallel or related action) before a foreign court. Although some commentators have

[84] Masato Dogauchi, 'Kokusai Sosho Kyogo' in Akira Takakuwa and Masato Dogauchi (eds), *Shin Saiban Jitsumu Taikei (3): Kokusai Minji Soshoho (Zaisanho Kankei) (International Civil Litigation Law (Proprietary Matters))* (Seirinshoin, 2002) 148.

[85] Judgment of Tokyo District Court, 29 January 1991, HJ 1390, 98.

[86] Sato=Kobayashi (n 62) 159 and 179.

[87] Judgment of Supreme Court, 10 March 2016, *Minshu* 70(3), 846 ((2017) 60 *JYIL* 488).

opined that anti-suit injunctions may be issued as interim measures,[88] it is generally understood that anti-suit injunctions are not possible under Japanese law.[89]

v. *Interim Measures*

In 2011 the first black-letter rules on international jurisdiction in respect of interim measures were introduced in CPRA. According to CPRA article 11, a party may file a petition for interim measures when (a) an action on the merits may be brought before the Japanese courts or (b) the property to be temporally seised or the object in dispute is found in Japan. The first ground is justified by the fact that such petition is subordinate to the merits of the case and it is convenient for a court seised to deal with the petition and the substantive matter.[90] But, if the parties have agreed on the exclusive jurisdiction of a foreign court or arbitration abroad, jurisdiction over the substantive proceeding will be refused, with the result that jurisdiction in respect of the petition will also be denied.[91] In this case, the party seeking an interim measure in Japan will need to rely on the second ground. This latter ground is justified by the fact that the court of the place where the relevant property or disputed subject matter is located is in a good position to decide the necessity of a provisional remedy and is able to execute such remedy effectively.[92] Pursuant to CPRA article 7, the provisions of CCP apply *mutatis mutandis* except as otherwise provided. CPRA does not explicitly eliminate the applicability of the special circumstances test in article 3-9.[93] Thus, when deciding jurisdiction in respect of interim measures, the court may apply the corrective rule in theory. Nevertheless, the court is unlikely to decline jurisdiction in practice, in particular when the relevant property or disputed subject matter is in Japan. Typically, a decision whether or not to grant an interim measure will have to be taken urgently and efficiently. A consideration of the corrective rule in article 3-9 would delay matters and therefore should not normally come into play in the context of interim measures.[94] The court should instead take into account the circumstances of each case when assessing the necessity of interim measures under CPRA article 20.[95]

[88] Masato Dogauchi, 'Concurrent Litigations in Japan and the United States' (1994) 37 *JAIL* 72 (Dogauchi/Concurrent Litigations). For possible anti-suit injunctions in support of cross-border insolvency proceedings in Japan, see Satoshi Watanabe, '*Gaikoku Sosho Sashitome Meirei: Nihon no Saibansho ha Meirei Dekiruka*' in Y Matsui et al (eds), *Global-ka suru Sekai to Ho no Kadai: Heiwa, Jinken, Keizai wo tegakari ni* (Toshindo, 2006) 244–53.

[89] Nishitani/Jurisdiction (n 74) 273. *cf* Yoshimasa Furuta, 'Sosho Sashitome Meirei' in Akira Takakuwa and Masato Dogauchi (eds), *Shin Saiban Jitsumu Taikei (3): Kokusai Minji Soshoho (Zaisanho Kankei) (International Civil Litigation Law (Proprietary Matters))* (Seirinshoin, 2002) 157–60.

[90] Yoshiaki Sakurada, *Kokusai Shiho (Private International Law)*, 7th edn (Yuhikaku, 2020) 373–74 (Sakurada); Sato=Kobayashi (n 62) 183; Sawaki=Dogauchi (n 23) 358; Muneki Uchino (ed), *Ichimon Itto Heisei 30 Nen Jinji Soshoho Kaji Jiken Tetsuzukiho to Kaisei: Kokusai Saiban Kankatsu Hosei no Seibi (Explanatory Note on the 2018 Reform of the Personal Status Litigation Act, Domestic Relations Case Procedure Act: Improvement of the institution on International Adjudicative Jurisdiction)* (Shojihomu, 2019) 70–71 (Uchino).

[91] Decision of Tokyo District Court, 28 August 2007, HJ 1991 89; Yasunori Honma, Shun'ichiro Nakano and Hajime Sakai, *Kokusai Minji Tetsuzuki-ho (International Procedure Law)*, 2nd edn (Yuhikaku, 2012) 205 (Honma/Nakano/Sakai).

[92] Sakurada (n 90) 374; Sato=Kobayashi (n 62) 183; Sawaki=Dogauchi (n 23) 358; Uchino (n 90) 70–71.

[93] Sato=Kobayashi (n 62) 187.

[94] Sawaki=Dogauchi (n 23) 358–59.

[95] ibid. Also, Decision of Asahikawa District Court, 9 February 1996, HJ 1610, 106.

vi. Choice of Court Agreements

A choice of court agreement is largely governed by CCP article 3-7.[96] That stipulates:

(1) Parties may establish, by agreement, the country in which they are permitted to file an action with the courts.

(2) The agreement as referred to in the preceding paragraph is not valid unless it is made regarding actions that are based on a specific legal relationship, and executed by means of a paper document.

(3) If electronic or magnetic records (meaning records used in computer data processing which are created in electronic form, magnetic form, or any other form that is otherwise impossible to perceive through the human senses alone; the same applies hereinafter) in which the content of the agreement is recorded are used to execute the agreement as referred to in paragraph (1), the agreement is deemed to have been executed by means of a paper document and the provisions of the preceding paragraph apply.

(4) An agreement that an action may be filed only with the courts of a foreign country may not be invoked if those courts are unable to exercise jurisdiction by law or in fact.

(5) An agreement as referred to in paragraph (1) which covers Consumer Contract disputes that may arise in the future is valid only in the following cases:

(i) if the agreement provides that an action may be filed with the courts of the country where the Consumer was domiciled at the time the Consumer Contract was concluded (except in the case set forth in the following item, any agreement that an action may be filed only with a court of such a country is deemed not to preclude the filing of an action with a court of any other country);

(ii) if the Consumer, in accordance with said agreement, has filed an action with the courts of the agreed-upon country, or if an Enterprise has filed an action with the Japanese courts or with the courts of a foreign country and the Consumer has invoked said agreement.

(6) An agreement as referred to in paragraph (1) which covers an Individual Civil Labour Dispute that may arise in the future is valid only in the following cases:

(i) if the agreement is made at the time a labour contract ends, and establishes that an action may be filed with the courts of the country where the place that the labour was being provided as of that time is located (except in the case set forth in the following item, an agreement that an action may be filed only with the courts of such a country is deemed not to preclude the filing of an action with the courts of any other country);

(ii) if the worker, in accordance with said agreement, files an action with the courts of the agreed-upon country; or if the enterprise files an action with the Japanese courts or with the courts of a foreign country and the worker invokes said agreement.

Under article 3-7, parties may agree to the exclusive or non-exclusive jurisdiction of a court or courts in Japan or elsewhere, unless the special rules on exclusive jurisdiction in article 3-5 or on consumer contracts and employment relations in articles 3-7(5) and (6) apply. To be valid, a choice of court agreement must be in writing and 'concerned with an action arising from a particular legal relationship' (article 3-7(2)). An agreement conferring exclusive

[96] For details, see, eg, Shunichiro Nakano, 'Agreement on Jurisdiction' (2011) 54 *JYIL* 278 (Nakano/Agreement); Shiho Kato, 'Recent Developments in Rules on Choice of Court Agreements in Japan: New Codification and Remaining Problems' in Alexander Bruns and Masabumi Suzuki, *Preventive Instruments of Social Governance* (Mohr Siebeck, 2017) (Kato/CCA).

jurisdiction on a foreign court may not be invoked in a case where the designated court is legally or factually unable to exercise jurisdiction (article 3-7(4)). The special circumstances test under article 3-9 does not apply when the parties agree to confer exclusive jurisdiction on the Japanese courts. This rule aims to secure stability and predictability in respect of the validity of choice of court agreements.[97] Furthermore, under article 3-7, a choice of court agreement is not deemed to confer exclusive jurisdiction on the designated court, unlike in other jurisdictions.[98] Whether an agreement is exclusive or prerogative will be determined by the law applicable to that agreement because this is a matter of parties' intention and the interpretation of an agreement.

The prevailing view[99] is that an exclusive choice of court agreement must further satisfy an unwritten requirement, namely, the public policy requirement introduced by the Supreme Court in the *Chisadane* case (1975). According to this, an agreement will be unenforceable 'if it is excessively unreasonable and is against public policy rules'.[100] Lower courts have applied the public policy requirement on a case-by-case basis, checking whether an agreement is unreasonable in light of all the circumstances. For instance, in determining unreasonableness, courts have taken into account factual elements such as (a) connection with Japan, (b) connection with the *situs* of the designated court, (c) any difficulties in accessing the designated court, (d) the location of evidence, (e) the process whereby the agreement was concluded, and (f) the necessity of protecting consumers.[101] Consequently, the public policy requirement functions as a safety valve for invalidating agreements that are found to be unreasonable and does not deal with the question of derogation.[102] In the 2011 CCP amendment, some provisions which might be characterised as embodying a public policy requirement were introduced. For instance, article 3-7(4) now deals with situations in which the designated court is legally or factually unable to exercise jurisdiction over a case. Articles 3-7(5) and (6) provide special protection for weaker parties, such as consumers and employees. These recent provisions come into play prior to any consideration of

[97] Sato=Kobayashi (n 62) 162.

[98] eg, Brussels *Ibis* article 25; SPIL article 5. Also HCC article 3(2).

[99] See, eg, Sato=Kobayashi (n 62) 140; Sawaki=Dogauchi (n 23) 306; Koji Takahashi, 'Choice of Court Agreement' (2012) 210 *Bessatsu Jurist* 202; Masato Dogauchi, 'Kokusai Saiban Kankatsu Goui no Yukosei – Tokyo Chisai Heisei 28 nen 2 gatsu 15 nichi Chukan Hanketsu wo megutte' (2016) 1077 *NBL* 29–30.

[100] Judgment of Supreme Court, 28 November 1975, *Minshu* 29(4), 572 ((1976) 20 *JAIL* 106). In *Chisadane*, the Supreme Court established the aforementioned public policy requirement. The case involved an action for damages by a Japanese insurance company (appellant, plaintiff) (as a subrogated party to a claim by a Japanese trading company) against a Dutch shipping company (appellee, defendant). The issue was the validity of an exclusive choice of court agreement contained in a bill of lading conferring jurisdiction on the court in Amsterdam. The appellant argued that such agreement was against public policy (here, presumably, some mandatory provisions of the International Convention for the Unification of Certain Law Relating to Bills of Lading (the Hague–Visby Rules)). However, the Court held that the relevant clause should be regarded as 'valid in principle unless such agreement is excessively unreasonable and against public policy rules'. This judgment thus suggests that an exclusive choice of court agreement designating a foreign court may not be enforced in exceptional situations. For details, see Nakano/Agreement (n 96) 280–83.

[101] For instance, Kato/CCA (n 96) 182–91. There have been some cases in which Japanese courts have held that choice of court agreements are contrary to public policy rules: Interim Judgment of Tokyo District Court, 13 September 1999, *Kaiji-ho Kenkyu Kai Shi* 154, 89; Judgment of Tokyo District Court, 14 November 2012, *Rohan* 1066, 5; Judgment of Tokyo High Court, 28 June 2012, LEX/DB25504140; Judgment of Osaka High Court, 20 February 2014, HJ 2225, 77; Judgment of Tokyo High Court, 17 November 2014, HJ 2243, 28.

[102] Most commentators support this fact-based or case-by-case analytical framework. For example, Masatsugu Mitsuki, 'Goui Kankatsu' in Takao Sawaki and Jun'ichi Akiba, *Shinban, Kokusai Shiho no Soten* (Yuhikaku, 1996) 232.

the unwritten public policy requirement.[103] The public policy control would then only be engaged when the national or public interest might be harmed by reason of a choice of court agreement.[104]

Insofar as an exclusive choice of court agreement is concerned, an important question is whether an exclusive selection of a foreign court should be regarded as valid, even if it would lead to a derogation from overriding mandatory rules of the court seised. In this regard, in a case involving competition law, Japanese courts adopted an interesting approach.[105] According to this, a choice of court agreement should be respected, even if it would lead to a derogation from domestic competition law. The exception is where there would be such a wide discrepancy between the outcomes before the designated foreign court and the Japanese court, that it would be intolerable to enforce the choice of court agreement from the standpoint of maintaining the public policy objectives of Japanese competition law. The problem, however, is that proceeding as the Japanese courts have held would mean deciding at the jurisdictional stage on the basis of alleged facts whether or not there would be a wide discrepancy between the likely findings of the Japanese and foreign courts. The allegations may later turn out to be untrue. It would be impermissibly straying into the merits. It is instead submitted that choice of court agreements should generally be respected, unless they are obviously unreasonable or contrary to public policy on their face. At the jurisdictional stage, a court should not treat an agreement as invalid merely because it could potentially lead to a derogation from the substantive domestic laws of the forum, even where such law is regarded as a body of overriding mandatory rules.[106]

It is disputed in Japan how best to determine the substantive validity of a choice of court agreement, which is severable from the main contract. A previous opinion advocated that criteria appropriate to Japanese international civil procedure law should apply, although without specifying the content of such criteria.[107] For the sake of legal certainty, recent authors have increasingly pointed to the law chosen by the parties to govern their choice of court agreement. In the absence of an expression of the governing law by the parties, the system of law with the closest connection should apply. That will usually coincide with the law governing the main contract (*cf* the Act on General Rules for Application of Laws (AGRAL) articles 7 and 8).[108] While these solutions take the private international law of the forum as a starting point, HCC articles 5(1), 6(a) and 9(a) and Brussels I*bis* article 25(1) seek uniformity and coordination among Contracting States or Member States by referring to the law of the designated forum, including its private international

[103] Miyuki Watanabe, 'Kankatsu ni kansuru Goui to Ouso ni yoru Kankatsu' in Hiroyuki Kobayashi (ed), *Kokusai Saiban Kankatsu no Riron to Jitsumu* (Shin Nippon Hoki, 2017) 202.

[104] Masato Dogauchi, 'Kokusai Saiban Kankatsu Goui no Yukosei – Tokyo Chisai Heisei 28 nen 2 gatsu 15 nichi Chukan Hanketsu wo megutte' (2016) 1077 *NBL* 30.

[105] Judgment of Tokyo District Court, 6 October 2016, *Kinyu Shoji Hanrei* 1515, 42; Judgment of Tokyo High Court, 25 October 2017, 2017WLJPCA10256010 ((2018) 61 *JYIL* 416).

[106] For details, see Kazuaki Nishioka, 'Choice of Court Agreements and Derogation from Competition Law' (2020) 16 *JPIL* 300.

[107] Sueo Ikehara, 'Kokusaiteki Saiban Kankatsuken' in Chu'ichi Suzuki and Akira Mikazuki (eds), *Shin Jitsumu Minji-Soshoho Koza* (*New Series on Practice of Civil Procedure Law*) (Nihon Hyoronsha, 1982) 36 (Ikehara/Jurisdiction).

[108] Tadashi Kanzaki, 'Goi ni yoru Kankatsuken' in Akira Takakuwa and Masato Dogauchi (eds), *Kokusai Minji Soshoho: Zaisanhô Kankei* (Seirin Shoin, 2002) 138–40; Nakano/Agreement (n 96) 287–88.

law. From the perspective of promoting legal certainty and predictability, this solution would seem appropriate.

vii. Submission

CCP article 3-8 provides an alternative ground for jurisdiction: 'The courts shall have jurisdiction when the defendant, without objecting to the jurisdiction, made an oral argument on the merits or made a statement in preparatory proceedings'. As is evident from the wording, the defendant's submission to the court can ground jurisdiction, even if other jurisdictional heads under CCP articles 3-2–3-7 are not satisfied. However, it would not constitute a submission to the court if the defendant only appears before it to object to jurisdiction. The defendant must reply to the merits of the case, without opposing jurisdiction.[109] Even if the defendant's objection to jurisdiction is rejected, article 3-8 will not apply as a basis for jurisdiction unless the defendant replies to the merits. Pursuant to CCP article 3-10, however, article 3-8 'shall have no application where, with respect to the action in question, the exclusive jurisdiction of the Japanese courts is prescribed by legislation'. Conversely, the Japanese courts are obliged to dismiss a claim which falls within the exclusive jurisdiction of a foreign court by applying CCP article 3-5 analogously, even where a defendant submits to the Japanese court.[110]

viii. Exclusive Jurisdiction

With the public interest in mind, Japan has reserved certain matters to the exclusive jurisdiction of the Japanese courts. CCP article 3-5 lists those matters:

(1) Actions in Chapter II (except those set out in sections 4 and 6) of Part VII of the Companies Act, actions in section 2 of Chapter VI of the Act on General Incorporated Associations and General Incorporated Foundations (Act No 48 of 2006) and analogous actions relating to associations or foundations incorporated under other Japanese legislation shall be subject to the exclusive jurisdiction of the Japanese courts.
(2) An action with respect to registration shall be subject to the exclusive jurisdiction of the Japanese courts if the place of registration is located in Japan.
(3) An action with respect to the existence and effect of an intellectual property right (viz the right as defined by article 2(2) of the Basic Act of Intellectual Property (Act No 122 of 2002)) which comes into existence by registration shall be subject to the exclusive jurisdiction of the Japanese courts if the registration was effected in Japan.

The first set covers corporation matters. Japanese courts have exclusive jurisdiction over disputes concerning the validity of the constitution or dissolution of a company or other entity and the nullity of the decisions of their organs. Also, it covers the liability and discharge of corporate officers, aiming at uniform decisions and procedural convenience for companies and shareholders.[111] An action against former and present individual members of a company, on the other hand, is not subject to exclusive jurisdiction, but to the non-exclusive and ordinary jurisdiction of the courts under article 3-3(7) (see section II.B.iii).

[109] Sato=Kobayashi (n 62) 155.
[110] ibid 155–56.
[111] *Hosoku Setsumei* (CCP) 17–20, available at: www.e-gov.go.jp/; Sato=Kobayashi (n 62) 102–03.

The second deals with matters relating to registration. Japanese courts have exclusive jurisdiction for disputes over a registration to be made in Japan. This provision specifically covers the entries in public registers about immovable property situated in Japan and the registration of intellectual property rights (including patent rights, trademark, design rights and utility model rights).[112] Furthermore, insofar as the action relates to the registration, all categories of IP rights – including copyrights that come into existence without formalities but can be registered in order to be opposed to third parties – are subject to the exclusive jurisdiction of the country of protection or registration.[113] This rule is justified by public interest, such registration being inseparable from the public registry system, and the court's capability in the relevant state of administrating the sound and prompt trial.[114]

The third set covers the existence and validity of intellectual property rights registered in Japan. The term 'intellectual property rights' covers rights established by registration (article 2(2) of the Basic Act of Intellectual Property), such as a patent, utility model, design or trademark. This jurisdictional ground is justified because the country of registration is considered as the most appropriate forum, patents, trademarks and comparable IP rights being granted by an administrative act and subject to specific proceedings for their invalidation or revocation with *erga omnes* effect.[115] Insofar as rights which need to be registered in Japan are concerned, disputes as to their existence or validity come within the exclusive jurisdiction of the Japanese courts. In contrast, actions relating to intellectual property rights (including actions to seek damages for the infringement of intellectual property rights) are not subject to the exclusive jurisdiction of the Japanese courts. The courts may hear such actions if any of the jurisdictional grounds in CCP articles 3-2–3-9 are applicable (see section II.B.ii.c).

CCP article 3-5(1)–(3) are understood as being applicable by analogy to foreign courts. This means that, where (for instance) an intellectual property right of one of the abovementioned categories, like patent, is registered in Japan, the Japanese courts will have exclusive jurisdiction in respect of the validity and existence of that right. Conversely, where an intellectual property right is registered abroad, then although not explicitly stated in CCP article 3-5, the court in the place of registration is treated as having exclusive jurisdiction by analogy. This means that the Japanese court must decline jurisdiction in such case, even where an alternative ground is present for founding jurisdiction, such as the defendant's domicile under CCP article 3-2.[116] Accordingly, when a ground of exclusive jurisdiction under CCP article 3-5 points by analogy to a foreign state having jurisdiction, the indirect jurisdiction of the latter is confirmed and the direct jurisdiction of the Japanese courts is denied by definition.[117]

[112] Sato=Kobayashi (n 62) 109.
[113] ibid 109.
[114] ibid 107–08.
[115] *Hosoku Setsumei* (CCP) 36–37, available at: www.e-gov.go.jp/. It does not comprise disputes over the ownership of intellectual property rights, which do not require any special technique or expertise on the part of the courts of the country of registration. Sato=Kobayashi (n 62) 111.
[116] Sato=Kobayashi (n 62) 108.
[117] Nishitani/Jurisdiction (n 74) 264; Sawaki=Dogauchi (n 23) 293; Yasuhiro Okuda, *Kokusai Zaisanho (Private International Law in Business)* (Akashi Shoten, 2019) 277 (Okuda/Business). *cf* Dai Yokomizo, 'Kokusai Senzoku Kankatsu' (2012) 245 *Nagoya Daigaku Hosei Ronshu* 123.

ix. Plurality of Parties or Claims

CCP article 3-6 grants Japanese courts international jurisdiction over a joint claim, provided that:

> If multiple claims are involved in a single action and the Japanese courts have jurisdiction over one of those claims and no jurisdiction over the others, the action may be filed with the Japanese courts only if the one claim is closely connected with the other claims; provided, however, that with regard to an action brought by multiple persons or an action brought against multiple persons, this applies only in the case specified in the first sentence of article 38.

Once Japanese courts are competent to decide a claim, other claims between the same parties that are closely related to the principal claim can be joined ('objective joinder of claims': CCP article 3-6). As opposed to the domestic jurisdiction rule (article 7), a close connection between the claims is required, aiming at the protection of the defendant and procedural economy.[118]

By CCP Article 146(3) jurisdiction can be extended to a counterclaim that is closely related to the subject matter of the principal claim or the allegations and evidence of the defence.[119] The requirement of 'a close connection' aims to prevent proceedings from being protracted due to a counterclaim without such connection. This requirement can be satisfied, for instance, where the principal claim is for payment of a construction fee and the counterclaim is for damages based on defects in respect of the same construction.[120]

Furthermore, plaintiffs or defendants can be joined with the principal parties insofar as rights or obligations constituting the subject matter of the claim are common between them or arise out of the same factual or legal grounds ('subjective joinder of claims': CCP article 3-6 and article 38, first sentence).[121] The broad scope of objective and subjective joinder of claims is a specific aspect of Japanese rules.

As an exception, the objective or subjective joinder of claims is not admissible for claims governed by the exclusive jurisdiction of foreign states *ex lege* (CCP article 3-5 *mutatis mutandis*; Articles 3-10 and 146(3), second sentence). For instance, where a plaintiff (seller) claims payment of money for the sale of immovable property situated abroad, the defendant (buyer) may not file a counterclaim for registration of transfer of that immovable property in the absence of jurisdiction of the Japanese courts.[122] This principle, however, does not apply to an exclusive choice of court agreement designating a foreign court, as the legislature was of the view that choice of court agreements do not involve the public interest and are therefore unconstrained by the judicial policy of deciding related issues in the same proceedings.[123] Consequently, for example, an obligee who has agreed with a guarantor to confer exclusive jurisdiction on a foreign court can require the latter to appear before the Japanese court by suing the main obligor domiciled in Japan.[124]

[118] *Hosoku Setsumei* (CCP) 47–48, available at: www.e-gov.go.jp/; Sato=Kobayashi (n 62) 118.

[119] Sato=Kobayashi (n 62) 125–26.

[120] ibid 126.

[121] It is not required, though, that the parties be joined *ex lege* as under CCP article 40. *Hosoku Setsumei* (CCP) 50, available at: www.e-gov.go.jp/; for the previous state of the discussion, see Nishitani/Baum/Bälz (n 6) [143–144].

[122] Sato=Kobayashi (n 62) 127.

[123] ibid 121–23 and 127–28.

[124] Yoshihisa Hayakawa, 'Zadankai: Kokusai Saibankankatsu Ruru no Horeika ni atatte' [Comments by Yoshihisa Hayakawa] in Nihon Bengoshi Rengokai Kokusai Saibankakatsukisoku no Horeika ni kansuru Kento Kaigi (ed), *Atarashii Kokusai Saibankankatsu Hosei: Jitsumuka no Shiten kara* (Shojihomu, 2012) 28; Sato=Kobayashi (n 62) 127–28.

B. Special Rules

CCP articles 3-3 and 3-4 provide specific jurisdictional grounds that are available in particular situations, for instance, the place of performance, situs of the property, the place of the defendant's office and business activities. Japanese courts may assume jurisdiction when any of general or specific jurisdictional grounds point to Japan, subject to the special circumstances test under Article 3-9 (see section II.A.ii).

i. Law of Obligations

a. Contract

Introduction

Specific jurisdictional grounds often function in all the contractual disputes and in practical terms play a very important role. However, applicable jurisdictional grounds widely differ in accordance with the type of contractual dispute and, in particular, the status of the parties. For instance, pursuant to CCP article 3-4(3) covering disputes relating to consumer contracts and individual labour relations, CCP article 3-3

> shall have no application to an action brought by a business operator against a consumer with respect to a consumer contract or to an action brought by an employer against its employee with respect to a civil dispute over individual employment relations.

Consequently, the jurisdictional grounds in article 3-3 are not available in such cases. Also, CCP article 3-7(5) imposes some additional conditions on choice of courts agreements relating to consumer contracts and individual labour relations. The following passages will first describe relevant specific jurisdictional grounds in ordinary contractual disputes and then deal with special rules in consumer contracts and individual labour relations.

Place of Performance Jurisdiction

CCP article 3-3(1) provides for the place of performance as an alternative and specific basis of jurisdiction in contractual disputes (including unjust enrichment and *negotiorum getio* arising out of contractual relationships; for unjust enrichment, see section II.B.i.c). It stipulates as follows:

> An action for the enforcement of a contractual obligation, an action arising from *negotiorum gestio* (management of another's affairs without mandate) performed in connection with a contractual obligation, an action relating to unjust enrichment arising in connection with a contractual obligation, an action seeking damages for the breach of a contractual obligation, or any other action relating to a contractual obligation:
>
> - when the place of performance of the obligation as specified in the contract is located in Japan or when the place of performance of the obligation is located in Japan according to the governing law chosen in the contract.

As is evident from the wording, international jurisdiction based on the place of performance relates exclusively to contractual obligations, whereas the domestic jurisdiction of the place of performance in CCP article 5(1)[125] covers contractual and non-contractual obligations. The legislature restricted its scope for the purpose of international jurisdiction, following the previous prevailing opinion,[126] which is in line with Brussels I article 5(1) (Brussels I Recast article 7(1)). In fact, the defendant can hardly ascertain for sure the place of performance of a non-contractual obligation arising under the law of tort, unjust enrichment or *negotiorum gestio* (AGRAL articles 14–21). Moreover, jurisdiction based on the place of a tort is more suitable to tortious claims than the place of performance of an underlying obligation, as it has a closer connection to the subject matter of the claim and evidence (CCP article 3-3(8)).[127]

Despite this distinction, some authors take the view that tortious claims arising out of a breach of contractual obligations fall within the place of performance jurisdiction,[128] while prevailing opinion favours concurrent jurisdiction with the place of tort under article 3-3(8).[129] In any event, actions in relation to an underlying contract can be joined and heard together pursuant to article 3-6 (see section II.A.i.x). Furthermore, since article 3-3(1) deals with legal issues arising from an 'existing contract', the place of performance ground will not be available, if no contract exists as when a party brings a damage claim for *culpa in contrahendo*. The latter type of claim would be subject to the place of tort ground of jurisdiction under article 3-3(8).[130]

Pursuant to article 3-3(1), the place of performance is determined by reference to the contractual obligation in question. The legislature did not envisage a specific rule comparable to Brussels I article 5(1)(b) (Brussels I Recast article 7(1)(b)), which uniformly points to the place of characteristic performance in contracts for the sale of goods or the provision of services.[131] CCP article 3-3(1) not only covers validity and primary claims relating to the contract, but also claims pertaining to accessory duties and remedies for non-performance, including restitution and damages. Consequently, in the event of non-performance, the court at the place of performance of the underlying contractual obligation can take jurisdiction. In a sales contract, for instance, the seller's claim for restitution of delivered goods in default of a buyer's payment is subject to Japan's jurisdiction, insofar as payment was to be made in Japan, independently of the place where restitution is supposed to be made.[132]

[125] CCP article 5 reads as follows: 'An action set forth in one of the following items may be filed with the court of jurisdiction in the place specified in said item: (i) an action involving a property right: the place of performance of the obligation'.

[126] Nishitani/Baum/Bälz (n 6) [122–125]; Satoshi Watanabe and Mari Nagata, 'Gimu Rikochi no Kankatsuken' in Akira Takakuwa and Masato Dogauchi (eds), *Shin Saiban Jitsumu Taikei (3): Kokusai Minji Soshoho (Zaisanho Kankei) (International Civil Litigation Law (Proprietary Matters))* (Seirinshoin, 2002) 75–76; also, Judgment of Tokyo District Court, 15 February 1984, HJ 1135, 70; Judgment of Tokyo District Court, 1 June 1987, *Kinsho* 790, 32; Judgment of Tokyo District Court, 25 April 1995, HJ 1561, 84; Judgment of Tokyo District Court, 31 October 2006, HT 1241, 338; *contra*, Judgment of Tokyo District Court, 28 August 1989, HJ 1338, 121 ((1990) 33 *JAIL* 206).

[127] *Hosoku Setsumei* (CCP) 8–9, available at: www.e-gov.go.jp/.

[128] Sawaki=Dogauchi (n 23) 272.

[129] Nozomi Tada, 'International Civil Jurisdiction Based on the Place of the Tort' (2012) 55 *JYIL* 287, 295 (Tada/Tort); Judgment of Tokyo District Court, 19 June 1989, HT 703, 246; Judgment of Tokyo District Court, 4 April 2006, HJ 1940, 130.

[130] Sawaki=Dogauchi (n 23) 273.

[131] Also DHC-1999 article 6 (a)–(c); Watanabe and Nagata (n 126) 77.

[132] *Hosoku Setsumei* (CCP) 9–11, available at: www.e-gov.go.jp/; Akira Saito, 'International Civil Jurisdiction Based on the Place of Performance of Obligation Relating to a Contract' (2011) 54 *JYIL* 295, 304–08; also, Judgment of Osaka District Court, 25 March 1991, HJ 1408, 100; *contra*, Judgment of Nagoya High Court, 12 November 1979, HT 402, 102.

To ensure certainty and foreseeability, CCP article 3-3(1) restricts the relevant place of performance to the one designated in the contract[133] or determined by the applicable law explicitly or implicitly chosen by the parties (AGRAL article 7; see chapter three, section II).[134] Accordingly, applicable law as determined by an objective connecting factor in the absence of an express or implied choice of law (AGRAL article 8) will not ground place of performance jurisdiction. Arguably, the place of performance under United Nations Convention on Contracts for the International Sales of Goods of 11 April 1980 (CISG) article 31 or 57(1) is also to be disregarded, unless the parties explicitly or implicitly refer to it in their contract or choose a national law (including CISG) to govern their contract (*cf* CISG article 1(1)(b)).[135]

Situs of Property Jurisdiction

CCP article 3-3(3) can often come into play. This provision sets out the situs of property as an alternative jurisdictional ground and stipulates as follows:

(iii) An action relating to a property right:
- when the object of the claim is located in Japan; or
- if the action is for the payment of money, when the defendant's asset capable of being seized is located in Japan (except where the value of the asset is extremely low).

With regard to the situs of property, it is reasonable to confer international jurisdiction when the subject matter of a claim is in Japan.[136] However, international jurisdiction based on the situs of the defendant's seizable property in general is questionable. Brussels I not only precludes a general situs jurisdiction, but even outlaws the relevant rule in Member States' domestic legislation (Austria and Germany)[137] as exorbitant jurisdiction (Brussels I articles 3(2) and 4(2) (Brussels I Recast articles 5(2) and 6(2))). By the same token, DHC-1999 Article 18(2)(a) placed the situs jurisdiction on the blacklist. Nevertheless, the Japanese legislature adopted situs jurisdiction under CCP article 3-3(3), with a view to guaranteeing enforcement of claims against the defendant's assets in accordance with the corresponding domestic jurisdiction rule (article 5(4)).[138] The situs jurisdiction may well have an impact on cross-border litigation, since a party with tangible or intangible seizable property, including claims or intellectual property rights in Japan, is in principle subject to the jurisdiction of the Japanese courts.[139] In 2017 the Tokyo District Court denied the

[133] Also Judgment of Tokyo High Court, 31 May 1993, *Minshu* 51(10), 4073; Judgment of Tokyo District Court, 25 April 1995, HJ 1561, 84.

[134] Minutes of 2nd Meeting (AGRAL); Sawaki=Dogauchi (n 23) 278–79.

[135] Sakurada (n 90) 360; Sato=Kobayashi (n 62) 37–38; Sawaki=Dogauchi (n 23) 279. According to the majority of commentators, a choice of non-state law including conventions such as CISG as applicable law is not permissible in court proceedings. See Yuko Nishitani, 'Ist das Kollisionsrecht für den internationalen Rechts- und Wirtschaftsverkehr ein ausreichendes Instrumentarium? – Unter besonderer Berücksichtigung der "lex mercatoria"' in Karl Riesenhuber and Kanako Takayama (eds), *Rechtsangleichung: Grundlagen, Methoden und Inhalte – Deutsch-Japanische Perspektiven* (de Gruyter Verlag, 2006).

[136] Kazuhiko Yamamoto, 'International Jurisdiction Based on the Location of Property' (2011) 54 *JYIL* 311, 312–13 (Yamamoto/Property).

[137] §99(1) Austrian Jurisdiktionsnorm; §23 German Zivilprozessordnung; see annex I of Brussels I.

[138] *Hokokusho* (CCP) 20, available at: www.moj.go.jp/content/000012193.pdf; Sato=Kobayashi (n 62) 45.

[139] Yamamoto/Property (n 136) 313 and 319–20.

application of this head of jurisdiction where a plaintiff claimed a negative declaration of liability.[140]

To restrict the scope of the situs jurisdiction, the relevant subject matter of the claim is limited to the payment of money. Furthermore, pursuant to CCP article 3-3(3), the situs jurisdiction is precluded when the value of property is extremely low. The value is not assessed in relation to the amount in dispute, but according to absolute criteria that at least allows minor assets such as samples of goods or utensils to be disregarded.[141] For a lack of clear criteria, a nexus between the claim, the seizable property and the forum is not required.[142]

In fact, the 2009 Interim Draft envisaged two other methods of limiting situs jurisdiction. One proposal was to allow situs jurisdiction only as a ground of direct jurisdiction for Japanese courts, while declining to recognise a foreign judgment rendered on the basis of situs jurisdiction.[143] It aimed to restrict the effect of Japanese judgments relying on situs jurisdiction to the territory of Japan, expecting that foreign states would refuse to recognise such Japanese judgments.[144] This proposal was not approved, however, due to the fact that it was too complicated and could send a wrong message that Japan advocated protectionism.[145] The other proposal was to make the provisional seizure of property a prerequisite for situs jurisdiction following Swiss Private International Law (Bundesgesetz über das Internationale Privatrecht, SR 291) (SPIL) article 4.[146] This proposal was also not adopted, as it would have placed an excessive burden on an obligee and would have unduly restricted the situs jurisdiction when provisional measures were not available due to a lack of an urgent need for protection (CPRA article 15). Moreover, it would not have functioned to prevent the abusive seizure of insignificant property as a way of establishing jurisdiction.[147]

Although CCP article 3-3(3) adopted the aforementioned limitations, the risk of exorbitant jurisdiction is still inherent. As a last resort *de lege lata*, the Japanese judge could circumvent the exercise of exorbitant jurisdiction by referring to the corrective rule in article 3-9 and exceptionally dismiss the claim (see section II.A.ii). In contrast to domestic jurisdiction (CCP article 5 No 4), international situs jurisdiction based on the subject matter of security (such as property) provided in respect of a claim has rightly been excluded. The reasoning was that (a) such security could be executed without an enforcement title pursuant to CEA articles 180–95, thereby making jurisdiction on the merits superfluous, and (b) the obligor should not be subject to Japan's jurisdiction simply because the guarantor is domiciled in Japan.[148]

[140] Judgment of Tokyo District Court, 27 July 2017, 2017WLJPCA07279006.

[141] Minutes of 13th Meeting (CCP); Sato=Kobayashi (n 62) 45–46; *contra*, Sawaki=Dogauchi (n 23) 276.

[142] *Hosoku Setsumei* (CCP) 14, available at: www.e-gov.go.jp/.

[143] Interim Draft (CCP) II-1, 1st alternative.

[144] *Hosoku Setsumei* (CCP) 13, available at: www.e-gov.go.jp/; also advocated by Hiroshi Takahashi, 'Kokusai Saiban Kankatsu: Zaisankankei Jiken wo Chushin ni shite' in Takao Sawaki and Yoshimitsu Aoyama (eds), *Kokusai Minji Soshoho no Riron* (Yuhikaku, 1987) 61.

[145] Yamamoto/Property (n 136) 318.

[146] See Interim Draft (CCP) II-1, 2nd alternative.

[147] Yamamoto/Property (n 136) 318.

[148] Sato=Kobayashi (n 62) 50; Yamamoto/Property (n 136) 313–14. For maritime securities, however, the situs of the ship constitutes the jurisdiction of the Japanese courts in accordance with established maritime business practice (CCP article 3-3(6)).

Branch Office Jurisdiction

Pursuant to CCP article 3-3(4), the court at the place where the defendant's office (other than the principal office) is situated may take jurisdiction insofar as an action relates to business conducted at that office. The provision stipulates:

> An action which is against a person having an office and relates to the activities carried out in that office
>
> – when the office is located in Japan.

This provision is generally understood as correcting the precedent set by the *Malaysia Airlines* case,[149] in which Japan's general jurisdiction was based on the Tokyo branch office of the defendant Malaysian company in a damages claim arising out of the defendant's business and operation of domestic flights in Malaysia.[150] Article 3-3(4) should be understood as only addressing the business directly conducted at the relevant office, not the business in abstract terms that could have been undertaken by that office.[151] In principle, this jurisdictional ground accords with Brussels I article 5(5) (Brussels I Recast article 7(5)). The notion of an office under CCP article 3-3(4) is, however, narrower than the 'branch, agency or other establishment' of the latter which also comprises subsidiaries with independent legal personality.[152]

Business Activities Jurisdiction

CCP article 3-3(v) provides a new jurisdictional ground based on the defendant's business activities. It stipulates as follows:

> An action against a person engaged in business in Japan (including a foreign company (as defined by CA Article 2 (2) which continuously carries out transactions in Japan):
>
> – when the action relates to the business in Japan.

It primarily targets foreign companies that are continuously doing business in Japan. Since 2002, such foreign companies are no longer required to establish an office in Japan, but only to designate a principal representative (Company Act (CA) article 817(1)(2)),[153] so CCP article 3-3(4) would not suffice consistently to subject them to Japan's jurisdiction.

Jurisdiction based on business activities is comparable to the US 'doing business' jurisdiction and represents a foreign importation into the civil law system. It is to be noted, however, that the US activity-based jurisdiction principally comprised all kinds of disputes

[149] Masato Dogauchi, 'Nihon no Atarashii Kokusai Saibankankatsu Rippo ni tsuite' (2010) 12 *JYPIL* 194; Mari Nagata, 'Kokusai Saibankankatsu Kitei no Rippo to Kokusai Torihiki he no Eikyo' (2011) 13 *Kokusai Shotorihiki Gakkai Nenpo* 205, 206–08 (Nagata/Jurisdiction); *cf* Minutes of 13th Meeting (CCP).

[150] See, *Malaysia Airlines* case (n 1).

[151] Sato=Kobayashi (n 62) 52; Jun Yokoyama, *Kokusai Shiho* (*Private International Law*) (Sanseido, 2012) 334 (Yokoyama/PIL). Otherwise, Japan would have the branch office jurisdiction under the same facts as in the *Malaysia Airlines* case. *Contra* Yoshiaki Muto, 'Hikoku no Jusho, Eigyousho Shozaichi nado ni yoru Kankatsuken' in Nihon Bengoshi Rengokai Kokusai Saibankakatsukisoku no Horeika ni kansuru Kento Kaigi (ed), *Atarashii Kokusai Saibankankatsu Hosei: Jitsumuka no Shiten kara* (Shojihomu, 2012) 37–38.

[152] CJEU 9 December 1987 – Case C-218/86 *SAR Schotte v Parfums Rothschild* [1987] ECR 4905; see, inter alia, Peter Mankowski, 'Article 5' in Ulrich Magnus and Peter Mankowski (eds), *Brussels I Regulation*, 2nd edn (Sellier, 2012) 281–85.

[153] See Yoshiaki Nomura, 'Activity-Based Jurisdiction of Japanese Courts – A Bold But Unnecessary Departure' (2012) 55 *JYIL* 263, 269–72 (Nomura/Activity).

as a general ground of jurisdiction[154] and was often deemed exorbitant,[155] while CCP article 3-3(5) only provides for special jurisdiction and is limited to disputes arising out of the defendant's business activities in Japan.[156] For instance, where a foreign company directly enters into transactions with Japanese companies through its website without its Japanese office being involved, disputes arising out of those business activities can be decided by Japanese courts pursuant to CCP article 3-3(5).[157] On the other hand, where the Tokyo office of a foreign company administers all business activities in Asia without directly undertaking transactions in Japan, disputes arising out of business activities in (say) Hong Kong and elsewhere would be subject to Japan's jurisdiction in accordance with article 3-3(4).[158] In all contractual disputes (except for certain cases of consumer contracts and individual labour relationships), Japanese courts may assume jurisdiction where any of the aforementioned requirements is fulfilled. That said, Japanese courts may decline jurisdiction in accordance with the special circumstances test under CCP article 3-9, even if one of the jurisdictional grounds is met.

Consumer and Employment Contracts

Consumer contracts and individual labour relationships are subject to the special jurisdictional rules in CCP articles 3-4 and 3-7(5) and (6), enacted for the protection of weaker parties. CCP article 3-4 stipulates:

(1) An action involving a contract concluded between a Consumer (meaning an individual (except for an individual that becomes a party to a contract as a part of a business undertaking or for business purposes; the same applies hereinafter) and an Enterprise (meaning a corporation or any other association or foundation or an individual that becomes a party to a contract as a part of a business undertaking or for business purposes; the same applies hereinafter) (this excludes a labour contract; hereinafter referred to as a 'Consumer Contract'), which is brought by the Consumer against the Enterprise, may be filed with the Japanese courts if the Consumer is domiciled in Japan at the time the action is filed or at the time the Consumer Contract is concluded.

(2) An action involving a dispute over a civil matter that arises between an individual worker and that worker's employer with regard to the existence or absence of a labour contract or any other particulars of their labour relations (hereinafter referred to as an 'Individual Civil Labour Dispute'), which is brought by the worker against the employer, may be filed with the Japanese courts if the place where the labour is to be provided as per the labour contract to which the Individual Civil Labour Dispute pertains (or if such a place is not established, the location of the place of business that hired the worker) is within Japan.

(3) The provisions of the preceding Article [Article 3-3] do not apply to an action involving a Consumer Contract which is brought by an Enterprise against a Consumer, or an action involving Individual Civil Labour Dispute which is brought by an employer against a worker.

[154] See *International Shoe Co v Washington* 326 US 310 (1945); *Perkins v Benguet Consol Mining Co* 342 US 437 (1952); *World-Wide Volkswagen Co v Woodson* 444 US 286 (1980); *Helicopteros Nacionales de Colombia SA v Hall* 466 US 408 (1984); *Goodyear Dunlop Tires Operations v Brown* 131 S Ct 2846 (2011).

[155] The admissibility of the 'doing business' jurisdiction was one of the most disputed points in the original Hague Judgments Project. DHC-1999 article 18(2)(e) placed it on the blacklist. See Peter Nygh and Fausto Pocar, *Report on the Preliminary Draft Convention on Jurisdiction and Foreign Judgments in Civil and Commercial Matters adopted by the Special Commission* (2000) 80–81, available at: www.hcch.net/upload/wop/jdgmpd11.pdf.

[156] Dogauchi/Jurisdiction (n 3) 273–74; Nagata/Jurisdiction (n 149) 208–09; Nomura/Activity (n 153) 277–86.

[157] Sato=Kobayashi (n 62) 55–58; Yokoyama/PIL (n 151) 335.

[158] *Hosoku Setsumei* (CCP) 16, available at: www.e-gov.go.jp/; Sato=Kobayashi (n 62) 56.

Article 3-4(3) must be noted. Pursuant to that provision, jurisdictional grounds in article 3-3 are not available, where a business operator or employer brings a suit against a consumer or employee. In such cases, the available forum is restricted to that of the consumer's or employee's domicile. There are some exceptions, where the parties have entered into a choice of court agreement (article 3-7(5) and (6)) or entered an appearance in court (article 3-8) (see sections II.A.vi and II.A.vii).[159] Conversely, a consumer can file an action against a business operator before the courts of the locality in which the consumer was domiciled at the time of the filing of the action or at the conclusion of the contract (CCP article 3-4(1)), in addition to the competent courts pursuant to CCP articles 3-2 and 3-3. The employee can sue the employer at the place of performance of work under the contract[160] or, if that is not ascertainable, at the place of the office through which the employee was employed (article 3-4(2)), in addition to the venues provided by articles 3-2 and 3-3.[161] While these rules largely correspond to Brussels I articles 16(1) and 19(1) and (2) (Brussels I Recast articles 18(1) and 21(1)(a)(b)), Japanese courts are more broadly available due to the applicable special jurisdiction rules (CCP article 3-3) and the possibility of joinder of claims (articles 3-6 and 146(3)).

Unlike the choice of law rules in AGRAL article 11(6), CCP article 3-4(1) protects a 'passive' as well as an 'active' consumer who on his or her initiative travels to a foreign state in which the business operator is established and concludes a contract or receives complete performance there. For the purpose of international jurisdiction, even an active consumer deserves protection.[162] Disadvantages that a foreign business operator may incur are to be mitigated by referring to the corrective rule under CCP article 3-9 (see section II.A.ii).[163]

With regard to a choice of court agreement after a dispute has arisen out of a consumer or employment contract, the parties are free to designate a competent court (CCP article 3-7(5) and (6)). Prior to that date, a choice of court agreement is valid if (a) the parties confer non-exclusive jurisdiction on the courts of a state where the consumer was domiciled at the time of the conclusion of the consumer contract or the employee carried out his or her work at the time of termination of the employment contract (article 3-7(5) No 1 or (6)).[164] This is also the case if (b) the consumer or employee institutes proceedings at the chosen forum or invokes the choice of court agreement when sued in a different forum (article 3-7(5) No 2 or (6) No 2). Situation (b) is a unique Japanese rule and is justified as the subsequent consent

[159] It is still debatable whether CCP article 3-6 on the joinder of claims should be applicable as well. See Tadashi Kanzaki, 'Jurisdiction over Consumer Contracts and Individual Labor-Related Civil Disputes' (2012) 55 *JYIL* 306, 312–13 and 315–16 (Kanzaki/Jurisdiction).

[160] When the employee performs his or her labour at several ascertainable places, all of them can constitute jurisdiction. Atsushi Fukuda, 'Kokusai Saiban Kankatsu ni kansuru Minji Soshoho no Kaisei no Gaiyo' (2011) 1931 *Kinyu Homu Jijo* 79; Kanzaki/Jurisdiction (n 159) 311–12; Minutes of 8th Meeting (CCP).

[161] Kanzaki/Jurisdiction (n 159) 310–12.

[162] *Hosoku Setsumei* (CCP) 43–44, available at: www.e-gov.go.jp/; Sato=Kobayashi (n 62) 88; *contra Hokokusho* (CCP) 73–74, available at: www.moj.go.jp/content/000012193.pdf.

[163] Dogauchi/Jurisdiction (n 3) 197–98; Kanzaki/Jurisdiction (n 159) 317–19; Yasuhiro Okuda, 'New Provisions on International Jurisdiction of Japanese Courts' (2011) 13 *YPIL* 366, 374.

[164] An exclusive choice of court selection clause is understood *ex lege* as non-exclusive (CCP article 3-7(5) No 1 and (6) No 1). The choice of court agreement in employment contracts under situation (a) can only be made at the time of terminating the contract (for instance, together with a non-disclosure or non-competition clause). Sawaki=Dogauchi (n 23) 291–92; Kanzaki/Jurisdiction (n 159) 313–14.

of a consumer or employee to a renunciation of the right to sue or be sued before a different court.[165]

Other Types of Contract

For other types of contract such as insurance contracts, contracts for the sale of immovable property, contracts for sale of goods, contracts for hire of goods, contracts for the carriage of goods by sea, air, or land, letters of credit, contracts involving the transfer of foreign currency, and agency, the legislature has not adopted any special rules. Therefore, they are also subject to the jurisdictional rules discussed above, unless a contract is regarded as either a consumer contract or an individual labour contract.

Although it may or may not be related to contractual obligations, pursuant to CCP article 3-3(2), Japanese courts may take jurisdiction over claims to seek payment of a bill of exchange, promissory note or cheque, where such payment of the bill, note or cheque is to be made in Japan.

b. Tort

When it comes to tortious disputes, unlike the conflict of laws rules in AGRAL articles 17 to 22 (see chapter three, section II.C), CCP does not adopt jurisdictional rules for specific torts. The legislature sets out one specific jurisdictional ground in CCP article 3-3 (8). That provision stipulates as follows:

> An action relating to a tort:
>
> - when the tort occurred in Japan (except where the result of a harmful act committed abroad has occurred in Japan and the occurrence of that result in Japan would have been normally unforeseeable).

This ground is justified by the fact that the place of tort is closely connected with the subject matter of the claim and the evidence. Moreover, it facilitates access to justice and enhances the protection of the victim.[166] The scope of article 3-3(8) basically extends to all tortious cases such as product liability and defamation[167] and covers all tortious claims including damages and injunctions.[168] Also, it extends to negative declarations of liability,[169] despite a previous minority view which precluded it from being used to prevent a tortfeasor from strategically instituting proceedings at his or her own domicile.[170] On the other hand, indemnification among tortfeasors should be left out of the scope of this provision.[171]

[165] See Sato=Kobayashi (n 62) 147–48; Kanzaki/Jurisdiction (n 159) 314–15. On the other hand, Japan lacks a provision that corresponds to Brussels I article 17(3) (Brussels I Recast article 19(3)), which upholds an exclusive jurisdiction clause in favour of the common domicile or habitual residence of the consumer and the business operator at the time of the conclusion of the contract.

[166] Sato=Kobayashi (n 62) 68; Tada/Tort (n 129) 290–91.

[167] Sawaki=Dogauchi (n 23) 280.

[168] Judgment of Supreme Court, 24 April 2014, *Minshu* 68(4), 329 ((2015) 58 *JYIL* 463); Nishitani/Jurisdiction (n 74) 263; Sato=Kobayashi (n 62) 69.

[169] Nishitani/Baum/Bälz (n 6) [132]; Sawaki=Dogauchi (n 23) 282; Tada/Tort (n 129) 296–97; Judgment of Tokyo District Court, 27 November 1998, HT 1037, 235.

[170] For instance, Ikehara/Jurisdiction (n 107) 32.

[171] Nishitani/Baum/Bälz (n 6) [129–131]; Hiroshi Sano, 'Fuhokoichi no Kankatsuken' in Akira Takakuwa and Masato Dogauchi (eds), *Shin Saiban Jitsumu Taikei (3): Kokusai Minji Soshoho (Zaisanho Kankei) (International Civil Litigation Law (Proprietary Matters))* (Seirinshoin, 2002) 122–24. *Contra*, Tada/Tort (n 129) 294–95.

The notion of 'the place of tort' comprises both 'the place where the harmful act was committed (*locus delicti commissi*)' and 'the place where the injury occurred or is likely to occur (*locus damni*)'. Accordingly, as long as either of these grounds is in Japan, Japanese courts may hear and determine the tortious claim in question. However, it should be noted that the place where the injury occurred or is likely to occur (*locus damni*) may be inapposite, when the occurrence of the injury at that place could not be predicted (CCP article 3-3 (8), second sentence). It is understood that the place where indirect or secondary injury occurred or is likely to occur does not constitute a jurisdictional ground,[172] even if one follows a minority view including it in the broad concept of *locus damni*.[173]

The predictability requirement for the place of injury under the second sentence of CCP article 3-3(8) aims to balance the parties' interests and correspond with their risk calculation.[174] It restricts indirect jurisdiction of foreign courts insofar as recognising their judgments in Japan, especially in product liability cases.[175] 'Predictability' only concerns the possibility of injury occurring under normal circumstances and does not concern the likelihood of injury occurring by reason of the act in question (for instance, releasing a product into the 'stream of commerce').[176] In deciding whether the occurrence of the injury is predictable, only objective factors are considered and subjective factors such as the tortfeasor's intention are not considered,[177] just as under AGRAL article 17 (see section II.C).

Whereas the court *ex officio* examines international jurisdiction (CCP article 3-11), the plaintiff victim has the burden of proving the objective factual relationships underlying the wrongful act and the violation of the legally protected right to establish the jurisdiction of the court at the place of the tort.[178] On the other hand, the facts for determining the predictability of the occurrence of injury at the *locus damni* are to be proven by the defendant tortfeasor.[179] The place of tort (both the place of a harmful act and the place of injury) is a general concept. Therefore, it must be determined in individual cases. In specific torts such as product liability, defamation and environmental damage, each of those places should be determined in light of the characteristics of the tort in question. Further, in working out the place of a tort, the focus of article 3-3(8) is on where a harmful act and the resultant injury have occurred, no matter whether liability is based on negligence, nuisance or otherwise.

When it comes to product liability, the legislature deliberated on whether to set out a special jurisdictional rule on product liability as with the choice of law rules in AGRAL article 18. It was eventually decided not to adopt a special jurisdictional rule for several

[172] Sato=Kobayashi (n 62) 69; Okuda/Business (n 117) 254; in this sense also Ikehara/*Kokusai Shiho* (n 4) 31; Judgment of Tokyo District Court, 15 February 1984, HJ 1135, 70; Judgment of Tokyo District Court, 31 October 2006, HT 1241, 338.

[173] Tada/Tort (n 129) 299–302; Judgment of Shizuoka District Court, Numazu Branch, 30 April 1993, HT 824, 241.

[174] Sato=Kobayashi (n 62) 70–71.

[175] *Hosoku Setsumei* (CCP) 21–22, available at: www.e-gov.go.jp/.

[176] See the discussion in the US compared with the criterion of 'purposeful availment' at *World-Wide Volkswagen Co v Woodson* 444 US 286 (1980); *Asahi Metal Industry Co v Superior Court of Cal* 480 US 102 (1987); *J McIntyre v Nicastro* 131 S Ct 2780 (2011); *Goodyear Dunlop Tires Operations v Brown* 131 S Ct 2846 (2011).

[177] Sato=Kobayashi (n 62) 71.

[178] ibid 72; also, Judgment of Supreme Court, 8 June 2001, *Minshu* 55(4), 727 (*Ultraman* case). *Contra*, Sawaki=Dogauchi (n 23) 282–83.

[179] Minutes of 2nd Meeting (CCP).

reasons. For instance: (a) claims for product liability may often involve third parties; (b) it may not serve the parties' convenience and the sound and prompt administration of justice to proceed with lawsuits at the place where a product has been delivered in the course of distribution; and (c) important evidence may not be situated in one particular place.[180] Therefore, this question is open to interpretation. On the one hand, the place of injury is literally where an injury arising from a defective product has been sustained. Under CCP article 3-3(8), the predictability of the injury occurring at such place must be assessed, as opposed to AGRAL article 18, according to which one considers the predictability of a product being delivered at a given place by a producer. On the other hand, the place of a harmful act may be understood as involving a range of locations. It is submitted that, in light of the likely whereabouts of the evidence and the ease of finding the defendant, the place of a harmful act should be regarded as the place where a defective product has been produced.[181]

As for defamation, the legislature did not adopt a special rule, unlike the conflict of laws rules in AGRAL (see section II.C.ii.b). Therefore, the jurisdictional rule in CCP article 3-3(8) applies. In comparison to tort in general, defamation has some peculiarities: (a) it is not easy to situate the place of a harmful act (in particular, in cases of defamation via the internet or mass media); (b) defamation may occur simultaneously in various states; and (c) it is difficult to situate where the injury occurs because abstract concepts such as reputation being harmed by the communication of a false statement, may not be so readily pinned down to a defined locality.[182]

It is suggested that the place of a harmful act should be regarded as (a) the place where a statement is edited and published in cases of defamation (libel) through printed media such as newspapers and magazines,[183] and (b) the place from which a broadcaster has transmitted a statement in cases of defamation (slander) via radio or television.[184] This would also serve the purposes of jurisdiction based on the place of tort in the sense that the evidence would likely be found in the suggested locations and the possibility of inflicting harm on a defendant would be foreseeable by a wrongdoer so situated.

This basis for jurisdiction should likewise be applied to cyberspace defamation, as where a wrongdoer in Japan uploads a defamatory statement via a foreign server or where a wrongdoer overseas uploads such statement via a server in Japan.[185] When it comes to

[180] Sato=Kobayashi (n 62) 73; *Hosoku Setsumei* (CCP) 23, available at: www.e-gov.go.jp/.

[181] Okuda/Business (n 117) 254. Although prior to the 2011 amendment, lower courts held that the place of a harmful act was the place of designing and producing defective products. For instance, Interlocutory Judgment of Osaka District Court, 9 October 1973, HJ 728, 76; Interlocutory Judgment of Tokyo District Court, 24 July 1974, *Kaminshu*, 25(5-8), 639; Interlocutory Judgment of Tokyo District Court, 27 March 1984, *Kaminshu* 35(1-4), 110; Judgment of Tokyo District Court, 29 January 1991, HJ 1390, 98.

[182] Yasushi Nakanishi, 'Mass media niyoru Meiyokison, cyberspace deno Chosakuken Shingai tono Kankatsuken' in Akira Takakuwa and Masato Dogauchi (eds), *Shin Saiban Jitsumu Taikei (3): Kokusai Minji Soshoho (Zaisanho Kankei) (International Civil Litigation Law (Proprietary Matters))* (Seirinshoin, 2002) 99.

[183] Although prior to the 2011 amendment, in a case involving the alleged defamation of a Japanese citizen living in the US by a Japanese magazine edited and published in Japan, but distributed in the US as well as Japan, the Tokyo District Court held that the tortious wrong complained of by the plaintiff was not the editing and publication of the magazine in Japan, but was instead the sales of the magazine in California which had infringed his fame. Judgment of Tokyo District Court, 28 August 1989, HJ 1338 121 ((1990) 33 *JAIL* 206).

[184] Nakanishi, 'Mass media niyoru Meiyokison, cyberspace deno Chosakuken Shingai tono Kankatsuken' (n 182) 100.

[185] ibid 101; for defamation via magazine, see also Okuda/Business (n 117) 254.

the place where the injury occurs, that place might be understood as the place where the plaintiff is domiciled because reputation is an intangible which attaches to the plaintiff as a personal right. According to this, the jurisdiction of the Japanese courts would always be grounded where a victim is domiciled in Japan. This interpretation would protect victims and would be consonant with an underlying rationale for jurisdiction based on the place of tort. However, such understanding would break down the balance between the parties. It is instead submitted that the place where the injury occurs should be regarded as: (a) the place where printed copies were distributed in the case of defamation via printed media such as newspaper and magazines; (b) the place where an allegedly harmful statement has been received in the case of defamation via radio or television); and (c) the place where an allegedly harmful statement is accessible (ie, can be downloaded) in the case of cyberspace defamation.[186] If the allegedly harmful statement is directed to the whole world, the injury might occur all over the globe. However, the place of the injury is not available as a jurisdictional ground when the occurrence of the injury at a specific place could not be predicted. Consequently, the 'valid' place is unlikely to be ubiquitous.

In situations of defamation or violation of privacy and personal rights cases where a single infringing act may cause harm in several states by distribution, the *Shevill* ruling of the Court of Justice of the European Union (CJEU)[187] restricted the scope of the *locus damni* jurisdiction to the damage that occurred in the respective state, while granting jurisdiction to award damages for the entire harm at the publisher's establishment.[188] This 'mosaic' approach of the *locus damni* jurisdiction is of little interest to Japan, not only because there is no need to deter *forum shopping*, but because all closely related claims between the same parties can be objectively joined pursuant to CCP article 3-6 (see section II.A.ix).

In respect of environmental damage and pollution, there has been no case law. Suppose that toxic gas is wrongly released from one state and borne by the wind to another state with detrimental effect to the environment and the health of the population in that other state. There is no doubt that the place of a harmful act should be the place where toxic gas was released,[189] and the place where the injury occurs should be the place where the damage occurs. Where either place is in Japan, the Japanese court may take jurisdiction. But the place where the injury occurs (*locus damni*) may be precluded when the occurrence of damage at such place could not be predicted.[190] Insofar as claims regarding oil pollution are concerned, relevant international conventions may apply (see section I.A).

[186] With regard to defamation over the internet, the Supreme Court has held that the uploading by a US company of an article on its website resulted in damage to the credit and reputation in Japan of a Japanese company and its directors and therefore the place of the injury was Japan. But the Court, after all, declined jurisdiction based on CCP article 3-9. Judgment of Supreme Court, 10 March 2016, *Minshu* 70(3), 846 ((2017) 60 *JYIL* 488). *cf* Nakanishi, 'Mass media niyoru Meiyokison, cyberspace deno Chosakuken Shingai tono Kankatsuken' (n 182) 103–05.

[187] Case C-68/93 *Shevill v Presse Alliance SA*, ECLI:EU:C:1995:61.

[188] As an exception for defamation via the internet, the plaintiff can claim compensation for the whole damage both at the place of his or her centre of interest as well as at the defendant's establishment. See Case C-509/09 *eDate Advertising GmbH* v *X & Olivier Martinez* and Case C-161/10 *Robert Martinez* v *MGN Limited*, ECLI:EU:C:2011:192.

[189] Okuda/Business (n 117) 254.

[190] Where environmental damage occurs abroad, in reality it seems more or less impossible to predict the occurrence of damage in Japan because of its distance from neighbouring countries. The exception would be where a plaintiff intentionally directs a harmful act to Japan's territory or possibly a catastrophic event such as significant nuclear leakage.

In addition to CCP article 3-3(8), other jurisdictional grounds in articles 3-2–3-8 may ground the jurisdiction of the Japanese courts, in particular, article 3-3(3), (4) and (5) often come into play (for these grounds, see section II.B). Pursuant to article 3-3(3), Japanese courts may take jurisdiction, 'if the action is for the payment of money, when the defendant's asset capable of being seized is located in Japan (except where the value of the asset is extremely low)'. Considering that most tortious claims seek damages and a plaintiff normally brings a case before courts in the country where the defendant's assets are located, this head of jurisdiction will easily ground the jurisdiction of the Japanese courts. Also, the jurisdiction of the Japanese courts will be grounded in accordance with article 3-3(4), if a defendant has an office in Japan and an action relates to activities carried out from that office. Furthermore, pursuant to article 3-3(5), Japanese courts may assume jurisdiction where an alleged tort derives from the defendant's business in Japan.

c. Unjust Enrichment

CCP article 3-3(1) sets out a special jurisdictional rule for an action involving a contractual obligation according to which a party may file an action relating to 'unjust enrichment arising in connection with a contractual obligation' with Japanese courts' (a) when the place of performance of the obligation as specified in the contract is located in Japan, or (b) when the place of performance of the obligation is located in Japan according to the governing law chosen in the contract. Accordingly, where (for instance) a seller seeks restitution of delivered good after terminating a contract upon the buyer's failure to make a payment, Japanese courts may accept jurisdiction if payment was to be made in Japan.[191] As evident from the wording, this head of jurisdiction does not cover an action for unjust enrichment that has not arisen in connection with a contractual obligation. For such type of action, a party will be required to rely on other jurisdictional rules.

d. Trusts and Charitable Foundations

A trust can be established by a person's unilateral conduct or the parties' agreement. A person (trustor) transfers property to and asks another person (trustee) to administer or dispose of that property for the benefit of a third party (beneficiary), the trustor, or for a specified purpose. A charitable foundation is one type of trust in that a trustor transfers assets to a trustee to hold for charitable purposes. In addition, in common law jurisdictions, a trust can be imposed by the courts as equitable remedy (constructive trust) in the absence of consensus or legal relationship between the parties. This type of trust is unknown to most civil law jurisdictions (including Japan). In Japan, the institution of unjust enrichment instead has a similar function. In this light, the constructive trust in common law countries is regarded as a remedy for unjust enrichment for the purpose of deciding Japan's jurisdiction and choice of law rules.[192]

[191] Sato=Kobayashi (n 62) 36; Osamu Ito and Yoshimasa Furuta, 'Keiyaku jo no Saimu ni kansuru Uttae nado no Kanakatsuken' in Nihon Bengoshi Rengokai Kokusai Saibankakatsukisoku no Horeika ni kansuru Kento Kaigi (ed), *Atarashii Kokusai Saibankankatsu Hosei: Jitsumuka no Shiten kara* (Shojihomu, 2012) 41.

[192] For the characterisation in choice of law context, Tadashi Kanzaki, 'Shintaku' in Yoshiaki Sakurada and Masato Dogauchi (eds), *Chushaku Kokusai Shiho: Dai 1 kan (Commentary on Private International Law: Volume 1)* (Yuhikaku, 2011) 352.

As regards trusts, as in the choice of law context, there are no special jurisdictional rules.[193] It is left to interpretation when Japanese courts may take jurisdiction over matters relating to trusts. Various disputes may arise out of trusts. Those disputes occur in the context of either (a) the internal relationship among trustee, trustor and beneficiary, or (b) an external relationship (for instance, contractual or tortious disputes between a trustee and a third party). In the latter relationship, a trustee simply appears as the owner of a set of assets and the dispute has nothing to do with administration of the trust itself. Therefore, disputes arising out of an external relationship are simply regarded as ordinary disputes and so subject to the ordinary jurisdictional rules of the CCP. With regard to an internal relationship, ordinary jurisdictional rules in CCP are also to be applied, in view of a shortage of explicit jurisdictional rules. There is no doubt that the defendant's domicile under article 3-2 is the principal ground. In addition, the defendant's branch office or business activities in Japan under article 3-3(4) and (5) may ground Japan's jurisdiction, where a claim is brought against a trustee for an alleged breach of obligation of management and the trustee is a business operator. Furthermore, the defendant's assets in Japan may function as an alternative ground, in accordance with article 3-3(3). When a trust asset is immovable property in Japan, the Japanese court may assume jurisdiction on the basis of the situs of that property in accordance with article 3-3(11). When a beneficiary alleges that a trustee has diverted a trust asset, the place of tort under article 3-3(8) may function. When the parties to a trust agreement have agreed on a particular court by a choice of court agreement, such agreement may ground Japan's jurisdiction. When a trust agreement is regarded as a consumer contract, a trustee (sometimes a beneficiary as well) is a consumer and the special rule for consumer contracts in article 3-4 applies.

There are some peculiarities to be considered. The first is whether the place of performance under article 3-3(1) is available. There is no doubt that such place may found jurisdiction when the trust is established by the parties' agreement. For instance, where a trustee fails to distribute the earnings of a trust to the beneficiary, the place of performance under article 3-3(1) may ground jurisdiction of the Japanese courts. On the other hand, if the trust is established by a person's unilateral conduct, there exists no contractual obligations. One may take the view that the place of performance should not ground jurisdiction. However, it is instead submitted that Japanese courts should be allowed to assume jurisdiction, through applying article 3-3(1) by analogy.[194] In such case, a trustee undertakes obligations voluntarily and can foresee the place where he or she is supposed to perform such obligations, much as in the contractual context. Therefore, basing jurisdiction upon the place of performance will not come as a surprise to the trustee. It would rather cater for the parties' expectations. The second is that a trust has similar characteristics to those of legal persons or organisations in the way that internal relationships among relevant parties (for instance, trustor, trustee and beneficiary) in connection with the management of trust assets. Consequently, jurisdictional rules for legal persons or organisations should be applied by analogy to those internal relationships. Specifically, Japanese courts should be

[193] In contrast, articles 7(6) and 25(3) of Brussels I Recast and Article Swiss Private International law contain several jurisdictional rules that are similar to those applicable to corporations or organisations.

[194] See Makoto Shimada, 'Shintaku Sosho no Kokusai Saiban Kankatsu' (2014) 28 *Keio Hogaku* 222.

authorised to take jurisdiction, where the central administration of a trust lies in Japan.[195] This approach would result in relevant parties solving their disputes in a single forum and thereby serve procedural economy.

ii. Law of Property

a. Immovable Property

With regard to disputes over immovable property, CCP article 3-3(11) provides for situs jurisdiction. It stipulates:

> An action set forth in one of the following items may be filed with the Japanese courts in the case specified in said item:
>
> (xi) An action related to real property: if the real property is located within Japan.

It is conceived, though, as non-exclusive jurisdiction for all kinds of litigation, including rights *in rem*, which is in contrast to Brussels I Recast article 24(1).[196] The reasoning was that the exclusive jurisdiction limited to disputes *in rem* would require a delineation of its scope, while rights or claims *in rem* cannot be defined categorically. Nor can claims for restitution anchored in contract be clearly differentiated from claims for restitution *in rem*. Furthermore, it was opined that Japanese courts should always be available to parties domiciled in Japan, even for disputes concerning immovable property located abroad.[197] As a result, it is only for disputes over entries in public registers that the situs of immovable property is exclusively competent pursuant to CCP article 3-5(2) (see section II.A.viii).

CCP article 3-3(11) covers claims whose subject matter is a right relating to immovable property, as for instance the right to a declaration of ownership of immovable property, the right to quiet possession based on ownership of immovable property, the right to restitution of immovable property based on ownership.[198] To the contrary, it does not cover claims for the payment of the purchase price or rent for immovable property.[199] The principle of non-exclusivity will often lead to limping legal relationships, as foreign states may not enforce a Japanese judgment deciding rights *in rem* in immovable property located in their territory.

b. Intangible Property

Intangible property covers a very wide range of property and rights, such as contractual debts (claims), shares in companies, securities and other financial instruments, and intellectual property (for intellectual property, see section II.B.ii.c). Intangible property (except for certain matters relating to registration of intellectual property) does not fall under the

[195] As a similar position in a legislative proposal, Miho Tanaka, 'Shintaku wo meguru Kokusai Saibankankatsu Kettei jou no Mondai' (2014) 16 *YJPIL* 220.
[196] Also DHC-1999 article 12(1) and HCC article 2(2)(l).
[197] *Hosoku Setsumei* (CCP) 23–24, available at: www.e-gov.go.jp/; Minutes of 7th Meeting (CCP).
[198] Sato=Kobayashi (n 62) 78; Sawaki=Dogauchi (n 23) 284.
[199] Sato=Kobayashi (n 62) 78.

exclusive jurisdiction of the Japanese courts. Disputes over intangible property are subject to the jurisdictional rules in CCP articles 3-2–3-8. Most disputes relating to intangible property are in nature contractual (for instance, disputes arising out of the sale or assignment of contractual debts and securities). In such a case, relevant jurisdictional rules in contractual cases (in particular, article 3-3(1), (4) and (5)) should be considered. There are also non-contractual disputes relating to intangible property, such as the right to sue a tortfeasor and rights arising from trusts. For these matters, relevant jurisdictional rules (eg, those dealing with tort or trusts as the case may be) would apply.

c. Intellectual Property

With regard to disputes over intellectual property rights (including patents, trademarks and copyright),[200] there is a distinction to be made: (a) disputes relating to the existence, registration or validity of such rights, and (b) other disputes relating to contractual obligations and infringements of such rights. Given the public interest, Japan subjects disputes in the former category (ie, registration of intellectual property rights and the validity and existence of intellectual property rights that are established by registration) to the exclusive jurisdiction of Japanese courts (see section II.A.viii). The latter category of disputes (for instance, contractual obligations arising out of an assignment or licence contract of intellectual property rights and tortious claims to seek damages or injunctions based upon an infringement of intellectual property rights) are not subject to exclusive jurisdiction, but simply to ordinary and non-exclusive jurisdiction. Therefore, Japanese courts may hear and determine those cases if any of the jurisdictional grounds in CCP articles 3-2–3-8 apply, subject to the special circumstance test of article 3-9. For contractual disputes in which intellectual property is the subject matter of a contract (such as an assignment contract and a licence contract), the principal jurisdictional ground is the defendant's domicile (or principal office) under article 3-2. In addition, article 3-3(1), (4) and (5) may come into play (see section II.B.i.a).

In respect of tortious claims seeking damages or injunctions based on an infringement of intellectual property rights, the principal jurisdictional ground is the defendant's domicile (or principal office).[201] Other specific jurisdictional grounds (in particular, CCP article 3-3(4) and (5)) may also come into play. Furthermore, Japanese courts may take jurisdiction based on the place of tort under article 3-3(8). Nevertheless, as the place of tort under article 3-3(8) is a general concept, it must be interpreted considering the characteristics of intellectual property grounded on the principle of territoriality. In this regard, it is submitted that the place of a harmful act (*locus delicti commissi*) should be regarded

[200] For the international jurisdiction of Japan in intellectual property matters, see, for instance, Toshiyuki Kono, 'Recent Judgments in Japan on Intellectual Property Rights, Conflict of Laws and International Jurisdiction' in Josef Drexl and Annette Kur (eds), *Intellectual Property and Private International Law. Heading for the Future* (Hart Publishing, 2005); Yuko Nishitani, 'Intellectual Property in Japanese Private International Law' (2005) 48 *JAIL* 87; Shigeki Chaen, Toshiyuki Kono and Dai Yokomizo, 'Jurisdiction in Intellectual Property Cases: The Transparency Proposal' in Jürgen Basedow, Toshiyuki Kono and Andreas Metzger (eds), *Intellectual Property in the Global Arena* (2010).

[201] See Judgment of Supreme Court, 26 September 2002, *Minshu* 56(7), 1551 ((2002) 45 *JAIL* 175). In the case involving alleged infringements of US patents between a Japanese national and a Japanese company, the Supreme Court accepted jurisdiction, although it did not touch upon and decide on whether it had jurisdiction.

as the place where the tortfeasor acted or induced the infringement, including acts taken outside the country of protection or registration, and the place where the injury occurs (*locus damni*) should be regarded as the country of protection or registration, namely, in which an intellectual property right is effective and damage is felt.[202]

With regard to jurisdiction based on the place of tort, it should be noted that article 3-3(8) is intended to cover an action for the infringement of rights granted under foreign law.[203] This is because, if only Japanese parties are involved in disputes relating to infringements of foreign intellectual property rights and they wish to bring their lawsuits at Japanese courts, hearing and determining the disputes in Japan would serve the convenience of the parties. Where parties have agreed to resolve before a foreign court, infringements of intellectual property rights registered or granted in Japan, there is no basis to invalidate such a choice of court agreement.[204] Since such claims seek a private law remedy *inter partes*, there is no good reason to deny an action relating to infringements of foreign intellectual property rights.

There is an additional question, namely, whether Japanese courts having jurisdiction over the infringement of a foreign patent can incidentally decide on the validity issue when raised as a defence. The Tokyo District Court held that the fact that the invalidity of a foreign patent will have to be considered as an incidental question will not preclude the jurisdiction of countries other than the country of registration, because the decision does not have *erga omnes* effects, but only binds the parties to the action.[205] Accordingly, Japan's jurisdiction will not be precluded due to the raising of such a defence. For the sake of effective remedies, instead, the Japanese court should be allowed to decide on the validity of foreign patents purely as between the parties, insofar as the applicable substantive rules provide for this.[206] This would be in line with the Japanese rule in domestic cases that permits an incidental decision on the validity of a patent registration in infringement suits (Patent Act article 104), independently of the invalidation by the Patent Office with *erga omnes* effects (article 123). Furthermore, where invalidity proceedings are pending in the foreign country of registration, Japanese courts may suspend infringement proceedings in Japan by reference to article 168(2) *mutatis mutandis*.[207] In the case of an infringement of parallel patents in different countries, especially through a Japanese parent company and its foreign subsidiaries, all the claims can be heard together before the Japanese court by way of an objective and subjective joinder of claims pursuant to CCP article 3-6 (see section II.A.ix).

[202] Nishitani/Jurisdiction (n 74) 267; Yuko Nishitani, 'Supreme Court 26 September 2002, *Fujimoto v Neuron Co Ltd* (*Card Reader* case)' in Moritz Bälz et al (eds), *Business Law in Japan* (Kluwer Law International 2012).

[203] Sato=Kobayashi (n 62) 69 and 113–14; *Hosoku Setsumei* (CCP) 37–38, available at: www.e-gov.go.jp/. In fact, Japanese courts have not declined jurisdiction simply because claims were based on a foreign patent law. For instance, Judgment of Supreme Court, 26 September 2002, *Minshu* 56(7), 1551 ((2002) 45 *JAIL* 175); Judgment of Tokyo District Court, 12 June 1953, *Kaminshu* 4(6), 847; Judgment of Tokyo District Court, 16 October 2003, HJ 1874, 23.

[204] Sato=Kobayashi (n 62) 113–14; *Hosoku Setsumei* (CCP) 37–38, available at: www.e-gov.go.jp/.

[205] Judgment of Tokyo District Court, 16 October 2003, HJ 1874, 23.

[206] For the substantive law solution, Sato=Kobayashi (n 62) 69 and 111–13; for granting jurisdiction without regard to the applicable substantive law, Honma/Nakano/Sakai (n 91) 65.

[207] *Hokokusho* (CCP) 68, available at: www.moj.go.jp/content/000012193.pdf; Minutes of 4th Meeting (CCP). Also, Sato=Kobayashi (n 62) 116.

iii. Law of Corporations

In respect of matters relating to corporations or legal persons, it should be noted that in order to protect the public interest, Japan has designated certain matters as falling within the exclusive jurisdiction of the Japanese courts (see section II.A.viii). Other matters relating to corporations or legal persons are governed by ordinary and non-exclusive jurisdictional rules. Among others, specific grounds in CCP article 3-3(7) are noteworthy. Pursuant to that provision, 'if the association or foundation is a legal person, when it was incorporated under Japanese law; and if it is not a legal person, when its principal office is located in Japan', Japanese courts may have jurisdiction over the following actions:

(a) An action by a company or other association against its present or former member, an action by a member against a present or former member, or an action by a former member against a present member, each of which is based on his/her status as a member.
(b) An action by an association or foundation against its present or former officer based on his/her status as an officer.
(c) An action by a company against its present or former incorporator or inspector, based on his/her status as an incorporator or inspector.
(d) An action by a creditor of a company or other association against its present or former member, based on his/her status as a member.

Each of these items covers various claims.[208] For instance, item (a) covers a damages claim by a membership company (*mochibun kaisha*)[209] against a member for failure to make contributions in that company pursuant to CA article 582(1) and a damages claim by a membership company against a member conducting its business for failure to perform one's duty pursuant to CA article 596. Item (b) covers a damages claim by a membership company against its liquidator for failure to perform one's duty pursuant to CA article 652. Item (c) covers a damages claim by a company against an inspector. Item (d) includes a claim by a creditor of a membership company seeking performance of the company's obligations pursuant to CA article 580(1).[210] A claim by a creditor of the company or other associations against an officer of the company based on the latter's status as an officer (for instance, a damages claim by a third party against a director of the company pursuant to CA article 429 (1)) is not covered by any of those items. This is because such claim can be covered by other jurisdictional grounds, in particular, the place of tort under CCP article 3-3(8).[211] Under this special rule for corporations or legal persons, it is not required that a defendant be domiciled in Japan.[212] For contractual or tortious matters arising out of the activities of corporations or legal persons, the location of the defendant's principal office in Japan is the main jurisdictional ground for the Japanese courts. Other jurisdictional

[208] For details, see Sato=Kobayashi (n 62) 219–23.

[209] *Mochibun kaisha* is a class of corporations with legal personality under Japanese law. There are three types of *mochibun kaisha*: (1) *gomei gaisha* (in which all members have unlimited liability for the company's debt); (2) *goshi gaisha* (in which some members have unlimited liability and others have limited liability for the company's debt); and (3) *godo gaisha* (in which all members have limited liability for the company's debt).

[210] Sato=Kobayashi (n 62) 66.

[211] ibid 67.

[212] Sawaki=Dogauchi (n 23) 279; Sakurada (n 90) 361; Okuda/Business (n 117) 253.

grounds in CCP articles 3-3–3-8 and the special circumstances test under article 3-9 may also come into play.

III. Status and Family Matters

A. General Part

i. Jurisdictional Rules in PSLA

a. Introduction

PSLA covers matters relating to personal status. Article 2 defines 'personal status litigation' as 'litigation related to … actions seeking the formation, or a declaration of the existence, of family relationships'.[213] Specifically, 'personal status litigation' covers actions: (a) to seek invalidation or annulment of a marriage; (b) to seek a divorce; (c) to seek invalidation or annulment of a consensual divorce; (d) to seek a declaratory judgment on the existence of a marital relationship; (e) to rebut the paternity presumption of a child in wedlock; (f) to seek establishment of legal parentage (or filiation); (g) to seek invalidation or annulment of acknowledgement; (h) to seek a declaratory judgment on the existence of legal parentage; (i) to seek invalidation or revocation of adoption; (j) to seek dissolution of an adoptive relationship; (k) to seek invalidation or annulment of a consensual dissolution of an adoptive relationship; and (l) to seek a declaratory judgment on the existence of an adoptive parent–child relationship. In addition, actions relating to other matters that are not enumerated under Japanese law (such as legal separation) are also likely to come under the definition.[214]

b. Previous Case Law

Prior to the 2018 amendment of PSLA, there were no written rules on international jurisdiction in personal status matters. Thus, Japanese courts determined jurisdiction in accordance with a few Supreme Court precedents involving a cross-border divorce.[215] They were the (a) 1964 Supreme Court judgment,[216] and (b) 1996 Supreme Court judgment.[217]

Case (a) concerned the divorce of a Japanese wife, who had left her Korean husband in Korea by agreement and returned to Japan after their marriage broke down over

[213] PSLA article 2 reads: 'The term "personal status litigation" as used in this Act means litigation related to the following actions and other actions seeking the formation, or a declaration of the existence, of family relationships (hereinafter referred to as "actions concerning personal status")'.

[214] Uchino (n 90) 25; Yoshio Tameike, *Kokusai Shiho Kogi* (*Private International Law Course*), 3rd edn (Yuhikaku, 2005) 478 (Tameike); Ryoichi Yamada, *Kokusai Shiho*, 3rd edn (*Private International Law*) (Yuhikaku, 2014) 457. At the choice of law level, separation has been handled in a similar way to divorce.

[215] For developments prior to the 2018 amendment, see, for instance, Ai Murakami, 'International Adjudicatory Jurisdiction for Divorce Cases' (2009) 52 *JYIL* 583; Yasuhiro Okuda, 'New Rules on International Jurisdiction over Divorce in Japanese Courts' (2018/19) 20 *YPIL* 66, 66–68 (Okuda/New Rules); Yuko Nishitani, 'Jinji Sosho Jiken oyobi Kaji Jiken no Kokusai Saibankankatsu tou ni kansuru Shin Hosei (1)' (2019) 71 *Hoso Jiho* 489, 506–10 (Nishitani (1)).

[216] Judgment of Supreme Court, Grand Bench, 25 March 1964, *Minshu* 18(3), 486 ((1964) 8 *JAIL* 175). Also, Hidebumi Egawa, 'International Divorce Jurisdiction in Japan' (1964) 8 *JAIL* 1.

[217] Judgment of Supreme Court, Second Petty Bench, 24 June 1996, *Minshu* 50(7), 1451 ((1997) 40 *JAIL* 132).

15 years before. The wife had neither been in touch with the husband, nor known his whereabouts since then. The Supreme Court stated that the Japanese courts may assume jurisdiction, (i) where a defendant is domiciled in Japan, since granting jurisdiction based on the defendant's domicile 'would live up to the demand of due process and deter the creation of a limping marriage'. Moreover, the Japanese courts may take jurisdiction based on the plaintiff's domicile in Japan, (ii) where the plaintiff has been abandoned, where the defendant's whereabouts are unknown, or where there are other similar exceptional circumstances. In this case, due to the unknown whereabouts of the defendant, the Supreme Court ultimately granted jurisdiction based on the plaintiff's domicile in Japan.[218]

Case (b) concerned the divorce of a Japanese husband, who had left his German wife without her consent in Germany and returned to Japan with their daughter in 1989. The determination of parental authority over their child was also disputed. The Supreme Court apparently took a different approach in this case. According to the Justices, Japanese courts may assume jurisdiction where the defendant is domiciled in Japan. However, even if the defendant is not domiciled in Japan, the courts may decide to accept jurisdiction 'in accordance with the principles of justice and reason based upon fairness between the parties and the sound and prompt administration of justice'. Under this test, the courts are supposed to take into consideration, among others, the burden on the defendant (who will be obliged to appear before the Japanese courts) and de jure or *de facto* obstacles for the plaintiff to claim divorce at the defendant's domicile. In this case, the couple had been divorced by a judgment in Germany, which did not fulfil the requirements of recognition in Japan, so their marriage persisted in Japan, but the plaintiff would have been hampered to bring a divorce claim afresh to the German courts due to the *res judicata* effects. The Supreme Court eventually accepted jurisdiction on grounds of special circumstances justifying the exercise of jurisdiction, presumably to deter a limping marital relationship as a *forum necessitatis*.[219]

c. 2018 Amendments of PSLA

In 2018, by largely relying on previous case law, the legislator introduced the following new jurisdictional rules into PSLA.[220] Article 3-2 sets out seven jurisdictional grounds, stipulating as follows:

> [a]ctions concerning personal status may be filed with the courts of Japan in cases where:[221]
>
> (1) An action is filed against either party to the family relationship and the party has his/her domicile in Japan (or residence in Japan, if he/she has no domicile or his/her domicile is unknown).

[218] Soon after this judgment, in a case involving the divorce of American spouses, the Supreme Court followed the judgment and denied exercising jurisdiction based on the plaintiff's domicile, holding that there existed no such exceptional circumstances. Judgment of Supreme Court, First Petty Bench, 9 April 1965, *Saiban Syumin* 73, 51. With the Supreme Court judgment of 1964, the two decisions were often referred to as '1964 (*Showa 39-nen*) rules'.

[219] In this case, a Japanese husband who returned from Germany to Japan with his child claimed divorce and parental authority over the child before a Japanese court. His German wife had already obtained a German judgment for divorce and parental authority in her favour. However, the German judgment was not eligible to be recognised in Japan because the suit had begun with service of process by publication and without the husband's appearance, and thereby the requirement of article 200(2) (present, article 118(2)) was not fulfilled.

[220] Minutes of 18th Meeting 1–2; Keisuke Takeshita, 'Atarashii Jinji Sosho Jiken no Kokusai Saiban Kankatsu Kitei' (2018) 27 *Ronkyu Juristo* 31 (Takeshita).

[221] Translation cited from (2019) 62 *JYIL* 486–95.

(2) An action is filed against both parties to the family relationship and one or both of the parties have their domicile in Japan (or residence in Japan, when one or both of the parties have no domicile, or their domicile is unknown).
(3) An action is filed by either party to the family relationship and the other party had his/her domicile in Japan at the time of his/her death.
(4) Both parties to the family relationship have died and one or both of them had their domicile in Japan at the time of their death.
(5) Both parties to the family relationship have the Japanese nationality (including cases where one or both of them had the Japanese nationality at the time of their death).
(6) An action is filed by either party to the family relationship who has his/her domicile in Japan and both parties had their last common domicile in Japan.
(7) An action is filed by either party to the family relationship who has his/her domicile in Japan and
   - the whereabouts of the other party are unknown;
   - final and binding judgment concerning the same family relationship as the action at hand rendered in the state where the other party has his/her domicile does not have effects in Japan; or
   - there are any other special circumstances under which a trial and judicial decision by the courts of Japan would support equity between the parties or ensure the realisation of a proper and prompt trial.

These new rules are grounded on previous case law, sophisticating or adding some new jurisdictional grounds (more particularly, PSLA article 3-2(1), (4), (6) and (7)). In this sense, it clarifies the Supreme Court's approaches[222] and renders jurisdiction more certain and foreseeable. Notably, these new rules cover not only divorce cases, but also other matters relating to personal status. The term 'either party (or both of the parties) to the family relationship' refers to the person or persons who are the subject of the relevant matrimonial, parental or other proceedings.[223] Accordingly, where a third party seeks annulment of a couple's marriage, the plaintiff would not come under the definition of 'a party (or parties) to the family relationship'.

d. Defendant's Domicile

PSLA article 3-2 adopts as principal indicators, both domicile (or residence) under article 3-2(1)–(4) and (6) and nationality under article 3-2(5) and (7) (for each definition, see chapter one, section V). For instance, article 3-2(1) grounds Japan's jurisdiction on the defendant's domicile in Japan (or residence, if the defendant has no or no known domicile) as in CCP article 3-2(1). This rule adopts the traditional principle of *actor sequitur forum rei* and aims to balance the parties' interests.[224] The principle is also seen in the Supreme Court judgments just discussed. In the absence of a domicile in Japan, article 3-2(1) and (2) refer to the defendant's residence in Japan. In this regard, as in CCP, a defendant 'having no domicile' means that the defendant has no domicile in Japan or anywhere else in the world.[225]

[222] Takeshita (n 220) 32.
[223] Uchino (n 90) 26–27.
[224] Sato=Kobayashi (n 62) 22.
[225] Nishitani (1) (n 215) 515; Sawaki=Dogauchi (n 23) 271; Takeshita (n 220) 32, fn 8.

PSLA article 3-2(2), (3) and (4), ground Japan's jurisdiction on the basis of domicile in Japan of a party or parties.[226]

e. Last Common Domicile

Article 3-2(6) establishes Japan's jurisdiction on the 'last common domicile' in Japan of both parties, subject to the condition that a plaintiff is still domiciled in Japan.[227] This condition aims to ensure sufficient connection between the case and Japan.[228] Pursuant to this rule, the court may assume jurisdiction, for instance, where one spouse has abandoned and left the other spouse who remains domiciled in Japan. In such a case, the remaining spouse will not be compelled to bring a divorce action before the court of the state where the other party has moved. It would be reasonable for the other spouse to be sued before the Japanese court, because evidence for the claim (eg, extramarital relationship of the defendant) is often located at the parties' last common domicile and responding to the claim there should not pose a huge burden on the defendant.[229]

f. Common Nationality

Prior to the 2018 amendment, it was unclear whether and when Japanese nationality served as a basis for jurisdiction of the Japanese courts (as opposed to 'the defendant's domicile').[230] PSLA article 3-2(5) clarifies that the Japanese nationalities of both parties ground Japan's jurisdiction. It is not required that a plaintiff is domiciled in Japan, as the common Japanese nationality would sufficiently prove a close connection with Japan.[231] Thus, where both parties have Japanese nationality, Japanese courts may take jurisdiction, even where the defendant lives abroad or where both spouses live abroad.[232] This provision is based on the idea that Japan has an interest in the personal status of Japanese nationals, particularly to ensure their right to claim divorce, and that such jurisdiction is deemed fair for the Japanese spouses in that their relatives are likely to be domiciled in Japan and thereby have some connection with Japan.[233] From the viewpoint of administrating the family registry, such jurisdiction may also be justified. For instance, in actions seeking a declaration of invalidity of a marriage or of the non-existence of parentage, the party and the state have

[226] Before the 2018 amendment, in the cases where a person who would be the defendant had already died, some lower courts accepted jurisdiction, where such person had a last domicile in Japan. For instance, Judgment of Osaka High Court, 9 May 2014, HJ 2231, 53.

[227] Although it is unclear from the wording what the term 'last common domicile' exactly means, it is generally understood as the last place (not country) where the parties lived together. Uchino (n 90) 33; Masanori Takeda, 'Rikon, Kon'in no Torikeshi nado ni kansuru Kokusai Saibankankatsu' in Ayako Ikeda (ed), *Kokusai Kaji Jiken no Saiban Kankatsu* (*International Jurisdiction in Cross-border Family Law Matters*) (Nihon Kajo Syuppan, 2019) 48 (Takeda/Ikeda). *cf Zadankai* (PSLA and DRCPA) 11 [Comments by Dogauchi].

[228] Uchino (n 90) 33.

[229] Sawaki=Dogauchi (n 23) 316.

[230] For developments prior to the 2018 amendment, see, for instance, Tameike (n 214) 472. In some cross-border divorce cases between Japanese spouse, lower courts have exercised jurisdiction based on their Japanese nationality. Judgment of Tokyo Family Court, 27 March 2014, unpublished; Judgment of Tokyo District Court, 4 November 1999, HT 1023, 267.

[231] Minutes of 13th Meeting (PSLA and DRCPA).

[232] Nishitani (1) (n 215) 516; Sawaki=Dogauchi (n 23) 315; Takeda/Ikeda (n 227) 46.

[233] Uchino (n 90) 29; *Zadankai* (PSLA and DRCPA) 14–15 [Comments by Dogauchi and Uchino].

legitimate interests in maintaining correct personal records in the family registry. Since the family registry only takes up Japanese nationals, grounding Japan's jurisdiction on common Japanese nationality is justified.[234]

This jurisdictional ground applies even where a party has one or several foreign nationalities besides Japanese.[235] On the other hand, the Japanese courts may not accept jurisdiction simply based on the Japanese nationality of one party (a plaintiff), as in the case where, for instance, a Japanese wife who used to live abroad with her husband of foreign nationality, comes back to Japan and claims divorce before the Japanese court. This is because the nationality of only one party does not constitute a sufficient connection with Japan, imposing an excessive burden on the defendant and running counter to fairness between the parties.[236]

g. Plaintiff's Domicile

Unlike the defendant's domicile under PSLA article 3-2(1) as the primary ground of jurisdiction, the Japanese courts are not allowed to accept jurisdiction merely based on the plaintiff's domicile in light of fairness between the parties.[237] Therefore, additional factors are needed to establish a plaintiff's jurisdiction pursuant to PSLA article 3-2(7). This provision exceptionally constitutes Japan's jurisdiction based on the plaintiff's domicile in Japan where:[238] (a) the whereabouts of the other party are unknown; (b) a final and binding judgment concerning the same family relationship as the action at hand rendered in the state where the other party has a domicile does not have effect in Japan; or (c) there are any other special circumstances under which a trial and judicial decision by the courts of Japan would support equity between the parties or ensure the realisation of a proper and prompt trial.

Items (a) and (c) modified the ruling in the 1964 Supreme Court judgment and item (b) reflects the ruling in the 1996 Supreme Court judgment.[239] It is understood that item (a) covers situations such as, for instance, where the defendant's factual domicile is not ascertainable with reasonable effort and service cannot be effectuated on the defendant.[240] In such cases, service will be made by publication, with the result that the defendant may not have due process protection. Therefore, when deciding whether a defendant has been missing, it is necessary to look carefully into the circumstances.[241]

While the 1996 Supreme Court judgment granted a *forum necessitatis* in Japan, item (b) arguably has a different meaning. Item (b) does not automatically confer jurisdiction to

[234] Nishitani (1) (n 215) 517; Sawaki=Dogauchi (n 23) 315.

[235] Nishitani (1) 518.

[236] Uchino (n 90) 31.

[237] ibid 28.

[238] PSLA article 3-2(7) does not refer to the situation where the plaintiff has been abandoned which the 1964 Supreme Court judgment mentioned. This is because it is unclear what precisely 'abandonment' means and it is necessary to look into the culpability of one party (ie, stray into the merits). *Hosoku Setsumei* (PSLA and DRCPA) 7.

[239] Uchino (n 90) 36–37; Takeshita (n 220) 34. *cf* Sawaki=Dogauchi (n 23) 316 (which takes the view that article 3-2(7) effectively provides emergency jurisdiction, subject to the condition that a plaintiff is domiciled in Japan).

[240] Uchino (n 90) 40. Also, Judgment of Nagoya High Court, 30 May 1996, HT 891, 248. In this case, the Court exercised jurisdiction on the basis that the defendant's exact domicile was unknown, although the state where the defendant was staying was known and the defendant could be reached via e-mails and other means.

[241] Nishitani (1) (n 215) 521.

the Japanese courts on the ground that a plaintiff cannot bring a claim before any foreign courts. It simply requires the Japanese courts to consider that a final and binding judgment rendered at the defendant's domicile cannot be recognised in Japan, when deciding whether to take jurisdiction based on the plaintiff's domicile. Indeed, the plaintiff may be able to avail himself or herself of an alternative forum in a foreign state other than that of the defendant's domicile, and the resulting judgment could be recognised in Japan, but this factor is not taken into account in item (b). Thus, item (b) should be understood as applying the reasonable circumstances test, instead of establishing a *forum necessitatis*.[242]

h. Joinder of Claims

In addition, Japanese courts may extend jurisdiction to some related matters pursuant to PSLA articles 3-3 and 3-4. In respect of matters relating to personal status such as divorce, claims for damages may often arise between the parties, when, for instance, a wife seeking divorce also claims compensation for her pain and suffering due to her husband's adultery. Although such claims, being of a pecuniary nature, would generally come under the jurisdictional rules of CCP, PSLA article 3-3 allows a joinder of claims, so a plaintiff may pursue related damages claim against the defendant before a single court.[243] This would duly resolve the entire dispute at once, allowing the court seised to determine, based on the same evidence, both the divorce and damages claims (including, where appropriate, the amount of solatium),[244] even where the Japanese courts would not have jurisdiction over such pecuniary claims under CCP.[245]

In connection with divorce or annulment of a marriage, some ancillary issues often arise, such as the determination of a child's custodian or guardian, access to the child and payment of child support. In this light, PSLA article 3-4(1) grounds jurisdiction of the Japanese courts over such ancillary issues, where Japanese courts have jurisdiction over an action regarding divorce or annulment of a marriage.[246] It is not required that Japan has international jurisdiction on such ancillary issues separately under DRCPA articles 3-8 or 3-10.[247] On the other hand, pursuant to PSLA article 3-4(2), Japanese courts may take

[242] Nishitani (1) (n 215) 522–23; Takeshita (n 220) 34, fn 21.

[243] PSLA article 3-3 reads as follows: 'In cases where the party seeks to join a claim for personal status litigation with a claim for damages arising from the facts underlying the original claim in a single action (limited to a claim by either party of the personal status litigation against the other party), the action may be filed with the courts in Japan only if the courts in Japan have jurisdiction over the original claim for personal status litigation'.

[244] Uchino (n 90) 49.

[245] ibid.

[246] PSLA article 3-4 reads:

> '(1) In cases where the courts of Japan have jurisdiction over an action seeking the revocation of marriage or divorce, the courts also have jurisdiction over a case concerning a judicial decision on the designation of a person who will have custody over the child or any other disposition pertaining to the custody of the child as set forth under Article 32, paragraph (1), as well as over a judicial decision on the designation of a person who will have parental authority as set forth in paragraph (3) of the said Article.
> (2) In cases where the courts of Japan have jurisdiction over an action seeking the revocation of marriage or divorce, the courts also have jurisdiction over a case concerning a judicial decision on a disposition pertaining to the distribution of property as set forth in Article 32, paragraph (1) when any condition specified in the items of Article 3-12 of DRCPA is fulfilled'.

[247] Even before the 2018 amendment, lower courts had upheld jurisdiction on the same ground. See, for instance, Judgment of Nagoya District Court, 24 November 1999, HJ 1728, 58; Judgment of Tokyo District Court,

jurisdiction over matters regarding distribution of property, where they have jurisdiction over an action for divorce or annulment of a marriage and the jurisdictional requirements under DRCPA article 3-12 are satisfied. In other words, in the case of distribution of property, this joinder of claims that duly serves for procedural economy[248] can only be granted when DRCPA article 3-12 separately confers jurisdiction proper to distribution of property to the Japanese courts (see section III.C.ii).

i. Special Circumstances Test

PSLA also has in article 3-5 a corrective rule similar to that in CCP article 3-9. That provision stipulates as follows:

> Even where the courts of Japan have jurisdiction over an action, the court may dismiss the whole or a part of such action when it finds special circumstances under which a trial and judicial decision by the courts of Japan would undermine the equity between the parties or disturb the realisation of a proper and prompt trial, considering the nature of the case, the degree of the defendant's burden of submitting a defense, the location of evidence, the interests of the minor child of the parties to the family relationship involved in the action, and any other relevant circumstances.

Compared with CCP article 3-9, there are two differences to be noted. First, because PSLA does not allow choice of court agreements between the parties in personal status matters geared towards stability and mandatory regulation,[249] PSLA article 3-5 does not have a specific exception in the case of an exclusive choice of court agreement for Japanese courts.[250] Second, PSLA article 3-5 expressly requires the interests of a minor child to be taken into consideration.[251] This requirement shows that great value should be attached to the best interests of a minor child in cases relating to family relationships.[252] Thus, Japanese courts may decline jurisdiction, where hearing the case in Japan would not serve the best interests of a minor child.[253]

Like CCP article 3-9, PSLA article 3-5 allows the Japanese courts to decline jurisdiction in the absence of a close connection between the case and the forum state. This might be the case when spouses, for example, had their last common domicile in Japan and the plaintiff still resides in Japan (PSLA article 3-2 (6)), but the defendant has not visited Japan for a significant period of time after moving abroad.[254] This might also be the case when both parties to divorce proceedings are Japanese nationals (PSLA article 3-2 (5)) but have been

26 December 1995, HT 922, 276; Judgment of Chiba District Court, 31 March 1972, HJ 682, 50. *cf* Decision of Tokyo Family Court, 13 June 1969, *Kagetsu* 22(3), 104.

[248] Uchino (n 90) 60.

[249] The parties can agree on the jurisdiction of the Japanese courts limited to conciliation pursuant to DRCPA article 13-3(1)(3). Ayako Ikeda, 'Soron' in Ayako Ikeda (ed), *Kokusai Kaji Jiken no Saiban Kankatsu* (*International Jurisdiction in Cross-border Family Law Matters*) (Nihon Kajo Syuppan, 2019) 17 (Ikeda/Ikeda).

[250] Sawaki=Dogauchi (n 23) 320.

[251] Uchino (n 90) 63. The legislator takes a hypothetical divorce case involving a minor child as example, mentioning that it will be considered whether the child is able to appear before the Japanese court to deliver a statement, and, if not, whether there are alternative methods of understanding his or her opinion correctly.

[252] Sawaki=Dogauchi (n 23) 320.

[253] For instance, where, following PSLA article 3-4, a Japanese court may take jurisdiction over divorce and disposition of a child custody, but the child is not found in Japan. *Zadankai* (PSLA and DRCPA) 16 [Comments by Otani].

[254] Uchino (n 90) 61.

living abroad all the time,[255] or when a third party brings a petition against both spouses of Japanese nationality domiciled abroad to seek annulment of their marriage.[256] So far, there have been no reported cases where PSLA article 3-5 was exceptionally applied.

Furthermore, pursuant to PSLA article 18(1), a plaintiff may amend a claim or statement of claims (and a defendant may file a counterclaim) until the conclusion of the oral arguments in the first or second instance. Such amendment may take time, and in the meantime, a defendant may have moved abroad. PSLA article 18(2) allows Japanese courts before which the principal claim has been pending to extend jurisdiction to an amended claim, where the amended claim is to seek a declaration of the formation or existence of one and the same relationship that the principal claim addresses. This would be the case with, for instance, a wife who first sought divorce but later amended her claim to seek annulment of her marriage.[257] However, Japanese courts may decline jurisdiction over an amended claim under the special circumstances test in PSLA article 3-5.[258]

A similar issue may arise in the context of counterclaims by a defendant. Pursuant to PSLA article 18(3), Japan's jurisdiction can be extended to a counterclaim in principle, if the counterclaim is (a) to seek a declaration of the formation or existence of one and the same personal status which is the subject matter of the principal claim (for instance, where the claim is for divorce and the counterclaim for annulment),[259] or (b) to seek compensation for alleged damage or loss arising out of the cause grounding the principal claim pending before the Japanese court. This is because it is necessary that disputes relating to personal status should be resolved in a single action to stabilise the personal status of the relevant parties. However, jurisdiction may be declined for the counterclaim for lack of sufficient connection with Japan under PSLA article 3-5.[260]

j. International Parallel Proceedings

PSLA does not contain any explicit rule on *lis alibi pendens*. During the legislative process, it was discussed whether to adopt a specific rule to regulate international parallel proceedings. It was suggested[261] that the judge be authorised to stay proceedings involving the same cause of action between the same parties before a foreign court seised first, if that court is likely to render a judgment on the merits, which would fulfil the recognition requirements under CCP article 118. The suggestion was eventually abandoned as the Legislative Subcommittee did not see any reason to adopt an explicit rule for parallel proceedings in status and family matters, while a comparable rule had been given up for civil and commercial matters (see section II.A.iii).

k. Choice of Court Agreements and Submission

PSLA neither allows choice of court agreements nor submission, since personal status matters require stability and certainty, in addition to the exclusion of parties' disposition

[255] Ikeda/Ikeda (n 249) 9.
[256] Takeshita (n 220) 37, fn 45.
[257] Uchino (n 90) 64.
[258] ibid 65.
[259] ibid 66.
[260] ibid 66–67.
[261] Interim Draft (PSLA and DRCPA) 8; *Hosoku Setsumei* (PSLA and DRCPA) 59–62.

for jurisdictional grounds. There is no room for party autonomy in personal status matters under PSLA. Accordingly, Japanese courts may not take jurisdiction simply based on the parties' choice of court agreements or the defendant's submission pursuant to PSLA.[262] Nevertheless, as a matter of fact, the parties' agreements to sue before the Japanese courts or the defendant's submission there may be taken into consideration when determining jurisdiction based on the plaintiff's domicile under article 3-2(7).[263]

ii. Jurisdictional Rules in Domestic Relations (DRCPA and AGRAL)

a. Introduction

DRCPA principally covers non-contentious matters, for instance, administration of an absentee's property, annulment of disappearance adjudication, permission to adopt, and establishment of special adoption. It offers two methods for dispute resolution: adjudication by court and conciliation by court. Both proceedings are closed, as opposed to litigation under CCP or PSLA. DRCPA contains jurisdictional rules for both adjudication by court and conciliation by court. Insofar as matters supposed to be addressed in court adjudication are concerned, DRCPA articles 3-2–3-12 provide specific grounds in particular cases (for details, see sections III.B–E). As opposed to CCP or PSLA, DRCPA does not provide general grounds for jurisdiction (ie, 'all-purpose jurisdiction').

b. Conciliation

With regard to conciliation by the court, DRCPA article 3-13 offers three jurisdictional grounds.[264] According to article 3-13(1), a court may hold conciliation: (a) where it has jurisdiction over an action or case for a particular issue that would constitute the subject matter of the conciliation; (b) where the respondent has a domicile in Japan (or residence in Japan, when the respondent has no or no known domicile); (c) where the parties have agreed that a petition for conciliation should be filed with a court or the courts of Japan. However, insofar as personal status matters other than divorce and dissolution

[262] Ikeda/Ikeda (n 249) 23.

[263] Takeshita (n 220) 38; Takeda/Ikeda (n 227) 52; *cf Zadankai* (PSLA and DRCPA) 18 [Comments by Dogauchi]. Prior to the 2018 amendment, some lower courts accepted jurisdiction on the basis of the fact that the defendant submitted him/herself to the court, in addition to the plaintiff's domicile in Japan, for instance, Judgment of Mito Family Court, 16 December 2016, HT 1439, 251; Judgment of Kobe District Court, 30 January 1991, HT 764, 240.

[264] DRCPA article 3-13 reads as follows:

'(1) The courts have jurisdiction over conciliation cases pertaining to domestic relations in cases where:

(i) the courts of Japan have jurisdiction over an action or case for a particular issue that constitutes the subject-matter of the conciliation;
(ii) the respondent has his/her domicile in Japan (or residence in Japan, when he/she has no domicile or his/her domicile is unknown); or
(iii) the parties agreed that a petition for conciliation should be filed with a court or courts of Japan.

(2) The provisions of CCP Article 3-7, paragraphs (2) and (3) shall apply mutatis mutandis to the agreement referred to in item (iii) of the preceding paragraph.
(3) The provision of paragraph (1) (limited to items (ii) and (iii) herein) shall not apply to conciliation cases for particulars for which actions concerning personal status set forth in PSLA article 2 (excluding actions for divorce or dissolution of an adoptive relationship) may be filed'.

are concerned, (b) and (c) are not available (article 3-13(3)). Where parties agree on conciliation by the court in accordance with DRCPA article 3-13, such agreement must satisfy the requirements of CCP article 3-7(2) and (3) (DRCPA article 3-13(2)). It is not required that a petitioner has a domicile in Japan.

c. Special Circumstances Test

DRCPA also contains a corrective rule in article 3-14 as follows:

> Even where the courts of Japan have jurisdiction over a case specified under Articles 3-2 to the preceding Article (excluding a case pertaining to the division of an estate being filed on the ground of an agreement designating the courts of Japan as having exclusive jurisdiction), the court may dismiss the whole or a part of such case when it finds special circumstances under which a trial and judicial decision by the courts of Japan would disturb the realization of a proper and prompt trial or, in contentious cases, undermine the equity between the parties, considering the nature of the case, the degree of the burden of persons concerned other than the petitioner, the location of evidence, the interests of a minor child, and any other circumstances.

This corrective rule contains a reservation of non-application to cases of a pecuniary nature pertaining to the division of an estate, where parties agree on exclusive jurisdiction of the Japanese courts. This aims to respect party autonomy and certainty.[265] On the other hand, where parties simply agree on the (non-exclusive) jurisdiction of the Japanese courts, the court seised may decline jurisdiction, applying the special circumstances test under DRCPA article 3-14. Therefore, the Japanese courts may decline jurisdiction where Japan has little connection with a case except for parties' choice of court agreement. This would be the case, for instance, when several heirs visited Japan for a short period of time, but the deceased had never lived in Japan before dying and there is no property to be inherited in Japan.[266]

Likewise, DRCPA article 3-14 follows the framework of CCP article 3-9. However, reflecting the fact that DRCPA covers a wide range of domestic relations (not only contentious but also non-contentious matters), article 3-14 sets forth additional factors to be considered, such as 'the burden on persons other than the petitioner' and 'the interests of a minor child'. A Japanese court is thus required to consider circumstances in individual cases, depending on the nature of the case. The court examines whether there are special circumstances that would impair fairness as between the petitioner and the opposing party. When there is no opposing party, the court examines whether there are special circumstances that would hinder the sound and prompt administration of justice. As for *lis pendens* and submission, there exist no explicit rules in DRCPA. DRCPA allows parties to agree on a specific court for adjudication in cases relating to the division of estates and dispositions of special contributory portions (DRCPA article 3-11(4)). To be valid, such agreements must satisfy the requirements of CCP article 3-7(2)–(4) (DRCPA article 3-11(5)). Furthermore, pursuant to DRCPA article 3-13, parties may agree to refer matters to conciliation by the Japanese court (article 3-13(3)). Such agreements are governed by CCP article 3-7(2) and (3).

[265] Sawaki=Dogauchi (n 23) 332.
[266] Uchino (n 90) 154–55.

d. Remaining Jurisdictional Rules in AGRAL

Notably, AGRAL, which generally provides for conflicts rules to determine the applicable law, also comprises some jurisdictional rules. AGRAL articles 5 and 6 sets forth jurisdictional rules on disappearance and protection of adults, which are no longer transferred to DRCPA since its 2018 reform. This primarily owes to the limited mandate of the Legislative Subcommittee and the character of AGRAL articles 5 and 6, which also designate Japanese law to be applicable as the *lex fori*. In the following, the relevant jurisdictional rules in AGRAL are also discussed.

B. Capacity and Protective Measures

i. Disappearance

AGRAL and DRCPA provide specific jurisdictional rules on matters of persons. AGRAL article 6 applies concerning a declaration of disappearance, which brings about the presumption of death under Japanese law. According to AGRAL article 6(1) providing general jurisdictional grounds, the court may make an adjudication of disappearance 'where an absentee had domicile in Japan or had Japanese nationality, at the latest point of time when found to be alive'. The rule first grounds the principal jurisdiction on an absentee's last domicile in Japan,[267] irrespective of his or her nationality. It is reasonable to investigate an absentee's situation at the latter's last domicile, where the centre of the individual's life was arguably situated.[268] In addition, article 6(1) grounds Japan's jurisdiction on an absentee's Japanese nationality. This means that Japan exercises jurisdiction to protect its own nationals living overseas after they have disappeared.

Even if an absentee did not have his or her last domicile in Japan nor Japanese nationality at the relevant time, AGRAL article 6(2) authorises the courts to make an adjudication in two exceptional cases: (a) 'if an absentee's property is situated in Japan', or (b) 'if an absentee's legal relationship should be governed by Japanese law or is connected with Japan in light of the nature of the legal relationship, the person's domicile or nationality, and any other circumstances'. These exceptional grounds of jurisdiction are geared towards protecting a third party's or public interest.[269] As is evident from the wording of the provision, however, Japan's jurisdiction only extends to the relevant property or legal relationship respectively.[270]

Item (a) refers to 'property'. This covers not only tangible property (ie, immovable and movable property), but also intangible property such as intellectual property rights (for instance, patents and copyright) and claims.[271] While the physical location of tangible

[267] In contrast, *Horei* article 6 exceptionally grounded Japan's jurisdiction for an allegedly missing foreigner based on the latter's property being situated in Japan.

[268] *Hosoku Setsumei* (AGRAL) 131.

[269] Sawaki=Dogauchi (n 23) 151.

[270] AGRAL article 6(2) reads as follows: '[e]ven in the case where the preceding paragraph does not apply, if an absentee's property is situated in Japan, or if an absentee's legal relationship should be governed by Japanese law or is connected with Japan in light of the nature of the legal relationship, the domicile or nationality of the party and any other circumstances concerned, the court may, by applying Japanese law, make an adjudication of the absentee's disappearance only with regard to said property or said legal relationship, respectively'.

[271] Yasushi Nakanishi, 'Article 6 (Shisso no Senkoku)' in Yoshiaki Sakurada and Masato Dogauchi (eds), *Chushaku Kokusai Shiho: Dai 1 kan (Commentary on Private International Law: Volume 1)* (Yuhikaku, 2011) 128.

property can easily be ascertained, this is not the case with intangible property. For the purpose of AGRAL article 6(2), intangible property should be understood as referring to intellectual property rights registered or granted under Japanese law, as well as claims[272] that can be made before the Japanese courts.[273]

Item (b) mentions two situations where (i) an absentee's legal relationship should be governed by Japanese law, or (ii) an absentee's legal relationship is linked to Japan in light of the nature of the legal relationship, the domicile or nationality of the party, and any other circumstances. The first situation arises when, for example, an absentee's marriage is governed by Japanese law pursuant to AGRAL article 25 (see chapter three, section V.A) and a relevant contract is governed by Japanese law pursuant to AGRAL articles 7–9 (see chapter three, section II.A).[274] The second situation arises where a Japanese wife who used to live abroad returns to Japan after her foreign husband's disappearance and seeks a declaration of his disappearance.[275]

On the other hand, when it comes to (i) the administration of an absentee's property and (ii) the annulment of a disappearance adjudication, DRCPA articles 3-2 and 3-3 apply respectively. (i) Under DRCPA article 3-2,[276] the court may make an adjudication on a disposition regarding the administration of the absentee's property, if an absentee's property is situated in Japan. This is because the court is in the best position to decide on the administration of the absentee's relevant property.[277] Following this reasoning, Japan's jurisdiction should be limited to the property located in Japan. The nationality of an absentee does not come into play. (ii) With regard to the annulment of a disappearance adjudication, by article 3-3,[278] jurisdiction will be established (a) where such adjudication has been made in Japan, (b) where the absentee is domiciled in Japan or has Japanese nationality, or (c) where an absentee had his or her last domicile in Japan or Japanese nationality prior to being found to be alive. The third ground corresponds to AGRAL article 6(1). In addition, as discussed in the previous paragraph, the court may make a declaration of disappearance in two exceptional cases. Where property ought to be administered in Japan, the first exceptional ground would apply.

ii. Protection of Adults

As with other jurisdictions, Japan has some legal institutions to protect mentally incapacitated adults due to impaired intelligence or age-related illness such as Alzheimer's disease.

[272] See BA article 4(2).

[273] Nakanishi, 'Article 6 (Shisso no Senkoku)' (n 271) 129; Sawaki=Dogauchi (n 23) 151; Sakurada (n 90) 162–63; Yasuhiro Okuda, *Kokusai Kazokuho* (*International Family Law*) (Akashi Shoten, 2015) 443 (Okuda/Family).

[274] Sawaki=Dogauchi (n 23) 151; Sakurada (n 90) 163; Okuda/Family (n 273) 444.

[275] Sawaki=Dogauchi (n 23) 151; Okuda/Family (n 273) 444; Yasushi Nakanishi, Aki Kitazawa, Dai Yokomizo and Takami Hayashi, *Kokusai Shiho* (*Private International Law*), 2nd edn (Yuhikaku, 2018) 377.

[276] DRCPA article 3-2 reads as follows: 'The courts have jurisdiction over cases for dispositions pertaining to the administration of the property of an absentee … in cases where the property of the absentee is located in Japan'.

[277] Uchino (n 90) 89.

[278] DRCPA article 3-3 reads as follows: 'The courts have jurisdiction over the adjudication of cases for the revocation of the adjudication of disappearance … in cases where:

(i) an adjudication of disappearance was made in Japan;
(ii) an absentee is domiciled in Japan or has the Japanese nationality; or
(iii) an absentee was domiciled in Japan or had the Japanese nationality at the last time where the absentee was deemed to be alive'.

Japanese substantive law offers guardianship (*kouken*), curatorship (*hosa*) or assistance (*hojo*), depending on the degree of mental incapacity of the adult concerned. With regard to the jurisdiction on the commencement of guardianship, curatorship or assistance, AGRAL article 5 applies. The Japanese courts may make such a ruling 'where a person who is to become an adult ward, person under curatorship, or person under assistance has domicile or residence in Japan or has Japanese nationality'. This rule grounds jurisdiction on a party's nationality, domicile, or residence in Japan. It is easy to ascertain whether a person has Japanese nationality or has domicile or residence in Japan. These jurisdictional grounds allow the Japanese courts to provide necessary protection for adults who are domiciled or temporarily staying in Japan, or who reside abroad but have Japanese nationality. The legislature did not adopt the location of property as an alternative jurisdictional ground, as such ground might be regarded as exorbitant.[279] Arguably, the Japanese courts could also exercise jurisdiction as a *forum necessitatis*, when neither the person's home state nor state of residence has an equivalent institution and no authority other than the Japanese could make the ruling.[280]

As to other matters regarding guardianship of adults, such as annulment of a ruling for commencement of guardianship, curatorship, or assistance of adults, or relevant protective measures (including designation or dismissal of a guardian, and appointment of a special agent), similar jurisdictional rules were proposed in the Interim Draft,[281] but are no longer adopted. In particular, opinions were divided on whether a foreign court decision ordering the commencement of guardianship ought to be recognised in Japan. This is because there is no registration system in Japan to enter the effects of the foreign decision (eg, restriction of the individual's legal capacity and enumeration of legal acts to be undertaken by his or her legal representative), which could cause uncertainty in transactions taking place in Japan. It was thought inappropriate to set out jurisdictional rules that would clearly presuppose the recognition of foreign decisions and determine jurisdiction of the Japanese courts to appoint, for example, a guardian or supervisor of a guardian subsequent to the commencement of guardianship abroad.[282] Therefore, it remains an open question when Japanese courts may have jurisdiction over these matters.

iii. Protection of Minors

In respect of guardianship for a minor child, DRCPA article 3-9 sets out only one jurisdictional rule on an adjudication by court for appointment of a guardian for a minor child.[283] According to this rule, the court may make such adjudication, where a minor child has a

[279] Kunio Koide (ed), *Chikujo Kaisetsu Ho no Tekiyo ni kansuru Tsusokuho* (*Commentary on the Act on General Rules for Application of Law*) (Shojihomu, expanded edn, 2015) 58.

[280] Sakurada (n 90) 174; Tadashi Kanzaki, *Kaisetsu Ho no Tekiyou ni kansuru Tsuusokuho* (*Commentary on the Act on General Rules for Application of Law*) (Kobundo, 2006) 39–40.

[281] Interim Draft (PSLA and DRCPA) 16. Under the proposed rules, the domicile or residence and the nationality of a guardian, curator, assistant as well as the adjudication that a Japanese court has made would also be jurisdictional grounds.

[282] *Hosoku Setsumei* (PSLA and DRCPA) 32.

[283] DRCPA article 3-9 stipulates as follows: 'The courts have jurisdiction over cases pertaining to the appointment of a person as a guardian of a minor after the dissolution of his/her adoptive relationship … or adjudication of cases for the appointment of a guardian of a minor … in cases in which a person who is to be a minor ward or is a minor ward has his/her domicile or residence in Japan or he/she has the Japanese nationality'.

domicile or residence in Japan or has Japanese nationality. Due to a lack of explicit jurisdictional rules, it is unclear when Japanese courts may assert jurisdiction over other subsequent matters relating to the guardianship of minors, such as dismissal of a guardian, appointment of a supervisor of a guardian, or taking of other protective measures. In the course of the legislative process, jurisdictional rules similar to those on guardianship of adults were proposed, but are no longer adopted (except for one proposed rule which became DRCPA article 3-9) for the similar reasons discussed above as to guardianship etc of adults.[284]

iv. Contractual Guardianship

Likewise, there are no explicit jurisdictional rules in adjudication cases relating to voluntary or contractual guardianship. Under Japanese law, a party may appoint a guardian through an agreement in accordance with the Act on Voluntary Guardianship Contract (AVGC). In the Interim Draft, a jurisdictional rule based on the domicile and residence of a mandator (namely, a principal) was proposed. However, such proposal was not adopted for the reason that depending on applicable law, such form of guardianship is diverse and therefore difficult to deal with comprehensively in jurisdictional rules.[285] Therefore, it is still an open question when the Japanese court may assume jurisdiction here. But Japanese courts should be authorised to take jurisdiction, at least, where an underlying contract has been registered pursuant to AVGC.[286] For contractual or tortious matters arising out of a natural person's activities, the defendant's domicile in Japan is the principal jurisdictional ground. Other grounds in CCP articles 3-3–3-8 and the special circumstances test under article 3-9 may come into play (see section II).

C. Matrimonial Matters

i. Patrimonial Effects of Marriage

To be valid, a marriage must satisfy the requirements of applicable laws designated in AGRAL article 24 (see chapter three, section V.A). Disputes relating to the formation of marriage arise as to its invalidity or annulment as personal status matters (for these matters, see section III.C.ii).

Apart from the validity or annulment of marriage, some disputes may arise out of cross-border marriages. As to cooperation and mutual assistance between spouses and the sharing of living expenses, DRCPA article 3-10 determines international jurisdiction.[287] The Japanese courts may accept jurisdiction, where the party obliged to provide support

[284] Minutes of 16th Meeting (PSLA and DRCPA) 33–34.

[285] Minutes of 14th Meeting (PSLA and DRCPA) 16–22.

[286] *Hosoku Setsumei* (PSLA and DRCPA) 37.

[287] DRCPA article 3-10 reads as follows: 'The courts have jurisdiction over cases pertaining to maintenance obligations arising from matrimonial, parental, or other family relationships … if a maintenance obligor (or a person to be a maintenance obligor in cases pertaining to the particulars set forth in Appended Table 1, row (84)), who is not a petitioner, or a maintenance obligee (or a person who has custody of the child, or the child, in cases involving dispositions pertaining to the sharing of expenses required for the custody of a child) has his/her domicile in Japan (or residence in Japan in the case where he/she has no domicile or his/her domicile is unknown'.

or the person entitled to support is domiciled in Japan (or resident if the latter has no or no known domicile). Also, the court may assume jurisdiction to conduct conciliation on these matters, where parties have agreed to refer them to conciliation by the Japanese courts in accordance with DRCPA article 3-13(1)(iii). For the parties to select Japanese courts, no connection between the case and Japan is required (eg, domicile of the petitioner). Although this point was discussed in the course of legislative proceedings, the legislature ultimately decided not to impose such a condition.[288]

DRPCA does not contain jurisdictional rules on matrimonial property matters during marriage, such as the change of an administrator of property (including upon the commencement of bankruptcy proceedings), but only in relation to distribution of property at divorce (DRCPA article 3-12). Consequently, whether the Japanese courts have jurisdiction on matrimonial property matters during marriage will be determined based on *jori*. In this regard, it is submitted that Japanese courts should be able to assume jurisdiction at least where a petitioner, an administrator, or an insolvent is domiciled in Japan or where, even if none of the parties is domiciled in Japan, the parties have entered into a marriage and registered their matrimonial contract in accordance with Japanese law.[289]

ii. Divorce, Nullity and Separation

Insofar as divorce (or nullity of marriage and separation) claims are concerned, the court has jurisdiction where any of the following situations specified in PSLA article 3-2 is fulfilled (for each item, see section III.A.i): (a) where the defendant has a domicile in Japan (or residence in Japan if the latter has no or no known domicile) (article 3-2(1)); (b) where the plaintiff and defendant are Japanese nationals (article 3-2(5)); (c) where the last common domicile of the plaintiff and defendant was Japan and the plaintiff currently resides in Japan (article 3-2(6)); or (d) in the special circumstances where (i) the plaintiff is domiciled in Japan and the defendant has been missing, (ii) a final and conclusive judgment on the same personal status rendered by the courts of the defendant's domicile has no effect in Japan, or (iii) there are circumstances favouring the hearing and determination of the case in Japan in the interests of fairness and the proper and efficient administration of court proceedings (article 3-2(7)). The court may dismiss the whole or part of the proceedings under a corrective rule of PSLA article 3-5.

For issues ancillary to divorce, that is, claims for damages, designation of a person having parental authority (*shinken*)[290] or custody (*kangoken*),[291] and arrangements relating

[288] *Hosoku Setsumei* (PSLA and DRCPA) 62–63.

[289] Ikeda/Ikeda (n 249) 34.

[290] Pursuant to CC article 820, a person who exercises 'parental authority (*shinken*)' holds the right and bears the duty to care for and educate the child for the child's interests. More particularly, such person has the right to determine the child's residence (article 821); the right to discipline the child to the extent necessary for the care and education under the provisions of article 820 (article 822); the right to give, revoke, or limit the permission for occupation to the child (article 823); and the right to administer the child's property and represent the child in any legal act in respect of the child's property (article 824). CC article 818(3) stipulates that '[p]arental authority shall be exercised jointly by married parents'. Joint *shinken* is not granted under Japanese law.

[291] *Kangokaen* is a part of *shinken* and akin to physical custody (for instance, taking care of the child on a daily basis). It does not include the right to administer the child's property and represent the child in any legal act in respect of the child's property. CC article 766(1) provides: 'If parents divorce by agreement, the matters of who will have custody over a child, visitation and other contacts between the father or mother and the child, sharing of

to the custody of the child including access and child support, the courts may always exercise jurisdiction grounded on joinder of claims when the requirements of PSLA article 3-2 are fulfilled (PSLA articles 3-3 and 3-4(1)). On the other hand, for distribution of property at divorce, PSLA article 3-4(2) does not automatically confer jurisdiction by joinder of claims on divorce or annulment of a marriage but requires separately that jurisdictional grounds under DRCPA article 3-12 are fulfilled.[292] Notably, however, DRCPA article 3-12 grants jurisdiction on the division of property: (a) where the defendant is domiciled in Japan; (b) where the spouses have Japanese nationality; (c) where the spouses had their last common domicile in Japan and the petitioner currently resides there; or (d) where there are special circumstances such that the hearing and determination of the case in Japan would be conducive to fairness between the parties and secure the sound and prompt administration of justice. These jurisdictional grounds are *de facto* identical to the grounds in PSLA article 3-2. Therefore, where a court accepts jurisdiction over claims seeking divorce or annulment of a marriage, it may generally extend its jurisdiction to related disputes over the division of property.[293]

D. Matters Relating to the Wellbeing of the Child

i. *Introduction*

A wide range of matters may arise in relation to children. In accordance with the nature of disputes, they can be divided into two groups: (a) matters that come under the definition of 'personal status litigation' in PSLA article 2; and (b) matters that are subject to adjudication by the court under DRCPA.

The first group covers, for instance: (a) rebuttal of the presumption of a child being born in wedlock; (b) recognition of parentage (legitimation by recognition); (c) invalidation or annulment of a recognition of parentage; (d) determination of paternity pursuant to the provisions of CC article 773;[294] (e) declaration of the existence of parentage between

expenses required for custody of the child and any other necessary matters regarding custody over the child shall be determined by that agreement. In this case, the child's interests shall be considered with the highest priority'.

[292] DRCPA article 3-12 reads: 'The courts have jurisdiction over cases for a disposition pertaining to the distribution of property … in cases where:

(i) a petition is filed by the former husband or wife and the other party has his/her domicile in Japan (or residence in Japan, when he/she has no domicile or his/her domicile is unknown);
(ii) both former spouses have the Japanese nationality;
(iii) a petition is filed by the former husband or wife who has his/her domicile in Japan and both former spouses had their last common domicile in Japan; or,
(iv) a petition is filed by the former husband or wife who has his/her domicile in Japan, and

- the whereabout of the other party are unknown;
- a final and binding decision for a disposition pertaining to the distribution of property rendered in the state where the other party has his/her domicile does not have effects in Japan; or,
- there are any other special circumstances under which a trial and judicial decision by the courts of Japan would support equity between the parties or ensure the realization of a proper and prompt trial.'

[293] Yuko Nishitani, 'Jinji Sosho Jiken oyobi Kaji Jiken no Kokusai Saibankankatsu tou ni kansuru Shin Hosei (2)' (2019) 71 *Hoso Jiho* 715, 744 (Nishitani (2)).

[294] Under CC articles 733 and 773, a person may bring an action seeking a determination of paternity. This is needed, for instance, where the presumption of legitimacy is directed at both the current and the previous husband

a natural parent and a child; (f) invalidation or annulment of adoption; (g) dissolution of an adoptive relationship; (h) invalidation or revocation of the dissolution of an adoptive relationship by agreement; (i) declaration of the existence of an adoptive parent–child relationship.

Where one party to a family relationship brings an action against the other party, the same jurisdictional rules as divorce apply (see the discussion in section III.C.ii). Thus, Japanese courts may take jurisdiction, where any of the requirements under PSLA article 3-2(1), (5), (6) and (7) is fulfilled. In addition, where one party to the family relationship died before a party brings an action, pursuant to article 3-2(3) the court may accept jurisdiction, when the defendant was domiciled in Japan at the time of death. Further, with regard to some matters coming under the first group, a third party or a person who is not a subject of the family relationship, may also bring an action seeking invalidation or annulment of the relevant status. For instance, a child may bring an action seeking a declaratory judgment on the invalidity of acknowledgement declared by his or her father or, in the case where a man has adopted a child as a simple adoption, his wife (or even their children) may bring an action for a declaratory judgment on the invalidity of such adoption. In such cases, by article 3-2(2) and (5), Japanese courts may assume jurisdiction, where one or both parties to the family relationship are domiciled or resident in Japan or where both parties are Japanese nationals.

The second group covers, for instance: (a) permission to adopt; (b) establishment of special adoption; (c) dissolution of the parental relationships based on adoption; (d) dissolution of special adoption; (e) appointment of a special agent for a child; (f) change of a guardian; (g) loss of guardianship, suspension of guardianship or loss of right of administration of property; (h) a disposition regarding the custody of a child; and (i) child support.

a. Adoption

Insofar as (a) permission to adopt and (b) establishment of special adoption are concerned, by DRCPA article 3-5, the court may have jurisdiction where an adoptive parent or a child to be adopted is domiciled in Japan (or has residence in Japan if the latter has no or no known domicile).[295] This ground is justified by the fact that the Japanese courts are in a good position to determine whether adoption would serve the child's interests, as relevant evidence (including living conditions of the involved persons) would be located in Japan.[296] Where an adoptive parent is domiciled in Japan, it usually coincides with the future domicile of the child, so the Japanese courts can duly examine the eligibility of the adoptive parents, as well as the child's living conditions, educational policy and social environment.

of the child's mother. Pursuant to PSLA articles 43(1) and (2), (a) a child or mother may bring an action against the present and previous husband (after the death of either); (b) the current husband may bring an action against the previous husband; and (c) the previous husband may bring an action against the current husband. If, at the time a plaintiff brings an action, all possible defendants have died, the public prosecutor will stand as a defendant. Article 773 prohibits women from giving birth within 100 days of a remarriage. It is not apparent why there needs to be such a prohibition insofar as proof of legitimacy is concerned and why the violation of the prohibition should only be attributed to women. Considering that AGRAL article 28 designates several applicable laws to parentage, it is necessary to determine paternity, even where there exists no such violation. See Sawaki=Dogauchi (n 23) 323.

[295] DRCPA article 3-5 reads: 'Courts have jurisdiction over cases seeking permission to adopt … and over cases seeking the establishment of special adoption … in cases where an adoptive parent or the person to be adopted has his/her domicile in Japan (or residence in Japan, when he/she has no domicile or his/her domicile is unknown)'.

[296] *Hosoku Setsumei* (PSLA and DRCPA) 17; Sawaki=Dogauchi (n 23) 324; Uchino (n 90) 96.

On the other hand, where a child to be adopted is domiciled in Japan, the court will be capable of effectively examining the child's character, maturity, needs, cultural or religious background, and the necessity of adoption.[297] In exceptional circumstances, the courts may decline jurisdiction under DRCPA article 3-14.

b. Dissolution of Adoptive Filiation by Death

A parental relationship established through an adoption is not automatically dissolved, even where either the adoptive parent or adopted child has died. In order to dissolve adoptive filiation, a petition to the courts needs to be filed. According to DRCPA article 3-6,[298] the courts may adjudicate on the matter, if any of the following requirements is satisfied: (a) the surviving adoptive parent or adopted child is domiciled in Japan (or has residence, if there is no or no known domicile); (b) the deceased adoptive parent or adopted child was domiciled in Japan at the time of his or her death; or (c) both the adoptive parent and adopted child had Japanese nationality. The first two heads of jurisdiction are premised on the likelihood of relevant evidence being located in Japan, while the last head is based on the national interest in determining the status of Japanese nationals.[299]

c. Dissolution of Full Adoption

Dissolution of full adoption is subject to DRCPA article 3-7.[300] This provision mainly covers situations where the adoptive parents turned out to be abusing, abandoning or

[297] Uchino (n 90) 96.

[298] DRCPA article 3-6 reads: 'Courts have jurisdiction over cases seeking permission for the dissolution of an adoptive relationship after the death of a party to adoption … in cases where:

(i) an adoptive parent or an adopted child has his/her domicile in Japan (or residence in Japan, when he/she has no domicile or his/her domicile is unknown);
(ii) an adoptive parent or an adopted child had his/domicile in Japan at the time of his/her death; or,
(iii) either an adoptive parent or an adopted child has Japanese nationality and the other party had the Japanese nationality at the time of his/her death'.

[299] *Hosoku Setsumei* (PSLA and DRCPA) 19; Sawaki=Dogauchi (n 23) 327; Uchino (n 90) 106–07. The third head of jurisdiction was not in the Interim Draft.

[300] DRCPA article 3-7 reads: 'The courts have jurisdiction over cases for the dissolution of special adoptions … in cases where:

(i) an adoptive parent has his/her domicile in Japan (or residence in Japan, when he/she has no domicile or his/her domicile is unknown);
(ii) the petition is filed by a natural parent of the adopted child or a public prosecutor and the adopted child has his/her domicile in Japan (or residence in Japan, when he/she has no domicile or his/her domicile is unknown);
(iii) both an adoptive and the adopted child have Japanese nationalities;
(iv) the petition is filed by the adopted child domiciled in Japan and both an adoptive parent and the adopted child have had their last common domicile in Japan, or
(v) the petition is filed by the adopted child domiciled in Japan and:

- the whereabouts of the adoptive parents are unknown;
- a final and binding decision concerning the dissolution of their adoption rendered in the state where the adoptive parents are domiciled does not have effects in Japan; or
- there are any other special circumstances under which a trial and judicial decision by the courts of Japan would support equity between an adoptive parent or an adopted child or ensure the realisation of a proper and prompt trial'.

causing significant harm to the adopted child, or were unable to provide reasonable care for the adopted child, so the biological parents or the public prosecutor petitions against the adoptive parents for the dissolution of full adoption. DRCPA article 3-7 offers similar jurisdictional grounds as PSLA article 3-2, taking into consideration that there may well exist a serious conflict of interests between adoptive parents and adopted child.[301] Pursuant to DRCPA article 3-7, the Japanese courts have jurisdiction if any of the following requirements is met: (a) the adoptive parents are domiciled in Japan (or have residence, if there is no or no known domicile); (b) in the case where natural parents or a prosecutor brings such petition, the adopted child is domiciled in Japan (or has residence, if there is no or no known domicile); (c) the adoptive parents and adopted child are Japanese nationals; (d) in the case where the adopted child domiciled in Japan makes such petition, the child and the adoptive parents had their last common domicile in Japan; or (e) in the case where the adopted child domiciled in Japan makes such petition, (i) the adoptive parents have been missing, (ii) a final judgment on dissolution given by the state where the adoptive parents are domiciled has no legal effect in Japan, or (iii) there are other special circumstances favouring the hearing and determination of the case in Japan in the interests of fairness between the parties or sound and prompt administration of justice. The last head of jurisdiction aims to meet the necessity of protecting the child in such special circumstances.[302]

d. Appointment of a Guardian of Minors

DRCPA article 3-9 provides a special jurisdictional rule in matters of the appointment of a guardian of a minor child.[303] This provision comes into play where the child is left without legal biological or adoptive parents and needs to be taken care of by a guardian as the child's legal representative. This is the case when, for example, both biological parents die in a traffic accident, so there is no legal representative for the child left behind. This is also the case when the adoptive filiation between the adoptive parents and the child, grounded on simple adoption or full adoption, has been dissolved and there is no legal representative for the child. In such a case, when, for example, the child's uncle intends to look after the child in the place of the biological or adoptive parents, he needs to petition to the courts to be appointed as a guardian of the child. Pursuant to DRCPA article 3-9, Japanese courts may take jurisdiction so to adjudicate, where a minor child has a domicile or residence in Japan or is a Japanese national. These jurisdictional rules are defined in the same way as AGRAL article 5 on the protection of adults, considering that the child concerned is similarly in need of immediate and efficient protection. Japan ought to duly exercise jurisdiction to protect such children in danger, insofar as they are living continuously or staying temporarily in Japan or belong to Japan as its national.

[301] *Hosoku Setsumei* (PSLA and DRCPA) 18–19.

[302] Uchino (n 90) 108.

[303] DRCPA article 3-9 reads: 'The courts have jurisdiction over cases pertaining to the appointment of a person as a guardian of a minor after the dissolution of his/her adoptive relationship … or adjudication of cases for the appointment of a guardian of a minor … in cases in which a person who is to be a minor ward or is a minor ward has his/her domicile or residence in Japan or he/she has the Japanese nationality'.

e. Parental Authority and Custody

Pursuant to DRCPA article 3-8,[304] the court has jurisdiction on matters of parental authority, arrangements regarding the custody of the child, and related issues, when a child is domiciled in Japan (or resident in Japan, if there is no or no known domicile). The premise underlying this jurisdictional ground is that the Japanese courts will be in a good position to assess where the child's best interests lie, as the relevant evidence will normally be found in Japan and the courts are readily accessible and able to investigate the child's living conditions, social environment and the child's wishes and opinions.[305] Adjudication on the sharing of the expenses arising from the custody of the child, that is, child support, is subject to DRCPA article 3-10, not article 3-8.

With regard to parental responsibility or custody of a child, special consideration is needed where the Convention on the Civil Aspects of International Child Abduction (HCAC) applies.[306] According to HCAC, where one parent wrongfully removes a child from State A where the child habitually resides to State B, or retains the child in State B although the child is supposed to be returned to State A, the authority of State B is in principle obliged to promptly order return of the child to State A without deciding on the merits of custody. The contents and exercise of parental responsibilities need to be determined by the authority of State A as the natural forum grounded on the child's habitual residence. Because Japan has been a party to HCAC since 2014, when determining jurisdiction on the merits of custody pursuant to DRCPA article 3-8, the Japanese court is required to respect and fulfil the demands and functioning of HCAC.

In an outgoing case, where a child has been abducted from Japan to another Contracting State of HCAC, that child will be returned from that foreign state to Japan in accordance with HCAC. The Japanese courts are supposed to decide on the merits of parental

[304] DRCPA article 3-8 reads: 'The courts have jurisdiction over cases pertaining to parental authority … adjudication of cases for a disposition pertaining to the custody of a child … (excluding the adjudication of cases of a disposition pertaining to the sharing of expenses required for the custody of a child) and the adjudication of cases for the loss of the right to the administration of property upon the commencement of bankruptcy proceedings against a person exercising parental authority … in cases where the child has his/her domiciled in Japan (or residence in Japan, when he/she has no domicile or his/her domicile is unknown)'.

[305] Uchino (n 90) 116–18; Mizuho Hata, 'Kaji Jiken nikakaru Kokusai Saiban Kankatsu' (2018) 27 *Ronkyu Juristo* 39, 41 (Hata); Sawaki=Dogauchi (n 23) 328. This jurisdiction has been supported by lower courts as well as commentators. For instance, Decision of Tokyo Family Court, 20 June 1969, *Kagetsu* 22(3), 110; Decision of Tokyo Family Court, 18 October 1973, *Kagetsu* 26(7), 50; Decision of Tokyo Family Court, 12 August 1975, *Kagetsu* 28(6), 87; Decision of Matsuyama Family Court, Uwajima Branch, 9 January 1976, *Kagetsu* 29(3), 101; Decision of Sendai Family Court, 16 March 1982, *Kagetsu* 35(8), 149; Decision of Tokyo Family Court, 27 April 1987, *Kagetsu* 39(10), 101; Decision of Shizuoka Family Court, 27 May 1987, *Kagetsu* 40(5), 164; Decision of Tokyo Family Court, 22 September 1989, *Kagetsu* 42(4), 65 ((1991) 34 *JAIL* 179); Decision of Naha Family Court, 1 April 1991, *Kagetsu* 43(10), 44; Decision of Kobe Family Court, Itami Branch, 10 May 1993, *Kagetsu* 46(6), 72 ((1995) 38 *JAIL* 148); Decision of Osaka Family Court, 2 December 1994, *Kagetsu* 48(2), 150; Decision of Kanazawa Family Court, Komatsu Branch, 11 March 1996, *Kagetsu* 48(8), 102; Decision of Nagoya Family Court, Toyohashi Branch, 16 February 1998, *Kagetsu* 50(10), 150; Decision of Tokyo High Court, 16 September 2008, *Kagetsu* 61(11), 63; Decision of Osaka High Court, 23 January 2009, 2009WLJPCA01238013; Decision of Yokohama Family Court, Odawara Branch, 12 January 2010, *Kagetsu* 63(1), 140; Decision of Tokyo Family Court, 15 July 2010, *Kagetsu* 63(5), 58; Decision of Tokyo High Court, 19 May 2017, *Katei no Ho to Saiban* 12, 58. For cases on child visitation, for instance, Decision of Kyoto Family Court, 31 March 1994, HJ 1545, 81 ((1996) 39 *JAIL* 275); Decision of Tokyo Family Court, 9 October 1995, *Kagetsu* 48(3), 69; Decision of Kyoto Family Court, 31 March 2006, *Kagetsu* 58(11), 62; Decision of Tokyo Family Court, 7 May 2008, *Kagetsu* 60(12), 71.

[306] See Masako Murakami, 'International Jurisdiction of Child-Related Cases in Japan' (2019) 62 *JYIL* 189, 204–08.

responsibilities. Thus, references in DRCPA article 3-8 to the child's domicile should be understood as coinciding with the child's habitual residence under HCAC, so domicile will remain in Japan for a certain period of time even after the wrongful removal or retention of the child.[307]

In an incoming case, where a child has been abducted from another Contracting State of HCAC to Japan, the authority of the child's habitual residence retains jurisdiction for a certain period of time to decide on the merits of parental responsibilities. Under the Act for Implementation of the Convention on the Civil Aspects of International Child Abduction article 152, once informed that the child has been wrongfully removed to or retained in Japan, the Japanese court seised of the determination of parental authority or related custody issues ought to refrain from rendering a decision, insofar as (a) a petition for the return of child is filed within a reasonable period of time following the wrongful removal, or (b) the petition for the return of the child has been dismissed. On the other hand, while the abducted child is staying in Japan, the Japanese courts should determine the exercise of access by the left-behind parent, given that the HCAC aims to ensure access of a parent residing in a different state from the child.[308] Furthermore, the Japanese courts ought to take interim measures to appoint a custodian for the abducted child, particularly in cases where the taking parent cannot provide proper care and protection for the child. It is, however, unclear when and on what grounds Japanese courts may accept jurisdiction in these situations. Considering that domicile of the child under DRCPA article 3-8 should be understood as being located in the state of origin where the child habitually resides, it is hard to interpret that provision as allowing a child to be treated as having a domicile in Japan only for the purpose of deciding rights of access or designating a temporary custodian of the child. In addition, provisions concerning jurisdiction on interim measures prior to adjudication have been abandoned in the legislative process of DRCPA. Thus, to take jurisdiction, Japanese courts have to rely on the provisions of HCAC or *jori* or assume emergency jurisdiction as a *forum necessitatis*.[309]

f. Child Support

Questions of child support are subject to DRCPA article 3-10. That covers, in particular, the establishment of an obligation to support, the determination of the terms of support and the change[310] or annulment of such determination. According to that provision, Japanese courts may assume jurisdiction in the case where a party (other than the petitioner) who is under a duty to support or who is entitled to receive support has domicile in Japan (or residence, if there is no or no known domicile). The provision aims to balance between the interests of obligees and obligors.[311] When a obligee in need of child support (the child and/or custodial parent is entitled, depending on the applicable substantive law) petitions for the payment of child support against an obligor, the Japanese courts can hear the case insofar as either the obligee or obligor has domicile in Japan. On the other hand, when an obligor files a petition

[307] Nishitani (2) (n 293) 729–32.
[308] ibid 733.
[309] ibid 733–34.
[310] Minutes of 4th, 13th and 16th Meetings (PSLA and DRCPA); Hata (n 305) 42.
[311] Uchino (n 90) 131–32; Hata (n 305) 42; Sawaki=Dogauchi (n 23) 329.

for a change or reduction of child support against an obligee, jurisdiction of the Japanese courts is provided only when the obligee is domiciled in Japan.

When several claims are involved in child support disputes, the court must assess whether it has jurisdiction over each of those claims by looking into the individual circumstances.[312] Suppose that A is the first obligor and B is the second, and that A seeks to switch the order of child support obligations, lowering A's responsibility from first to second (matter A) and raising B's responsibility from second to first (matter B). To determine jurisdiction, the court is required to consider the respective relationships between A and B, on the one hand, and the person to whom support is owed, on the other.[313] Where an obligee has domicile in Japan, the courts may take jurisdiction over both A and B. Where an obligee has no domicile in Japan, only the domicile of a respondent may ground jurisdiction. In the scenario above, as A is petitioning against B, the court may only take jurisdiction over matter A if B has domicile in Japan, whereas no jurisdiction over matter B is provided unless A is also domiciled in Japan.

E. Succession

Depending on the nature of disputes, matters arising out of succession are subject to different jurisdictional rules.[314] For contentious matters, CCP article 3-3(12) provides jurisdiction of district courts for an action relating to an inheritance right or a hereditary reserve, and an action relating to a testamentary gift (or bequest) or any other legal act taking effect upon death.[315] Specifically, that provision covers an action to seek confirmation of the existence of an inheritance right, an action to seek confirmation (or to claim) of a hereditary reserve (*légitime*), and an action to seek for the performance of obligations arising out of a testamentary gift or *donatio causa mortis* (ie, a gift made with the expectation that the donor will soon die).[316] Insofar as these contentious matters are concerned, Japanese courts may take jurisdiction, in addition to usual jurisdictional grounds under CCP article 3-2 ff, by CCP article 3-3(12) when any of the following requirements is fulfilled: (a) the deceased was domiciled in Japan at the commencement of succession; (b) if the deceased had no or no known domicile, the deceased was resident in Japan at the commencement of succession; or (c) if the deceased had no or no known residence, the deceased had been domiciled in

[312] Uchino (n 90) 133–34; Takeda/Ikeda (n 227) 143.

[313] Uchino (n 90)136–38; Takeda/Ikeda (n 227) 143.

[314] For the situation prior to the introduction of statutory rules, see, Takami Hayashi, 'International Jurisdiction in Cases Related to Succession: New Rules in Japan' (2019) 62 *JYIL* 209, 210–14.

[315] CCP article 3-3(12) reads: 'An action set forth in one of the following items may be filed with the Japanese courts in the case specified in said item: …

> (xii) an action related to a right of inheritance or legitime, or an action related to a legacy or any other act that comes into effect upon a person's death: if at the time of the opening of the succession, the decedent was domiciled in Japan; if at the time of the opening of the succession, the decedent was without a domicile or was of domicile unknown, but had a residence in Japan; or if at the time of the opening of the succession, the decedent was without a residence or was of residence unknown, but before the opening of the succession, the decedent had been domiciled in Japan (unless the decedent was domiciled in a foreign country after last being domiciled in Japan'.

[316] Sato=Kobayashi (n 62) 81.

Japan prior to the commencement of succession (except where the deceased became domiciled abroad after having been domiciled in Japan).

This head of jurisdiction is justified by the fact that most inheritable property and the evidence relating to the same would normally be situated in the place where the deceased was domiciled or resident.[317] This reasoning is widely applied in terms of establishing jurisdiction in matters of succession. As it is preferable to settle questions of inheritance promptly (in particular in respect of the attribution of property among the heirs), matters arising out of succession should be handled uniformly at the place regarded as the centre of the succession relationship.[318] Therefore, Japan's jurisdiction may be grounded even though there might be no inheritable property in Japan.[319]

CCP article 3-3(13) covers matters relating to an obligation or encumbrance on inheritable property which does not fall under article 3-3(12).[320] An example is an action for the performance of an obligation owed by the deceased that an heir is supposed to assume by reason of succession and an action for payment of expenses consequent upon the death of the deceased, such as funeral expenses and expenses in carrying out a will.[321] For the reason mentioned in the previous paragraph, the court may accept jurisdiction over these matters, where any of the requirements under article 3-3(12) is fulfilled.

On the other hand, DRCPA article 3-11 provides jurisdictional rules on non-contentious matters to be decided by family court adjudication or in-court conciliation.[322] They are,

[317] ibid 79–81; *Hosoku Setsumei* (PSLA and DRCPA) 23.

[318] Sawaki=Dogauchi (n 23) 285.

[319] Decision of Tokyo High Court, 9 May 2011, *Kagetsu* 63(11), 60.

[320] CCP article 3-3(13) reads: 'An action set forth in one of the following items may be filed with the Japanese courts in the case specified in said item: …

(xiii) an action involving a claim against a succession or any other charge on an estate which does not fall under the category of an action set forth in the preceding item: as specified in that item'.

[321] Sato=Kobayashi (n 62) 81.

[322] DRCPA article 3-11 reads: '(1) The courts have jurisdiction over cases pertaining to inheritance …

- if the decedent has his/her domicile in Japan at the time of the commencement of inheritance; or
- if the decedent has his/her residence in Japan at the time of the commencement of inheritance, when he/she has no domicile or his/her domicile is unknown; or
- if the decedent had his/her domicile in Japan prior to the commencement of inheritance, when he/she has no residence or his/her residence is unknown (excluding cases in which he/she has his/her domicile in a foreign state after the date when he/she had his/her last domicile in Japan).

(2) In applying the provision of the preceding paragraph to an application filed in one of the following cases, the wording "at the time of the commencement of inheritance" shall be disregarded, and the wording "prior to the commencement of inheritance" shall be replaced by "prior to the application":

- adjudication of cases for the disinheritance of a presumptive heir;
- adjudication of cases for the revocation of disinheritance of a presumptive heir;
- adjudication of cases for the confirmation of a will … or
- adjudication of cases involving permission for the renunciation of an heir's reserved share ..

(3) In addition to the circumstances referred to in paragraph (1), the courts have jurisdiction over the following cases, if any property belonging to the estate is located in Japan:

- adjudication of cases for a disposition pertaining to the administration of an estate for a period before a ruling on the disinheritance of a presumptive heir, or a ruling to revoke such a ruling, becomes final and binding …
- adjudication of cases for a disposition pertaining to the preservation or administration of an estate;
- adjudication of cases for the appointment of an administrator of estate upon entering a qualified acceptance of inheritance …

in particular, the disinheritance of presumptive heirs, the renunciation of inheritance, the separation of property, the distribution of inheritable property to persons with special connections, the confirmation of a will, the appointment or dismissal of an executor, the renunciation of a hereditary reserve, and the division of estates.

DRCPA article 3-11(1) provides for general jurisdiction in succession matters to be determined by family court adjudication. Pursuant to article 3-11(1), the Japanese court may assume jurisdiction: (a) when the deceased was domiciled in Japan at the time of the commencement of succession; (b) if the deceased had no or no known domicile at that time, when the deceased was resident in Japan at the time of the commencement of succession; or (c) if the deceased had no or no known residence, when the deceased had been domiciled in Japan prior to the commencement of succession (except where the deceased became domiciled abroad after having been domiciled in Japan). This head of jurisdiction is geared towards uniform determination of the entire issues in succession matters and justified for the same reasons as CCP article 3-3(11) and (12), as discussed above.

In the determination of presumptive heirs and other acts taken prior to the commencement of inheritance, by DRCPA article 3-11(2) the court may accept jurisdiction under the same conditions as set out in article 3-11(1). Only the relevant timing is different, as article 3-11(2) points to the time of petition to the courts, instead of the commencement of inheritance.

In addition to these jurisdictional grounds, DRCPA article 3-11(3) provides for jurisdiction of the situs of inheritance properties for the exclusion of presumptive heirs, preservation or administration of inheritance properties, appointment of an administrator, among others. This provision opens supplementary jurisdiction, in addition to DRCPA article 3-11(1), at the situs of inheritance properties to ensure proper and effective preservation and administration of properties and to cater for the convenience of heirs and other parties.[323] The scope of DRCPA article 3-11(3) is restricted in order not to hamper the uniform determination of the entire succession matters at the last domicile of the deceased (article 3-11(1)). Nor does this head of jurisdiction extend to cases relating to division of estates.[324]

Moreover, under DPCRA article 3-11(4), parties may designate the Japanese courts for the division of estates, prohibition of the division of estates, and the determination of an heir's contribution portion. Allowing such choice of court agreement makes sense, as these matters principally involve the heirs' interests, who are, in actuality, free to dispose of the assets as they see fit.[325] To be valid, such agreement must satisfy the requirements set forth in CCP article 3-7 (article 3-11(5)). When parties enter into an exclusive choice of court

- adjudication of cases for a disposition pertaining to the administration of an estate after the request for a separation from an heir's property … or
- adjudication of cases for a disposition pertaining to the administration of an estate in the absence of heirs …

(4) The parties may determine by prior agreement the state with whose court or courts a petition for a case pertaining to the division of an estate between them … may be filed.
(5) The provisions under CCP Article 3-7, paragraphs (2) to (4) shall apply mutatis mutandis to the agreement referred to in the preceding paragraph'.

[323] Uchino (n 90) 145.

[324] Hata (n 305) 43.

[325] Katsuhisa Masuda, 'Sozoku ni kansuru Jiken no Kokusai Saibankankatsu' in Ayako Ikeda (ed), *Kokusai Kaji Jiken no Saiban Kankatsu* (*International Jurisdiction in Cross-border Family Law Matters*) (Nihon Kajo Syuppan, 2019) 149; Uchino (n 90) 143; Sawaki=Dogauchi (n 23) 330–31.

agreement, the designated Japanese courts may not decline jurisdiction under the special circumstances test of DPCRA article 3-14. Further, pursuant to DRCPA article 3-13, a court can conduct conciliation: (a) where it has jurisdiction over the subject matter of the conciliation; (b) where the other party has domicile in Japan (or residence, if there is no or no known domicile); or (c) where the parties have agreed to petition the court for conciliation.

IV. Other Matters

A. Insolvency Law

A party basically may file a petition for commencement of bankruptcy or civil rehabilitation proceedings in Japan, only (a) if the debtor, who is an individual, has a business office, domicile, residence or property in Japan, or (b) if the debtor, who is a legal person or any other association or foundation, has a business or other office or property in Japan (Bankruptcy Act (BA) article 4; Civil Rehabilitation Act (CIRA) article 4). In addition, by BA and CIRA article 4(2), 'a claim for which demand by litigation may be made pursuant to the provisions of CCP shall be deemed to exist in Japan'. Accordingly, where the claim is the subject matter of an action, the Japanese courts will have jurisdiction over related insolvency cases.[326]

Insofar as corporate reorganisation proceedings are concerned, on the other hand, a stock company may only file a petition, if it has a business office in Japan (Corporate Reorganisation Act article 4). As opposed to bankruptcy and civil rehabilitation proceedings, Japanese courts may not assume jurisdiction merely due to the fact that a company has properties in Japan.

BA provides special jurisdictional rules over certain bankruptcy cases, namely, those relating to inherited property (article 222) and trust property (article 244-2). In the former cases, a party may file a petition for the commencement of bankruptcy proceedings under BA against inherited property, only if the deceased's domicile as at the time of commencement of inheritance was in Japan or property forming part of the property exists in Japan. This rule is justified by the fact that most inherited property and the heirs to the same are likely to be found in Japan and that, when inherited property is in Japan, it may be expected that claims would be made against those properties.[327] In the latter cases, a party may file a petition for the commencement of bankruptcy proceedings under BA against trust property, only if the property that belongs to the trust property or the trustee's domicile exists in Japan. This jurisdiction is justifiable. If trust property is located in Japan, a trust creditor or beneficiary expects to collect revenue from those properties. Even where trust property is not located in Japan, if a trustee is domiciled in Japan, such trust creditor or beneficiary normally expects a trustee to perform his or her obligations in Japan and it can reasonably be expected that information concerning the trust property is to be found in Japan.[328]

[326] Commentary on Bankruptcy Act 2004, 51.
[327] ibid 1479.
[328] ibid 1552.

B. Competition Law

Competition law is concerned with a broad range of legal areas and consequently various legal relationships may arise. Depending on their nature, these relationships may be broken into two groups: (a) contractual and (b) tortious relationships. Competition law matters do not fall under the exclusive jurisdiction of the Japanese courts. Also, there exist no special jurisdictional rules for competition law matters. Therefore, such matters are subject to the ordinary jurisdictional rules in CCP articles 3-2–3-9 (see section II).

The first group covers situations such as where a party to a contract sues the other party for a declaration as to the nullity of the contract or unfair terms within the contract, due to the defendant having infringed competition law. In this context, the infringement of competition law may give rise to a ground for nullification of a contract. Such a claim would be an ordinary contractual claim and therefore jurisdiction rules for contract are relevant. In particular, CCP article 3-3(1), (3), (4) and (5) may come into play. As explained above, the Japanese court has jurisdiction when the place of performance of an obligation is in Japan, when the defendant's property is in Japan, when the defendant's office is in Japan and the action is related to that office, or when the defendant has been continuously doing business in Japan. In addition, where the parties to a contract have entered into a choice of forum agreement designating a particular court, such agreement may play an important role.[329]

The second group covers situations such as, for instance, where a victim of a cartel sues cartel participants for damages or an injunction based on their infringements of competition law or where a party to a contract sues the other party for damages in relation to an abuse of dominant position in breach of competition law. Claims based on competition law infringement are by their nature tortious and therefore subject to the jurisdictional rules applicable to torts. In particular, CCP article 3-3(3), (4), (5) and (8) may establish Japan's jurisdiction. As a typical competition law claim is for pecuniary damages, the court has jurisdiction when the defendant's seizable property is situated in Japan. Also, a competition law infringement (such as a cartel agreement or an abuse of dominant position) normally occurs in a business context. Therefore, the court may also accept jurisdiction, when the infringement involves or relates to activities of the defendant's office in Japan or the defendant's continuous business in Japan.

Pursuant to CCP Article 3-3(8), Japanese courts may take jurisdiction where either the place of a harmful act or the place of injury is in Japan. Both the place of a harmful act and the place of injury must be identified, in light of the nature of a competition law claim. Suppose a company A and a company B enter into a price-fixing cartel agreement in respect of product C and inflate the price of C. Due to the cartel, purchasers of C had to pay the inflated price and suffered financial loss as a result (for instance, the difference between the cartel price and the market price if there had been no cartel). In such a case, one may take the view that the place of injury should be the place where the victims incurred loss.[330] However, a cartel is primarily intended to harm and distort healthy competition in the

[329] Judgment of Tokyo District Court, 6 October 2016, *Kinyu Shoji Hanrei* 1515, 42; Judgment of Tokyo High Court, 25 October 2017, 2017WLJPCA10256010 ((2018) 61 *JYIL* 416).

[330] Case C-352/13 *Cartel Damages Claims (CDC) Hydrogen Peroxide SA v Akzo Nobel NV, Slovay SA/NV, Kemira Oyj, FMC Foret SA*, EU:C:2015:335.

market. It is detrimental to the interests of market players in the sense that they are unable to purchase a product or service at the market price. Competition law maintains market order and promotes economic development by regulating anti-competitive activities. In this light, it is submitted that the place of injury should be regarded as the place where the market has been (or is likely to be) affected by a cartel's anti-competitive activities, not the place where a given victim has suffered financial loss. This reasoning should likewise apply in cases concerning an abuse of dominant position.

Japanese courts may not accept jurisdiction based on the place of injury, if the occurrence of the injury at that place was not foreseeable (see section II.B.i.b). But the occurrence of harm is normally predictable in the competition law context, because anti-competitive activities, such as a cartel or the abuse of a dominant position, are directed to specific markets or specific players in a given market.

On the other hand, the place of a harmful act should be interpreted depending on the type of anti-competitive activity involved. This is because competition law regulates various anti-competitive activities by applying different standards. For instance, in the case of abuse of a dominant position or market power, the abuse gives rise to injury and constitutes an infringement of competition law at the substantive law level.[331] The place of a harmful act should therefore be the place where such dominant position or market power was abused, that is, the location of the relevant market.

In the case of a cartel, the implementation of a cartel agreement is an important factor in determining the place of a harmful act because such implementation gives rise to actual injury. Without such implementation, any distortion of market order and loss would not occur. However, it should be noted that as opposed to an abuse of dominant position or market power, entry into a cartel may, per se, be a violation of competition law at a substantive law level. It cannot be denied that the place where the cartel agreement was concluded is therefore also closely connected with the case. Indeed, it may be reasonably expected that relevant evidence would be found in that place. Thus, in the case of a cartel, the place of a harmful act should be the place where the agreement was implemented as well as the place where the agreement was concluded.[332]

Nevertheless, it may be hard or even impossible to identify the place where an agreement was concluded, because cartel participants normally enter into such agreement in secret. An exception is where competition authorities have already engaged in an investigation or completed public enforcement against a cartel or upon applications by cartel participants to leniency programmes. In those cases, a victim might be able to ascertain details of relevant cartel activity, including the place of conclusion or negotiation of an agreement. Following this approach, where cartel participants conclude, renew and modify cartel agreements through a series of meetings in various countries or by way of teleconference, it appears that the place of a harmful act would be spread out all over the world and lead to an 'extraordinary inflation' of places. To ground jurisdiction, however, such places must have a causal connection with the injury. With this filter, such an 'over-inflation' is unlikely to occur.

[331] At the substantive law level, an abuse of dominant position or market power is regulated and prohibited, while it is not prohibited to gain such position or market power. In other words, it is necessary that such activities are actually implemented.

[332] *cf* Case C-352/13 *Cartel Damages Claims* (n 330).

C. Jurisdiction in Shipping Claims

i. *Jurisdiction of the Japanese Court*

It is undisputed that the jurisdictional rules under CCP articles 3-2–3-9 have application in cases relating to shipping claims. Among others, specific jurisdictional grounds in article 3-3 (3), (4), (9) and (10) play an important role.

For instance, pursuant to article 3-3(3), the Japanese courts have jurisdiction where the defendant's ship is situated in Japan. To the contrary, where the defendant is not the owner of the ship situated in Japan, article 3-3(3) is not available because seizable property grounding Japan's jurisdiction has to belong to the defendant. But, by article 3-3(6),[333] a party may file an action based on a maritime lien or any other claim secured by a ship, when the ship is situated in Japan, whether the defendant is the shipowner or not. Accordingly, even where the defendant is a charterer, if the ship is situated in Japan, the Japanese court will have jurisdiction as far as a maritime lien claim or other claim secured by a ship is concerned.

In the case of a collision of ships and other accident at sea, there exist additional grounds. Where a ship collision or other accident occurs within the territorial waters of Japan, the place of torts under CCP article 3-3(8) is available (see section II.B.i.b). Where a collision or other accident occurs on the high seas, a party seeking damages may not rely on this ground.[334] However, under article 3-3(9),[335] a party may file an action before a Japanese court to seek damages, when the first place at which the damaged ship arrived is in Japan.[336] This ground is available, no matter where a collision or other accident occurs.

Insofar as claims relating to salvage are concerned, pursuant to CCP article 3-3(10),[337] no matter whether a salvage is contractual or not, a party may file an action before the Japanese court, when the salvage was performed in Japan, or where the first port which the salvaged ship reached is located in Japan. This ground is justified on the idea that the relevant evidence (eg, the ship's log and other records) will normally lie in those places and it is convenient to take evidence there.[338] Where a contractual salvage was performed and a party seeks remuneration, Japan's jurisdiction may be founded on article 3-3(1), if the place of payment is Japan.[339]

[333] CCP article 3-3(6) reads: 'An action set forth in one of the following items may be filed with the Japanese courts in the case specified in said item:...

> (xiii) an action based on a ship claim or any other claim secured by a ship: if the ship is located within Japan'.

[334] Sato=Kobayashi (n 62) 74; Sawaki=Dogauchi (n 23) 283.

[335] CCP Article 3-3(9) reads as follows: 'An action set forth in one of the following items may be filed with the Japanese courts in the case specified in said item:

> (ix) an action for damages due to the collision of a ship or any other accident at sea: if the first place where the damaged ship docked is within Japan'.

[336] *cf* Judgment of Sendai High Court, 22 September 2011, HT 1367, 240. In the case where a ship's collision occurred on high seas and the first place at which the damaged ships arrived was in Japan, the Court declined to exercise jurisdiction based on special circumstances (although this judgment was rendered before the black-letter rules are introduced).

[337] CCP Article 3-3(9) reads as follows: 'An action set forth in one of the following items may be filed with the Japanese courts in the case specified in said item:...

> (x) an action related to a maritime rescue: if the place where the maritime rescue took place or the first place where the salvaged ship docked is within Japan'.

[338] Sawaki=Dogauchi (n 23) 284; Sato=Kobayashi (n 62) 76.

[339] Sawaki=Dogauchi (n 23) 284.

ii. The Process of Ship Arrest in Japan

Under Japanese law, ship arrest can be made as a provisional seizure under CPRA. A party seeking an order for a provisional remedy may file a petition only if an action on the merits may be filed with a court in Japan, or if the property to be provisionally seized or the disputed subject matter is located in Japan (CPRA article 11). Thus, under CPRA article 11, two heads of jurisdiction are available: jurisdiction over the merits of the case,[340] and the location of property. But the former head is not available when the parties have agreed on the exclusive jurisdiction of a foreign court or dispute resolution by way of arbitration.[341]

When making an application for provisional seizure, a party may be required to deposit security (CPRA article 4). CPRA article 20(1) stipulates that '[a]n order for provisional seizure may be issued when it is likely that compulsory execution regarding a claim for payment of money will not be possible or will result in the occurrence of significant difficulties'. Article 48(1) provides that the provisional seizure of a vessel can be executed in two ways: by way of registration of the provisional seizure, or by way of the surrender of 'the document proving the nationality of the vessel and any other documents necessary for the navigation of the vessel' to the court executing the provisional remedy. In the latter, the court will order a court execution officer to confiscate those documents.[342]

For the execution of a provisional seizure, CPRA article 48(2) stipulates that:

> The court that issued the order for provisional seizure has jurisdiction over the execution of a provisional seizure that is carried out by way of registration of the provisional seizure as the court executing the provisional remedy, and the district court that has jurisdiction over the location of the vessel has jurisdiction over the execution of a provisional seizure that is carried out by way of ordering the confiscation of the certificate of the vessel's nationality, etc.

It should be noted that, pursuant to Commercial Code article 689, seizure or provisional seizure (excluding provisional seizure by means of registration) cannot be executed against a ship which is at sea, while it can be executed against a ship anchored in harbour.

V. Immunities from Jurisdiction

A. Sovereign Immunity

As for sovereign immunity from the foreign judicial power in civil and commercial matters, Japan adhered to the absolute immunity doctrine until recently.[343] In 2002 the Supreme

[340] Before the black-letter rules were introduced, many courts grounded jurisdiction on the fact that they also had jurisdiction over the merits of the case. For instance, Decision of Asahikawa District Court, 9 February 1996, HJ 1610, 106; Judgment of Yokohama District Court, 29 September 1966, *Kaminshu* 17(9–10), 874; Decision of Tokyo District Court, 26 April 1965, HJ 408, 14; Decision of Tokyo District Court, 5 December 1983, *Rominshu* 39(6), 658.

[341] Decision of Tokyo District Court, 28 August 2007, HJ 1991, 89. Honma/Nakano/Sakai (n 91) 205.

[342] For detailed process, see also Rules of Civil Provisional Remedies.

[343] Before 2006, Decision of Great Court of Cassation (the Supreme Court (in pre-war Japan)), 28 December 1928, *Minshu* (7), 1128 was the established case law. For discussions and developments in Japan, see, for instance, Yuji Iwasawa, 'Gaikoku Kokka oyobi Kokusai Kikan no Saibanken Menjo' in Akira Takakuwa and Masato Dogauchi (eds), *Shin Saiban Jitsumu Taikei (3): Kokusai Minji Soshoho (Zaisanho Kankei) (International Civil Litigation Law (Proprietary Matters))* (Seirinshoin, 2002).

Court referred to the practice of restrictive immunity theory that was predominant in other states, but accepted the state immunity of the US in the underlying case on its military base.[344] Four years later, the Supreme Court changed its position and eventually adopted the restrictive immunity theory, holding that

> a foreign state shall not be immune from the civil jurisdiction of the Japanese courts for its acts under private law or acts for business administration, unless there are special circumstances where the exercise of civil jurisdiction by Japanese courts is likely to infringe the state's sovereignty.[345]

Also, in deciding whether the acts are of private law nature or for business administration, the Court held that:

> These acts conducted by the appellee are, in nature, commercial transactions that can be conducted by a private person, and therefore it should be deemed that these acts fall within the category of acts under private law or acts for business administration, irrespective of the purpose of the acts.[346]

As is evident from the wording, the criterion for determining whether a foreign state can enjoy immunity from Japan's civil jurisdiction is the nature of the act, not its purpose. Following this judgment, the Supreme Court later denied state immunity in the case of the termination of an employment contract between a Japanese national and the US State of Georgia.[347]

Japan is a party to United Nations Convention on Jurisdictional Immunities of States and Their Property of 2 December 2004 (UNCJI) (not yet entered into force).[348] Largely based on UNCJI, it has enacted the Act on Civil Jurisdiction of Japan with respect to a Foreign State, etc (ACJJ).[349] After ACJJ came into force in 2010, the question of sovereign immunity has been governed by it. ACJJ is based on the restrictive immunity doctrine. Thus, a 'foreign state' can be immune from the civil jurisdiction of the Japanese courts only in limited situations. ACJJ article 2 defines a 'foreign state' as including: (a) a state and its various organ of government; (b) constituent units of a federal state and other equivalent administrative divisions of a state, which are entitled to perform acts in the exercise of sovereign authority; (c) entities that are entitled to perform acts in the exercise of sovereign authority (limited to cases in which such authority is exercised); and (d) representatives of the entity in the previous three acting in that capacity.

Pursuant to ACJJ article 4, a foreign state shall generally be immune from Japan's jurisdiction. Yet, ACJJ articles 5–16 (Section 2) list situations in which a foreign state will

[344] Judgment of Supreme Court, 12 April 2002, *Minshu* 56(4), 729. This case was concerned with claims to prohibit night flights of US military aircraft departing from and back to Yokota base and to damages based on the infringement of personal rights. Since such flights constituted sovereign activities (*iure imperii*) by the US, state immunity was accepted.

[345] Judgment of Supreme Court, 21 July 2006, *Minshu* 60(6), 2542. Before this judgment, there had been one judgment given by a lower court which denied state immunity on the ground of the restrictive immunity theory (Decision of Tokyo District Court, 31 July 2003, HJ 1850, 84).

[346] ibid.

[347] Judgment of Supreme Court, 16 October 2009, *Minshu* 63(8), 1799. Also, the Court referred to the 2004 UN Convention and the ACJJ, although neither had entered into force at the time.

[348] Adopted by the UN General Assembly on 2 December 2004. General Assembly Resolution 59/38, annex, Official Records of the General Assembly, Fifty-ninth Session, Supplement No 49 (A/59/49).

[349] For details, see Kimio Yakushiji, 'Legislation of the Act on Civil Jurisdiction Over Foreign States, Acceptance of the UN Convention on Jurisdictional Immunity of States and Their Property, and Their Possible Effects upon the Jurisprudence of Japanese Domestic Courts on State Immunity' (2010) 53 *JYIL* 202.

exceptionally not enjoy sovereign immunity. Articles 5–7 cover situations where a foreign state explicitly by words or implicitly by conduct consents to the jurisdiction of a Japanese court. Articles 8–16 list specific matters where a foreign state will not enjoy sovereign immunity. They include such matters as commercial transactions,[350] labour contracts, death or injury of persons, loss of tangible objects, rights and interests pertaining to real property, rights and interests pertaining to the administration or disposition of property in which the court participates, intellectual property rights, operation of ships, and arbitration agreements.

Further, there are multilateral and bilateral treaties or arrangements dealing with immunity for diplomats, for instance, the Vienna Convention on Diplomatic Relations of 18 April 1961 (VCDR), the Vienna Convention on Consular Relations of 24 April 1963 (VCCR), and bilateral consular treaties with the US, the UK, the former Soviet Union[351] and the PRC.[352] With regard to immunity of international organisations and their staff, the Convention on the Privileges and Immunities of the United Nations has application. In addition, there is a special agreement between Japan and the US in respect of US armed forces in Japan.[353]

B. State-Owned Enterprises (SOEs)

When it comes to state-owned enterprises (SOEs), the first question is whether SOEs can be regarded as a 'foreign state' within the meaning of the ACJJ (in particular, article 2(iii) and (iv)). Some SOEs, such as a central bank, may come under the definition of a 'foreign state'.[354] However, it should be noted that, according to article 2(iii), SOEs must perform an act in the exercise of sovereign power so as to enjoy state immunity. If SOEs engage in a purely private transaction by not exercising sovereign power, they are not regarded as a foreign state and thereby subject to the civil jurisdiction of the Japanese courts. If SOEs are regarded as a foreign state, they can be immune from Japan's jurisdiction.

Having said that, SOEs exceptionally cannot enjoy immunity insofar as certain activities listed in ACJJ articles 5–16 (for instance, commercial transaction and labour contracts) are concerned. In respect of commercial transaction, pursuant to article 8,[355] SOEs in principle

[350] Judgment of Tokyo District Court, 18 September 2014, 2014WLJPCA09188002.

[351] Consular Convention between Japan and the Union of Soviet Socialist Republics (USSR) (Treaty No 9 of 15 August 1967).

[352] Agreement on Consular Relations between Japan and the People's Republic of China (PRC) (Treaty No 1 of 18 January 2010).

[353] Agreement under Article VI of the Treaty of Mutual Cooperation and Security between Japan and the US, regarding Facilities and Areas and the Status of the US Armed Forces in Japan (Treaty No 7 of 23 June 1960).

[354] Honma/Nakano/Sakai (n 91) 20.

[355] Article 8 reads as follows:

> '(1) A foreign state, etc shall not be immune from jurisdiction with respect to judicial proceedings regarding commercial transactions (meaning contracts or transactions relating to the civil or commercial buying and selling of commodities, procurement of services, lending of money, or other matters (excluding labour contracts); the same shall apply in the following paragraph and Article 16) between said foreign state, etc and a citizen of a state other than said foreign state, etc (for those other than a state, the state to which they belong, hereinafter the same shall apply in this paragraph) or a judicial person or any other entity established based on the laws and regulations of the state or the state, etc which belongs to the state.

cannot be immune from Japan's jurisdiction. However, SOEs can enjoy immunity, where they engage in commercial transactions with citizens or enterprises of their own state or with other states, or where the parties to a commercial transaction have expressly agreed otherwise. The term 'commercial transaction' means 'contracts or transactions relating to the civil or commercial buying and selling of commodities, procurement of services, lending of money, or other matters' and excludes 'labour contracts'. The nature of the relevant act determines whether a given transaction is commercial in nature.[356]

As regards labour contracts, ACJJ provides in article 9 a special rule. Pursuant to article 9(1),[357] SOEs cannot be immune from Japan's jurisdiction with respect to labour contracts between the SOE and an individual, according to which all or part of the employment is, or is to be, performed in Japan. The exceptions are where an individual is: (a) a person who enjoys diplomatic immunity (such as a diplomat within the meaning of VCDR article 1(e) and a consular officer in the meaning of VCCR article 1(d)); (b) a person who has been employed to perform duties pertaining to the security, diplomatic secrets, or other

(2) The provision of the preceding paragraph shall not apply in the cases listed below:

(i) Cases of commercial transactions between said foreign state, etc. and a state, etc other than said foreign state, etc;
(ii) Cases in which parties to said commercial transactions have expressly agreed otherwise'.

[356] Tomoyuki Tobisawa, *Chikujo Kaisetsu Taigai Minji Saibanken Ho: Wagakuni no Shuken Menjo Hosei ni tsuite* (Shoji Homu, 2009) 35–37.

[357] Article 9(1) reads:

'(1) A foreign state, etc shall not be immune from jurisdiction with respect to judicial proceedings regarding labour contracts between said foreign state, etc and an individual wherein all or part of the labour is, or is to be, provided in Japan.
(2) The provision of the preceding paragraph shall not apply in the cases listed below:

(i) Where said individual is one of the following persons:

(a) A diplomat as provided in Article 1 (e) of the Vienna Convention on Diplomatic Relations;
(b) A consular officer as provided in Article 1(d) of the Vienna Convention on Consular Relations;
(c) A diplomatic staff of a permanent missions or a special mission to international organisations or person employed to represent said foreign state, etc (for those other than a State, the State to which they belong; hereinafter the same shall apply in this paragraph) at international conferences;
(d) In addition to those persons listed in (a) through (c), persons enjoying diplomatic immunity.

(ii) In addition to the cases listed in the preceding item, cases where said individual has been employed in order to perform duties pertaining to the security, diplomatic secrets, or other important interests of said foreign state, etc;
(iii) An action or petition regarding the existence or nonexistence of the contract for the employment or re-employment of the individual (excluding those seeking compensation for damages);
(iv) An action or petition regarding the effect of a dismissal or other termination of the labour contracts (excluding those seeking compensation for damages) where the head of said foreign state, etc, the head of its government, or its Minister of Foreign Affairs finds that there is a risk that judicial proceedings pertaining to said action or petition would harm the security interests of said foreign state, etc;
(v) Cases where the individual is a citizen of said foreign state, etc at the time of the filing of the action or any other petition for commencement of Judicial Proceedings; provided however, that this shall not apply where said individual has the permanent residence in Japan;
(vi) Cases where the parties to said labour contract have otherwise agreed in writing; provided however, that this shall not apply where the lack of jurisdiction over the action or petition regarding said labour contract by Japanese courts is contrary to public order from the viewpoint of protecting workers'.

important interests of the foreign state; and (c) a citizen of that foreign state who does not have permanent residence in Japan. In addition, SOEs enjoy immunity in respect of actions or petitions (a) relating to the existence of a contract for the employment or re-employment of an individual (ACJJ article 9(2)(iii)), or (b) regarding the effect of a dismissal or other termination of a labour contract that would, from the perspective of the foreign state involved, harm that state's security interests (article 9(2)(iv). Actions seeking damages based on labour relationships are subject to Japan's jurisdiction. This is because a judgment in such actions would not compel a foreign state to employ or fire an individual. By ACJJ article 9(2)(vi), where the parties to the labour contract have so agreed in writing, SOEs can be immune from Japan's jurisdiction, subject to public policy controls in the interests of employee protection.

3

Choice of Law

I. Persons

A. Natural Persons

i. Legal Capacity to Act

The Act on General Rules for Application of Laws (AGRAL) article 4(1) adopts the nationality principle as to a natural person's capacity to act, stipulating that 'the legal capacity of a person to act shall be governed by his or her national law'. Thus, a natural person's capacity to act is determined in accordance with the *lex partriae*. In contrast, there exists no explicit provision on the legal capacity to hold rights. It is therefore left for interpretation which law determines this question. That said, it has been widely accepted that a natural person's general capacity to hold rights is also subject to his or her national law,[1] while a capacity to hold rights in specific situations such as a capacity to inherit and an embryo's capacity to seek damages is governed by relevant applicable law (*lex causae*) designated by choice of law rules of AGARAL. As to a general capacity to hold rights, as any legal institution in our time authorises such capacity to every natural person, the law applicable to it would not in practice give rise to any problem.

AGRAL article 4(2) contains a reservation with regard to a natural person's capacity to act, aiming at securing the protection of transaction.[2] Pursuant to this provision, even if a natural person has limited capacity to act according to his or her national law, one is deemed to have full capacity, when one has full capacity in accordance with the law of the place where an act is done (*lex loci actus*) and both parties to a contract are present in the place where the same law applies at the time of the conclusion of their agreement. It is irrelevant whether the other party to the contract knew or must have known of the other natural person's capacity being limited because proving such a subjective requirement is difficult and might protract legal proceedings.[3]

[1] Yoshiaki Sakurada, *Kokusai Shiho* (*Private International Law*), 7th edn (Yuhikaku, 2020) 159–69); Takao Sawaki and Masato Dogauchi, *Kokusai Shiho Nyumon* (*Introduction to Private International Law*), 8th edn (Yuhikaku, 2018) 140–50 (Sawaki=Dogauchi); Jun Yokoyama, *Kokusai Shiho* (*Private International Law*) (Sanseido, 2012) (Yokoyama/PIL) 106.

[2] AGRAL article 4(2) reads: 'Notwithstanding the preceding paragraph, when a person who has performed a juridical act is subject to the limitation of his/her capacity to act under his/her national law but has full capacity to act under the law of the place where the act is done (*lex loci actus*), that person shall be deemed to have full capacity to act, only in cases where all the parties were present in a place governed by the same law at the time of the juridical act'.

[3] Minutes of 26th and 27th Meetings (AGRAL).

Pursuant to article 4(3),[4] this reservation in article 4(2) does not apply to a juridical act, when (a) a juridical act is to be governed by the provisions of family law or succession law, or (b) a juridical act relates to real property situated in a jurisdiction different from where the act was done. In the first scenario, the act is simply subject to the *lex causae* of the relevant family or succession law relationship. In the second scenario such as where both parties (A and B) are present in State X but the real property is situated in State Y, article 4(2) has no application. To the contrary, where both parties (A and B) are present also in State Y, article 4(2) applies.

ii. Protection of Adults

As to the commencement of guardianship, curatorship, or assistance (thereafter, collectively 'guardianship') of adults who have no or limited capacity due to dementia or mental disorder, AGRAL article 5 sets out jurisdictional and choice of law rules.[5] Pursuant to this provision, Japanese courts have jurisdiction to decide on the commencement of guardianship when an adult is domiciled or resident in Japan or has Japanese nationality (see chapter two, section III.B). In that case, courts always apply Japanese law. AGRAL adopts such a unilateral reference to Japanese law on the ground that in non-contentions cases, applicable law is closely linked to the proceedings and applying the *lex fori* is able to provide parties with an effective protection.[6]

Notably, article 5 only deals with the grounds and immediate effects of the commencement of guardianship, namely, limiting a natural person's legal capacity to act and implementing protective measures. Other matters, such as the appointment or supervision of a guardian and the powers of a guardian, are subject to the law governing guardianship under AGRAL article 35.[7] While AGRAL article 35(1) points to the law of nationality of the person concerned, article 35(2)(ii) refers to Japanese law by definition when the Japanese courts commenced guardianship for a foreign national. Thus, judicial guardianship of adults is always governed by Japanese law, to the exclusion of guardianship *ex lege* (see section V.G).

iii. Disappearance

AGRAL article 6 covers disappearance of persons, providing both jurisdictional and choice of law rules, as in the case of AGRAL article 5.[8] Pursuant to article 6(1), Japanese

[4] AGRAL article 4(3) reads: 'The preceding paragraph shall not apply to a juridical act to be governed by the provisions of family law or inheritance law, or a juridical act relating to real property situated in a place governed by a different law from the law of the place where the act was done'.

[5] AGRAL article 5 reads: 'The court may make a ruling for commencement of guardianship, curatorship or assistance (hereinafter collectively referred to as a "Ruling for Commencement of Guardianship, etc") under Japanese law where a person who is to become an adult ward, person under curatorship or person under assistance has domicile or residence in Japan or has Japanese nationality'.

[6] *Hosoku Setsumei* (AGRAL) 128–29.

[7] Sakurada, *Kokusai Shiho* (*Private International Law*) (n 1) 175.

[8] AGRAL article 6 reads:

> '(1) The court may make an adjudication of his/her disappearance under Japanese law where an absentee had domicile in Japan or had Japanese nationality, at the latest point of time when he/she was found to be alive.

courts may take jurisdiction to declare a person's disappearance when an absentee had domicile in Japan or Japanese nationality at the time when last found to be alive. Further, according to article 6(2), Japanese courts may take jurisdiction, (a) when an absentee's property is situated in Japan, or (b) when an absentee's legal relationship is governed by Japanese law or connected with Japan in light of the nature of the legal relationship, domicile or nationality of the parties and other circumstances (for details, see chapter three, section III.B). As to disappearance of persons, Japanese courts always apply the *lex fori* in accordance with AGRAL article 6(1) or (2). The *lex fori* covers only the requirements and immediate effects of the declaration of disappearance, in particular, the irrebuttable presumption of death Civil Code (CC) article 31). To the contrary, 'indirect effects', such as commencement of succession or dissolution of marriage, are subject to the law governing those matters (*lex causae*) in accordance with the relevant choice of law rules (with regard to succession, AGRAL article 36; with regard to dissolution of marriage, AGRAL article 25).

iv. Name

Concerning the law governing the name of a natural person, AGRAL does not contain any choice of law rule. In this regard, academic opinions are divided into three groups. (i) Some authors opine, with an emphasis on the aspects of family relationship, that the person's name should be subject to the law governing his or her family relationship causing change to his or her name, such as marriage or adoption. (ii) Other authors argue, with an emphasis on the aspects of personality, that the person's name should be governed by his or her *lex patriae*, or national law. This position is now the prevailing opinion among commentators and found some resonance in lower court decisions.[9] (iii) A few other commentators consider that name is used by the authority to identify people as a purely public law matter, grounded on the practice and tradition of the Japanese family register system. According to this position, only Japanese nationals have an official name to be entered into the family register and can therefore not legally take the name of a foreign national. Thus, Japanese law always governs the name of Japanese nationals, to the exclusion of CC article 750.[10] On the other hand, the

(2) Even in the case where the preceding paragraph does not apply, if an absentee's property is situated in Japan, or if an absentee's legal relationship should be governed by Japanese law or is connected with Japan in light of the nature of the legal relationship, the domicile or nationality of the party and any other circumstances concerned, the court may, by applying Japanese law, make an adjudication of the absentee's disappearance only with regard to said property or said legal relationship, respectively'.

[9] Decision of Shizuoka Family Court, Atami Branch, 29 May 1974, *Kagetsu* 27(5), 155; Decision of Kyoto Family Court, 28 February 1980, *Kagetsu* 33(5), 90; Aki Kitazawa, 'Uji' in Yoshiaki Sakurada and Masato Dogauchi (eds), *Chushaku Kokusai Shiho: Dai 2 kan (Commentary on Private International Law: Volume 2)* (Yuhikaku, 2011) 180–83; Jun Yokoyama, *Private International Law in Japan*, 2nd edn (Kluwer Law International, 2019) 53 (Yokoyama/PILJ).

[10] CC article 750 stipulates that '[a] husband and wife shall adopt the surname of the husband or wife in accordance with that which is decided at the time of marriage'. Accordingly, when a Japanese couple marry, the spouses may choose either of their surnames as the uniform family name to be recorded in their family register. When a foreign man and a Japanese woman marry, the change in her status will be recorded in the family register, but her surname will officially never change. When she decides to assume her husband's surname, it will simply be treated as an unofficial calling name. CC article 750 does not apply here. The surname system in Japan is unique by identifying and controlling the status of all Japanese nationals, to the exclusion of foreign nationals.

name of foreign nationals is always determined by the state to which they belong, and Japan solely accepts it. This official position of the family registry is grounded on the unilateral application of public law and does not leave room for a choice of law rule.[11]

B. Corporations and Other Entities

i. Choice of Law Rule and Incorporation Theory

As opposed to natural persons, there exists no explicit choice of law rule as to legal persons including corporations or entities in general (*lex societatis*). Nor has there been any explicit case law established by the Supreme Court.[12] In the course of legislating AGRAL, it was discussed whether a special choice of law rule for corporations should be adopted, but the legislator decided not to do so mainly for two reasons. First, there had not yet been sufficient academic discussions on how to determine the scope of the *lex societatis* or follow the recognition approach of foreign corporations, and how to treat organisations without legal personality. Second, comparatively speaking, there were not yet clear rules for international company law, especially in the EU with the evolving case law of the Court of Justice of the European Union at that time. Since no notable problems had occurred in Japan without written conflicts rules on *lex societatis*, it was held appropriate to leave room for further developments in case law.[13]

That said, it is generally accepted by a majority of practitioners and commentators that the incorporation theory should be followed.[14] Therefore, corporations are subject to the law of the country where they were established and incorporated, with the result that they have legal capacity under that law. The advantage of the incorporation theory is that a company's capacity can be easily ascertained and resistant to change or manipulation.[15] Furthermore, this theory caters for the founder's autonomy and freedom of establishment, readily allowing companies to unfold its transactions across borders. As to entities without legal personality, the connecting factor can be a place analogous to the place of incorporation. As an exception, where an entity is formed without any act (such as registration) but by legal effects, the place where the centre of its activity lies (namely, its seat) ought to be decisive.

[11] Sawaki=Dogauchi (n 1) 144–45.

[12] *cf* Judgment of Supreme Court, 15 July 1975, 29(6) *Minshu* 1061. The Supreme Court has once dealt with this question but did not expressly proclaim the incorporation or seat theories.

[13] *Hosoku Setsumei* (AGRAL) 119–21. Also because CA was being enacted at that time, the Legislative Subcommittee for AGRAL refrained from setting out rules that could bind the legislative work for CA.

[14] Judgment of Tokyo District Court, 25 December 1973, HJ 747, 80; Judgment of Tokyo District Court, 28 January 1992, HJ 1437, 122; Dai Yokomizo, 'International Company Law in Japan' in Jürgen Basedow, Harald Baum and Yuko Nishitani (eds), *Japanese and European Private International Law in Comparative Perspective* (Mohr Siebeck, 2008); Sakurada, *Kokusai Shiho* (*Private International Law*) (n 1) 85; Yokoyama/PIL (n 1) 120. But some commentators deny the choice of law approach (both the incorporation and seat theories) and instead argue that, as imbuing a company with legal personality is an act of state and the effects of legal personality are limited to the territory of that state, the question is whether the legal personality of a foreign company is recognised in Japan within the framework of CC article 35 and the requirements of CCP article 118. See, eg, Sawaki=Dogauchi (n 1) 163–65.

[15] Sakurada, *Kokusai Shiho* (*Private International Law*) (n 1) 85.

The problems of a 'pseudo foreign company' (*giji gaikoku kaisha*) which is incorporated abroad but carries out its business mainly in Japan, is handled under Japanese substantive rules regulating foreign persons (*gaijin ho*). According to the Company Act (CA) article 821(1), foreign companies that have their actual headquarters in Japan or intend to do business mainly in Japan are not allowed to do business in Japan continuously. However, transactions undertaken by pseudo foreign companies in Japan in breach of CA article 821(1) are not null and void but provided with legal effects. CA article 821(2) only stipulates that an individual transacting through such a bogus foreign company is held jointly liable towards the contracting party.

ii. Scope of the lex societatis

The *lex societatis* covers all the matters concerning a corporation from its establishment to dissolution. Thus, a corporation's general legal capacity is subject to the *lex societatis*. In this regard, the traditionally prevailing view was that AGRAL article 4(2) can be applied by analogy to corporations for the protection of a third party, unless the corporation is entered in the commercial register due to its long-term activity in Japan (*cf* CA article 818). According to this view, even if the governing law of a foreign corporation follows the ultra vires doctrine and the corporation's capacity is limited by its articles, the corporation is considered to have capacity in Japan, insofar as the transactions concerned are attributed to that corporation under Japanese law.[16] It is, however, widely recognised today that no such complicated choice of law construct is necessary and, for the purpose of protecting a third party, the recourse to public policy under AGRAL article 42 would suffice.[17]

The corporation's capacity to exercise individual rights (for instance, the right to inherit) is in principle governed by the law applicable to the relevant legal relationship, that is, the *lex causae* (eg, insofar as the right to inherit is concerned, the law governing succession). Notably, however, the capacity to exercise individual rights also concerns the question of whether and to what extent a corporation can enjoy such rights. It would be contradictory to accept that a corporation has capacity to inherit property only by virtue of the *lex causae*, where the law of incorporation of the company denies such rights. Consequently, a corporation should be granted capacity to hold a specific right, only when both the *lex causae* and *lex societatis* accept it. In this respect, both applicable laws ought to be applied cumulatively.[18]

Since a corporation cannot transact and do business of itself, its executive bodies or agents must instead do so on behalf of the corporation. Thus, a corporation's

[16] Yoshio Tameike, *Kokusai Shiho Kogi* (*Private International Law Course*), 3rd edn (Yuhikaku, 2005) 299 (Tameike); Ryoichi Yamada, *Kokusai Shiho*, 3rd edn (*Private International Law*) (Yuhikaku, 2014) 234–35 (Yamada).

[17] Yuko Nishitani, 'Hojin oyobi Gaijinho Kisei' in Yoshiaki Sakurada and Masato Dogauchi (eds), *Chushaku Kokusai Shiho: Dai 1 kan* (*Commentary on Private International Law: Volume 1*) (Yuhikaku, 2011) 162–63; Sakurada, *Kokusai Shiho* (*Private International Law*) (n 1) 183.

[18] Sakurada, *Kokusai Shiho* (*Private International Law*) (n 1) 184; Tameike (n 16) 298–00; Yamada, *Kokusai Shiho* (n 16) 234–35.

'legal capacity to act' needs to be determined, particularly: (a) whether the bodies purporting to act for the company have powers to represent the corporation; (b) to what extent they can exercise such powers; and (c) whether, as a matter of legal effects, their actions can be attributed to the corporation as principal. As these issues are primarily related to the characteristics of a corporation, they should be subject to the law governing the corporation (*lex societatis*).[19] For the protection of third parties, however, it will be reasonable to apply AGRAL article 4(2) by analogy, so that counterparts transacting with the corporation can rely on the legal capacity of the corporation under the law of the place of transaction.[20]

When the representatives or employees of a corporation commit a wrong within their business activities, some questions arise: for what kind of wrongs the corporation ought to bear legal responsibility and (in respect of such wrongs) whether the corporation is solely or jointly liable. The traditional majority view subjected these questions to the law governing corporations (*lex societatis*), with a view to protecting corporations and their shareholders. This will enable a corporation and its shareholders to predict the extent of a corporation's liability. On the other hand, the currently prevailing view characterises legal responsibility for a wrong as part of tortious legal relationship on the ground that it is simply about the attribution of liability. In fact, this position seems to be preferable, as it better protects the victims by allowing them to foresee whether they should sue the corporation and its representatives jointly, or only the latter.[21] Consequently, the legal responsibility of corporations ought to be governed by the law applicable to tort as designated by AGRAL articles 17–22.

Dissolution of a company or merger with another company is governed by the law applicable to corporations (*lex societatis*). In cases of cross-border merger, this would mean applying the respective *lex causae* of two companies cumulatively. However, a direct merger between a foreign and a Japanese company is not permitted in Japan.[22] Only a triangular merger is legally possible, typically involving a Japanese subsidiary as an intermediary of a purchasing foreign parent company. The shares of the parent company can be used to acquire shares in the triangular merger. Although such cross-border mergers have been supported by several legislative reforms, they rarely occur in practice as the disproportionately high amount of tax reduces the attractiveness of such a merger.[23]

As to the legal construct of 'piercing the corporate veil', the applicable law should be determined differently depending on the nature of the case. In cases concerning the internal relationship between the corporation and its shareholders (eg, where: (a) a loan from

[19] Nishitani, 'Hojin oyobi Gaijinho Kisei' (n 17) 164; Sakurada, *Kokusai Shiho* (*Private International Law*) (n 1) 184; Sawaki=Dogauchi (n 1) 165–66; Yamada *Kokusai Shiho* (n 16) 235.

[20] Nishitani, 'Hojin oyobi Gaijinho Kisei' (n 17) 164; Sakurada, *Kokusai Shiho* (*Private International Law*) (n 1) 184; Yamada, *Kokusai Shiho* (n 16) 235–36.

[21] Judgment of Osaka District Court, 6 December 1991, HT 760, 246; Nishitani, 'Hojin oyobi Gaijinho Kisei' (n 17) 164; Sakurada, *Kokusai Shiho* (*Private International Law*) (n 1) 184; Tameike (n 16) 301; Yamada, *Kokusai Shiho* (n 16) 236.

[22] The current trend among commentators is in favour of direct mergers. For example, Kenjiro Egashira, 'Shoho kitei no Kokusai teki Tekiyo Kankei' (2000) 2 *YJPIL* 139.

[23] Yamada, *Kokusai Shiho* (n 16) 239, fn 5. See Hiroshi Mitoma, 'Cross-Border M&As – Japanese Companies and Foreign Investors' (2007) 50 *JAIL* 124.

shareholders to an under-capitalised company is treated as an investment; (b) a parent company exploits a subsidiary; or (c) a dominant shareholder mixes up his or her personal assets with those of the corporation), the negation of separate legal personality should be determined by the law governing the company (or subsidiary). On the other hand, where an external relationship between a corporation and a third party is involved (for instance, where a contract with a third party was entered into by a dummy subsidiary and its parent company is held liable), the question of denying legal personality should be determined in accordance with the law applicable to the relevant legal relationship (in the example, the law governing the contract).[24] This is because in such situations the question of piercing the corporate veil would simply be among the issues arising from the circumstances of the specific relationship (in the example, whether the counterpart to the contract was intended to be).

iii. Regulation by Japanese Substantive Law

Even when incorporated in a foreign country under foreign law, a legal entity must receive an 'approval' (*ninkyo*) under CC article 35(1) to carry out activities in Japan under its own name. Notably, foreign corporations are not granted an approval upon individual application, but by definition insofar as they fall under the categories of legal entities in CC article 35(1). Those relevant foreign corporations are states and their administrative units, foreign companies[25] and foreign corporations approved by law[26] or international treaties (eg, the UN and its organisations).[27] Notably, foreign non-profit legal entities do not fall under any of these categories and can therefore not unfold their activities in their own name. Arguably, the scope of article 35(1) is too narrow, so even globally recognised non-profit legal entities, such as the Red Cross or the International Olympic Committee, cannot be approved. This provision ought to be lifted *de lege ferenda*, as non-approved foreign corporations, when operative in Japan, cannot obtain rights or incur obligations directly, nor enjoy the privilege of limited liability.[28]

Pursuant to the Civil Code (CC) article 35(2), approved foreign corporations generally have the same rights as comparable corporations established in Japan. As an exception, foreign corporations cannot enjoy any rights prohibited to foreign nationals or restricted by statutes or international treaties. Once approved in Japan, foreign corporations can carry out their activities under their name, subject to supervision by the competent authorities of Japan in accordance with CC articles 36 and 37, as well as CA articles 817–22.

[24] Judgment of Tokyo High Court, 30 January 2002, HJ 1797, 27. See Nishitani, 'Hojin oyobi Gaijinho Kisei' (n 17) 165.

[25] CA article 2(2) defines 'foreign company' as 'any corporation incorporated under the law of a foreign country or such other foreign organisation that is of the same kind as the company or is similar to a company'. The term 'corporation' is understood to include a company based on an international convention, not a national law, such as Scandinavian Airlines (SAS). Sakurada, *Kokusai Shiho* (*Private International Law*) (n 1) 187.

[26] For instance, Insurance Business Act articles 185–93.

[27] For instance, article 4 of the Treaty of Friendship, Commerce and Navigation between Japan and the US of 2 April 1953 (Treaty No 27 of 28 October 1953).

[28] Sakurada, *Kokusai Shiho* (*Private International Law*) (n 1) 188.

II. Law of Obligations

A. Contracts

i. Governing Law of a Contract

a. Contracts and Unilateral Juristic Acts

AGRAL article 7 has maintained the rule in *Horei* article 7(1),[29] allowing parties to choose the law governing the contract ('party autonomy').[30] This provision applies not only to contracts, but also unilateral juristic acts. Unlike the explanation given by the Ministry of Justice,[31] the unilateral juristic acts under AGRAL article 7 ought to be understood as independent legal relationships at the private international law level, such as donation, trust, offer of rewards, letter of intent, or advertisement of rewards.[32]

b. Modalities of Choice of Law

With a reservation of the rights of third parties, AGRAL article 9 allows the contracting parties to subsequently change the governing law. Such a subsequent change or choice of the applicable law has retroactive effects if the parties so wish.[33] Other issues relating to choice of law are left to the interpretation of AGRAL article 7 by court decisions and commentators.[34] It is generally accepted that contracting parties may select more than one law to govern their contract (*dépeçage*) (see chapter one, section IV.H).[35] As for the validity of the parties' choice of law, opinions are divided, but the current prevailing view seems to point to the law putatively chosen by the parties.[36]

[29] AGRAL article 7 reads: 'The formation and effect of a juridical act shall be governed by the law of the place chosen by the parties at the time of the act'.

[30] See Yuko Nishitani, 'Party Autonomy and its Restrictions by Mandatory Rules in Japanese Private International Law' in Jürgen Basedow, Harald Baum and Yuko Nishitani (eds), *Japanese and European Private International Law in Comparative Perspective* (Mohr Siebeck, 2008); Yuko Nishitani 'Parteiautonomie im internationalen Vertragsrecht Japans' in Karl Riesenhuber and Yuko Nishitani (eds), *Wandlungen oder Erosion der Privatautonomie?: Deusch-japanische Perspektiven des Vertragsrechts* (De Gruyter, 2007). For the legislative history of *Horei* article 7(1), see Yuko Nishitani, *Mancini und die Parteiautonomie im Internationalen Privatrecht – Eine Untersuchung auf der Grundlage der neu zutage gekommenen kollisionsrechtlichen Vorlesungen Mancinis* (Universitätsverlag Winter, 2000) 250 ff.

[31] The Ministry of Justice explained that AGRAL article 7 covers unilateral juristic acts such as rescission or nullification of a contract. *Hosoku Setsumei* (AGRAL) 136; Kunio Koide (ed), *Chikujo Kaisetsu Ho no Tekiyo ni kansuru Tsusokuho* (*Commentary on the Act on General Rules for Application of Law*) (Shojihomu, expanded edn, 2015) 78–79 (Koide). However, these unilateral juristic acts as a declaration ancillary to contractual issues ought to be governed by the law governing the contract itself, not by a different law proper to these acts.

[32] Yuko Nishitani, '§ 26: Internationales Privat- und Zivilverfahrensrecht' in Harald Baum and Moritz Bälz (eds), *Handbuch Japanisches Handels- und Wirtschaftsrecht* (*Handbook on Japanese Commercial law and Economic Law*) (Carl Heymanns Verlag, 2011) [64].

[33] Koide (n 31) 61. AGRAL article 9 provides: 'The parties may change the law otherwise applicable to the formation and effect of a juridical act; provided, however, that if such change prejudices the rights of a third party, it may not be asserted against the third party'.

[34] Minutes of 26th Meeting (AGRAL).

[35] Judgment, Tokyo District Court, 30 May 1977, HJ 880, 79; Judgment, Tokyo High Court, 9 February 2000, HJ 1749, 157; Judgment, Tokyo District Court, 26 February, 2002 (not published in any law reports); see also Judgment of Tokyo District Court, 28 May 2001, HT 1093, 174.

[36] For background, see Nishitani, 'Hojin oyobi Gaijinho Kisei' (n 17) 195–98; Sakurada, *Kokusai Shiho* (*Private International Law*) (n 1) 224–25.

Parties are free to choose any state law as the law governing the contract, including the law of a third country which the case or the parties are not related to. The choice of a neutral law may well be beneficial to strike a balance between both parties' interests. Parties can also take advantage of internationally recognised law of a certain state, regardless of its territorial link to their contract. With regard to insurance or carriage of goods by sea, in particular, English law is often selected as an established global standard without the transactions being connected with England. On the other hand, opinion is divided on whether to allow parties to select non-state law or *lex mercatoria*, such as the UNIDROIT Principles of International Commercial Contracts, as the law governing the contract in litigation. While some academics in Japan favour the choice of non-state law, the majority categorically deny it.[37]

c. Explicit or Implicit Intent of the Parties

Horei article 7(1) was interpreted as not requiring the parties to explicitly choose the applicable law, but sufficed it to implicitly refer to it.[38] In the absence of an explicit choice of law, the parties' tacit intent was discerned by considering various factors, including the characteristics and contents of the contract, place of performance, nationality and domicile of the parties, location of the object of the contract,[39] or even the registration of a foreign incorporation in Japan.[40] This approach could lead *de facto* to 'hypothetical' intent, or artificially induced intent. Such a broad interpretation of tacit intent was meant to avoid, at the expense of legal certainty, falling back to the objective reference to law of the place where the contract was concluded under *Horei* article 7(2).[41]

Notably, since AGRAL was adopted in 2006, the objective connecting factor in the absence of the parties' choice of law has been switched to the 'closest connection' under AGRAL article 8(1), supplemented by rules setting out a presumption for the 'closest connection' in AGRAL article 8(2) and (3). Because AGRAL article 8(1) appropriately subjects a contract or juristic act to the law that has the closest connection at the time of

[37] Yasushi Nakanishi, 'Article 8 (Tojisha ni yoru Junkyoho no Sentaku ga nai baai)' in Yoshiaki Sakurada and Masato Dogauchi (eds), *Chushaku Kokusai Shiho: Dai 1 kan* (*Commentary on Private International Law: Volume 1*) (Yuhikaku, 2011) 189–90; Sawaki=Dogauchi (n 1) 181–82; Sakurada, *Kokusai Shiho* (*Private International Law*) (n 1) 223; Yuko Nishitani, 'Ist das Kollisionsrecht für den internationalen Rechts- und Wirtschaftsverkehr ein ausreichendes Instrumentarium? – Unter besonderer Berücksichtigung der "lex mercatoria"' in Karl Riesenhuber and Kanako Takayama, *Rechtsangleichung: Grundlagen, Methoden und Inhalte – Deutsch-Japanische Perspektiven* (De Gruyter, 2006); Yuko Nishitani, 'Party Autonomy in Contemporary Private International Law: The Hague Principles on Choice of Law and East Asia' (2016) 59 *JYIL* 300, 338.

[38] eg, Judgment of Supreme Court, 20 April 1978, *Minshu* 32(3), 616; Judgment of Supreme Court, 4 September 1997, *Minshu* 51(8), 3657 ((1998) 41 *JAIL* 109); Yutaka Orimo, *Kokusai Shiho: Kakuron* (*Private International Law: Special Part*) (Yuuhikaku, 1972) 129–30; Tameike (n 16) 367–68.

[39] Judgment of Osaka High Court, 18 October 1962, *Kaminshu* 13(10), 2094.

[40] Judgment of Tokyo High Court, 19 July 1982, *Rominshu* 33(4), 673.

[41] As the place where the contract is concluded can be specified fortuitously, it will not cater for the characteristics of every type of contract appropriately. Under *Horei* article 9(2), the place of sending an offer was regarded as the place of conclusion if the parties to the contract were situated in different countries. In modern contract negotiations, however, offer and acceptance are often exchanged instantaneously by electronic means. As a result, such a place cannot be specified readily. Nishitani, '§ 26: Internationales Privat- und Zivilverfahrensrecht' (n 32) 1237.

entering into the contract or juristic act,[42] the parties' choice of law in the sense of AGRAL article 7 ought to be restricted to the parties' real intent that actually exists, to the exclusion of hypothetical intent. Thus, an implicit choice of law should only be accepted where the parties' intent clearly appears from the provisions of the contract or the entire circumstances of the case. In practice, while the initial court decisions under AGRAL article 7 still followed previous case law in inferring the parties' implicit choice of law, recent decisions gradually adopt a restrictive interpretation and readily refer to AGRAL article 8.[43]

While there are not yet established grounds to induce an implied choice of law in Japanese case law, some typical case scenarios can be considered. A tacit choice of law may be inferred, for example, when the parties select only a single place of performance for the entire obligations arising out of a synallagmatic contract. An implicit intent can also be presumed, when the provisions of the contract clearly point to a particular legal system, or when in long-term transactions the individual contracts for delivery of goods do not contain a choice of law clause, but obviously rely on the framework contract governed by a law chosen by the parties. Notably, recent authors do not equate a choice of court agreement or arbitration agreement as a choice of the law governing the contract as such, but only consider them as one of the relevant factors to derive the parties' implicit choice of law.[44]

d. Objective Connecting Factor

As mentioned above, in the absence of the parties' explicit or implicit choice of law, the judge determines the applicable law pursuant to the 'closest connection' under AGRAL article 8(1). The place having the closest connection with the contract is generally presumed to be the place where the party carrying out the characteristic performance of a contract or juristic act habitually resides (AGRAL article 8(2)). Only where the subject matter of a contract or juristic act is real property, is the closest connection presumed to coincide with the place where the property is situated (AGRAL article 8(3)). Comparatively speaking, similar constructs are often used in other jurisdictions, including the EU

[42] AGRAL article 8 stipulates:

'(1) In the absence of a choice of law under the preceding article, the formation and effect of a juridical act shall be governed by the law of the place with which the act is most closely connected at the time of the act.

(2) In the case referred to in the preceding paragraph, if only one of the parties is to provide a characteristic performance involved in a juridical act, the law of the habitual residence of the party providing said performance (in cases where said party has a place of business connected with the juridical act, the law of the place of business; in cases where said party has two or more such places of business which are connected with the juridical act and which are governed by different laws, the law of the principal place of business) shall be presumed to be the law of the place with which the act is most closely connected

In the case referred to in paragraph (1), if the subject matter of the juridical act is real property, notwithstanding the preceding paragraph, the law of the place where the real property is situated (*lex rei sitae*) shall be presumed to be the law of the place with which the act is most closely connected'.

[43] *cf* Yoshihisa Hayakawa, 'New Private International Law of Japan: General Rules on Contracts' (2007) 50 *JAIL* 25, 28–29; for further detail, see Yuko Nishitani, 'Japan' in Daniel Girsberger, Thomas Kadner Graziano and Jan L Neels (eds), *Choice of Law in International Commercial Contracts: Global Perspectives on the Hague Principles* (Oxford University Press, 2021).

[44] Nishitani, 'Japan' (n 43).

(Rome I article 4) and Switzerland (Swiss Private International Law (SPIL) article 117). During the legislative process in Japan, the 'characteristic performance' test was criticised for fear that it cannot help in finding out the closest connection in complex contracts, such as joint venture contracts. Nevertheless, AGRAL article 8(2) was adopted, considering that the characteristic performance test constitutes a mere rebuttable presumption without binding the court to apply it in determining the applicable law.[45]

e. Scope of Application of the Law Governing the Contract

The law governing the contract covers all the matters arising out of a contractual relationship such as the existence and validity of the contract, as well as legally binding effects, contents, illegality and the effects of non-performance of contractual obligations. Also the performance of a contractual obligation is principally governed by the law applicable to a contract. AGRAL does not contain a specific rule as to the performance of a contract in contrast to Rome I article 12(2) allowing a reference to the law of the place of performance. However, there have been some cases in which a court took into consideration, within the framework of public policy, the illegality of performance under the law of the place where the contractual obligation was to be performed.[46] Such a *de facto* reference to the law of the place of performance as 'data' ought also to be admissible in Japan *de lege lata*.

ii. Ascertainment and Application of the Governing Law

Under Japanese law, the ascertainment of the applicable foreign law is not a matter of fact, but a matter of law. Therefore, Japanese courts must *ex officio* ascertain and determine any applicable foreign law (*iura novit curia*). Parties do not bear the burden of proving the content of the applicable law, although they may be asked by courts to assist in finding out the content of the applicable law (see chapter one, section VII).

iii. Formal Validity

Formal validity of contracts or juristic acts is subject to AGRAL article 10. Pursuant to this provision, to be valid formally, a contract or juristic act must satisfy formal requirements under either (a) the law applicable to the formation of the contract or juristic act (article 10(1)), or (b) the law of the place where the relevant act was done (article 10(2)).

AGRAL article 10(3) and (4) specify the latter 'place of act' within the meaning of AGRAL article 10(2) in the case of a juristic act involving more than one country. When it comes to a unilateral juristic act (ie, a manifestation of intention by one party), pursuant to AGRAL article 10(3), the place where the person's declaration originates is deemed to be the place of act. Thus, such unilateral act is formally valid insofar as it satisfies the formal requirements of the law of the place of manifestation. In accordance with AGRAL article 10(4), a contract concluded between parties present in different countries

[45] *Hosoku Setsumei* (AGRAL) 145; Minutes of 15th and 26th Meetings (AGRAL); Koide (n 31) 108–09.
[46] Judgment of Tokyo High Court, 9 February 2000, HJ 1749, 157.

is formally valid when it satisfies the requirements of (a) the law of the place where the notice of offer was dispatched, or (b) the law of the place where the notice of acceptance was dispatched.

AGRAL article 10(5) sets out a special rule for juristic acts establishing or disposing of rights *in rem* in movable and immovable property. By this provision, article 10(2)–(4) does not apply. Thus, to be formally valid, those juristic acts must always satisfy the requirements under the law applicable to the juristic act (*lex causae*) in accordance with AGRAL articles 7 or 8. With regard to formal validity of consumer contracts, AGRAL article 11(3)–(5) special rules (see section II.B.i).

iv. Material Validity

While formal validity of contracts or juristic acts is separately dealt with under AGRAL article 10, material or substantive validity of contracts or juristic acts is subject to the law applicable to the contract or juristic act concerned pursuant to AGRAL articles 7–9. The law governing the contract determines what is deemed an offer or acceptance and whether a party's statement constitutes a misrepresentation or fraud.

v. Capacity

The law governing the contract designated under AGRAL articles 7–9 does not cover matters of capacity. AGRAL article 4 sets out a general rule for capacity. Pursuant to AGRAL article 4(1), legal capacity of a person is subject to the latter's national law in principle, subject to exceptions in AGRAL article 4(2) and (3). For the capacity of adults for whom guardianship etc has been commenced, Japanese law determines to what extent the adult's legal capacity is restricted and how it is supplemented pursuant to AGRAL article 5. The appointment of a guardian etc is also determined by Japanese law in accordance with AGRAL article 35(1) and (2)(ii) (see section I.A).

vi. Overriding Mandatory Rules

Although there exists no explicit provision under AGRAL dictating the application of overriding mandatory rules in Japan, it is widely accepted that courts must apply such rules insofar as the requirements for their application are satisfied (see chapter one, section VIII.A).[47] To the contrary, it is unclear whether overriding mandatory rules of a third state (other than the state whose law governs the contract) can be directly applied or taken into consideration when interpreting or applying the applicable law.

In a case involving a claim arising from a shipping contract governed by Japanese law, the Tokyo High Court once showed a positive attitude towards considering the effect of overriding mandatory rules of a foreign state within the framework of public policy.

[47] Decision of Tokyo District Court, 26 April 1965, HJ 408, 14; Judgment of Tokyo District Court, 24 February 2004, HJ 1853, 38 ((2005) 48 *JAIL* 191). Also, Yuko Nishitani, 'New Private International Law of Japan: Protection of Weaker Parties and Mandatory Rules' (2007) 50 *JAIL* 40, 53–58; Sakurada, *Kokusai Shiho* (*Private International Law*) (n 1) 221; Sawaki=Dogauchi (n 1) 177; Yokoyama/PILJ (n 9) 46.

In that case, the insurer contended that the marine cargo insurance policy was invalid due to the US executive order against Iran which made the cargo contraband. The first instance held the insurance policy null and void as it ran counter to public policy in Japan at the substantive law level, on the ground that recognising the validity of the policy for the transportation of contraband to the US would foster an illegal transaction.[48] The Tokyo High Court seems to have principally followed the approach taken by the first instance court, but reached a different conclusion, holding that the insurance policy did not violate public policy in Japan.[49] On the other hand, a lower court recently denied the applicability of overriding mandatory rules of a third state, contending that the effects of those rules should not be taken into account as factual circumstances when interpreting and applying substantive rules of the applicable law (in this case, Japanese law).[50] The issue is left to further developments in case law and academic discussions.

Notably, while AGRAL articles 11 and 12 have specific rules for the protection of weaker parties, Japan's overriding mandatory rules always have priority over these provisions.[51] Under AGRAL articles 11 and 12, consumers and employees in certain circumstances can ask Japanese courts to apply the mandatory rules of the law of the consumer's habitual residence (article 11(1)) or the law that is most closely connected with the employment contract (article 12(1)), in addition to the law governing the contract designated by the parties (see sections II.B.i and II.B.ii). The relevant mandatory rules of the law, which would otherwise govern the consumer or employment contract in the absence of choice of law, cannot be applied *ex officio* by courts, but only by invocation of the consumer or employee as the weaker party, as a result of a misguided decision of the legislature. To the contrary, overriding mandatory rules of Japan are applied by the judge *ex suo motu*, even if the consumer or employee fails to make such a request under AGRAL article 11(1) or article 12(1). In this respect, the insufficient protective norms for consumers or employees can duly be complemented by an *ex officio* application of the overriding mandatory rules of Japan.[52]

B. Specific Contracts

i. Consumer Contracts

a. Party Autonomy and Consumer Protection

Like usual contracts, consumer contracts are subject to party autonomy under AGRAL articles 7 and 11(1). Parties are free to agree on the law(s) applicable to their contract. However, to tackle an arbitrary choice of law by the enterprise, article 11(1) provides for a special norm of consumer protection. Pursuant to this provision, consumers can

[48] Judgment of Tokyo District Court, 13 May 1998, HJ 1676, 129.
[49] Judgment of Tokyo High Court, 9 February 2000, HJ 1749, 157.
[50] Judgment of Tokyo District Court, 26 March 2018, 2018WLJPCA03268007.
[51] Koide (n 31) 88; Nishitani, 'New Private International Law of Japan' (n 47) 57; Nishitani, '§ 26: Internationales Privat- und Zivilverfahrensrecht' (n 32) 82.
[52] Koide (n 31) 88–89; Interim Draft (AGRAL) Nos 5 and 6, 96.

seek the application of the mandatory rules of the law of the place where they have their habitual residence, when a different law has been designated as applicable to the contract (article 11(1)).[53] In other words, consumers have to invoke those rules, as the court cannot apply them of their own initiative.

During the legislative drafting of AGRAL, there was discussion whether the 'favourability principle' or 'preferential law approach' (*Günstigkeitsprinzip*), similarly to Rome Convention article 5(2), should be introduced. According to this principle, the court has to determine *ex officio* which law is more favourable to the consumer by comparing the law applicable to the contract with the law of the consumer's habitual residence.[54] This proposal, however, was criticised, on the ground that such a rule would put an excessive burden on judges, given that under Japanese civil procedure law judges always incur the task of ascertaining and applying foreign law *ex officio* (see chapter one, section VII). Thus, the legislature decided to require instead that the consumer invoke the law of his or her habitual residence,[55] both in court proceedings (ie, before the court) and outside courts. Moreover, consumers are required not only to submit relevant facts, but also specify the legal effects of the mandatory rules (such as withdrawal from the contract, or rescission or invalidity of the contract).[56]

It is obvious that AGRAL article 11 does not provide sufficient protection to consumers. It would be difficult for the ordinary consumer to understand the complicated choice of law rules involved, as well as to know the content of the chosen law and the law of his or her habitual residence well enough to invoke the latter's mandatory rules in his or her favour. To ensure effective protection, judges should at least be given procedural discretion to draw attention to the point that the law of the consumer's habitual residence could possibly be applied.[57] Despite its drawbacks, AGRAL article 11(1) may still have impact on the behaviour of enterprises to the extent that, being aware of the risk that the mandatory rules of a consumer's habitual residence may apply, they may consider the relevant rules when designing their products or drawing up their standard terms.[58]

Objective Connecting Factor

In the absence of choice of law by the parties, by AGRAL article 11(2), consumer contracts are objectively governed by the law of the consumer's habitual residence. For the sake of an effective protection of consumers, this provision, unlike AGRAL article 8(1), does not allow deviating from the law of habitual residence to refer to a different law that is more closely connected with the case.[59]

Substantive Scope of Application

The concept of 'consumer contracts' is in line with the Consumer Contract Act article 2(1)(2)(3), which follows a comparatively broad notion extending to all contracts

[53] Judgment of Tokyo District Court, 17 January 2017, LEX/DB25538954. In this case, the Court applied Consumer Contract Act article 4(1) based on AGRAL article 11(1).

[54] Minutes of 3rd, 15th and 20th Meetings (AGRAL).

[55] Minutes of 15th and 20th Meetings (AGRAL).

[56] *Hosoku Setsumei* (AGRAL) 153–54; Koide (n 31) 137.

[57] *Zadankai* (AGRAL) 24–25.

[58] 'Nishitani, 'New Private International Law of Japan' (n 47) 45–48.

[59] *Hosoku Setsumei* (AGRAL) 154–55; Koide (n 31) 139–40.

that are entered into between a person contracting outside business purposes ('consumer') and an enterprise acting for business purposes. The consumer contracts in this sense include purchase contracts of goods, immovable property and financial instruments, tenancy contracts of residence, service contracts, transport contracts and licence contracts of intellectual property.[60]

Personal Scope of Application: Passive Consumer

As for the territorial and personal scope of the application of AGRAL article 11(1)–(5), it only covers 'passive consumers', to the exclusion of 'active consumers' who go abroad on their own initiative to a state different from their habitual residence and, therefore, do not deserve protection. In this sense, AGRAL article 11(6)(i) and (ii) stipulate that protection is denied to a consumer who (a) goes to a state where the enterprise's office is located and concludes a contract there, or (b) goes to a state where the enterprise's office is located and that office has performed or is supposed to perform obligations under the contract in question. Yet, this rule does not apply, insofar as the enterprise solicited the consumer (*Kan-yu*) to go to that state of the enterprise's office under (a) or (b).[61]

Furthermore, AGRAL article 11(6)(iii) and (iv) adopted exceptions for consumer protection in e-commerce. A consumer does not enjoy protection provided by AGRAL article 11(1)–(5), insofar as (c) the enterprise did not know for legitimate grounds where the actual habitual residence of the consumer was located at the time of conclusion of a contract (AGRAL article 11(6)(iii)), or (d) the enterprise misunderstood for legitimate grounds that the other party was not a consumer (article 11(6)(iv)).[62] Both (c) and (d) extend to situations that would not justify protecting the consumer, on the grounds that the consumer did not indicate his or her actual habitual residence in State A but misrepresented it as being in State B, or the consumer pretended to be a merchant, with a view to taking advantage of favourable conditions of contracts.

Formal Requirements

AGRAL articles 11(3)–(5) set out special rules in respect of the formal validity of consumer contracts. These conflicts rules accommodate some substantive law rules that provide for consumer protection by requiring specific formal requirements to be abided by. Thus, notwithstanding the parties' choice of the law governing the contract, once the consumer invokes mandatory rules of the law of his or her habitual residence, the contract needs to satisfy the formal requirements of that law pursuant to AGRAL article 11(3) and (4).[63] Accordingly, the contract may be held null and void, even though it satisfies the formal requirements under the law of the place of act in accordance with

[60] *Hosoku Setsumei* (AGRAL) 155.

[61] With regard to '*Kan-yu*' by enterprises that solicit consumers to enter into contracts, article 4 of the Consumer Contract Act mentions, for instance, actions to solicit consumers to join a day trip or action to tempt the consumer to negotiate in the country where the office of the enterprise is located. General advertisement in the country where the consumer has a habitual residence or the setting up of a passive website enabling consumers to access the same from the country of their habitual resident do not constitute '*Kan-yu*'. *Gaiyo* (AGRAL) 55.

[62] *Hosoku Setsumei* (AGRAL) 156; Koide (n 31) 141–42.

[63] Article 11(3) covers situations where the parties have chosen as governing law a law other than the law of the place where the consumer has a habitual residence, while article 11(4) deals with situations where the parties have chosen the law of the place where the consumer has a habitual residence.

AGRAL article 10(1), (2) or (4). In the absence of choice of law by the parties, by article 11(5), the consumer contract must satisfy the formal requirements of the law of the place where the consumer habitually resides.

ii. Employment Contracts

a. Definition of Employment Contracts

AGRAL article 12 does not define the term 'employment contracts', as opposed to 'consumer contracts' in article 11. Pursuant to the legislature, to be characterised as an employment contract, a contract must meet the following three requirements: (a) an employee carries out work; (b) an employee is subordinate to directions or orders of an employer in carrying out such work; and (c) an employer pays his or her wages for such work.[64]

b. Employee Protection

On employment contracts, the same protection mechanism as with consumer contracts is basically applicable (see section II.B.i). Employment contracts are primarily subject to party autonomy under AGRAL articles 7 and 9. Yet, to combat an arbitrary choice of law by an employer, article 12(1) provides employees with special protection. According to AGRAL article 12(1), employees can claim the application of the mandatory rules of the law of the place most closely connected with the employment contract, if a different law has been designated by the parties. As in the case of consumer contracts, Japanese courts will not apply such rules *ex officio*, but only upon invocation by the employee.

Closest Connection

Pursuant to article 12, the place where an employee carries out work in performing the employment contract is presumed to be most closely connected with the contract.[65] If such place cannot be ascertained (eg, in the case of flight attendants carrying out work in multiple states continuously), the place of establishment which hired an employee is considered to have the closest connection with the contract.

Objective Connecting Factor

In the absence of a choice of law by the parties under AGRAL article 7, the applicable law is determined by AGRAL article 8(1) in accordance with the closest connection test. In employment contracts, AGRAL article 8(2) does not apply, but AGRAL article 12(2) is applied to look for the closest connection. As above, the closest connection is presumed to coincide with the place where an employee carries out work in performance of the contract in principle and, if it cannot be ascertained, with the place of establishment which hired

[64] *Hosoku Setsumei* (AGRAL) 158; Koide (n 31) 156–57.

[65] Judgment of Tokyo District Court, 20 May 2016, 2016WLJPCA05208002. In this case, despite the parties' agreement on Hong Kong law as the governing law of the contract, the Court applied article 16 of the Japanese Labour Contract Law (abuse of the right of dismissal) as Japan was the place where the employee carried out work and that provision is a mandatory rule. Judgment of Tokyo District Court, 26 September 2016, 2016WLJPCA09268020. In this case, although the parties chose 'UK law', the Court applied article 19 of the Japanese Labour Contract Law (termination of employment) based on a similar reason.

the employee (AGRAL article 12(3)). Notably, unlike AGRAL article 11(2), the objective reference under AGRAL article 12(3) is only a rebuttable presumption, so a different law may take precedence by article 8(1) in exceptional cases. This would be the case where an employee is hired in State A where the employer's headquarters is located, is sent to State B to be engaged in work there for 10 years, and is temporarily (for six months) carrying out work in State C when a labour dispute arises. In such a case, notwithstanding AGRAL article 12(2), neither State C as the place of carrying out work nor State A as the place of hiring the employee, but State B may be considered as having the closest connection with the contract.[66]

As opposed to AGRAL article 11(3)–(5), article 12 sets out no special choice of law rules in respect of the formal validity of employment contracts. This makes sense, as the collective and individual regulations for employee protection in substantive law are not geared towards the conclusion of the contract, but rather towards the performance of contractual obligations to carry out work (eg, labour conditions, participation in a trade union, binding force of a collective agreement, etc). Consequently, the law governing the formal validity of employee contracts is determined by the general choice of law rules in AGRAL article 10 (see section II.A.iii).

iii. Insurance Contracts

There exists no special choice of law rule for insurance contracts. Consequently, insurance contracts are subject to the general rule for contracts under AGRAL articles 7–9. Party autonomy first comes into play. Absent a choice of law by the parties (normally, conditions of insurance contain a choice of law clause), the applicable law must be determined based on a statutorily defined connecting factor in article 8, that is, the habitual residence of the party who performs an obligation characteristic to the contract. For insurance contracts, it will be the law of the place where the habitual residence or the relevant office of the insurer is situated.[67] This presumption is rebuttable. If rebutted, the law most closely connected with the contract will apply. If a party to the contract is a 'consumer' within the meaning of AGRAL article 11(1), then article 11 prevails over articles 7–9 (see section II.B.i).

iv. Contracts for the Sale of Immovable Property

While the structure is different, applying the general choice of law rules in AGRAL articles 7–9 to contracts relating to immovable property generally brings about the same result as under Rome I article 4 and SPIL article 119. First, parties to the contract can agree on the law governing the contract on immovable property in accordance with AGRAL article 7. In the absence of choice of law by the parties, the applicable law is determined by AGRAL article 8(1), pointing to the place that is most closely connected with the contract. Unlike other contracts, pursuant to AGRAL article 8(3), the situs of the immovable property

[66] *cf* Sawaki=Dogauchi (n 1) 209; Naoshi Takasugi, 'Article 12 (Rodo Keiyaku no Tokurei)' in Yoshiaki Sakurada and Masato Dogauchi (eds), *Chushaku Kokusai Shiho: Dai 1 kan* (*Commentary on Private International Law: Volume 1*) (Yuhikaku, 2011) 288–89.

[67] Nakanishi, 'Article 8' (n 37) 209.

as the subject matter of the contract is presumed to have the closest connection with the contract. This presumption is though rebuttable when there is another law constituting a closer connection. When it comes to a contract for building or repairing an immovable property, the contract is regarded as a service contract, so AGRAL article 8(3) does not apply.[68] In a case in which a party to the contract is a 'consumer' in the sense of AGRAL article 11(1), article 11 is given priority over articles 7–9 (see section II.B.i).

v. *Contracts for the Sale of Goods*

Despite a different construct, applying general choice of law rules in AGRAL articles 7–9 to contracts for the sale of goods generally leads to the same result as under Rome I article 4. Parties to a contract are free to choose and change the law applicable to the sales contract. In the absence of choice of law by the parties, the applicable law is determined pursuant to AGRAL article 8. The closest connection in the sense of AGRAL article 8(1) is presumed to lie in the place of habitual residence or establishment of the seller as the characteristic performer, unless other facts allow rebutting this presumption. If a party to the contract falls under the category of 'consumer' under AGRAL article 11(1), article 11 takes precedence over articles 7–9 (see section II.B.i).

Notably, although Japan has joined the United Nations Convention on Contracts for the International Sales of Goods (CISG), it scarcely has practical impacts because the parties generally exclude the application of CISG (CISG article 6). Thus, choice of law rules for the sale of goods under AGRAL articles 7–9 remain highly relevant before the Japanese courts.

vi. *Contracts for the Hire of Goods*

As for contracts for the hire of goods, there is no special choice of law rules. These contracts, too, are subject to the general choice of law rules in AGRAL articles 7–9. A similar analysis, as discussed above in relation to contracts for the sale of goods, will generally apply. In a case in which a party to the contract is a 'consumer' within the meaning of AGRAL article 11(1), article 11 prevails over articles 7–9 (see section II.B.i).

vii. *Contracts for the Carriage of Goods by Sea, Air or Land*

For lack of special choice of law rules for contracts for the carriage of goods by sea, air or land, these contracts are subject to the general choice of law rules in AGRAL articles 7–9. Party autonomy first comes into play. In the absence of choice of law by the parties, the applicable law is determined grounded on the closest connection test under AGRAL article 8. In this case, the closest connection is rebuttably presumed to lie at the place, where the carrier's establishment involved in the transaction is situated.[69] With a successful

[68] Koide (n 31) 110; Nakanishi, 'Article 8' (n 37) 211.
[69] Sakurada, *Kokusai Shiho* (*Private International Law*) (n 1) 237.

rebuttal of the presumption, the judge applies another law more closely connected with the contract. Also, in a case in which a party to the contract is regarded as a 'consumer' within the meaning of AGRAL article 11, article 11 always prevails over articles 7–9 (see section II.B.i).

viii. Negotiable Instruments

As for bills of exchange and cheques, the Bills of Exchange Act (BEA) and the Cheques Act (CHA) contain some choice of law rules. These rules always override the relevant choice of law rules in AGRAL (in particular, articles 7–10).[70] Bills of exchange and promissory notes as well as cheques are mostly subject to the comparable choice of law rules. For bills of exchange and promissory notes, BEA (modelled on the 1930 Geneva Convention Providing a Uniform Law for Bills of Exchange and Promissory Notes and the Convention for the Settlement of Certain Conflicts of Laws in connection with Bills of Exchange and Promissory Notes) sets out choice of law rules in articles 88–94. For cheques, CHA (modelled on the 1931 Geneva Convention for the Settlement of Certain Conflict of laws in Connection with Cheques) provides choice of law rules in articles 76–81.

A person's capacity to bind oneself by a bill of exchange, promissory note or a cheque is basically subject to one's national law. *Renvoi* is also allowed (BEA article 88(1); CHA article 76(1)). Even if a person lacks capacity according to the law designated under article 88(1), the person is deemed to be bound by a bill of exchange, if that person has capacity under the law of the place where one's signature has actually been given (BEA article 88(2); CHA article 76(2)). This rule aims to tie a transaction to the place of execution (signature). These rules are also applied to corporations.

The form of a bill of exchange, promissory note or cheque is subject to of the territory in which the bill of exchange or cheque has been signed (BEA article 89(1); CHA article 78(1)). As for cheques, it is sufficient if the forms prescribed by the law of the place of payment are observed (CHA article 78(1)). If, however, the obligations initially entered into by means of a bill of exchange, promissory note or cheque are not valid according to the law of the place of act, but conform to the laws of the country where a subsequent contract has been entered into, the initial lack of validity does not invalidate the subsequent contract (BEA article 89(2); CHA article 78(2)). Further, contracts by means of a bill of exchange, promissory note or cheque signed abroad by a Japanese national are valid and can be invoked against another Japanese national, provided that they satisfy the formal requirements of Japanese law (BEA article 89(3); CHA article 78(3)). The person on whom a cheque may be drawn is governed by the law of the country in which the cheque is payable (CHA article 77(1)). If the instrument is not valid as a cheque by reason of the person on whom it is drawn, the obligations arising out of the signatures affixed thereto in other countries whose laws provide otherwise is nevertheless deemed valid (article 77(2)).

Obligations of the acceptor of a bill of exchange or of the maker of a promissory note (BEA article 91(1)) are subject to the law of the place in which these instruments are payable.

[70] Naoshi Takasugi 'Tegataho, Kogitteho no Kokusai Shihokitei' in Yoshiaki Sakurada and Masato Dogauchi (eds), *Chushaku Kokusai Shiho: Dai 2 kan* (*Commentary on Private International Law: Volume 2*) (Yuhikaku, 2011).

Questions arising from the partial acceptance of a bill of exchange are subject to the law of the place in which a bill of exchange is payable (BEA article 92). The time limitation for exercising rights of recourse is governed by the law of the place where the instrument was created (BEA article 90(2); CHA article 79). The question whether there has been an assignment to the holder of the debt which has given rise to the issue of the instrument is subject to the law of the place in which the instrument was issued (BEA article 91). The question whether the holder has special rights against an acceptor, payor or endorser and the nature of such rights is subject to the law of the place in which the cheque is payable (CHA article 80(6)).

The form of and the limits of time for protest as well as the form of the other measures necessary for the exercise or preservation of rights concerning a bill of exchange, promissory note or cheque, are governed by the law of the country in whose territory the protest must be drawn up or the measures in question taken (BEA article 93; CHA article 81). The measures to be taken in case of the loss or theft of a bill of exchange, promissory note or cheque are determined by the law of the country in which the instrument is payable (BEA article 94; CHA article 80(8)). Other matters concerning a cheque, such as the effects of a post-dated cheque and the time of limit for presentation, are governed by the law of the state in which the cheque is payable (CHA article 80).

ix. Letters of Credit

Letter of credit transactions involve various and multiple legal relationships. In addition to the buyer and the seller, a series of banks (an issuing bank, a corresponding bank, a confirming bank etc) may be involved in the transaction. When the underlying main contract is for the sale of goods, a legal relationship obviously first arises between the buyer and the seller. A second legal relationship arises between the buyer and the issuing bank when the former asks the latter to open a letter of credit in favour of the seller. The third arises between the issuing bank and the correspondent bank engaged in making payments or receiving and checking documents. The fourth may arise between the confirming (correspondent) bank and the seller if the bank confirms the credit. The fifth is grounded between the seller and the issuing bank which ought to make payment against the presentation of documents. Each relationship needs to be handled separately in light of its nature.

For letters of credit, there is no special choice of law rules in AGRAL. Although the precise legal characterisations of letter of credit transactions may be debatable, it is widely accepted in conflict of laws that a letter of credit falls within the law of obligations.[71] As a result, a letter of credit is governed by AGRAL articles 7–9 as general choice of law rules for juristic acts.[72] Under these rules, party autonomy initially comes into play. Absent a choice

[71] Toru Sugie, 'Shinyo jo no Junkyoho' in Sawaki, Takao and Jun'ichi Akiba, *Shinban Kokusai Shiho no Ronten* (Yuuhikaku, 1996) 135.

[72] Judgment of Tokyo District Court, 26 September 2003, *Kinho* 1706, 40 (upheld by Tokyo High Court, Judgment of Tokyo High Court, 30 March, 2004 *Kinho* 1714, 110 ((2005) 48 *JAIL* 184). Some commentators take the view that, as legal relationships arising from a letter of credit involving various parties concerned are required to be handled uniformly, they should not be referred to the law chosen by the parties, but to the law designated by *jori*. Akira Takakuwa, *Shinban – Kokusai Shotorihiki Ho* (*Law of Cross-border Business Transactions [New Edition]*) (Toshindo, 2019) 205 (Takakuwa/Business).

of law by the parties, the applicable law is by the closest connection test under article 8(1), which is presumed to point to the place of habitual residence or an establishment involved in the transaction of the characteristic performer (see section II.A.i).

First, there is no doubt about the underlying main contract (the contract for the sale of goods) being governed by the applicable law proper to it pursuant to AGRAL articles 7–9. Second, for the contract between the buyer and the issuing bank, absent choice of law by the parties, the state, where the establishment of the issuing bank as the characteristic performer is situated, is presumed to have the closest connection under AGRAL article 8(1)(2).[73] Third, as for the relationship between the issuing bank and the correspondent or confirming bank (namely, an engagement agreement), for lack of the parties' choice of law, the law of the state of establishment belonging to the characteristic performer, namely the bank making payments or receiving and checking documents, will generally apply pursuant to AGRAL article 8(1)(2). Fourth, the independent relationship between the confirming bank and the seller is held to be closely related to the obligation of the issuing bank. In this light, it would be reasonable to objectively refer to the law of the place where the issuing bank transacts. This would generally ensure uniformity in handling letters of credit transactions.

In Japan, there has so far been one court decision that discussed the law governing the relationship between the issuing bank and the seller.[74] In the underlying case, the parties did not explicitly agree on the law applicable to the letter of credit. By applying *Horei* article 7, the Tokyo District Court looked into the parties' implicit intent and contended that the law of the place of payment (fixed in the contract) was tacitly selected, considering that the issuing bank generally plays the lead role in letter of credit transactions, and the payment obligation under the letter of credit is of the greatest importance to the parties.

However, it is doubtful whether the same reasoning should be followed under AGRAL, which is understood as restricting the parties' implied intent (article 7) to give priority to an objective connecting factor (article 8). Arguably, in the underlying case, an implicit choice of law ought to be denied under AGRAL article 7. Instead, by virtue of AGRAL article 8, the establishment of the issuing bank making payments against the presentation of documents will be presumed to point to the closest connection, as this obligation constitutes the core of letter of credit transactions.[75] This presumption may though be rebutted depending on the case, leading to a reference to the place of payment, as did the Tokyo District Court. In any case, choice of law issues over letters of credit are seldom raised in practice, because the UCP (Uniform Customs and Practice for Documentary Credits latest version: UCP 600) of the International Chamber of Commerce (ICC) normally defines the parties' substantive rights and obligations directly, once the UCP is incorporated into the contract by virtue of the parties' agreement or trade usage.

x. Contracts Involving the Transfer of Foreign Currency

In international contracts, a debt (ie, the value of goods or services) may be expressed in a foreign currency. Such a contract entails the transfer of foreign currency, which gives rise

[73] Also, Takakuwa/Business (n 72) 205.

[74] Judgment of Tokyo District Court, 26 September 2003, *Kinho* 1706, 40. This judgment was upheld by Tokyo High Court (Judgment, 30 March 2004, *Kinho*, 1714 110 ((2005) 48 *JAIL* 184)).

[75] Also, Takakuwa/Business (n 72) 205.

to some questions, as for instance: (a) the existence and definition of a currency; (b) the effects of changes in specific monetary systems on contractual obligations; and (c) whether a debtor can discharge an obligation to make payment in a different currency from the one expressed in a contract. The law applicable to each issue must be determined in light of its nature.

First, legal tender operates as currency. The question whether there exists a specific legal tender is determined by the (public) law of the state to which that currency belongs (*lex monetae*) (for Japan, the Act on Currency Units and Issuance of Coins).[76] This can be justified on the ground that each state has sovereignty in specifying a currency for its territory. This law covers questions relating to the currency itself, including switchover, devaluation and cancellation of convertibility.

Second, the effects of switchover and devaluation on the contractual obligation (in particular, the amount of a debt) should be subject to the law applicable to the value of goods or services (normally, the contract out of which the debt arises). This would not be a matter of currency itself, but a matter of the substantive debt (including under what circumstances a debtor can be exempted from the debt and whether a debtor can invoke the principle of *clausula rebus sic stantibus*).[77] The applicable law covers, for example, the effects of financial switchover, devaluation, abolition of convertibility, revalorisation and exchange rate changes.[78]

Third, it remains unclear which law determines whether a debtor can tender payment for a debt in a different currency from the one expressed in a contract. At the substantive law level, CC article 403 stipulates that a debtor is capable to tender payment in Japanese currency (ie, the Japanese Yen) pursuant to the exchange rate at the place of performance, even if the debt is expressed in a foreign currency. The Supreme Court, however, gave creditors the right to seek payment in a different currency, holding that:

> A money claim for which the amount of claim is designated in foreign currency is a discretionary claim, and the creditor may seek payment of the claim from the debtor either in foreign currency or Japanese currency. JCC article 403 only provides that where the creditor seeks payment in foreign currency, the debtor may make payment in Japanese currency. In the case of payment in Japanese currency of a money claim for which the amount of claim is designated in foreign currency, the amount of claim to be paid should be converted based on the exchange rate at the time of payment. However, when making judgment upon an action filed to seek payment in Japanese currency of a money claim for which the amount of claim is designated in foreign currency, the court shall convert the amount of claim based on the foreign exchange rate as of the date of completion of the oral hearings in the fact-finding proceedings. Therefore, the court shall not take into account any change in the exchange rate during the period until the delivery of the judgment, including that argued by the appellant.[79]

At the choice of law level, there exists no written rule in this respect. Accordingly, it is left for interpretation as to which law determines whether and (if at all) to what extent a party

[76] Orimo, *Kokusai Shiho* (n 38) 188–89; Yamada, *Kokusai Shiho* (n 16) 383.

[77] Tetsuo Morishita, 'Tsuka Ho' in Yoshiaki Sakurada and Masato Dogauchi (eds), *Chushaku Kokusai Shiho: Dai 1 kan* (*Commentary on Private International Law: Volume 1*) (Yuhikaku, 2011) 658; Orimo, *Kokusai Shiho* (n 38) 189; Tameike (n 16) 404.

[78] Morishita (n 77) 658.

[79] Judgment of Supreme Court, 15 July 1975, *Minshu* 29(6), 1029. Practice in Japan has been following this judgment, but commentators have heavily criticised it. See Morishita (n 77) 661–62.

has such right. While opinions are divided,[80] in the authors' view, the point here is, after all, how a debtor can perform his or her obligation, that is, make payment (more particularly, in what currency). Since this is most closely linked with the place of performance (payment), it should be subject to the law of the place of payment.[81]

xi. Agency

AGRAL does not contain any specific choice of law rules for agency, and therefore the governing law of an agency is left to interpretation. Agency is characterised as a triangular relationship between an agent, a principal and a third party. Each leg of the triangle should be separately handled in light of the nature of the relationship.

The relationship between agent and principal should be governed by the law giving rise to the agency relationship between the two persons. Where the agency arises out of a contract between the two, the law regulating the incidents of the agent's authority (including the scope of the agent's authority) should be the law applicable to the contract of mandate or employment (AGRAL articles 7, 8 and 12). Where the agency arises by reason of some statutory or other legal relationship between the parties, the governing law should be the law applicable to that underlying relationship (*lex causae*). For example, in the case of a parent's authority to act on behalf of a child, the determination of the applicable law would be subject to AGRAL articles 32 and 35 dealing with child custody or guardianship.[82]

For relationships between an agent and a third party, the juristic acts between them should be governed by the law applicable to the legal relationship in question. Accordingly, if an agent is authorised by a principal to purchase a property, the law governing the purchase agreement will be the law applicable to the contractual relationship between an agent and a third party (here, the seller) (AGRAL articles 7–9). If the act concerns an *in rem* transaction in movable or immovable property, the law governing the property right applies under AGRAL article 13.

It is debatable how the relationship between a principal and a third party (in particular, the requirements under which a principal is legally bound by the action of an actual or purported agent) should be dealt with. There have been many opinions expressed.[83] In this regard, the interests of a principal and a third party ought to be properly balanced. (a) The prevailing view is that such relationship should be governed by the law applicable to the underlying relationship between the principal and the agent. This approach would serve the principal in terms of predictability. However, the third party cannot be assumed to have known this law at the time of the relationship. (b) Some commentators take the view that the law applicable to the legal relationship between the agent and the third party should govern this issue. This approach would cater for certainty insofar as the third party is concerned. But the principal would not necessarily be aware of that law. (c) With a view to

[80] See Morishita (n 77) 660–65.

[81] ibid 664.

[82] Sakurada, *Kokusai Shiho* (*Private International Law*) (n 1) 191; Sawaki=Dogauchi (n 1) 213; Tameike (n 16) 314; Yamada, *Kokusai Shiho* (n 16) 275.

[83] For details of the development under Japanese law, see Yoshiaki Sakurada, 'Dairi' in Yoshiaki Sakurada and Masato Dogauchi (eds), *Chushaku Kokusai Shiho: Dai 1 kan* (*Commentary on Private International Law: Volume 1*) (Yuhikaku, 2011).

securing certainty for both parties in a balanced way, it would be reasonable and appropriate to subject this issue to the law of the place where the agent acts, that is, where an agent and a third party enter into a transaction.[84]

The law governing the relationship between a principal and a third party will deal with situations of, for instance, apparent authority (where A represents that B has authority to act on A's behalf (but B has in fact never been appointed as A's agent)), undisclosed agency and undisclosed principal. The power of representing a corporation or other entity should in principle be governed by the law applicable to the corporation or other entity (see section I.B).[85] One may argue that this relationship has a similarity to contractual agency in the way that a corporation grants authority to a specific person to act as the corporation's agent. However, as this is simply one of the internal matters within a corporation or other entity, it should be governed by the law governing the corporation or entity. Such authorisation normally has to be registered and made known to the public.

C. Torts

i. Governing Law in Tort Generally

a. General Principles

To determine the law governing torts, *Horei* article 11(1) used to follow the *lex loci delicti* principle. It is a generally accepted principle, on the grounds that tort as a mechanism of compensation for wrongful acts is embedded in public interest of the place of tort, and the place of tort is neutral, predictable and readily ascertainable for the parties. However, the inflexible, fixed reference to the place of tort under *Horei* article 11(1) would not necessarily correspond with the place that has the 'closest connection' with the case at hand, nor did it function well for specific torts such as product liability and defamation.[86] Moreover, there was no consensus among academics on how to deal with a cross-border complex tort (*Distanzdelikt*), in which the injury was suffered in a place (*locus damni*) different from a place where the wrongful act was committed (*locus delicti commissi*).[87] Considering these drawbacks, new choice of law rules for torts have been adopted in AGRAL articles 17–22.[88]

[84] Sakurada, 'Dairi' (n 83) 337–39; Sawaki=Dogauchi (n 1) 214. Also, Decision of Kobe District Court, 2 September 1959, *Kaminshu* 10(9), 1849.

[85] Sakurada, 'Dairi' (n 83) 336; Sawaki=Dogauchi (n 1) 213.

[86] In a case involving a ski accident in Canada between two Japanese, the court applied the choice of law rule in *Horei* article 11(1), applying Japanese law on the ground that economic loss occurred in Japan and both parties had made arguments based on Japanese law. Judgment of Chiba District Court, 24 July 1997, HJ 1639, 86.

[87] The prevailing view was that *Horei* article 11(1) distinguishes between fault-based and strict liability and subjects the former to the law of the place where the harmful act originates and the latter to the law of the place where the injury is sustained. However, this opinion was criticised by many commentators on the grounds that there were no concrete criteria for drawing lines between the two kinds of liability at the private international law level. For instance, Tameike (n 16) 394 ff.

[88] Yasushi Nakanishi, 'Torts' (2007) 50 *JAIL* 60, 62. For the comparison between AGRAL and Rome II, see Yuko Nishitani, 'The Rome II Regulation from a Japanese Point of View' (2007) 9 *YPIL* 175; Yuko Nishitani, 'La loi applicable à la responsabilité délictuelle – Le règlement « Rome II » du point de vue japonais' (2008) 60 *Revue internationale de droit comparé* 639.

While AGRAL article 17 continues to follow the *lex loci delicti* principle, it brings about a clear definition of the place of tort. This provision requires focusing on those who are directly involved in the tort (ie, the wrongdoer and the victim), to the exclusion of successor or assignee of claims or obligations.[89] With regard to cross-border complex torts, to ensure protection of victims and equality of competition among tortfeasors, the law of the place in which the result of the harmful event occurred primarily applies (article 17, first sentence). However, when it was not predictable that a harmful act would result in injury in this place, the law of the place in which the harmful act was committed applies instead (article 17, second sentence).[90]

To determine whether the occurrence of the harm was predictable, the decisive factor is the geographical location. For instance, when a person in State A sends goods contaminated with an unknown, new type of virus to a person in State B and the virus damages the recipient's health, the requirement of predictability in AGRAL article 17 will be met. This is because the sender intentionally directed the goods to State B and could have predicted that a certain result of his or her action could occur in State B.[91] Whether the sender could have anticipated the existence of a virus or occurrence of the harm to the recipient is considered pursuant to the substantive law governing the tort when determining the sender's liability.[92]

On the other hand, when, in the same example, the sender intended to send the goods to a person in State B, but the intermediary made a mistake and sent the goods to another person in State C, who suffered from harm due to the unknown virus, the predictability in the sense of AGRAL article 17, second sentence, will be denied. This is because the sender could not have reasonably foreseen that the goods would end up in State C.

The legislature left it for interpretation whether the elements constituting predictability belong to a question of fact or law.[93] In the authors' eyes, it ought to be characterised as a matter of law to be decided by the courts *ex officio*, which accords with the procedural rules of determining connecting factors. A classification as a matter of law also allows deterring any 'manipulation' by the defendant, as otherwise the defendant could select whether or not to plead and prove the relevant facts, thereby influencing the determination of the applicable law.[94]

b. Specific Torts

While AGRAL article 17 covers torts in general, the legislature set forth other choice of law rules for specific categories of torts, that is, product liability (article 18) and defamation (article 19) (see section II.C.ii). During the legislative process, other choice of law rules were envisaged, which pointed to the country of protection for the infringement of intellectual

[89] Koide (n 31) 235.

[90] The legislative proceedings deliberated on whether torts were always referred to the law of the place of the result of the harmful event. Interim Draft (AGRAL), No 6 98. But the option was not adopted. See, Minutes of 26th and 27th Meetings.

[91] Predictability under AGRAL article 17 is in respect of a specific place and has to be distinguished from the predictability of a concrete result at the substantive law level. *Gaiyo* (AGRAL) 57; Koide (n 31) 194.

[92] Koide (n 31) 194–95.

[93] ibid 195.

[94] Nakanishi, 'Torts' (n 88) 64.

property rights, or to the marketplace for acts violating antitrust law, or acts violating unfair competition law geared towards a market and not individuals. These rules, however, were no longer adopted in AGRAL due to uncertainties in determining the connecting factor or unclear relationship with public law regulation by the authority.

c. Escape Clause

Considering the variety of categories of torts and situations surrounding them, the legislature set out an escape clause in AGRAL article 20 (see chapter one, section VIII.C). This provision allows deviating from the law designated by AGRAL articles 17–19 to point to another law of the place, with which the tort is clearly more closely connected. As indicators of the close connection, AGRAL article 20 explicitly requires considering the facts that the parties had a common habitual residence at the time of the tort[95] or had a contractual relationship which gave rise to the tort.

The common habitual residence of the parties is the social environment in which they are embedded. This place reflects their living standard and offers a proper criterion for calculating the quantum of damages. Where the parties have the same habitual residence (say, Japan), they would both return there after the injury caused by the tort. They would then bring the case before the court of their common habitual residence seeking damages. As a result, their common habitual residence should strongly point to the *lex fori* (Japanese law, where the common habitual residence is Japan).[96] Reference to the law of such place would cater for the parties' interests.[97]

Where an act constitutes a tort and also breaches an obligation arising out of a contract between the parties, an ancillary reference to the law governing the contract will synchronise the applicable law to avoid potential contradiction and characterisation issues and facilitate the assessment of damages. Notably, under *Horei* article 11(1), a minority view contended that both contractual and tortious claims should be uniformly characterised as 'contractual' as a matter of choice of law.[98] The prevailing view and court practice, however, opined that the claim arising out of a wrongful act ought to be characterised as a tort in nature.[99] The legislature followed the latter position in AGRAL article 20, but enables reaching the same appropriate result as the minority view by allowing an ancillary reference to the law governing the contract.

d. Party Autonomy

AGRAL article 21 introduces party autonomy in torts. The parties may choose the applicable law subsequent to the occurrence of the tort. Unlike Rome II article 14(1)(b),

[95] Although *Horei* does not contain this escape clause, a lower court came to a similar conclusion in a case involving a ski accident between two Japanese in Canada. Judgment of Chiba District Court, 24 July 1997, HJ 1639, 86. See, Judgment of Fukuoka High Court, 10 February 2009, HJ 2043, 89.

[96] *Hosoku Setsumei* (AGRAL) 184–86.

[97] Koide (n 31) 234.

[98] Yutaka Orimo, *Shogai Fuhokoi Ho Ron* (Yuhikaku, 1976) 165 ff; Akihiko Kunitomo, *Kokusai Shiho-jo no Tojishariekini yoru Seishitsu Kettei* (Yuhikaku, 2002) 44 ff.

[99] *Hosoku Setsumei* (AGRAL) 187–89; for previous legal situations, Judgment of Tokyo District Court, 25 September 2000, HJ 1745, 102; Judgment of Tokyo District Court, 27 May 1998, HJ 1668, 89; Judgment of Osaka District Court, 23 May 1995, HJ 1554, 91. See Tameike (n 16) 398–99; Yamada, *Kokusai Shiho* (n 16) 363–64.

however, AGRAL article 21 does not leave room for a choice of law prior to the occurrence of damage, considering the risk that the stronger party abuses his or her dominant position to impose a favourable law. Furthermore, it was felt that there was little necessity to allow the parties to choose the applicable law *ex ante*, because an accessory reference to the law governing the contract under AGRAL article 20 will generally lead to the same result.[100]

As in AGRAL articles 7 and 9, there is no limitation as to the eligible laws that parties may choose (see section II.A.i). With this generous approach, the legislature sought to meet the needs of international transactions and avoid the criticism that such limitation would enhance a homeward trend.[101] The law chosen by the parties subsequent to the tort cannot be opposed by a third party, when his or her rights are prejudiced by that law. This would be the case, for example, when an insurer enters into a contract to cover damage to be caused by the insured. After the occurrence of tort falling within the insurance policy, the insured and the victim agree on the application of a law different from the law designated by AGRAL articles 17–20. In such a case, if the law chosen by the insured and victim prejudices the insurer's rights and obliges the insurer to pay a higher amount of money, the effects of the choice of law remains limited to the parties, without binding the insurer, who can invoke the law originally designated by AGRAL articles 17–20.[102]

e. Double Actionability

The double actionability rule in *Horei* article 11(2) and (3) provided for a cumulative application of Japanese law, in addition to the *lex loci delicti*, concerning the existence and effects of torts. The Japanese courts, in particular, would only grant damages to the extent permitted under Japanese law, rather than any larger amount available under foreign law. Japanese companies were thereby protected from (especially the US) punitive damages and other extraordinary tortious claims under foreign law for sure.[103] Commentators, however, generally opined that the double actionability rule was outdated and unduly favoured defendants, claiming to abolish it *de lege ferenda*. In practice, the double actionability rule led to an unnecessarily complicated and artificial application of both Japanese and foreign law.[104] Moreover, to defend against punitive damages and other unusual tortious claims, it is sufficient to refer to public policy under article 42, along the lines of the Supreme Court decision which refused to recognise and enforce a Californian punitive damages judgment.[105]

Unfortunately, however, the double actionability rule has been upheld in AGRAL article 22 due to requests from Japanese industry. This is regrettable, considering the prevalent academic opinions opposed to the double actionability rule. It is also contradictory to the purpose of an accessory reference to the law governing the contract (AGRAL article 20)

[100] *Hosoku Setsumei* (AGRAL) 192–93; Koide (n 31) 243.

[101] Minutes of 6th and 7th Meetings (AGRAL).

[102] Koide (n 31) 249–50.

[103] Minutes of 26th Meeting (AGRAL).

[104] In most jurisdictions, similar double actionability rules have been abolished. But, there are some jurisdictions such as the UK, Hong Kong and Singapore that retain the rule (only in the case of defamation).

[105] Judgment of Supreme Court, 11 July 1997, *Minshu* 51(6), 2530 ((1998) 41 *JAIL* 104). See ch 4, section I.C.iv.

and party autonomy (AGRAL article 21). AGRAL article 22 ought to be abolished *de lege ferenda*, and at least be subject to a narrow interpretation *de lege lata*, restricting its scope of application. For instance, AGRAL article 22 could be limited to cases where there is a strong connection with Japan, or limited to the application of mandatory rules of Japan.[106]

ii. Specific Torts

As mentioned above, AGRAL sets out only two special choice of law rules for specific torts, that is, product liability (article 18) and defamation (article 19). These special rules prevail over the general rule in AGRAL article 17. Other torts will essentially be subject to the general choice of law rules in torts in articles 17, 20, 21 and 22. In fact, article 17 uses the term 'torts' to cover all types of tortious activities. The choice of law rule itself does not change, depending on the nature of the tort. Instead, the connecting factors in article 17 (ie, the place where the harmful act occurred and the place where the result of the harmful act occurred) must be identified in light of the elements constituting a given tort.[107] Even if the special choice of law rules in AGRAL articles 18 and 19 are applied, the escape clause and choice of law by the parties subsequent to alleged torts are also available (AGRAL articles 20 and 21). Further, even when foreign law is designated as applicable to the tort in question, Japanese law will always apply cumulatively due to the double actionability rule in AGRAL article 22.

a. Product Liability

Law Governing the Product Liability

Product liability is governed by AGRAL article 18. This provision has adopted the principle of the marketplace (article 18, first sentence), so that claims based on alleged product liability are referred to the law of the place where the victim received the product. Receiving a product means acquiring legal possession of the product, not merely putting a product under one's physical control.[108] Accordingly, when an agent manifests an intention to hold a product on behalf of a principal, such constructive transfer is regarded as a delivery of the product. The locality of the market for the product is a neutral connecting factor not only for victims, but also for producers and therefore can secure an appropriate balance of the parties' interests, as well as the equality of competition between producers engaged in business activities in the same marketplace.[109]

However, where a product (for instance, a used car) has been resold outside the normal stream of commerce and delivered in a place that was not predictable by the producer, reference to the marketplace would not strike a fair balance between the parties' interests. In such a case, pursuant to AGRAL article 18, second sentence, the law of the place where the producer has a principal establishment (or the law of habitual residence for a natural person)

[106] Nakanishi, 'Torts' (n 88) 73.
[107] Koide (n 31) 193.
[108] ibid 205.
[109] ibid 203.

is applied for the purpose of protecting producers.[110] The notion of predictability under AGRAL article 18, second sentence, is defined as that of AGRAL article 17, second sentence, and determined objectively in light of the circumstances surrounding the harmful event at hand.

Depending on the case, the determination of the applicable law by AGRAL article 18 can be substituted by the law of a state which is more closely connected with the case at hand under the escape clause (article 20), or the law chosen by the parties (article 21). In addition, Japanese law is always cumulatively applied pursuant to the double actionability rule (article 22), which will serve to exclude punitive damages and other extraordinary remedies that do not exist in Japanese substantive law, as mentioned above (see section II.C.i).

Scope of Application

While the Japanese product liability law (Product Liability Act (PLA))[111] solely includes movable property that has been produced or processed, AGRAL article 18 has a much broader scope and also covers unprocessed natural products and immovable property (for instance, buildings and developed residential land).

Along with this policy, as is obvious from the wording of AGRAL article 18, the concept of 'a producer' is wider than that of 'a manufacturer' in PLA article 2(3).[112] AGRAL article 18 covers not only a person who has produced, processed, imported, or exported, but also a person who has distributed or sold a product in their own name in the course of transactions. Accordingly, a wholesale distributor, a retailer, a forwarder or a warehouse keeper may also come under the definition of 'a producer' and can be called to account for product liability at the choice of law level, as long as one is engaged in the distribution or sale of a product at issue.[113] Further, the definition of 'defect' in article 18 AGRAL is broader than that in PLA article 2(2) and refers to the situation where a product lacks the ordinary nature that it is supposed to entail.[114]

On the other hand, AGRAL article 18 is understood not to extend to liability against a bystander who is by chance involved in an accident caused by a defective product. An example would be passengers on an aircraft which has crashed due to design defects. The bystander would be subject to the general choice of law rule for torts in AGRAL article 17,

[110] *Gaiyo* (AGRAL) 60–61; Koide (n 31) 203.

[111] Article 2(1) reads: 'The term "product" as used in this Act shall mean a movable which is manufactured or processed'.

[112] Article 2(3) reads: 'The term 'manufacturer, etc' as used in this Act shall mean the following:

(i) any person who manufactured, processed, or imported the product in the course of trade (hereinafter referred to as 'manufacturer');

(ii) any person who provides his/her name, trade name, trademark or other indication (hereinafter referred to as 'representation of name, etc') on the product as the manufacturer of such product, or any person who provides the representation of name, etc. on the product which misleads the others into believing that he/she is the manufacturer;

(iii) apart from any person mentioned in the preceding item, any person who provides any representation of name, etc on the product which, in light of the manner concerning the manufacturing, processing, importation or sales of the product, and other circumstances, holds himself/herself out as its substantial manufacturer'.

[113] Koide (n 31) 204.

[114] ibid 204.

in addition to articles 20, 21 and 22. This is because the bystander would not fall within the stream of commerce for the product.[115] It is left to court interpretation who falls under the notion of 'bystander'.

b. Defamation

General Remarks

AGRAL article 19 has a specific choice of law rule for defamation. It not only encompasses claims of individuals for the infringement of honour or fame as a part of personality rights,[116] but also the claims of corporations for the infringement of business reputation[117] (ie, causing damage to credibility). This choice of law rule adopts as a specific connecting factor the victim's habitual residence (or principal place of business in case of a corporation or other association), where the victim's interests are arguably centred by being integrated in the society and known to the public. This choice of law rule deviates from AGRAL article 17, considering that the protected interest, that is, honour, fame or credibility as an intangible value, can hardly be located pursuant to AGRAL article 17,[118] particularly in a case of defamation on the internet. Thus, defamation is in principle governed by the law of the victim's habitual residence, even if the defamatory event occurs concurrently in more than one jurisdiction.[119]

Notably, the designation of the law of the victim's habitual residence by AGRAL article 19 can be substituted by a different law pursuant to the escape clause (article 20) or the parties' choice of law (article 21). In addition, Japanese law is always cumulatively applied pursuant to the double actionability rule (article 22), which will *de facto* serve to ensure the constitutional right to freedom of expression of Japanese mass media[120] (see section II.C.i).

Remedies

Some jurisdictions (for instance, SPIL article 139(2)) have specific choice of law rules on non-monetary remedies for defamation, such as the right to reply or the right to seek

[115] *Hosoku Setsumei* (AGRAL) 196–97; Koide (n 31) 206–07; Hiroshi Sano, 'Article 18 (Seisanbutsu Sekinin no Tokurei)' in Yoshiaki Sakurada and Masato Dogauchi (eds), *Chushaku Kokusai Shiho: Dai 1 kan (Commentary on Private International Law: Volume 1)* (Yuhikaku, 2011) 469. *cf* Yasuhiro Okuda, *Kokusai Zaisanho (Private International Law in Business)* (Akashi Shoten, 2019) 130–31.

[116] Judgment of Tokyo District Court, 28 October 2013, HT 1419, 331; Judgment of Tokyo District Court, 5 September 2014, HJ 2259, 75; Judgment of Tokyo District Court, 27 April 2017, 2017WLJPCA04276002.

[117] Judgment of Intellectual Property High Court, 25 March 2015, 2015WLJPCA03259001. Nevertheless, since some types of business defamation are closely connected to financial credibility in a market (for instance, the announcement or dissemination of a falsehood that is injurious to the business reputation of a competitor (Unfair Competition Prevention Act (UCPA) article 2 (14)) can constitute unfair competition or the breach of competition laws. In this regard, it would be reasonable to refer such activities not to the law of the victim's habitual residence, but to the law of the market where that credibility is centred by reason of AGRAL article 20.

[118] *Hosoku Setsumei* (AGRAL) 198; Koide (n 31) 222.

[119] Koide (n 31) 224. In this sense, it can safely be said that AGRAL article 19 does not adopt the mosaic approach. But since article 20 still applies to defamation cases, it cannot be denied that harmful activity resulting in defamation in various jurisdictions simultaneously can be referred to several laws pursuant to that provision.

[120] This solution to the freedom of press question based on the double actionability rule has also been adopted in England.

corrective or remedial advertisement. Because AGRAL does not have such specific rules, the question of remedies is left to the law governing the defamation itself.[121]

Scope of Application

The wording of AGRAL article 19 solely covers defamation and infringement of credibility. It does not explicitly provide for the infringement of other personality rights, such as privacy, publicity or 'right to be forgotten'. The legislature opined that the scope of personal rights largely differs among states, and few jurisdictions have set out choice of law rules extending beyond defamation.[122] Thus, it is left to interpretation whether to subsume the infringement of other types of personality rights under AGRAL article 19 or the general choice of law rules under AGRAL article 17.[123]

c. Other Specific Torts

Private Nuisance

Private nuisance is an unreasonable interference by a neighbour with the employment or use of land (namely, a land-based tort). AGRAL does not contain any special choice of law rules for nuisance, unlike SPIL article 138.[124] Nor is there any explicit provision on private nuisance at the substantive law level. Nevertheless, it is generally understood that victims of nuisance may seek compensation for loss or damage as a matter of tort. Therefore, the claim is subject to the general choice of law rules in tort (AGRAL articles 17–22). Pursuant to AGRAL article 17, the law of the place where a harmful act generates its effect will be applicable, unless the occurrence of harm at that place was not predictable. Nuisance being an unreasonable interference by a neighbour, the occurrence of the effect will usually be predictable. Even if unpredictable, the place of a harmful act comes into play, which ought to be interpreted as the place where the land in question is situated due to the nature of nuisance. Accordingly, the law of the place where the land concerned is situated applies under AGRAL article 17.

Interference with Goods

Wrongful interference with goods, too, is subject to the general choice of law rules for tort in AGRAL articles 17–22. If someone wrongly interferes with the claimant's goods and damages them or injures an interest in goods (eg, conversion and trespass), such conduct constitutes a tort (namely, a goods-based tort). In this case, physical interference with goods

[121] Insofar as remedies that are unknown to Japanese law (in particular, the right of reply) are concerned, the application of foreign laws will inevitably give rise to public policy concerns and may trigger the public policy control in AGRAL article 42.

[122] Koide (n 31) 224.

[123] ibid. Some commentators take the view that certain personal rights such as privacy are also subject to AGRAL article 19. See Tadashi Kanzaki, *Kaisetsu Ho no Tekiyou ni kansuru Tsuusokuho* (*Commentary on the Act on General Rules for Application of Law*) (Kobundo, 2006) 134; Koji Deguchi, 'Article 19 (Meiyo mataha Shinyo no Kison no Tokurei)' in Yoshiaki Sakurada and Masato Dogauchi (eds), *Chushaku Kokusai Shiho: Dai 1 kan* (*Commentary on Private International Law: Volume 1*) (Yuhikaku, 2011) 486; Sawaki=Dogauchi (n 1) 227.

[124] SPIL article 138 allows victims to choose either the law of the state in which the real property is located or the law of the state in which the result occurred.

and the resultant damage normally occur in the same place. Therefore, the place of the harmful act and the place of its result are normally the same. Pursuant to article 17, the place of injury first comes into play, and the law of the place where the goods have been damaged or injured applies. Since a physical interference gives rise to a damage or injury, it is normally predictable for a wrongdoer that such damage or injury will occur at that place. Therefore, wrongful interference with goods is basically governed by the law of the place in which the injury occurred.

Environmental Damage

AGRAL does not have special choice of law rules for environmental damage and pollution, as opposed to Rome II article 7.[125] As with other tortious claims, claims based on environmental damage and pollution will be subject to the general choice of law rules for tort in articles 17–22. Suppose that a harmful gas emitted in another state is then windborne to the forum state, leading to widespread health damage. There is no doubt that the place of the harmful act is the place where a harmful gas is emitted and the place of the result is the place where the health damage occurs. Pursuant to article 17, the latter connecting factor comes into play, unless that place is not predictable. The predictability must be decided based on concrete circumstances. If unpredictable, the law of the place of harmful act applies. Insofar as nuclear damage is concerned, the Convention on Supplementary Compensation for Nuclear Damage of 12 September 1997 applies (article 14).

Unfair Competition

AGRAL does not set out special choice of law rules for competition-related matters, unlike Rome II article 6[126] and SPIL articles 136 and 137.[127] With regard to competition-related matters, there is one distinction to be drawn: unfair competition law and competition (anti-trust) law (for the latter, see section VII). As mentioned above, these two areas were discussed during the legislative process. The question was whether specific choice of law rules referring to the law of the market should be introduced. However, the legislature decided not to, on the grounds that unfair competition law involves various interests, which may render the application of the law of the market unreasonable,[128] and that the application of the law of the market to competition law matters, embedded in public law, could unduly lead to the application of foreign competition law before the Japanese courts.[129] Therefore, it is left to further developments of case law for how to deal with these matters in Japan.

As for unfair competition, despite the absence of explicit choice of law rules, it is clear from the wording of AGRAL article 19 that business defamation comes under the scope

[125] Rome II article 7 allows victims to choose either the law of the country in which the damage occurred or the law of the country in which the event giving rise to the damage occurred.

[126] Rome II article 6 covers not only unfair competition, but also restrictions free competition (that is, anti-competitive activity). It adopts the market principle (article 6(2), (3) and (4)). An exception is where unfair competition affects competitive relations or the collective interests of consumers (article 6(1)).

[127] SPIL article 136 deals with unfair competition, while article 137 concerns restraints on competition. As Rome II does, these articles follow the market principle. An exception to this principle is where unfair competition exclusively injures the business interests of a specific competitor.

[128] *Hosoku Setsumei* (AGRAL) 200; Koide (n 31) 229.

[129] Minutes of 6th and 17th Meetings (AGRAL); Koide (n 31) 228–29.

of article 19.[130] Insofar as claims based on alleged business defamation are concerned, the law of the victim's habitual residence (or establishment in case of a corporation or any other organisation) applies (see section II.A.ii.b).

To the contrary, it remains unclear how other unfair competition matters ought to be handled, such as false advertising, 'bait and switch' selling advertising, false representation of products or services, industrial espionage, labour piracy and infringement of know-how.[131] It is noteworthy that unfair competition is involved with different interests, depending on the nature and purpose of the relevant unfair competition. For instance, in cases of false advertising, unauthorised use of another person's goods or services and sale of imitations (passing-off), the market order may be affected. In this sense, the focus of unfair competition must be ensuring the regularity of markets and eliminating market distortions. But there can also be acts of unfair competition (such as industrial espionage, labour piracy and the infringement of know-how) which target a specific competitor, not a specific market (ie, individual-based unfair competition). In this case, it is not the effect on the market, but the effect on the parties' relationship that is brought to the fore. In this light, the law applicable to unfair competition should be determined in accordance with the nature of the relevant unfair competition. Consequently, market-based unfair competition should be governed by the law of the market that is (or likely to be) affected, while the law applicable to individual-based unfair competition should be determined in accordance with the general choice of law rules for tort in AGRAL articles 17 and 20–22.

Regrettably, however, Japanese courts have applied the general choice of law rules in torts (AGRAL articles 17 and 20–22), without distinguishing unfair competition matters into the above-mentioned two categories.[132] Further, insofar as injunction claims are concerned, lower courts have adopted different approaches. Basing themselves on *jori*, some courts have applied the law of the place most closely connected with a case.[133] Others, in cases of sales and exports by a Japanese company of imitation products, have applied Japanese unfair competition law, without mentioning the rationale for that application.[134] In recent cases involving claims for an injunction, banishment of products, or apology advertisements for the infringement of unfair competition law, the Intellectual Property High Court has held that the claims were in nature tortious and subject to AGRAL article 17.[135] Thus, since such

[130] Judgment of Intellectual Property High Court, 25 March 2015, 2015WLJPCA03259001. Also, Judgment of Intellectual Property High Court, 27 March 2014, 2014WLJPCA03279011.

[131] For conduct regulated under Japanese law, see UCPA article 2.

[132] eg, Judgment of Tokyo District Court, 24 September 1991, HJ 1429, 80 ((1992) 35 *JAIL* 175); Judgment of Tokyo District Court, 16 October 2003, HJ 1874, 23; Judgment of Osaka District Court, 9 November 2004, HJ 1897, 103 ((2006) 49 *JAIL* 197); Judgment of Intellectual Property High Court, 15 December 2009, 2009WLJPCA12159002; Judgment of Intellectual Property High Court, 27 March 2014, 2014WLJPCA03279011; Judgment of Intellectual Property High Court, 25 March 2015, 2015WLJPCA03259001; Judgment of Intellectual Property High Court, 15 January 2018, HT 1452, 80; Judgment of Intellectual Property High Court, 24 January 2019, HJ 2425, 88; Judgment of Intellectual Property High Court, 20 September 2019, 2019WLJPCA09209004.

[133] Decision of Intellectual Property High Court, 27 December 2005, 2005WLJPCA12279001; Decision of Tokyo District Court, 11 January, 2008, 2008WLJPCA01116003. With regard to a claim seeking an apology advertisement, the Tokyo District Court applied, based on *jori*, the law of the place which was most closely connected with the case (here, Japanese law). Judgment of Tokyo District Court, 4 July 2008, 2008WLJPCA07049004.

[134] Judgment of Osaka District Court, 9 November 2004, HJ 1897, 103 ((2006) 49 *JAIL* 197).

[135] Judgment of Intellectual Property High Court, 15 January 2018, HT 1452, 80; Judgment of Intellectual Property High Court, 24 January 2019, HJ 2425, 88.

claims for injunctions or other private law remedies are by nature tortious, they should be uniformly characterised as such and referred to the law governing the damages claim.

D. Unjust Enrichment and *negotiorum gestio*

Unjust enrichment and *negotiorum gestio* are subject to the law of the place where the facts constituting the cause of the enrichment occurred (AGRAL article 14). The provision has simply adopted the wordings of *Horei* article 11(1) and has not added any changes. As opposed to the choice of law rule in tort in AGRAL article 17, AGRAL article 14 leaves open the identification of the relevant place of unjust enrichment or *negotiorum gestio* in cases where more than one jurisdiction is involved (ie, the place where a fundamental act or event occurs is different from the place where its result occurs).

In the case of unjust enrichment based on a payment credited to the wrong account, the Tokyo High Court held that the place of unjust enrichment was the place where the payment was received (in that case, the Philippines), not the place where the payment originated (Japan).[136] In the case of non-contractual salvage within the territory of a specific country, the Hiroshima District Court has characterised the salvage as a type of *negotiorum gestio*, holding that it was subject to the law of the state where the salvage was performed.[137]

As special rules, the legislature set out two provisions: an escape clause (AGRAL article 15) and the choice of law by the parties subsequent to the event to change the governing law (article 16). Those provisions run in parallel with the choice of law rules in tort (articles 20 and 21). Under *Horei*, one of the biggest issues in unjust enrichment and tort was characterisation where there were pre-existing contractual relationships between the parties. Due to AGRAL article 15, the issue is in practical terms resolved within the framework of the escape clause, the same as AGRAL article 20 for torts. In the cases of unjust enrichment, the accessory reference to the law governing the contract under AGRAL article 15 is likely to play an important role. This is because unjust enrichment often arises out of performance of contractual obligations, as for instance in the case of invalidation of a contract or the revocation of a gift. In such cases, the unjust enrichment will be subject to the law applicable to the underlying contract.

E. Trusts and Charitable Foundations

A trust is a special instrument to invest and employ assets. The trust originates from common law jurisdictions. Yet, such an institution has been introduced ('localised') into a number of civil law jurisdictions. In the 1920s, Japan introduced the concept of 'trusts' into the Japanese legal system (*Shintaku*). It should be noted, however, that its concept and system is not same as in common law jurisdictions. For instance, a trust in Japan is in general set up by way of a contract pursuant to the Trust Act article 3(1). As mentioned

[136] Judgment of Tokyo High Court, 18 January 2012, HJ 2138, 42.
[137] Judgment of Hiroshima District Court, Kure Branch, 27 April 1970, *Kaminshu* 21(3–4), 607.

in the chapter on jurisdiction (see chapter two, section II.B.i.d), a trust is normally established by unilateral conduct or the parties' agreement (a trust agreement or instrument). A person (trustor or settlor) transfers property to another person (trustee) and asks the latter to administer or dispose of that transferred property for the benefit of a third party (beneficiary) or for a specified purpose. A charitable foundation is a type of trust in that a trustor establishes a set of assets for charitable purposes. In addition, in common law jurisdictions, a trust can be imposed by the court as an equitable remedy (constructive trust) in the absence of consensus or legal relationship between the parties. This type of trust is unknown in most civil law jurisdictions (including Japan). In Japan, insofar as the institution of unjust enrichment fulfils a similar function, it ought to be characterised as restitution for unjust enrichment.[138]

Japan is not a Contracting State to the Hague Convention of 1 July 1985 on the Law Applicable to Trusts and on their Recognition. Accordingly, the trust is subject to the domestic choice of law rules in AGRAL. AGRAL does not set out special choice of law rules for trusts. Choice of law issues over trusts are thus left for the court's interpretation. During the legislative process of AGRAL, there was deliberation over whether special choice of law rules for trusts should be introduced.[139] However, the legislature decided not to for several reasons. First, as trusts in Japan had been used mainly for commercial purpose and, for lack of public or academic discussion over civil trusts, it was held difficult to define their scope. Second, there was no consensus on the correct characterisation of trusts, especially whether contractual aspects and proprietary aspects should be characterised uniformly or separately. Third, there was no discernible trend among other civil law jurisdictions towards the amendment of domestic laws to deal with trusts. Fourth, in practice, no specific problems had been encountered.[140]

AGRAL articles 7–10 use the term *horitsukoui* to determine their scope of application. That term stems from the German concept of *Rechtsgeschäft* (juristic act). It is widely acknowledged that articles 7–10 are intended to cover not only contracts, but also unilateral juristic acts such as donations and reward advertisements.[141] Therefore, the law applicable to trusts (at least, concerning contractual obligations) is to be determined in accordance with articles 7–10.[142] A cardinal issue is whether a trust ought to be characterised as a contract or a unilateral juristic act. Although a trust is subject to articles 7–10 in any case, this question has a critical influence on the process of designating the governing law. Pursuant to articles 7 and 9, 'the parties' are free to choose the law applicable to a juristic act. If a trust is characterised as a unilateral act, a settlor alone can choose the law. If it is characterised as a contract, a settlor has to choose the law together with the trustee (ie, literally, the law

[138] For characterisation in choice of law, Tadashi Kanzaki, 'Shintaku' in Yoshiaki Sakurada and Masato Dogauchi (eds), *Chushaku Kokusai Shiho: Dai 1 kan* (*Commentary on Private International Law: Volume 1*) (Yuhikaku, 2011) 352.

[139] Minutes of 13th and 21st Meetings (AGRAL). Also, Kanzaki, 'Shintaku' (n 138) 343–44.

[140] *Hosoku Setsumei* (AGRAL) 168; Koide (n 31) 416–17.

[141] Yasushi Nakanishi, 'Article 7 (Tojisha ni yoru Junkyoho no Sentaku' in Yoshiaki Sakurada and Masato Dogauchi (eds), *Chushaku Kokusai Shiho: Dai 1 kan* (*Commentary on Private International Law: Volume 1*) (Yuhikaku, 2011) 183; Tameike (n 16) 364; Sakurada, *Kokusai Shiho* (*Private International Law*) (n 1) 222; Sawaki= Dogauchi (n 1) 211; Kanzaki, 'Shintaku' (n 138) 343–44.

[142] One commentator mentions that it may be possible to subject trusts to the choice of law rules for corporations and organisations on the ground that a trust is substantially a legal entity (Kanzaki, 'Shintaku' (n 138) 349).

must be chosen by the parties to the 'contract'). There has been no case law in this regard.[143] Furthermore, as mentioned, in common law jurisdictions, a trust can be established by courts as an equitable remedy, which in actuality plays a similar function as unjust enrichment under Japanese law. In this light, this type of trust should be regarded as a type of restitution.[144]

Trusts often are engaged in other legal relationships, such as real rights and inheritance, resulting in several laws being applicable to those relationships and covering the same issues. To avoid unnecessary overlap, the scope of the law governing trusts needs to be defined. For instance, when the trust is set up under the law of State A and the entrusted property is situated in State B, the question arises whether a trustee's creditor can enforce claims against that property. In this case, the first question is to whom the property belongs. It should be governed by the law of State B as the *lex situs*. If the property is segregated from other properties of the trustee pursuant to the law of State B, then the validity of the trust is to be examined. In relation to succession, a trust created by a will may impair the legitimate share (or legally reserved portion) of a successor in an inheritance. Such matters should be governed by the law governing a succession as in the cases of *donatio mortis causa* (a gift in prospect of death).[145] Further, if a trust is characterised as a consumer contract, it will be governed by AGRAL article 11. Therefore, a consumer (settlor)[146] can seek and enjoy the protection of the law of his or her habitual residence by actively invoking it.

F. Change and Extinction of Obligations

i. Voluntary Assignment of Receivables

a. General Remarks

A party (the assignor) may assign receivables to someone else (the assignee). To determine the law applicable to the validity and effects of such assignment of receivables, primarily the following three aspects ought to be differentiated: (i) first, the relationship between the assignor and assignee (question on whether the obligations grounded on the assignment contract have been fulfilled, and whether the receivables have been transferred); (ii) second, the effects of assignment towards the debtor (questions on whether the assignee can invoke the assignment against the debtor, and whether the debtor has been discharged); and (iii) third, third-party effects between competing assignees, or between an assignee and other creditors of the assignor (questions on whether the assignment has third-party effects, and which assignee has priority over the competing third parties).

In the absence of explicit provisions, it has always been taken for granted that the assignability of receivables (eg, prohibition or restriction of assignment by law or the

[143] For details of academic discussions, see, eg, Makoto Shimada, 'Kokusai Shintaku no Seiritsu oyobib Koryoku no Junkyoho (2)' (2009) 13 *Keio Hogaku* 23; Kanzaki, 'Shintaku' (n 138) 361–63.

[144] For characterisation in choice of law, Kanzaki, 'Shintaku' (n 138) 352.

[145] ibid 359; Sawaki=Dogauchi (n 1) 212.

[146] One commentator argues that, as the beneficiary's interest is centred on the legal relationship not the law of the consumer's habitual residence, the law of the beneficiary's habitual residence should be taken into consideration. Shimada (n 143) 64. *cf* Kanzaki, 'Shintaku' (n 138).

parties' agreement) is decided by the law governing the receivables themselves. It has also been presupposed that contractual obligations between the assignor and assignee are governed by the law governing the assignment contract. On the other hand, opinion has been divided on whether to subject the proprietary effects of the assignment between the assignor and assignee to the law governing their contract or to the law applicable to the receivable in question (for further detail, see below). As for (ii) and (iii), *Horei* article 12 provided that the effects of an assignment against the debtor and third parties were subject to the law of the place where the debtor was domiciled. While (i) remains unregulated in AGRAL, the connecting factor for (ii) and (iii) has been switched to the law governing the receivable concerned under AGRAL article 23.

b. AGRAL Article 23

During the legislative process, there was an extensive discussion whether (iii) the third-party effects of an assignment should be subject to the law of the place where the assignor is located, along the lines of articles 22 and 30 of the UN Convention on the Assignment of Receivables in International Trade (not yet entered into force).[147] The assignor's location rule has the advantage of subjecting the third-party effects and priority issues of all assignments to one single law, facilitating the assignor to be engaged in a bulk sale or factoring of a number of receivables, and assignment of future claims. However, such a rule was not adopted because the financial sector, mainly banks, set forth that there was scarcely any practical need to adopt this rule, owing to the limited number of cross-border assignments of multiple or future receivables. It was also argued that the third-party effects of assignment ought to be subject to the same law as the effects of assignment against the debtor to facilitate the law application.[148] Consequently, AGRAL article 23 stipulates for (ii) and (iii) that the effect of an assignment against the debtor and other third parties is governed by the law applicable to the assigned claim.

Insofar as relationships with the debtor under (ii) are concerned, the approach of AGRAL article 23 would be reasonable, as the law governing the receivables is readily ascertainable and foreseeable for the debtor without incurring an additional burden. It also guarantees that the debtor may invoke all defences and rights of set-off against an assignee as previously against the creditor (assignor). Further, this choice of law rule is generally acknowledged in various jurisdictions, including the UN Convention, the Hague Principles, Rome I and other domestic legal systems.

On the other hand, when it comes to relationships with third parties as (iii), there are some doubts about designating the law governing the receivables under AGRAL article 23. It is true that the proprietary effects of assignment concern the transfer of receivables without altering them, so they ought to be governed by the law applicable to the receivables. This choice of law policy also guarantees legal certainty, as the connecting factor does not change even if the assignor moves his or her place of business to a different country, assigns the same receivable to multiple assignees, or the receivable is subject to subsequent

[147] Interim Draft (AGRAL) 102 (No 8); *Hosoku Setsumei* (AGRAL) 102.
[148] *Gaiyo* (AGRAL) 61–63; Minutes of 26th Meeting (AGRAL).

assignments. Furthermore, by subjecting both (ii) relationships with the debtor and (iii) third-party effects to the same law governing the receivables, a characterisation and adaption problem is usually avoided.

However, this rule also has some disadvantages and encounters practical difficulties. The law governing the receivables is usually not publicised and is difficult to ascertain in the absence of the parties' choice of law. The applicable law may well not be identifiable or predictable for outsiders (ie, third parties other than the creditor and debtor) and is possibly subject to subsequent changes by agreement of the creditor and debtor. This conflicts policy does not function for future receivables either, as their applicable law is not yet ascertainable. Nor does it make sense to apply the law governing the receivables 'that [have] ceased to exist' insofar as the debt has been paid to an assignee and the dispute only concerns title to security interests. Most importantly, the conflicts rule of AGRAL article 23 is cumbersome and inapt for bulk assignments of existing and future receivables, given that the assignors and assignees need to look into the law that is (presumably) applicable to each receivable to decide priorities. Especially in the factoring or invoice-discounting industry, such practice is not suitable to the entire arrangement.[149] Considering these practical difficulties, it would be reasonable *de lege ferenda* to refer relationships with third parties to the law of the place where the assignor is situated, as adopted by the UN Convention, the Model Law and other jurisdictions, with a view to accommodating bulk assignment of existing or future receivables.

c. Assignment Contract and Proprietary Effects

AGRAL article 23 only deals with the effects of assignment against the debtor and other third parties. Therefore, other issues relating to the assignment of receivables (such as the formation and effects of the assignment between the assignor and the assignee) are left for the court's interpretation.

With regard to the formation of the assignment and its proprietary effects between the assignor and the assignee, the Tokyo District Court has held that those matters were subject to the law applicable to the assigned receivables.[150] This approach will have all the issues around the assigned claim subject to a single law and thereby enhance the liquidity of claims.[151]

The proprietary effects of the assignment of receivables concern whether and under what conditions the assignee can assert the 'right *in rem*' against the assignor. Further, fixing the time of the title transfer may be crucial in relation to the fruits of and income deriving from the assigned receivable, or when the assignor becomes insolvent before the assignee has recovered the debt. In actuality, the proprietary effects of assignment between the assignor and the assignee, on the one hand, and between the assignee and the debtor, on the other, ought to be governed by the same law. Otherwise, the law application will become cumbersome and may even lead to a contradictory result, although proprietary

[149] For comparative research on this point, Yuko Nishitani, 'Cross-border Assignment of Receivables: Choice of Laws in Secured Transactions' (2017) 22(4) *Uniform Law Review* 826.

[150] Judgment of Tokyo District Court, 11 July 1967, HT 210, 206.

[151] Sakurada, *Kokusai Shiho* (*Private International Law*) (n 1) 263–64.

effects of assignment ought to be determined uniformly to avoid relativity. In this light, the proprietary aspects of an assignment between the assignor and the assignee ought to be subject to the law governing the receivable, in the same way as (ii) the relationships with the debtor.

ii. Statutory Transfer of Receivables

The requirements and effects of a statutory transfer of receivables are governed by the law applicable to the underlying relationship. For instance, it is for the applicable law of an insurance contract that determines whether an insurer is subrogated to the damages claim of a victim against a wrongdoer, if the insurance company pays the insured amount to the victim.[152] On the other hand, the question whether a claim is assignable or is personal in nature and thus unassignable is subject to the law governing receivables, since it concerns the characteristics of the claims concerned.[153]

iii. Pledged Receivables

AGRAL does not contain a special choice of law rule for pledged receivables. During the legislative process of AGRAL, it was discussed whether a similar choice of law rule to that for the assignment of receivables should be introduced. The legislature ultimately refrained from adopting such a rule, on the ground that there were few jurisdictions that have explicit choice of law rules in this regard. It was also debatable how pledged receivables should be characterised (either as rights *in rem* or as a kind of assignment of receivables).[154]

Under *Horei*, the Supreme Court in 1978 regarded a pledged receivable as a species of right *in rem*. But the Court did not explicitly ground its conclusion on *Horei* article 10 (present, AGRAL article 13), holding that the proprietary effects of the pledged receivable (including the creditor's priority against a third party) as an intangible asset cannot be subject to the *lex rei sitae*. Rather, the justices reasoned that a pledge constitutes a title to dominate the receivable and dictate its destiny, so the proprietary effects of a pledge ought to be determined by the law governing the receivable itself.[155]

Some commentators have advocated that the matter of priority should be subject to the law of the debtor's domicile by analogy with *Horei* article 12 dealing with the effects of assignment of receivables towards the debtor and other third parties, so that priority between the assignee and the pledgee over the pledged receivables could be dealt with uniformly by that law. Since *Horei* article 12 has been replaced by AGRAL article 23, according to which the effects of assignment are subject to the law governing the assigned claim, it coincides with the ruling of the 1978 Supreme Court ruling to point to the law governing

[152] Judgment of Tokyo District Court, 20 June 1964, HJ 382, 42; Judgment of Tokyo High Court, 24 February 1969, *Kominshu* 22(1), 80; Judgment of Kobe District Court, 14 March 1970, HT 288, 283. *cf* Sawaki=Dogauchi (n 1) 241.

[153] Sakurada, *Kokusai Shiho* (*Private International Law*) (n 1) 263.

[154] Koide (n 31) 284.

[155] Judgment of Supreme Court, 20 April 1978, *Minshu* 32(3), 616.

the pledged claim. Although it remains debatable under AGRAL whether pledged receivables are characterised as rights *in rem* or as a sort of assignment of receivables,[156] this characterisation no longer has relevance in practical terms.

iv. Debt Assumption

A party may assume a debt by making a contract with someone else for reasons such as tax saving, resulting in a substitution of debtors.[157] AGRAL does not set out any choice of law rule for debt assumption. During the legislative process of AGRAL, there was discussion as to whether an explicit choice of law should be introduced for debt assumption. However, the legislature decided not to, on the ground that few jurisdictions had explicit choice of law rules dealing with this issue and there was no need to introduce an explicit rule which might rather give rise to practical difficulties.[158] There exists no case law on debt assumption. Accordingly, the applicable law is left for the court's interpretation. Considering that the framework of debt assumption is similar to the assignment of receivables, the principles for the latter should apply by analogy. Therefore, the formation and effects of debt assumption are subject to the law applicable to the assumed dept.[159]

v. Subrogation by Creditor

There exists no special choice of law rule for subrogation by creditor. After some debate on whether to adopt a special choice of law rule in AGRAL, it was abandoned due to lack of consensus. There were also few jurisdictions with explicit choice of law rules dealing with this issue and it was thought that introducing an explicit rule could cause difficulties in practice.[160]

Subrogation by creditor is a legal construct allowing the creditor to take the position of his or her debtor to enforce the debtor's claim against a third debtor. Although the Tokyo District Court once held that subrogation is a procedural right governed by the *lex fori*)[161] it is generally acknowledged today that subrogation by creditor belongs to a substantive law matter. The previously prevailing view set forth applying both the law governing the claim of the creditor (the subrogating party) against the debtor and the law governing the claim of the debtor (the subrogated party) against the third debtor. This is because subrogation concerns the effects of the claim belonging to the creditor and, at the same time, the position of the debtor needs to be protected by applying the law governing

[156] For developments and discussions in Japan, see Aki Kitazawa, 'Saiken Shichi' in Yoshiaki Sakurada and Masato Dogauchi (eds), *Chushaku Kokusai Shiho: Dai 1 kan* (*Commentary on Private International Law: Volume 1*) (Yuhikaku, 2011) 562–64.

[157] Under Japanese law, a surety may also assume a debt cumulatively (that is, by a collateral promise) A collateral promise will not change the debtor and instead operates similarly to a guarantee. Therefore, the creditor's interest will not be damaged by a collateral promise, but will instead be enhanced. In this light, it is not necessary to refer the formation and effects of a collateral promise to the law governing debt to protect the creditor's interest.

[158] Koide (n 31) 283.

[159] Koide (n 31) 283; Sawaki=Dogauchi (n 1) 241.

[160] Koide (n 31) 297.

[161] Judgment of Tokyo District Court, 20 July 1962, *Kaminshu* 13(7), 1482.

the claim belonging to the debtor. According to this view, subrogation by creditor is only admissible when it fulfils the requirements of both laws.[162]

The recent view, however, contends that the law governing the debtor's claim against the third debtor should not be applied, because subrogation by creditor does not change the position of the third debtor. Even if the creditor (the subrogating party) enforces the claim against the third debtor, that will not worsen the position or deprive any rights of the third debtor, who only needs to perform the same obligation to the creditor instead of the debtor. Thus, the subrogation can be subject only to the law governing the claim of the creditor.[163]

*vi. Fraudulent Conveyance (*action paulienne*)*

AGRAL does not contain any specific choice of law rule for fraudulent conveyance (*action paulienne*). After some reflection, the legislature decided not to adopt any provision for lack of consensus and comparative examples, and for fear of causing difficulties in practice.[164]

Fraudulent conveyance to a third party means a legal construct allowing the creditor to revoke the debtor's transaction with the third party before the judge, when the debtor transferred his or her assets to the third party with an intent to cause harm to the creditor. Once the judge accepts the claim of fraudulent conveyance, the transaction is cancelled, which directly affects the interests of the third party. Despite a minority view characterising fraudulent conveyance as a matter of procedural law to be governed by the *lex fori*, a majority of authors classify it as a matter of substantive law.[165]

According to the prevailing view, fraudulent conveyance ought to be governed cumulatively by the law applicable to the challenged transaction (in the case of a contract under AGRAL article 7 ff, in the case of a transfer of property under AGRAL article 13(2)), in addition to the law applicable to the creditor's claim. As a result, the creditor will only be successful when the requirements for fraudulent conveyance are fulfilled under both laws. The Tokyo District Court followed this position in 2015.[166]

Notably, some commentators take the view that fraudulent conveyance ought to be governed by the law of the situs of the property, reasoning that it is not appropriate to rely on the law chosen by the party (the debtor) who has acted in a fraudulent manner to harm the other party's (the creditor's) interests, because the debtor could then choose a legal order in which fraudulent conveyance is unknown or which sets out strict conditions

[162] Hidebumi Egawa, *Kokusaishiho* (*Private International Law*), 17th edn (Yuhikaku, 1988) 244–45; Yamada, *Kokusai Shiho* (n 16) 375.

[163] Tameike (n 16) 407; Sakurada, *Kokusai Shiho* (*Private International Law*) (n 1) 262. *cf* Sawaki=Dogauchi (n 1) 243.

[164] Koide (n 31) 297.

[165] For further detail, see Yuko Nishitani, 'Sagaikoi Torikeshiken no Junkyoho' (2016) 1492 *Jurist* 296.

[166] Sakurada, *Kokusai Shiho* (*Private International Law*) (n 1) 262–63; Tameike (n 16) 407; Yamada, *Kokusai Shiho* (n 16) 375; Aki Kitazawa, 'Saikensha Torikeshiken' in Yoshiaki Sakurada and Masato Dogauchi (eds), *Chushaku Kokusai Shiho: Dai 1 kan* (*Commentary on Private International Law: Volume 1*) (Yuhikaku, 2011) 574. See Judgment of Tokyo District Court, 31 March 2015, LEX/DB 25525135.

for establishing a claim for fraudulent conveyance.[167] With a view to deterring an abusive choice of law and protecting the creditor, this minor view may well have its justifications. Arguably, however, this minority view also entails certain drawbacks, considering that the location of property may not be easily ascertained (particularly in cases of assets located in several jurisdictions), and that the minority view may yield the same risk of abusive choice of law when the debtor has assigned his or her claim to the third party.

vii. Set-Off

In contrast to common law jurisdictions, set-off is characterised as a substantive law matter under Japanese private international law. Setting-off claims result in the mutual extinction of both claims. In a typical example, plaintiff creditor X makes a principal (or 'passive') claim against defendant debtor Y. By way of defence (an 'active' claim), defendant Y pleads a debt due from plaintiff X to him or her by way of reduction or extinction of the debt claimed by X. At the same time, Y may pursue a counterclaim for the repayment by X of the debt said to be due to the defendant.

AGRAL does not set out a special choice of law rule for set-off. During the drafting of AGRAL, there was discussion whether a special choice of law rule referring to the governing law of the passive claim (principal claim) should be introduced. But the proposal was not adopted, mainly due to difficulties in defining 'set-off' and 'passive claims'. The question of applicable law, therefore, is left for further developments in case law.

To determine the law applicable to set-off, authors traditionally argued that both the law governing the principal claim (passive claim) and the law governing the cross-claim (active claim) ought to apply cumulatively, considering that set-off concerns the destiny of both claims.[168] This cumulative application, however, may well impede set-off by requiring that the conditions for set-off are fulfilled under both laws. Today, a majority of authors take a different position, subjecting set-off solely to the law governing the passive claim. According to this view, the passive claim is the focal point of set-off, as the debtor of the passive claim (ie, defendant Y) declares set-off by using his or her claim against plaintiff X (active claim) to be exempted from his or her obligation, instead of making a liquid payment. Indeed, the cardinal role of set-off is to redeem or extinguish a passive claim. Furthermore, when X becomes insolvent, Y may use the passive claim to ensure the recovery of his or her claim against X (active claim), whereby set-off fulfils the function of securing Y's claim. In this light, it will make sense only to apply the law governing the passive claim.[169]

As for contractual set-off, there seems to be consensus that set-off of this kind is governed by the law designated under the choice of law rules for contract in AGRAL articles 7–9.[170]

[167] eg, Sawaki=Dogauchi (n 1) 243–44.
[168] Tameike (n 16) 413–14.
[169] Aki Kitazawa, 'Sosai' in Yoshiaki Sakurada and Masato Dogauchi (eds), *Chushaku Kokusai Shino: Dai 1 kan* (*Commentary on Private International Law: Volume 1*)(Yuhikaku, 2011) 583–84; Sawaki=Dogauchi (n 1) 242.
[170] Kitazawa, 'Sosai' (n 169) 584; Tameike (n 16) 414.

III. Law of Property

A. Governing Law of Property

i. General Rule

Pursuant to AGRAL article 13, rights *in rem* in movable and immovable property and other rights requiring registration[171] are subject to the law of the country in which the property is situated (*lex rei sitae*).[172] The legislature set out this provision by taking over *Horei* article 10 without adding any changes.[173] It was considered whether to introduce special rules for *res in transitu*, rights *in rem* on ships and aircraft, effects of rights *in rem* on securities and bills of lading, and security rights.[174] However, the legislature ended up deciding not to adopt these proposals for lack of consensus in court practice or academic opinion. A proposal for introducing a general escape clause[175] was also rejected for fear of compromising legal certainty.[176]

As is evident from its wording, AGRAL article 13(1) does not differentiate between movable and immovable property and refers rights *in rem* in both types of property to the *lex rei sitae*. This choice of law rule is based on the characteristics of property law, namely, the direct and exclusive disposition by the owner, the *erga ommnes* effects of the right, and a *numerus clausus* of the rights *in rem*. Such a unified reference to the *lex situs* makes redundant the characterisation between movable and immovable property at the choice of law level.

a. *Res in transitu*

Some specific issues may arise from movable property. When it comes to movable property in transit (for instance, goods being transported on international trains or ships sailing through an international strait) (so-called, *res in transitu*), a fixed and long-term situs of the property normally cannot be ascertained, as the transport keeps moving towards its destination and may often cross borders. While there have not been any court decisions on what law should govern the rights *in rem* in movable property in transit, the prevailing view refers to the law of the state of destination, which is presumably a stable place of situation in the future and the only material connection with the transaction, whereas the place of dispatch has lost its connection with the movable property. In exceptional circumstances, where an actual location of the movable property can be ascertained in a specific state (for instance, where the property is in storage), the law of that state ought to apply.[177]

[171] For instance, a right of redemption of immovable property (CC article 581) and a lease of immovable property (CC article 605).
[172] For intellectual property, see section IV.
[173] Koide (n 31) 163.
[174] Minutes of 8th and 18th Meetings (AGRAL).
[175] Interim Draft (AGRAL) 97 (No 6); see also *Hosoku Setsumei* (AGRAL) 171–78.
[176] Minutes of 26th Meeting (AGRAL).
[177] Sakurada, *Kokusai Shiho* (*Private International Law*) (n 1) 205; Sawaki=Dogauchi (n 1) 248.

When movable property is loaded onto transport by sea, a bill of lading is normally issued. Such document represents a right to seek the surrender of the property based on the transportation contract. Further, it is widely acknowledged that the delivery of the document is regarded as that of the property itself, resulting in such document having proprietary effect. With the document, therefore, the holder may dispose of the subject property of the bill. Looking at this proprietary effect, many commentators have taken the view that dispositions of that property should be governed by the law of the place where the bill of lading is situated.[178] According to this approach, that law will determine whether and under what circumstances the holder can dispose of the underlying property by delivering the bill of lading. However, a bill of lading does not represent the property itself, but simply a right to claim the surrender of the property based on the transportation contract. In this light, rights *in rem* in movable property shown in the bill of landing should always be governed by the law governing the property itself (or by the law of the destination, when the property is in transit).[179] Issuing a bill of lading itself and its contractual effects are subject to the law governing the transportation contract in accordance with AGRAL articles 7–10 (for instance, a claim of the holder against the carrier to seek the return of the property).[180] To the contrary, assignability of a bill of lading and the requirements for its disposition are subject to the law of the state in which the bill of lading is located.[181]

b. Means of Transport

Insofar as rights *in rem* on means of transport such as ships, aircraft and trains are concerned, it is often difficult to refer those rights to a *lex situs* because such transport may continually move and change their situs. Thus, Japanese courts have referred these matters to the law of the flag (the state under whose protection a ship is registered) or law of the state of registration.[182] Where the state of the flag and that of the registration are not identical (for instance, where, in the case of a demise charter, the charterer puts up a flag of a different state from the state of registration), it should be governed by the latter law, on the ground that the registration reflects the legal relationship *in rem* and is more permanent than the flag.

Rights *in rem* in vehicles were traditionally governed by the law of the state of registration. However, the Supreme Court in 2002 adopted a different approach. According to this, the law applicable to rights *in rem* in vehicles may differ, depending on whether the vehicle is legally and technically roadworthy.[183] If the vehicle is roadworthy, rights *in rem* are governed by the law of the home country because the vehicle can freely cross borders. If not roadworthy, such rights are governed by the law of the state in which the vehicle is

[178] Tameike (n 16) 343; Yamada, *Kokusai Shiho* (n 16) 311.
[179] Nishitani, '§ 26: Internationales Privat- und Zivilverfahrensrecht' (n 32) 1232; Sawaki=Dogauchi (n 1) 248.
[180] Takakuwa/Business (n 72) 132.
[181] ibid 132.
[182] For instance, Judgment of Yamaguchi District Court, Yanai Branch, 26 June 1967, *Kaminshu* 18(5–6), 711; Decision of Akita District Court, 23 January 1971, *Kaminshu* 22(1–2), 52; Judgment of Matsuyama District Court, 8 November 1994, HJ 1549, 109.
[183] Judgment of Supreme Court, 29 October 2002, 56(8) *Minshu* 1964.

physically situated. It is, however, doubtful whether such a distinction is appropriate. The distinction is rooted in substantive law (ie, the roadworthiness of the vehicle under administrative law) and no uniform criterion is provided at the choice of law level. Besides, there is no worldwide established registration system reflecting the ownership and security rights in vehicles, unlike ships and aircraft. Further, particularly in Europe, ordinary people or consumers often use vehicles for daily purposes, freely cross borders and sell or purchase vehicles, regardless of whether and where the vehicle is registered. Thus, the place of registration is not necessarily closely connected with the parties or transactions. With a view to ensuring legal certainty and predictability, rights *in rem* in a vehicle should generally be governed by the law of the state in which it is actually situated. Only in a case of vehicles in transit should the law of the home country apply.

c. Securities Held with an Intermediary

As for securities held with an intermediary there exists no special choice of law rule in Japan. Nor is Japan party to the Convention of 5 July 2006 on the Law Applicable to Certain Rights in Respect of Securities held with an Intermediary (Hague Securities Convention). There has been one case in which the law governing the transfer of rights in respect of securities held with an intermediary came into question.[184] This case concerned a bond with warrant in foreign currency which had been purchased by a Japanese investor (the plaintiff) from a Japanese securities company (the defendant). The plaintiff deposited the bond with Euroclear (a Belgian-based financial services company) via the defendant. The plaintiff brought a claim seeking reimbursement of the amount paid after the deduction of cross-trades. The plaintiff contended that it had terminated the contract by reason of the defendant's failure to deliver the stock warrant to the plaintiff, which allegedly amounted to non-performance by the defendant of its contractual obligations. The Yamagata District Court characterised this claim as concerning the effects of the contract, not as an issue of rights *in rem*. On this basis, the issue was held to be subject to the law governing the sale and purchase contract, not the *lex situs* of the bond (in this case, Belgian law).

B. Rights *in rem*

The existence, contents and effects of all rights *in rem* (including ownership, possessory rights, usufruct and leasehold) in movable and immovable property are governed by the law of the respective situs in accordance with AGRAL article 13(1).

Claims based on rights *in rem* are also subject to that law. Nevertheless, it is debatable whether a damages claim relating to a claim based on rights *in rem* such as one to reclaim the purchase price or to seek reimbursement of an expense is subject to the law applicable to rights *in rem* or is to be separately characterised as a non-contractual claim.[185]

[184] Judgment of Yamagata District Court, Sakata Branch, 11 November 1999, *Kinsho* 1106, 62; Judgment of Sendai High Court, Akita Branch, 4 October 2000, *Kinsho* 1098, 45.

[185] Judgment of Osaka District Court, 12 April 1960, *Kaminshu* 11(4), 817. Also, Sawaki=Dogauchi (n 1) 246.

The prevailing view is that such claims relating to rights *in rem* ought to be characterised depending on its respective nature.[186] For instance, where a plaintiff brings a claim seeking damages based on the neighbouring relationship such as a neighbour's right to use or pass the plaintiff's land, this claim should be subject to the *lex situs* as such a claim presupposes the existence of the proprietary right and is closely connected to such rights. On the other hand, where a plaintiff brings a claim seeking damages on the ground that a good has perished due to negligence of its possessor, this claim should be subject to the choice of law rule in torts, because such a claim is intended simply to seek compensation, not to recover the possession of the good.

C. Security Rights

With regard to security rights, there has traditionally been a distinction drawn between contractual and statutory security rights. When it comes to contractual security rights such as pledge and mortgage, there is a consensus that the formation and effects of such security rights are subject to the law of the situs.[187] Since the claim for which security has been granted is not directly related to the contractual right to exercise a security, the law governing the underlying claim should not be applied cumulatively.[188]

As for statutory security rights such as rights of retention and statutory liens, it is unclear whether the law applicable to the claim giving rise to the security is to be applied in addition to the law governing the right, that is, whether there should be a cumulative application. In the past, the Great Court of Cassation has held that a right of retention was governed by the law of the situs of the thing against which the right of retention was being exercised.[189] But contemporary court practice[190] and the prevailing view assert that, in addition to the law governing the right of retention, the law applicable to the underlying claim giving rise to a statutory security right ought to be applied cumulatively, because a statutory right to retain a thing pending (say) the performance by the debtor of some obligation has been created by the legislature to particularly secure the performance by the debtor of his or her obligation. In a recent case involving a lien on an insurance policy, the Tokyo High Court followed the prevailing view and cumulatively applied the law of the situs of the insurance policy and the law giving rise to the security right. The reasoning was that although the statutory

[186] Sakurada, *Kokusai Shiho* (*Private International Law*) (n 1) 206; Tameike (n 16) 336; Yamada, *Kokusai Shiho* (n 16) 297–98.

[187] Sakurada, *Kokusai Shiho* (*Private International Law*) (n 1) 208; Sawaki=Dogauchi (n 1) 249; Keisuke Takeshita, 'Article 13 (Bukken oyobi Sonota no Toki wo subeki Kenri)' in Yoshiaki Sakurada and Masato Dogauchi (eds), *Chushaku Kokusai Shiho: Dai 1 kan* (*Commentary on Private International Law: Volume 1*) (Yuhikaku, 2011) 382.

[188] Sakurada, *Kokusai Shiho* (*Private International Law*) (n 1) 208.

[189] Judgment of Great Court of Cassation, 15 September 1936, *Shinbun* 4033, 16.

[190] Judgment of Yamaguchi District Court, Yanai Branch, 26 June 1967, *Kaminshu* 18(5–6), 711; Decision of Akita District Court, 23 January 1971, *Kaminshu* 22(1–2), 52; Judgment of Tokyo District Court, 29 January 1976, *Kaminshu* 27(1–4), 23; Decision of Takamatsu High Court, 30 April 1985, HT 561, 150; Decision of Hiroshima High Court, 9 March 1987, HJ 1233, 83. But, some courts have followed the approach of the Great Court of Cassation (Decision of Kobe District Court, 2 September 1959, *Kaminshu* 10(9), 1849; Judgment of Hiroshima District Court, 27 April 1970, *Kaminshu* 21(3–4), 607), while others have applied the *lex fori* (Decision of Tokyo District Court, 18 August 1991, HJ 1402, 91; Decision of Tokyo District Court, 15 December 1992, HT 811, 229).

security right was a right *in rem*, it was a special right established by legislation to secure certain types of underlying claim and so must also be validated by the law governing the underlying claim.[191]

Insofar as statutory security rights against ships (maritime liens) are concerned, court practice and the prevailing view have been that it should be governed by the law of the ship's flag (ie, the law of registration) as the law of the situs and the law governing the maritime claim that has grounded the lien.[192] However, a growing number of commentators are of the opinion that, contrary to the currently prevailing view, statutory security rights are intended to protect creditors, not claims. Consequently, there may be little or no connection between a statutory security and the underlying claim for which it serves as collateral. If so, it should be sufficient to refer the formation and validity of a statutory security right over a thing to the law governing such right, namely, the law of the situs.[193] If this approach is adopted, there would be no need to differentiate contractual from statutory security rights, since both rights will simply be subject to the law of the situs.

Moreover, it is widely acknowledged that, since it is difficult to apply several laws to the effects of a statutory security right, the latter should only be governed by the law applicable to rights *in rem* (ie, the *lex situs*). This will ensure that priorities are handled in a uniform way.[194]

D. Acquisition and Loss of Rights *in rem*

Pursuant to AGRAL article 13(2), the acquisition and loss of rights *in rem* are governed by the law of the state in which the object is or was situated at the time when such rights were acquired or lost. A person's legal capacity for the act of disposal is not governed by the *lex situs*, but by his or her national law or, alternatively, the law of the place where the act is done as designated by AGRAL article 4. To be formally valid, pursuant to article 10(5), acquisition and loss of rights *in rem* must satisfy the formal requirements of the law governing rights *in rem*. Other questions over the disposition of property, for instance, whether ownership in property can be transferred to another by contractual agreement or by the delivery or registration of the property, are governed by the law applicable to the right *in rem*. To the contrary, the validity of the underlying transaction and rights and obligations that arise from that transaction are governed by the law applicable to such transaction.[195]

[191] Decision of Tokyo High Court, 30 June 2017, HT 1446, 93.

[192] See, cases cited in n 135. Also, Takeshita (n 187) 382–84. Considering that ships continuously change their location and maritime liens on ships are intended to secure certain claims (including the costs of foreclosure auctions, salvage costs and necessary expenses for continuing with a voyage), some commentators have expressed various views on whether maritime liens should be subject to the law governing the secured claims alone, the law of the ship's actual location (instead of the law of the ship's flag), or the *lex fori*.

[193] Sawaki=Dogauchi (n 1) 249.

[194] Decision of Hiroshima High Court, 9 March 1987, HJ 1233, 83. Also, Sakurada, *Kokusai Shiho* (*Private International Law*) (n 1) 210–11; Tameike (n 16) 338–39; Yamada, *Kokusai Shiho* (n 16) 296; Sawaki=Dogauchi (n 1) 249.

[195] Sakurada, *Kokusai Shiho* (*Private International Law*) (n 1) 213; Tameike (n 16) 340–41; Yamada, *Kokusai Shiho* (n 16) 301–02.

The period and other requirements for acquisitive prescription (including possession, good faith and the effects of interruption of possession) are governed by the law of the state in which the object is situated at the time of its alleged acquisition by prescription. Where the property's situs changes, the requirements for acquisitive prescription are subject to the law of the place where the property is currently situated, including whether the length of possession in other places can be combined with the length of possession in the latest situs.[196]

E. Expropriation

With regard to expropriation, the question arises as to how the effects of an expropriation by a foreign state may be dealt with in the forum state. There has been only one case in Japan. The case concerned the effect of the 1951 oil nationalisation order issued by the Iranian government in respect of the oil installation of a British company, whose equipment and oil had been confiscated and transferred to an Iranian state-owned company. After a Japanese company purchased oil from the Iranian company, transported it to and stored it in Yokohama, Japan, the British company sought before the Tokyo District Court provisional measures for an injunction of sales of the oil. Upon appeal, the Tokyo High Court held that the effects of the Iranian confiscation order were subject to the law of the situs as designated by *Horei* article 10 (currently, AGRAL article 13), that is, the issue is to be handled within the framework of the law applicable to rights *in rem* in the oil installation (in the case, Iranian law).[197]

Most scholars in Japan today, however, argue that such effects of a foreign confiscation order should not be subsumed under the application of the *lex rei sitae* designated by the traditional choice of law rule. Rather, they contend analysing the effects of a foreign confiscation order separately in terms of the recognition of foreign acts of state.[198] The expropriation by a foreign state is incidental to, but independent of the question of ownership of the property. While the validity of foreign acts of state within the territory of that state can generally not be questioned by the Japanese courts as a matter of public international law, the effects of a foreign expropriation need to be examined, to the extent that they affect the outcome of private law disputes over the ownership of the property. Some authors draw a parallel between the recognition of foreign acts of state and the foreign judgment recognition under the Code of Civil Procedure (CCP) article 118. Pursuant to this approach, such requirements as international prescriptive jurisdiction, due process and public policy (especially in relation to the payment of fair compensation) ought to be assessed *mutatis mutandis* by the Japanese courts.

[196] Sakurada, *Kokusai Shiho* (*Private International Law*) (n 1) 203; Tameike (n 16) 344–45; Yamada, *Kokusai Shiho* (n 16) 308.

[197] Judgment of Tokyo High Court, 11 September 1953, *Kominshu* 6(11), 702.

[198] Yokoyama/PIL (n 1) 159; Kazunori Ishiguro, *Gendai Kokusai Shiho: Jou* (*Modern Conflict of Laws in Japan: Volume One*) (University of Tokyo Press, 1986) 471–514; Dai Yokomizo, 'Gaikoku Kokuyuka, Shuyo Sochi no wagakuni ni okeru Koka' (1996) 113(2) *Hogaku Kyokai Zasshi* 326.

IV. Intellectual Property

A. General Remarks

Unlike other jurisdictions, AGRAL does not contain specific choice of law rules for intellectual property rights (IPRs). There was discussion during the drafting of AGRAL whether to adopt a choice of law rule on infringement of IPRs, designating the law of the country of protection.[199] However, that rule was not introduced due to a lack of consensus on how to deal with the public law nature of IPRs, the concern that international treaties already covered choice of law rules for IPRs, and a divergent notion of the 'state providing protection for an IPR'.[200] Therefore, the question on choice of law issues over IPRs is left to case law.

Since IPRs are generally governed by the principle of territoriality and their existence and effects are – in contrast to tangible property – limited to the territory of each country of protection,[201] determining the applicable law requires specific consideration and possible adjustment of the general principles of private international law. In so doing, a distinction needs to be drawn between two types of intellectual property: registered intellectual property (such as patents and trademarks), and non-registered intellectual property (such as copyright and related rights). Various legal issues arise from both types of intellectual property. Those issues can be categorised into three groups: (a) the existence and attributes of IPRs (such as their creation, scope, effects, protection, transferability and extinction); (b) contractual obligations arising out of contracts whose subject is an IPR (such as assignment or licence contracts); and (c) tortious liability for infringement of intellectual property. The applicable law may differ depending on the nature and characteristics of each category of IPR.

i. Registered Intellectual Property Rights

Issues over the existence and attributes of IPRs will depend on whether registration of the IPR is required. As regards registered IPRs such as patents and trademarks, the Paris Convention for the Protection of Industrial Property (PC) article 2 provides for the 'national treatment' of an individual belonging to a Member State of the Union.[202] This means that such individual will enjoy the same protection and remedies against an infringement of their rights as nationals of other Member States. Although foreign academics have bestowed a conflict of laws character to this provision and speak of the *lex loci protectionis*,

[199] Koide (n 31) 229–32.

[200] *Hosoku Setsumei* (AGRAL) 200–01; Koide (n 31) 230; Yuko Nishitani, 'Die Reform des internationalen Privatrechts in Japan' (2007) *IPRax* 556.

[201] The Supreme Court defined the 'territorial principle' as follows: '[T]he Principle of Territoriality as regards patents means that the existence, transfer, effect, etc of each country's patent are governed only by that country's law, and the patent is effective only in the territory of that country'. Judgment of Supreme Court, 1 July 1997, *Minshu* 51(6), 2299 ((1998) 41 *JAIL* 100) (*BBS* case).

[202] ie, the Union of member states to the Paris Convention for the Protection of Industrial Property of 20 March 1883, as revised at Brussels on 14 December 1900, at Washington on 2 June 1911, at the Hague on 6 November 1925, at London on 2 June 1934, at Lisbon on 31 October 3 1958 and at Stockholm on 14 July 1967.

a majority of Japanese conflicts scholars regard the provision as merely a rule of law relating to foreigners and not determinative of the governing law.[203] However, considering that patents as well as trademarks are conferred by an act of state, it makes sense, as a matter of Japanese choice of law to subject their existence, validity and effects to the law of the country where they are registered, that is, the *lex loci protectionis* (*cf* PC articles 4*bis* and 6(3)). In a case involving the effects of patent rights, the Supreme Court held:

> Regarding the law governing the validity [effects] of a patent right ... based on *jori*, it is appropriate to construe that it should be in accordance with the laws of the country having the closest bearing on the relevant patent right, namely, the county where the patent right was registered.[204]

The Court made clear its position of subjecting the effects of patent rights to a choice of law rule. Some commentators have emphasised the fact that patents are conferred by an act of state, suggesting that the existence, validity and effects of patent rights should not be subject to a choice of law rule at all. Instead, they say that IPRs should be handled within the framework of the recognition of foreign sovereign acts. Alternatively, they contend that the Japanese law of patents should be applied as overriding mandatory rules to IPR questions involving foreign elements.[205] Nevertheless, the likelihood is that, in keeping with the Supreme Court decision, Japanese courts will determine matters such as the effects of IPRs in accordance with the *lex loci protectionis*.

ii. Copyright and Other Non-Registered Rights

When it comes to copyright, the Berne Convention for the Protection of Literary and Artistic Works (BC) article 5(2) stipulates that 'apart from the provisions of the Convention, the extent of protection, as well as the means of redress afforded to the author to protect his rights, shall be governed exclusively by the laws of the country where protection is claimed'. In Japan, it remains uncertain whether the article is a choice of law rule or merely a law which may affect foreign nationals, but does not determine governing law. Some lower courts and many commentators understand the provision as a choice of law rule designating the *lex loci protectionis*,[206] while other academics deny the choice of law character of article 5(2), since BC provides only for the 'national treatment' and minimum standards of copyright protection.[207] Despite this, since copyright protection is provided by the law of each state within the Berne Union, the existence, content, effects and duration of copyright are to be determined by the relevant *lex loci protectionis* as a matter of Japanese choice of law.[208] There are similar provisions in BC articles 7(8), 10-2(1) and 14-2(2)(a). Although the

[203] eg, Shoichi Kidana, *Kokusai Kogyo Shoyukenho no Kenkyu* (Nihon Hyoronsha, 1989) 85–91.

[204] Judgment of Supreme Court, 26 September 2002, *Minshu* 56(7), 1551 ((2002) 45 *JAIL* 175).

[205] See, Masato Dogauchi, 'Chiteki Zaisanken' in Yoshiaki Sakurada and Masato Dogauchi (eds), *Chushaku Kokusai Shiho: Dai 1 kan* (*Commentary on Private International Law: Volume 1*) (Yuhikaku, 2011) 629–30.

[206] eg, Judgment of Tokyo District Court, 31 May 2004, HJ 1936, 140 ((2006) 49 *JAIL* 176); Judgment of Tokyo District Court, 14 December 2007, 2007WLJPCA12149002; Judgment of Tokyo District Court, 30 April 2009, HJ 2061, 83. Also Sawaki=Dogauchi (n 1) 254–55.

[207] eg, Shoichi Kidana, *Kokusai Chiteki Zaisan Ho* (Nippon Hyoronsha, 2009) 386.

[208] eg, Yasuto Komada, 'Chosakuken wo meguru Kokusai Saiban Kankatsu oyobi Junkyoho ni tsuite' (2004) 6 *JYPIL* 73.

understanding among scholars of these provisions is likewise split, it is submitted that the relevant applicable law is the *lex loci protectionis*.

As regards initial ownership of copyright, BC stipulates the application of the *lex loci protectionis* only with regard to initial ownership of cinematographic works (article 14*bis* (2)). Therefore, initial ownership of other works will be governed by the law designated by recourse to *jori*. On this, there have been a number of views expressed as to applicable law.[209] Among the suggested candidates are: the *lex loci protectionis* of each state and the law of the work's source country (*lex originis*) within the meaning of BC article 5(4) (ie, the law of the country of first publication or, for unpublished work, the law of the country in which the author is domiciled or of which he is a national).[210] Since copyright arises once the work is created and does not involve any act of state, the initial ownership should be uniformly determined across states. The designation of the *lex originis* has the advantage of avoiding limping legal relations among different protecting countries. Arguably, it is also in line with BC article 14*bis*(2).

On the other hand, the initial ownership of copyright with regard to works created by an employee within his or her duties requires different considerations. As a matter of Japanese national law, an employer acquires copyright – including moral rights – for work created by an employee (the 'work-for-hire' doctrine), unless the parties have agreed otherwise in the employment contract or service regulation (Copyright Law (CPA) article 15). In this regard, the Tokyo High Court has held that the copyright in an employee's work should be subject to the law applicable to the latter's employment contract.[211] The question of initial ownership is embedded in the relationship between employer and employee and the parties may reasonably determine the latter's remuneration according to which of them acquires initial ownership.[212] Also, 'work-for-hire' is generally a non-mandatory rule and can be deviated from by the parties' agreement to some other regime. In all the Berne Union states, in contrast to patents and trademarks, copyright is acquired instantaneously without any formal requirement upon the mere creation of a work. In those circumstances, it would seem reasonable, to achieve uniformity across states, to characterise work-for-hire as a matter of contract.

iii. Transfer and Licence Contracts and Infringements

As IPRs (in particular, patents) are economically valuable, they are often the subject matter of international trade, typically, in the form or transfer or licence agreements. When IPRs are transferred or licensed to another person, the parties enter into an agreement. In this case, the question is how to determine the law governing such legal relationship. It is widely accepted among Japanese courts that an underlying act (for instance, a transfer agreement) and the attribution of IPRs are to be characterised differently. The contractual

[209] See Dogauchi (n 205) 640–42.

[210] See Yuko Nishitani, 'Intellectual Property in Japanese Private International Law' (2005) 48 *JAIL* 96.

[211] Judgment of Tokyo High Court, 30 May 2001, HT 1797, 131. Some commentators advocate that it should be subject to the *lex loci protectionis*. *cf* Dogauchi (n 205) 639–42.

[212] eg, Nishitani, 'Intellectual Property in Japanese Private International Law' (n 210) 97.

aspects are governed by the choice of law rules for contract in AGRAL articles 7–10, while proprietary aspects such as registration, initial ownership and the requirements for transfer are governed by the *lex loci protectionis*.[213]

a. Employee's Invention

In relation to the transfer or license of a patent right, there has been intense discussion on which law ought to be applied to determine the amount of reasonable remuneration for an employee's invention created in the course of the latter's employment, when the employer is entitled to obtain a patent. The Supreme Court has held that this issue is governed by the law applicable to the underlying contract as designated in *Horei* article 7 (currently, AGRAL article 7).[214] This approach is likely to apply under AGRAL, too. It should be noted, however, that as the special choice of law rules in labour contracts were introduced in AGRAL article 12, the latter conflicts rule will apply where the circumstances in article 12 are satisfied.

With regard to the right to obtain a patent, especially the entitlement to a national (Japanese) or foreign patent in the case of an 'employee's invention', the Supreme Court stated, obiter, that as issues over the right to a patent (including its effects) should be separately analysed from issues over remuneration for the assignment of a patent, the right to obtain a patent should be governed by the law of the place of intended registration on the basis of the territorial principle.[215] As a matter of Japanese law, under PA article 35, all rights stemming from an employee's invention used to belong to an employee as the actual inventor, as in Germany, Austria and the US, whereas all rights belong to the employer in the UK, France, Switzerland and Italy. Since 2015 in Japan, however, the employer can be the original holder of the right to obtain a patent arising out of an employee's invention, when the employer and employee make a prior agreement in this sense (PA article 35(3)). Even if it is not the case, the employer can still obtain *ex lege* a non-exclusive licence in respect of the patent that the employee has acquired (article 35(1)).

When the employee entitles the employer to be the original holder of the right to obtain a patent, transfers the right to obtain a patent to the employer or sets up an exclusive licence on a patent for the employer, the employee has the right to claim a 'reasonable remuneration' (article 35(4)). Prior to the 2004 amendment, the provision on remuneration was generally regarded as a unilateral mandatory rule, since the initial amount agreed by the parties was valid if it was higher than or equal to the appropriate remuneration as determined by the court, but void if it was lower.[216] The court assessed an appropriate remuneration by reference to the profit an employer would make from the invention and the amount of the employer's contribution to the invention. However, after a series of lawsuits

[213] For instance, Judgment of Tokyo High Court, 30 May 2001, HJ 1797, 111; Judgment of Tokyo High Court, 28 May 2003, HJ 1831, 135. Also, Yamada, *Kokusai Shiho* (n 16) 339.

[214] Judgment of Supreme Court, 17 October 2006, *Minshu* 60(8), 2853. Also, Judgment of Intellectual Property High Court, 26 February 2009, HJ 2053, 74. Commentators have expressed different views on whether JPL article 35 should be applied as an overriding mandatory rule.

[215] Judgment of Supreme Court, 17 October 2006, *Minshu* 60(8), 2853. *cf* Kidana, *Kokusai Chiteki Zaisan Ho* (n 207) 478.

[216] See former case law (Judgment of Supreme Court, 22 April 2003, *Minshu* 57(4), 477).

were filed by former employees seeking an appropriate remuneration, the legislature amended PA article 35 in 2004 and 2015 to lower the standards for remuneration and strengthen the employer's position by entering into a prior agreement with the employee, which has been supported by Japanese industry. At present, PA article 35(5) and (6) provide that the initial amount agreed by the parties in their employment contract or employment regulation is held valid, insofar as its standards are reasonable in light of the circumstances of parties' negotiations, disclosure of the standards employed, the hearing of employees etc, considering also the Ministry of Economy, Trade and Industry (METI) guidelines.

With regard to the territorial scope of PA article 35, the Supreme Court has decided that it extends, by way of an analogy, to the right to obtain foreign patents. Accordingly, article 35 determines who has the right to a Japanese or foreign patent (the 'theory of application').[217] Some lower courts (including the second instance in the latter case) have adopted this approach, leading, inter alia, to the following arguments in support of the theory of application. First, the territoriality principle of patents solely applies to the procedure for the grant of a patent and the effects of a patent once granted. But the principle does not extend to the remuneration deriving from the transfer of the right to a foreign patent. Second, there would be no harmonisation with states which treats employee's inventions differently, so that a Japanese employee might be deprived of his or her rights in those jurisdictions. It would be cumbersome for a judge to apply the patent law of each foreign country in that circumstance. Third, the right to a patent is a 'universal right' to be granted to the inventor worldwide, as it exists before the right-holder applies for a patent and acquires an exclusive right over the invention as an intangible property in a certain country.[218]

b. Infringement of Intellectual Property

With the amendment of *Horei* in 2006, detailed conflicts rules on tort were adopted (AGRAL articles 17–22). As earlier mentioned, however, the reform ultimately left out an envisaged special rule on the infringement of IPRs with the law of the country of protection, due to a lack of any uniform understanding as to how that connecting factor should operate. Therefore, it was left for courts to determine how claims based on the infringement of intellectual property should be dealt with.

[217] Judgment of Supreme Court, 17 October 2006, *Minshu* 60(8), 2853. European countries (eg, France, Germany, the UK, Austria, Switzerland) generally subject this issue – together with the characterisation of an employee's invention and remuneration – to the law applicable to labour contracts, even though there are some deviating opinions. Also, article 60 of the European Patent Convention (EPC) subjects the initial entitlement to the law of the place where work is carried out, in order to attain a uniform solution among member states. See Yuko Nishitani, 'Employee's Invention and the Right to Obtain Foreign Patents: Current Trends in Japanese Law from a Comparative Perspective' in Vesna Tomljenovic, Johan A Erauw and Paul Volken (eds), *Liber Memorialis Petar Šarčević: Universalism, Tradition and the Individual* (Sellier, 2006).

[218] eg, Judgment of Tokyo High Court, 29 January 2004, HJ 1848, 25; Judgment of Tokyo District Court, 24 February 2004, HJ 1853, 38 ((2005) 48 *JAIL* 191); Judgment of Tokyo District Court, 27 March 2017, 2017WLJPCA03279007; Judgment of Tokyo District Court, 14 September 2018, 2018WLJPCA09149005. The first instance in that case adopted a different approach, concluding that according to the territorial principle, the existence, transfer and effects of every patent are subject to the law of the respective protecting country and the effects of a patent did not extend beyond its border (Judgment of Tokyo District Court, 29 November 2002, HJ 1807, 53). Some commentators opine that the applicability of PA article 35 to the right to a foreign patent should be dealt with as a matter of overriding mandatory rules.

c. Patent Infringement

On the infringement of patent rights, the Supreme Court decision in the *Card Reader* case[219] must be analysed, as it constitutes – despite some unclarity in its reasonings – a precedent in Japanese case law. In the underlying case, the plaintiff (appellant) X was a Japanese national and former employee of Japanese company Y. Out of X's invention while working for Y, X obtained a US patent, whereas Y acquired a parallel Japanese patent. Y produced machines in Japan, exported them to the US and had them sold by Y's 100 per cent US subsidiary in the US market. X alleged that the defendant (appellee) Y actively induced the infringement of X's US patent. X claimed: (a) an injunctive order prohibiting the production and export of the infringing products, (b) the destruction of the infringing products, and (c) compensation for Y's wrongful act.

The Supreme Court held that X's request for (a) and (b) should not be regarded as tort in nature, on the ground that tort is geared towards the payment of just and fair compensation in the form of damages for harm caused to a victim in the past. X's requests for relief were instead characterised as a question of the effects of X's patent.[220] Since *Horei* did not have an explicit provision on this issue, basing itself on *jori*, the justices referred the questions to US law as the law of the country, in which the patent was registered and which had the closest connection with the patent. According to US patent law (35 USC §271 (b) and §283), claims (a) and (b) should have been granted for Y's infringement. However, the Supreme Court reasoned that this result would unduly expand the effects of US patent law extraterritorially to Japan and would thus contravene the territoriality principle. Consequently, the application of US patent law was excluded as violating Japanese public policy under *Horei* article 33 (currently, AGRAL article 42).

The Supreme Court further found that claim (c) for damages was a civil law-based remedy against infringement of private property. Thus, that claim should be characterised as a tort to be governed by the *lex loci delicti* under *Horei* article 11(1) (currently, AGRAL article 17 with modifications). The *locus delicti* was held to be the US as the place where the inducement had been committed and where the resultant harm had been sustained. In this connection, the Court observed that: (i) the result of Y's wrong came about in the US, and (ii) Y could have foreseen the application of US law when it had exported its products to the US and had them sold there by its US subsidiary. Under US patent law (35 USC §271 (b) and §284), Y would have been liable for compensatory damages. But the Court reasoned that Japanese law also had to be cumulatively applied under *Horei* article 11(2) (now AGRAL article 22) and, since Japanese patent law (unlike US law) did not have a remedy for the infringement of a Japanese patent committed outside the territory of Japan, X would not be

[219] Judgment of Supreme Court, 26 September 2002, *Minshu* 56(7), 1551. See, eg, Yuko Nishitani, 'Case No 62: Infringement of a US Patent and Applicable Law' in Moritz Bälz, Marc Dernauer, Christopher Heath and Anja Petersen-Padberg (eds), *Business Law in Japan: Cases and Comments. Intellectual Property, Civil, Commercial and International Private Law* (Kluwer Law International, 2012); Shoichi Kidana, 'Private International Law Principles on Intellectual Property: Recent Development of Court Precedents in Japan and Current Characteristics' (2009) 52 *JYIL* 454.

[220] Also, Judgment of Tokyo District Court, 18 February 2015, HJ 2257, 87.

entitled to a remedy against Y. Thus, the Court concluded that none of claims (a), (b) or (c) could be granted.[221]

Following the reasonings of the Supreme Court, claims based on an infringement of IPRs ought to be categorised separately, depending on the remedy sought: claims seeking damages will be subject to the general choice of law rules in tort (ie, AGRAL articles 17–22), while claims seeking other remedies such as an injunction will trigger the law governing the effects of such rights (ie, the law of registration). The rationale for this dual characterisation appears to mirror Japanese substantive law, which treats a claim for an injunction and the prevention of infringing acts as *actio negatoria* and therefore subject to patent law (PA article 100(1) and (2)). In contrast, claims for damages to compensate a loss sustained in the past are classified by Japanese substantive law as tortious in nature (CC article 709).[222]

Such approach, however, contradicts the generally recognised principle that the criteria of characterisation must be found in the conflict of laws itself, independent of substantive law (see chapter one, section IV.C). While it is a matter of substantive law to stipulate the remedies available for particular breaches of rights or interests, patent infringement constitutes a legal phenomenon and the choice of law applicable to it must be decided on the basis of the characteristics of such phenomenon, regardless of the provisions of domestic substantive law. Furthermore, a characterisation based on the remedy sought runs the risk of possibly subjecting the claims to different applicable laws, leading to contradictory results. Comparatively speaking, under Rome II articles 8 and 15, all remedies for the infringement of intellectual property (injunctions to prevent infringement as well as damages) are duly governed by a single law, that is, the law of the country of protection. As at the jurisdictional stage (ie, to determine whether Japan has jurisdiction to hear the case of patent infringement), patent infringement ought to be uniformly characterised as a tort in relation to applicable law.[223] Thus, also in Japan, the law governing the infringement of patents ought to be determined uniformly by pointing to the law of the country of registration (*lex loci protectionis*) (ie, the US law in the *Card Reader* case), regardless of the remedies sought by the party (the legal basis is discussed below). An unacceptable result that may arise by applying the law of the country of registration should be countered by having recourse to public policy (AGRAL article 42).

[221] Justice Fujii, however, delivered a dissenting opinion. With regard to (c), he contended that a cumulative application of Japanese law under *Horei* article 11(2) (AGRAL article 22) means to examine whether the infringement of an equivalent right in Japan would constitute a wrongful act. In his opinion, the existence of the US patent was to be presupposed as an incidental question, even though the patent does not have extraterritorial effect in Japan. Since an active inducement of patent infringement constitutes a solicitation or assistance of a wrongful act according to CC articles 709 and 719(2), Y should have been held liable for damages as a joint tortfeasor.

[222] See, Makiko Takabe, 'Saiko Saibansho Chosakan Kaisetsu' in Hoso Kai (ed), *Saiko Saibansho Hanrei Kaisetsu Heisei 11 (2002) Nendo (Ge)* (Hoso Kai, 2002). Also, Ryu Kojima, Ryo Shimanami and Mari Nagata, 'Applicable Law to Exploitation of Intellectual Property Rights in the Transparency Proposal' in Jürgen Basedow, Toshiyuki Kono and Axel Metzger (eds), *Intellectual Property in the Global Arena* (Mohr Siebeck, 2010). The second instance held that claims (a) and (b) concerning the effects of a patent should be deemed to be matters of public law which would therefore not give rise to conflict of law question. The second instance took the view that claim (c) was tortious in nature. However, once granted and registered, patents can be licensed, assigned or pledged as an intangible property right. Infringement as a dispute between private persons is independent of the administrative procedure of conferring a patent and should consequently be subject to conflicts rules.

[223] Kojima, Shimanami and Nagata (n 222) 186.

In the underlying *Card Reader* case, X arguably could have obtained remedies for damages with regard to the past infringement of X's patent, considering that Y's conduct as an inducement of patent infringement would have qualified as a tort both under US law and Japanese law (AGRAL article 22). Moreover, an injunctive relief of prohibiting Y's export to the US could also have been granted pursuant to US law, even though Y's producing the products in Japan itself was grounded on Y's Japanese patent and therefore lawful under Japanese law.

d. Trademark Infringement

With regard to trademark, there has been one case involving damages claims based on the infringement of trademark in the People's Republic of China, Hong Kong and Taiwan.[224] The Tokyo District Court subjected those claims to the choice of law rules for torts in *Horei* article 11 (currently, AGRAL article 17 with modifications), applying the relevant choice of law rule to each infringement ('mosaic theory'). The Court applied Japanese law cumulatively in accordance with *Horei* article 11(2) and (3) (currently, AGRAL article 22). As the Court did not deal with the injunction claims for infringement of trademark, it is unclear whether such claims were subjected to the choice of law rules for torts in parallel with damages claims. If the principles in the *Card Reader* case apply here, the injunction claims for infringement of trademark should have been characterised as the effects of the trademark and governed by the *lex loci protectionis*. However, as argued above, those claims should be uniformly characterised as a tort and referred to a single law (the legal basis is discussed below).

e. Copyright Infringement

In the cases of the infringement of copyright (non-registered intellectual property), the approach may be different, depending on how the rules in BC articles 5(2), 6-2(3) and 10-2(1) and (2) are to be understood.[225] If those rules are regarded as choice of law rules, the *lex loci protectionis* applies pursuant to these rules. If not, the infringement of copyright will be governed by the general choice of law rules in tort or *jori*.

The lower courts have adopted the former approach. Again, as in the cases of patents, those courts have dealt with claims seeking injunctions and claims seeking damages differently, holding that while damages claims are subject to *Horei* article 11 (currently, AGRAL article 17 with modifications), injunction claims for infringement of copyright or an author's moral rights are governed by the *lex loci protectionis* by reason of BC articles 5(2) or 6(3).[226]

[224] Judgment of Tokyo District Court, 25 March 2011, 2011WLJPCA03258007.

[225] Matters that are not covered by those provisions, if any, will be subject to relevant choice of law rules or *jori*.

[226] eg, Judgment of Tokyo District Court, 31 May 2004, HJ 1936, 140 ((2006) 49 *JAIL* 176) (Tokyo High Court affirmed; Judgment of Tokyo High Court, 9 December 2004, HJ 1936, 140); Decision of Tokyo District Court, 11 July 2006, HJ 1933, 68; Judgment of Tokyo District Court, 29 August 2007, HJ 2021, 108; Judgment of Intellectual Property High Court, 28 February 2008, HJ 2021, 96; Judgment of Tokyo District Court, 14 December 2007, 2007WLJPCA12149002; Judgment of Intellectual Property High Court, 24 December 2008, 2008WLJPCA12249017; Judgment of Tokyo District Court, 30 April 2009, HJ 2061, 83; Judgment of Intellectual Property High Court, 28 October 2009, HJ 2061, 75; Judgment of Tokyo District Court, 2 March 2011, 2011WLJPCA03029001; Judgment of Intellectual Property High Court, 28 November 2011, 2011WLJPCA11289002;

A lower court has also held that the duration of protection was governed by the *lex loci protectionis* in accordance with BC article 7(8).[227] Although it is necessary to abide by the rules of the Berne Convention, the legislative history of the Berne Convention does not clearly indicate the choice of law character of BC articles 5 and 7. In this respect, the law governing the infringement of copyright should be a matter for Japanese private international law. For the reasons mentioned above, this yields a uniformly characterisation of copyright infringement as a tort, pointing to a single law, that is, the *lex loci protectionis* (the legal basis is discussed below).

Infringement of copyright presupposes that the copyright exists and can enjoy protection. As a matter of Japanese law, according to CPA article 6, only those works falling under one of the following classes are entitled to protection: (a) works of Japanese nationals ('Japanese nationals' include legal persons established under the laws and regulations of Japan and those who have their principal offices in Japan); (b) works first published in Japan, including those first published outside Japan and thereafter published in Japan within 30 days from the date from their first publication; (c) works in addition to those listed in the preceding two items, with respect to which Japan has an obligation to grant protection under an international treaty.

In this context, there is an important question: whether under BC article 3(1)(a) Japan is obliged to grant protection to works of nationals of a state not recognised by Japan. In a case on copyright in a cinematographic work produced in North Korea, the Supreme Court held that Japan did not incur the obligation to grant copyright protection to the work of North Korea, reasoning:

> In general, where a country not recognized as a State has acceded to a multilateral treaty which is already effective in relation to Japan, such country's accession to the treaty cannot be deemed to immediately give rise to the relationship between Japan and said country not recognized as a State in terms of rights and obligations under the treaty, unless the obligation to be assumed under the treaty by its contracting countries is an obligation under general international law which has universal value, so it is appropriate to construe that Japan has a choice of whether or not to give rise to the relationship with said country not recognized as a State in terms of rights and obligations under the treaty.
>
> In the case of BC, while protecting works whose authors are nationals of the countries of the Union (article 3(1)(a)), it does not generally protect works whose authors are nationals of countries outside the Union, but it protects the latter works only in the case where they were first published in one of the countries of the Union or simultaneously in a country outside the Union and in a country of the Union (article 3(1)(b)). Thus, BC aims to ensure protection of works on the basis of the framework of States in the capacity of the countries of the Union, and it does not intend to require the countries of the Union to assume any obligation under general international law which has universal value.

Judgment of Tokyo District Court, 31 May 2012, 2012WLJPCA05319003 (only for damages claims); Judgment of Tokyo District Court, 11 July 2012, HJ 2175, 98; Judgment of Tokyo District Court, 21 December 2012, HT 1408, 367 (only for damages claims); Judgment of Tokyo District Court, 17 May 2013, HT 1395, 319 (only for damages claims); Judgment of Tokyo District Court, 20 December 2013, 2013WLJPCA12209001 (only for damages claims); Judgment of Tokyo District Court, 5 September 2014, 2014WLJPCA09058017 (only for damages claims). There have been claims before some lower courts seeking non-monetary remedy such as injunction or an apology advertisement pursuant to AGRAL article 17 (Judgment of Tokyo District Court, 25 March 2013, 2013WLJPCA03259017; Judgment of Tokyo District Court, 29 September 2016, 2016WLJPCA09289009).

[227] Decision of Tokyo District Court, 11 July 2006, HJ 1933, 68.

> According to the facts mentioned above, when North Korea, a country not recognized as a State, acceded to BC, which was already effective in relation to Japan, the government of Japan did not give public notice to announce that BC took effect in relation to North Korea. MOFA and the Ministry of Education, Culture, Sports, Science and Technology have presented the view that they do not consider that Japan has the obligation to grant protection under BC with respect to works of nationals of North Korea as works of nationals of a country of the Union. In view of these facts, Japan takes the position that it has no relationship with North Korea, a country not recognized as a State, in terms of rights and obligations under BC, irrespective of whether North Korea has acceded to the Convention or not.[228]

It follows that works from non-recognised states are unlikely to enjoy copyright protection in Japan.

f. Legal Basis *de lege lata*

As mentioned above, court practice tends to deal with claims for the infringement of IPRs under the general choice of law rule in AGRAL article 17, in addition to articles 20 and 21. In AGRAL, however, the general conflicts rule for tort (article 17) and the escape clause (article 20), particularly the factors of common habitual residence and the underlying contractual relationship, focus on a close connection with the parties. Moreover, party autonomy (article 21) enables the parties to realise their private interests disregarding public interest and the fundamental policy of the country of protection. Arguably, these general conflict rules are not adequate to determine the law governing the infringement of IPRs. Notably, IPRs are exclusive rights grounded on the economic and industrial policy of the country concerned, whose validity and effects are confined territorially. Considering their characteristics, an appropriate conflicts rule will be to always point to the law of the country of protection based on *jori* to the exclusion of AGRAL articles 17, 20 and 21. This is actually the conflicts rule envisaged during the legislative process of AGRAL and ultimately discarded for lack of consensus.[229]

g. Specificities of IPRs Infringement on the Internet

The infringement of IPRs may occur on the internet (online infringement). Such cases should also be governed by the *lex loci protectionis* in principle. There may, however, be ubiquitous infringements occurring in numerous jurisdictions. This would mean that in cases of copyright infringement over the internet, the laws of each place of downloading will be applied as the *lex loci protectionis* to the infringement respectively. Some downloading may take place in jurisdictions which may be unidentifiable. The reference to each place of downloading could lead to multiple, perhaps an uncountable or indeterminate, number of governing laws and make the process cumbersome or even impossible for the judge.[230]

[228] Judgment of Supreme Court, 8 December 2011, *Minshu* 65(9), 3275.

[229] Yuko Nishitani, 'Article 17 (Fuho Koi)' in Yoshiaki Sakurada and Masato Dogauchi (eds), *Chushaku Kokusai Shiho: Dai 1 kan (Commentary on Private International Law: Volume 1)* (Yuhikaku, 2011) 453–56. Also, Nakanishi, 'Torts' (n 88) 65.

[230] A judge must apply foreign law *ex officio* in Japan. The case law even grants an appeal to the Supreme Court when lower courts wrongly interpret and apply a foreign law. Judgment of Supreme Court, 2 July 1981, *Minshu* 35(5), 881.

Considering that the downloading can also occur in a place fortuitously, reference should be made to the marketplaces that are significantly impacted by the alleged conduct and to which the infringer directed his activities (the market impact rule).[231]

Notably, as for copyright infringement, even if it is perpetrated over the internet, there will often be only one or a limited number of impacted marketplaces. For instance, in a case involving the infringement of copyright through peer-to-peer music filesharing (MP3),[232] the service provider was held liable. The defendant service provider and targeted users were Japanese, the programme was operated in Japanese, and only the host server was in Canada. In those circumstances, the traditional *lex loci protectionis* approach remains feasible and reasonable, since it leads to the application of Japanese law as the law of the protecting country, where the copyright infringement in question was concentrated.

On the other hand, where there are multiple, uncountable, or even unidentifiable marketplaces that are significantly impacted by a copyright infringement, reference may be made to a marketplace in which the infringement is deemed to be concentrated. The primary connecting factor would be the IPR holder's habitual residence or the latter's place of business where the harm is sustained. If it does not lie in one of the countries of downloading, the 'most significant relationship' test may apply by considering different elements, such as language and content of the website, the service provider's place of business and the server's location.

When it comes to the infringement of patent or trademark, the *lex loci protectionis* should govern the infringement, insofar as it has had an impact on the marketplace of that country. Since trademark and patent are, unlike copyright, registered in each country of protection and the number of impacted marketplaces is usually limited, an exceptional reference to a single connecting factor will seldom be required as compared with a case of copyright infringement.

V. Family and Succession Law

A. Marriage

i. Substantive Validity

In respect of celebrating marriage, there are two categories of choice of law issues to be considered. (i) The first issue is on the substantive requirements the parties must satisfy to marry legally. This category includes whether the prospective spouses each have capacity to marry, whether there exists consent between the parties, and whether there is any impediment to a marriage (such as the extent to which consanguineous marriage is allowed and whether a prospective bride is prohibited from remarrying for a certain period of time) (see this section). (ii) The second issue concerns the formality that the prospective spouses must observe. This category extends to whether it is necessary to go through a specific ritual

[231] Nishitani, 'Article 17 (Fuho Koi)' (n 229) 456.

[232] Judgment of Tokyo District Court, 9 April 2002, HJ 1780, 25.

or ceremony and whether it is necessary to submit a notification of marriage to the public authorities (see section V.A.ii).

As regards (i) the first category of substantive validity, AGRAL article 24(1) adopts the nationality of each party as the connecting factor (ie, nationality principle). It stipulates that 'the formation of a marriage shall be governed by the national law of each party', referring the substantive requirements to the national law of each party. When, for example, a German national and a Japanese national celebrate marriage, German law and Japanese law are applied respectively.

Notably, substantive requirements of marriage are classified into two categories: 'unilateral requirements' that only concern the respective party, and 'bilateral requirements' that need to be fulfilled by both parties.[233] Most substantive requirements of marriage constitute a unilateral requirement (such as minimum age, consent and mental capacity, absence of mistake, fraud or duress etc), which is governed by the national law of each party in a distributive way. Insofar as unilateral requirements are concerned, in the above example, German law is solely applied to the German party, and Japanese law solely to the Japanese party. On the other hand, some substantive requirements are conceived as bilateral involving both parties (such as prohibition of bigamy and incest). In this case, both parties are required to fulfil conditions of both national laws cumulatively. In the above example, the German party needs to satisfy the bilateral requirements of both German law and Japanese law, and the Japanese party likewise.

It is disputed among authors how to delineate between unilateral and bilateral requirements. Although some authors seek criteria in substantive law, most authors look for a reasonable standard in private international law, as this question is a presupposition of determining the applicable law. As a matter of interpretation, only those substantive requirements that are of fundamental importance and that both parties are obliged to fulfil should qualify as 'bilateral'. This is arguably the case with a waiting period for remarriage and prohibition of marriage based on religious grounds,[234] in addition to prohibition of bigamy and incest mentioned above.

The question of whether a marriage can be revoked or is null and void is determined by the respective law applicable to the substantive requirements. When applying national laws of the parties in a distributive or cumulative way, the stricter law prevails.[235] Accordingly, if a marriage can be annulled under the law of the prospective bridegroom, but it is null and void under the law of the prospective bride, the latter applies and holds the marriage null and void.

ii. Formal Validity

With regard to formal validity (formal requirements) of marriage, AGRAL article 24(2) and (3) set out choice of law rules. Under Japanese law (Family Register Act (FRA)

[233] Tameike (n 16) 422; Yamada, *Kokusai Shiho* (n 16) 409. *cf* Sawaki=Dogauchi (n 1) 88–89; Dai Yokomizo, 'Article 24 (Kon'in no Seiritsu oyobi Hoshiki)' in Yoshiaki Sakurada and Masato Dogauchi (eds), *Chushaku Kokusai Shiho: Dai 2 kan* (*Commentary on Private International Law: Volume 2*) (Yuhikaku, 2011) 13–14.

[234] Prohibition of marriage on religious grounds under foreign national law may well run counter to public policy in light of freedom of conscience and religion under the Constitution of Japan article 20. Judgment of Tokyo District Court, 29 March 1991, *Kagetsu* 45(3), 67; Sakurada, *Kokusai Shiho* (*Private International Law*) (n 1) 272.

[235] Judgment of Tokyo High Court, 25 April 2007, *Kagetsu* 59(10), 42.

article 74),[236] to marry legally, the prospective spouses are required to submit a marriage notification to the family registrar. The notification must be accompanied by the signatures of two adult witnesses (CC article 739(2)).[237] Once the notification is accepted by the family registrar, a marriage is deemed to be legally concluded.

AGRAL article 24(2) adopts the principle of *locus regit actum*, referring the formal validity of a marriage to the law of the place where the marriage is celebrated (*lex loci celebrationis*).

However, if the *lex loci celebrationis* is always rigidly applied as under *Horei* article 13, it would hamper celebration of marriage between prospective spouses in a country where it is required to abide by a certain customary or religious ritual. Moreover, a strict reference to the *lex loci celebrationis* would not be justified when the place of celebration only has a fortuitous connection (eg, tourist marriage in Nevada or Hawaii), or when the marriage is null and void under the *lex loci celebrationis*, but has validly been celebrated under the national law of the parties. Such a limping marriage would prejudice the parties' foreseeability, particularly when they discover it years later (for instance, at the succession of one spouse). Consequently, the 1989 reform of *Horei* introduced in article 13(3) an alternative reference to the national law of the parties, which is now AGRAL article 24(3). Pursuant to this provision, a marriage is deemed to be valid if it complies either with the *lex loci celebrationis* or the national law of either party.[238] As a result, in cases of a marriage between a German and a Swiss national in Japan, the marriage only needs to meet the formal requirements of either German or Swiss law.

An exception is where the prospective spouses celebrate their marriage in Japan and either party is a Japanese national. In this case, to marry legally, the prospective spouses must satisfy formal requirements under Japanese law and submit a marriage notification to the family registrar. Although, for instance, a Japanese and a German celebrate their marriage in Japan and satisfy the formal requirements of German law, their marriage is not deemed valid unless they also comply with the formal requirements of Japanese law. This rule was adopted for the family registrar to be informed of a Japanese national celebrated marriage in Japan and reflect it in the family registry, which has a particular system of entering all information on personal and family status of Japanese nationals.

Nationals abroad may celebrate their marriage before an ambassador, minister, or consular stationed in a foreign country. Insofar as both parties are Japanese nationals, pursuant to CC article 741[239] and FRA article 40,[240] they can celebrate their marriage

[236] FRA article 74 reads: 'Persons who wish to marry shall submit a notification to that effect, entering the following matters in the written notification: (i) the surname that the husband and wife will take; and (ii) other matters specified by Ordinance of the Ministry of Justice'.

[237] CC article 739 reads: '(1) Marriage shall take effect upon notification pursuant to FRA. (2) The notification in the preceding paragraph shall be given by document with the signatures of both parties and not less than two adult witnesses, or given orally by these persons'.

[238] AGRAL article 24(3) reads: 'Notwithstanding the preceding paragraph, the formalities that comply with the national law of either party to a marriage shall be valid; provided, however, that this shall not apply where a marriage is celebrated in Japan and either party to the marriage is a Japanese national'.

[239] CC article 741 stipulates: 'Two Japanese nationals in a foreign country who intend to marry may give notification to the Japanese ambassador or a minister of legation or consul stationed in that country. In this case, the provisions of the preceding two articles shall apply *mutatis mutandis*'.

[240] FRA article 40 stipulates: 'A Japanese national who is living in a foreign country may submit a notification to the Japanese ambassador, minister, or consul stationed in that country, in accordance with the provisions of this Act'.

abroad by providing a marriage notification to a Japanese ambassador, minister, or consul stationed in a foreign country.

The prospective spouses may also submit a marriage notification by mail from abroad to the Japanese authority at the family registry where either of them has a registered domicile. Prior to the 1989 amendment of *Horei* article 13, the term 'the place of celebration of marriage' in such a case used to be understood not as the place abroad where the parties were present and filled out the form to get married, but as the place where the notification of marriage is received by the authority in Japan. This interpretation enabled the marriage to be formally valid under *Horei* article 13, which always pointed to the *lex loci cerebrationis*. However, most commentators criticised such interpretation and advocated to regard the foreign country from where the parties dispatched the notification as the place of celebration, considering that this place, where the prospective spouses resided, agreed to their marriage, and undertook all the necessary acts to celebrate their marriage, had a substantial connection with the marriage.[241]

This issue has been overcome, when the 1989 reform of *Horei* introduced in its article 13(3) (currently, AGRAL article 24(3)) an alternative reference to the national law of the parties. While the place of celebration of marriage is now generally interpreted as the foreign country where a marriage notification originates, AGRAL article 24(3) renders the marriage legally valid under Japanese law, insofar as one of the parties is a Japanese national.[242] Thus, a prospective Japanese–foreign couple can readily satisfy formal requirements under Japanese law by sending a marriage notification to the family registrar from abroad.

iii. Same-Sex Marriages and Civil Unions

a. State of Discussion Worldwide

The number of jurisdictions allowing same-sex marriages (such as the Netherlands, France, Germany, Spain, Canada, the UK, the US, Australia, and soon Switzerland), or same-sex civil unions or registered partnerships (such as Italy, Ireland, the Czech Republic and Greece) has been increasing sharply since 2001. On the other hand, there are still many jurisdictions worldwide that strictly stick to the traditional institution of heterosexual marriage and are opposed to providing legal protection for same-sex couples. Thus, each state has taken a different approach to this subject.

b. Japanese Substantive Law

Japan has yet to recognise same-sex marriages or civil unions at the substantive law level. Notably, however, a number of municipalities have adopted an unofficial system of *de facto* partnerships and issue a certificate attesting the cohabitation of a same-sex couple, even

[241] Judgment of Kobe District Court, 29 January 1997, HJ 1638, 122; Sakurada, *Kokusai Shiho* (*Private International Law*) (n 1) 274.

[242] Circular Notice of Director General of the Civil Affairs Bureau (No 3900 of the Civil Affairs Second Division on 2 October 1989).

if without legally binding effects. This facilitates a social recognition of same-sex couples, enabling a partner to visit the other in hospital or receive cohabitation allowances. Further developments are possibly awaited, after the Sapporo District Court rendered a remarkable decision on 17 March 2021, stating that it is discriminatory and runs counter to the equality rights (Japanese Constitution (JC) article 14) that same-sex couples cannot enjoy any of the legal effects of marriage, while sexual orientation belongs to the nature of the person that cannot be chosen consciously.[243] Moreover, as a matter of immigration policy, permission to stay is issued to a foreign same-sex spouse of a highly qualified foreign worker resident in Japan, insofar as they validly contracted their same-sex marriage in their state of origin. Accordingly, such foreign same-sex couples are granted the same status as foreign heterosexual couples. In this sense, Japan has embraced same-sex marriage and civil unions to a certain extent and does not fully deny the institution of same-sex marriages or civil unions. Thus, sooner or later, Japanese courts will be faced with choice of law issues relating to same-sex marriage and civil unions.

c. Choice of Law Rules for Same-Sex Marriage

There is no explicit choice of law rule with regard to same-sex marriage or civil union. Nor has there been any case law rendered by the Supreme Court. Although there has scarcely been discussion among commentators, determining the law governing the same-sex marriage or civil union can arguably take one of the following avenues: namely, (i) pointing to the state where the same-sex marriage or civil union has been celebrated and registered, (ii) applying AGRAL articles 23 and 24 as a matter of 'other family relationships', or (iii) applying choice of law rules on marriage in AGRAL articles 24–26 *mutatis mutandis*.

Marriage under Japanese law is defined by JC article 24: '[m]arriage shall be based only on the mutual consent of both sexes and it shall be maintained through mutual cooperation with the equal rights of husband and wife as a basis'. While this provision is mostly understood as not covering same-sex marriages, the scope of 'marriage' under AGRAL articles 24–26 is not bound by Japanese substantive law. Still, one could argue that same-sex marriage is a particular institution different from heterosexual marriage by nature and AGRAL articles 24–26 are limited to the latter, considering that foreign law and domestic law are not yet equal or interchangeable.

Taking this as a starting point, one could contend, as (i), that the law of the state of celebration of registration of same-sex marriage applies to the substantive and formal requirements. Some other authors rather assert, as (ii), that same-sex marriages fall within the category of 'other family relationships' provided by AGRAL article 33 instead,[244] so

[243] Judgment of Sapporo District Court, 17 March 2021 (reported on the website of the Supreme Court of Japan: www.courts.go.jp/app/files/hanrei_jp/200/090200_hanrei.pdf) (in Japanese). Notably, the Tokyo High Court Judgment of 4 March 2020 (HJ 2473, 47) granted damages claims of a Japanese female spouse against her same-sex spouse on grounds of adultery with a male partner, after the spouses had legally entered into marriage in the US and lived together in Japan. This judgment can be regarded as indirectly honouring a peaceful cohabitation of a same-sex couple in Japan.

[244] Yokoyama/PILJ (n 9) 277–81.

their substantive requirements are governed by the national law of the parties (AGRAL article 33), whereas their formal requirements are either subject to the *lex loci celebrations* or the national laws of the parties concerned (AGRAL article 34).

On the other hand, one could also consider, as (iii), applying choice of law rules on marriage (AGRAL articles 24–26) by analogy. The underlying idea would be that 'marriage' is a legal institution creating a union and constituting rights and obligations between the spouses for social, emotional, financial and spiritual purposes, so heterosexual marriages and same-sex marriages ought to be treated equally.[245] Following this position, same-sex marriages fall within the category of marriage to be governed by AGRAL articles 24–26.

d. Choice of Law Rules for Civil Unions of Registered Partnerships

As for civil unions (or registered partnerships), a different consideration should apply. This is particularly because the legal effects of civil union at the substantive law level largely differ throughout various jurisdictions. For example, substantive rules are diverse as to whether civil unions are open to both same-sex and heterosexual couples, under which conditions parties can contract civil unions, and what legal effects civil unions provide for personal relationships (particularly the admissibility of joint adoption) and property consequences. In this respect, civil unions are, unlike marriage, a legal institution specific to the jurisdiction concerned and can hardly be conceived as equal or interchangeable among different legal systems. Due to a lack of equivalence among jurisdictions, a new category of family relationships as 'civil unions' can hardly be established at the level of private international law, nor can they be governed by bilateral choice of law rules. Considering the current state of discussion, it would be realistic to simply apply the law of the country of registration when dealing with choice of law issues on civil unions.[246]

B. Effects of Marriage

i. Personal Effects

a. Choice of Law Rule

Like other choice of law rules in AGRAL in relation to personal status and family relationships, article 25 follows the nationality principle at the outset. However, with a view to achieving equality of spouses instead of unilaterally applying the national law of the husband, AGRAL article 25 has adopted cascading connecting factors, seeking the closest connection that is common to both spouses in an appropriate order.[247] Thus, pursuant to AGRAL article 25, the personal effects of a marriage are primarily referred to the same national law of the spouses; in its absence, the law of the same habitual residence of the

[245] Yokomizo, 'Article 24 (Kon'in no Seiritsu oyobi Hoshiki)' (n 233) 10. In fact, there has been one case in which a lower court determined the formation of a same-sex marriage between a Japanese and a Filipino male by applying AGRAL article 24. See Decision of Saga Family Court, 7 January 1999, *Kagetsu* 51(6), 71.

[246] Sakurada, *Kokusai Shiho* (*Private International Law*) (n 1) 299.

[247] This is because *Horei* article 14, which used to designate the national law of the husband unilaterally to determine the personal effects of marriage, was held discriminatory and amended in 1989.

spouses applies; in its absence, the law of the place that is most closely connected with the case applies.

In determining whether the spouses have the same national law, the judge has to first identify the *lex personalis* for each spouse and see whether they coincide. The *lex personalis* is determined by AGRAL article 38(1) when either spouse has multiple nationality, and by AGRAL article 38(3) when either spouse belongs to a multi-unit state (eg, the US, the UK, Spain etc) (see chapter one, section V.A). When, for example, one spouse has both Japanese and Brazilian nationality and the other spouse only Brazilian nationality, the *lex personalis* is Japanese law and Brazilian law respectively. Thus, the judge cannot apply Brazilian law as the same national law of the spouses, but needs to move on to the next layer of cascading connecting factors.[248]

On the other hand, when either spouse belongs to a state consisting of multiple personal laws (eg, Egypt, Iran, Indonesia, Malaysia etc), the judge ought to simply apply the same national law of the spouses, instead of first seeking the *lex personalis* of each spouse among the relevant personal laws and see whether they coincide. When, for example, a Muslim husband is married to a Catholic wife and both are Egyptian nationals, the Japanese judge should not deny the existence of the same national law by considering that the *lex personalis* is Islamic personal law and Catholic personal law under AGRAL article 40(1) respectively. The judge should rather simply apply Egyptian law as the same national law of the spouses, because the Egyptian legal order has a specific interpersonal law rule and points to Islamic law in such a case (see chapter one, section V.A).

b. Substantive Scope of Application

Since AGRAL contains special choice of law rules for matrimonial property regimes and maintenance obligations between the spouses (see section V.B.ii), article 25 does not apply to those matters. AGRAL article 25 only covers personal effects, whose scope has not yet been clearly delineated.

While it is undisputed that AGRAL article 25 covers a duty to live together and cooperate for the spouses,[249] there is not yet unanimity whether to apply this provision to the determination of family name following marriage (see section I.A). Nor is it clear whether this provision extends to the emancipation of a minor through marriage. By defining this legal fiction as protecting the matrimonial community by liberating a minor spouse from parental authority, some commentators advocated applying AGRAL article 25.[250] Yet, recent authors rather characterise emancipation as a matter of capacity to be governed by AGRAL article 4, considering that this legal institution envisions honouring the mental maturity of a minor spouse.[251]

[248] This way of handling envisages avoiding the application of a law of common nationality, which could be easily brought about by an old-fashioned law of nationality that provides the wife with the nationality of the husband upon marriage. Such a simple common national law may well not represent the parties' actual connection with that state.

[249] Sakurada, *Kokusai Shiho (Private International Law)* (n 1) 280; Sawaki=Dogauchi (n 1) 95; Mao Uematsu, 'Article 25 (Kon'in no Koryoku)' in Yoshiaki Sakurada and Masato Dogauchi (eds), *Chushaku Kokusai Shiho: Dai 2 kan (Commentary on Private International Law: Volume 2)* (Yuhikaku, 2011) 28.

[250] Sakurada, *Kokusai Shiho (Private International Law)* (n 1) 278.

[251] Sawaki=Dogauchi (n 1) 95; Uematsu (n 249) 28.

Further, it is also disputable how to determine the law applicable to the question of whether spouses can legally represent the other party and are jointly or severally liable for their day-to-day household debts. Until recently, the prevailing view subjected this question to AGRAL article 26 on matrimonial property regimes rather than article 25, on the ground that it is immanently connected with the issue of the belonging of assets and debts between the spouses.[252]

ii. Matrimonial Property Regimes and Maintenance Obligations

a. Principle

As to matrimonial property regimes, AGRAL article 25 is applied *mutatis mutandis* via article 26(1).[253] Accordingly, the law application to matrimonial property regimes is primarily: (a) the same national law of the spouses; (b) in its absence, the law of the same habitual residence of the spouses; (c) in its absence, the law that has the closest connection with the spouses. In determining the closest connection as the third step of the cascading approach, the factors that have weight may differ between AGRAL article 25 (eg, future matrimonial residence or past habitual residence) and article 26 (eg, location of assets).

When the connecting factor alters over time, the change of the applicable law has only effect for the future to the exclusion of retroactive effect. Suppose, for example, German spouses living in Japan, who have not entered into a prenuptial agreement, naturalise in Japan subsequently. The applicable law of the same national law (AGRAL articles 26(1) and 25) changes from German law to Japanese law. In such a case, the assets obtained while German law was applicable are subject to the *Zugewinngemeinschaft*, the German legal matrimonial property regime,[254] whereas the other assets obtained under Japanese law are governed by the separation of assets as the Japanese legal matrimonial property regime.

[252] Sakurada, *Kokusai Shiho* (*Private International Law*) (n 1) 280; Sawaki=Dogauchi (n 1) 95; Uematsu (n 249) 28.

[253] AGRAL article 26 reads:

> '(1) The preceding article shall apply mutatis mutandis to the marital property regime.
> (2) Notwithstanding the preceding paragraph, if a husband and wife have designated one of the laws listed in the following as the governing law by means of a document signed by them and dated, their marital property regime shall be governed by the law thus designated. In this case, the designation shall be effective only for the future:
> (i) the law of the country where either husband or wife has nationality;
> (ii) the law of the habitual residence of either husband or wife; or
> (iii) with regard to marital property regime regarding real property, the law of the place where the real property is situated.
> (3) The marital property regime to which a foreign law should be applied pursuant to the preceding two paragraphs may not be asserted against a third party without knowledge, to the extent that it is related to any juridical act done in Japan or any property situated in Japan. In this case, in relation to such third party, the marital property regime shall be governed by Japanese law.
> (4) Notwithstanding the preceding paragraph, a contract on marital property concluded under a foreign law pursuant to paragraph (1) or (2) of this article may be asserted against a third party when it is registered in Japan'.

[254] The *Zugewinngemeinschaft* under German law is conceived as a separation of assets obtained during the marriage, in which both spouses mutually have a potential half portion respectively. The portion comes into effect when dissolving the matrimonial property regime by divorce.

Applying different laws to the matrimonial property regimes is cumbersome, but the legislator preferred the policy to apply the law that has the closest connection with the spouses at the relevant time. By excluding retroactive effect of the change of applicable law, the legislator ensures predictability for spouses and third parties, preventing that assets obtained under a certain matrimonial property regime be subsequently thwarted under a different law.

b. Party Autonomy

AGRAL article 26(2) provides for party autonomy in deviation from the objective connecting factors under article 26(1). Pursuant to AGRAL article 26(2), the spouses can choose the law governing their matrimonial property regime among the following options: (a) the national law of either spouse; (b) the law of habitual residence of either spouse; or (c) the law of the place of location for real property. As to (a), it should be noted that if a spouse has several nationalities like German and Swiss, both German law and Swiss law can be chosen by the spouses. In other words, the *lex personalis* eligible to be selected is not limited to one national law in the sense of AGRAL article 38(1). A subsequent designation of the applicable law is effective only for the future and has no retroactive effect, as under AGRAL article 26(1).

AGRAL article 26(2) contains a specific rule as to the formal validity of a choice of law agreement. According to this, a choice of law must be made by means of a dated document signed by both spouses. In contrast, AGRAL article 26(2) contains no choice of law rules as to the substantive validity of a choice of law agreement. Today, a majority of authors set forth, as in the case of contracts, subjecting the substantive validity of a choice of law agreement to the law chosen by the parties themselves (*lex causae* approach: see section II.A.i).[255]

c. Third-Party Protection

Pursuant to AGRAL article 26(1) and (2), foreign law may be designated as the law governing the matrimonial property regime. When one of the spouses signs a contract with a third party in Japan, there is a risk that the third party cannot foresee their matrimonial property regime governed by foreign law and finds out afterwards that the contract is not enforceable. Thus, AGRAL article 26(3) and (4) set forth several safeguards to secure transactions taking place in Japan for the third party.

Pursuant to AGRAL article 26(3), when the law governing matrimonial property is foreign law, it may not be opposed against a bona fide third party (ie is, a party without knowledge of the foreign law being applied) insofar as a juristic act performed in Japan or property situated in Japan is concerned. In such case, the relationship with the third party is subject to Japanese law. Yet, an exception is provided under AGRAL article 26(4), where

[255] Kiyoshi Aoki, 'Article 26 (Fufu Zaisansei)' in Yoshiaki Sakurada and Masato Dogauchi (eds), *Chushaku Kokusai Shiho: Dai 2 kan* (*Commentary on Private International Law: Volume 2*) (Yuhikaku, 2011) 41; Toshio Minami, *Kaisei Horei no Kaisetsu* (*Commentary on the Amended Horei*) (Hosokai, 1992) 76 (Minami); Sawaki=Dogauchi (n 1) 100.

a matrimonial property regime under foreign law is registered in Japan. In that case, it is expected that a third party will check the registration record when one or both spouses have foreign nationality. In Japan, such a registration can be made at a legal affairs bureau in the place where the spouses have their domicile or residence in accordance with the Act on Registration of Foreign Corporations and of Matrimonial Property Contracts.

d. Scope of Application

Notably, AGRAL article 26 deals with the proprietary effect of marriage, which extends to the matrimonial property regimes, their effects and dissolution, as well as the admissibility and validity of contracts between the spouses. On the other hand, some other proprietary matters arising out of marriage, particularly the issue of mutual legal representation and liability of the spouses for their household debts, are governed by AGRAL article 25. Moreover, matters of maintenance between the spouses (such as sharing of living expenses) come under the scope of the Act on the Law Applicable to the Obligation of Support (ALAOS), as is evident from ALAOS article 1 (for ALAOS, see section V.D.iv).[256]

C. Matrimonial Causes

i. Divorce and Separation

a. Principally Applicable Law

As to divorce, AGARAL article 27 primarily requires the choice of law rules in AGRAL article 25 to be applied *mutatis mutandis*. Accordingly, matters of divorce are also referred to: (a) the same national law of the spouses; (b) in its absence, the law of the same habitual residence of the spouses; (c) in its absence, the law of the place most closely connected with the spouses.

This reference to AGRAL article 25 is intended to uniformly determine the law governing the matrimonial relationship.[257] Nevertheless, the law of the place most closely connected with the spouses may differ for personal or proprietary effects of marriage and divorce. There are some notable judgments in this regard that have been given by the lower courts. In the case of divorce between a British husband and a French wife, the Mito Family Court found that Japan was most closely connected with their divorce, considering that the husband habitually resided in Japan and had spent most of his time there over the last two decades except for the time where he travelled on his yacht worldwide, and that the wife intended to stay in Japan after their divorce and planned to remarry a Japanese national.[258] Furthermore, in the case of divorce between a husband from the US State of Tennessee and a wife from the US State of Washington, the Tokyo District Court decided that Japan was

[256] Sakurada, *Kokusai Shiho* (*Private International Law*) (n 1) 280; Uematsu (n 249) 30. ALAOS article 1 reads: 'This Act shall provide the necessary matters concerning the law applicable to the obligation of support arising from the relationship between a husband and wife, parents and their child(ren), and other family relationships (hereinafter referred to as "obligation of support")'.

[257] Sakurada, *Kokusai Shiho* (*Private International Law*) (n 1) 290.

[258] Decision of Mito Family Court, 4 March 1991, *Kagetsu* 45(12), 57.

most closely connected with the spouses, on the ground that the spouses had celebrated their marriage and effectively reached an agreement on divorce in Japan, although in the meantime the wife had returned to the US.[259]

For the convenience of the family registrar that cannot exercise substantial control, the Ministry of Justice issued a particular guideline in 1993 to locate the closest connection of the spouses in Japan pursuant to AGRAL article 27: (i) where the spouses celebrated their marriage and have resided in Japan until they submitted a divorce notification; (ii) where the spouses, after celebrating their marriage abroad, have lived together and spent most of their marital life in Japan until they submitted a divorce notification; or (iii) where the spouses celebrated their marriage in Japan and no circumstances indicate they had their closest connection with a foreign country, even though one or both of the spouses do not reside in Japan at the time of submitting a divorce notification.[260]

b. 'Japanese Spouse' Clause

Notably, article 27 contains one reservation, according to which Japanese law applies, if either spouse is a Japanese national and habitually resides in Japan. This so-called 'Japanese spouse' clause, favouring the application of Japanese law when one of the spouses has Japanese nationality and habitual residence in Japan, should only intervene before moving to the closest connection as the third step (c) of the cascading connecting factors under AGRAL article 27. This is because, otherwise, Japanese law would already be designated on the first step (a) as the same national law of the spouses, or on the second step (b) as the law of the same habitual residence of the spouses.

The legislator adopted the 'Japanese spouse' clause, with a view to facilitating the determination of the applicable law where the spouses submit a divorce notification to the family registrar under Japanese law. This reservation, however, has been criticised both from theoretical and practical points of view, because it runs contrary to the principle of equality between domestic and foreign law in private international law and may even allow a Japanese spouse habitually resident in Japan to submit a divorce notification unilaterally.

In fact, the Ministry of Justice issued a guideline for family registrars, according to which the officers first apply the 'Japanese spouse' clause and determine whether Japanese law applies grounded on one spouse's Japanese nationality and habitual residence in Japan. This could have *de facto* a serious consequence that the nationality and habitual residence of the other foreign spouse is disregarded, who is not even summoned or required to appear before the family registrar when a divorce notification is submitted. As a result, it could remain unexamined whether that foreign spouse has agreed to divorce or even been informed of divorce.[261]

[259] Judgment of Tokyo District Court, 27 April 1990, HT 766, 25.

[260] Circular Notification of Director General of the Civil Affairs Bureau (No 2986 of the Civil Affairs Second Division on 5 April 1993).

[261] For further details, see Yuko Nishitani, 'Privat- und Schlichtungsscheidung deutscher Staatsangehöriger in Japan und die Scheidungsanerkennung in Deutschland' (2002) *IPRax* 49; Yuko Nishitani, 'Divorce of Brazilian Nationals in Japan' (2004) 18 *JJL* 215; Yuko Nishitani, 'Das japanische Familienregister und grenzüberschreitende Rechtsverhältnisse' (2002) 14 *JJL* 229.

c. Formal Validity

When the law applicable to divorce under AGRAL article 27 allows out-of-court divorce by a juristic act, such as consensual divorce or divorce by declaration before the administrative authority, its formal validity is governed by AGRAL article 34. Pursuant to AGRAL article 34, the couple must satisfy either the formal requirements of the law governing their divorce or those of the law of the place where the act is carried out. Thus, insofar as the law governing the divorce recognises out-of-court divorce by a juristic act, it can be effectuated by submitting a divorce notification to the family registrar under Japanese law insofar as it is compatible.[262]

d. Scope of Application

The applicable law designated by AGRAL article 27 determines all matters relating to divorce in principle, that is, the admissibility, requirements, methods, procedure and effects of divorce. It surely extends to the dissolution of the marital relationship between the couple as the direct effect of divorce. It is, however, debatable what law governs the ancillary effects of divorce.

In particular, as to the question of whether a spouse maintains his or her family name after marriage or readopts his or her family name prior to the marriage (maiden name), some authors characterise it as an issue of divorce to be governed by the law designated by AGRAL article 27,[263] whereas some other scholars classify it as a matter of personality right to be governed by the *lex personalis*, that is, the law of the state to which the person belongs.[264] Yet, the practice of family registrars follows a different approach, grounded on the public law theory of names, considering that Japanese law unilaterally determines the name of a Japanese spouse married to a foreign national (see section I.A). Following this approach, the Japanese spouse may resume his or her former family name by simply submitting a notification to the family registrar within three months after divorce (without obtaining permission from the family court) pursuant to FRA article 107(3).[265] By the same token, the family name of the foreign spouse after divorce is determined by the state to which he or she belongs.

As for capacity, a question may arise whether a minor, who was deemed as reaching majority upon marriage, loses his or her capacity afterwards. The prevailing view is that the

[262] In a notable case where a Muslim couple of Myanmar nationality effectuated *talaq* divorce under their national law (Myanmar Islamic law) in Japan, the Tokyo Family Court declared it null and void because of contravening public policy and rendered a divorce judgment under Myanmar Islamic law instead. See Judgment of Tokyo Family Court, 17 January 2019, 22 *Katei no Ho to Saiban* 121. It is not clear whether conducting *talaq* divorce in Japan would always not be permitted or could be acceptable under certain circumstances. In the latter case, the question further remains whether abiding by the formal requirements of consensual divorce under Japanese law would be compatible.

[263] Sakurada, *Kokusai Shiho* (*Private International Law*) (n 1) 294; Yamada, *Kokusai Shiho* (n 16) 450.

[264] Tameike (n 16) 468. One scholar characterises the matter of name as a whole as a matter of public law. Sawaki=Dogauchi (n 1) 107.

[265] FRA article 107(3) reads: 'When a person who has changed his/her surname pursuant to the provisions of the preceding paragraph intends, on or after the day of his/her divorce, annulment of his/her marriage, or the death of his/her spouse, to change his/her surname back to the surname he/she was using at the time that he/she first changed his/her surname, he/she may submit a notification to that effect, within the limit of three months from such day, without obtaining a permission of the family court'.

question should be regarded as an effect of divorce to be governed by the law applicable to divorce.[266] A preferable solution would be, however, to apply the law designated by AGRAL article 4, since capacity ought to be governed consistently by one law proper to the person, that is the *lex personalis*.[267]

At divorce of spouses, questions concerning parental authority, custody, access, or parenting plan of their minor child often arise. While a majority of authors traditionally referred these questions to the law governing the divorce as direct effects of divorce, the *Horei* reform of 1989 brought about clarification that they fall within the scope of the law applicable to the legal relationship between parents and children. This is because, since then, the law applicable to divorce is determined by cascading connecting factors that point to the law that is supposedly most closely connected with the spouses (*Horei* article 16, now AGRAL article 27), whereas the choice of law rule for the legal relationship between parents and children has adopted a child-centred approach to realise the best interests of the child at the level of choice of law (*Horei* article 21, now AGRAL article 32). Since then, court practice, family registrar practice[268] and commentators have followed this position and have the choice of law rules under AGRAL article 32 applied to parental authority and other related questions, primarily referring to the national law of the child when it is the same with either parent, and in its absence, to the law of the child's habitual residence. Arguably, this position is also justified in light of comparative law tendencies, where Western countries and others accept joint custody or co-parenting independently of the marital status of the parents and realise the equality of children born within and out of wedlock (see section V.D).[269]

Once the couple divorce, there are issues of distribution of assets obtained during marriage and payment after divorce. These issues include the dissolution of matrimonial property regime, compensation, child support and spousal maintenance after divorce. While child support and spousal maintenance are obviously subject to ALAOS article 4(1) pointing to the law applied to divorce,[270] the Supreme Court held that claims relating to compensation and damages are governed by the law applicable to divorce.[271] Due to the differing nature of respective claims, however, a more differentiated characterisation would be preferable.

Compensation after divorce is closely related to the matrimonial property regime. In Japanese substantive law, compensation is arguably granted because of the separation of assets as the legal matrimonial regime. When a foreign law governs the matrimonial property regime under AGRAL article 26 and provides for, for example, joint ownership

[266] eg, Egawa (n 162) 269.

[267] Kiyoshi Aoki, 'Article 27 (Rikon)' in Yoshiaki Sakurada and Masato Dogauchi (eds), *Chushaku Kokusai Shiho: Dai 2 kan* (*Commentary on Private International Law: Volume 2*) (Yuhikaku, 2011) 62; Sakurada, *Kokusai Shiho* (*Private International Law*) (n 1) 295; Sawaki=Dogauchi (n 1) 107; Tameike (n 16) 471; Yamada, *Kokusai Shiho* (n 16) 453.

[268] Circular Notice No 3900 (n 242).

[269] eg, Judgment of Tokyo District Court, 28 November 1990, HJ 1384, 71 ((1992) 35 *JAIL* 167); Sakurada, *Kokusai Shiho* (*Private International Law*) (n 1) 294; Sawaki=Dogauchi (n 1) 106–07.

[270] This law does not necessarily coincide with the law designated by AGRAL article 27, when, in particular, the judge excludes it by reference to public policy and applies Japanese law to the divorce case at hand.

[271] Judgment of Supreme Court, 20 July 1984, *Minshu* 38(8), 1051 ((1985) 28 *JAIL* 221). Some authors also support uniformly referring pecuniary claims to the law governing the divorce. Aoki (n 255) 60–61.

for assets obtained during marriage, that law ought to primarily determine how assets are distributed between the spouses at divorce. Only when the distribution of assets does not provide a spouse with sufficient payment, a compensatory claim proper to divorce should come into play pursuant to the law designated by AGRAL article 27. Thus, the dissolution of the matrimonial property regime, particularly the determination of the share of each spouse to be determined at divorce, ought to be determined by the law governing the couple's matrimonial property regime.[272]

For financial relief grounded on damages or solatium at divorce, further details are discussed below (see section V.C.ii).

e. Legal Separation

Legal separation is traditionally used in jurisdictions where divorce is prohibited, which is now limited to the Philippines, the Vatican and some remaining personal laws grounded on Canonic law (eg, Syria). The institution of legal separation may though still be observed in Catholic countries after introducing divorce. The purpose and function of legal separation is to dissolve socially the marital relationship between spouses and discharge them from obligations arising from their marriage (specifically, the obligations of living together, maintenance and parental responsibility), with the caveat that the marital bond is legally upheld, preventing the spouses from marrying another person.

At the private international law sphere, legal separation is normally regarded as a separate legal institution and distinguished from divorce. However, since legal separation is unknow to Japanese law there is neither procedural or substantive rules for claiming it, nor specific choice of law rules. Given that legal separation is akin to divorce in its purpose and effect, a majority of authors set forth analogously applying AGRAL article 27 to determine the applicable law.[273] When a claim seeking legal separation is brought before the Japanese courts, the procedure rules for divorce under the Personal Status Litigation Act may need to be adjusted.

ii. Financial Relief

On the occasion of divorce, a spouse may seek financial relief of damages or solatium caused either by the divorce itself or the other spouse's conduct leading to marriage breakdown, such as assault, violent acts and adultery.

According to the prevailing view, the former category of claim should be referred to the law designated by AGRAL article 27, as it aims to compensate the spouse's mental suffering from divorce and is therefore intertwined with divorce itself.[274] On the other hand, commentators are split over the characterisation of the second type of claim. Some argue that such a claim should be classified as a tort and be subject to the choice of law

[272] Aoki, 'Article 27 (Rikon)' (n 267) 60–61; Sawaki=Dogauchi (n 1) 107; Tameike (n 16) 469; Yamada, *Kokusai Shiho* (n 16) 541.

[273] Aoki, Article 27 (Rikon)' (n 267) 64; Sakurada, *Kokusai Shiho* (*Private International Law*) (n 1) 296; Sawaki=Dogauchi (n 1) 109.

[274] Judgment of Supreme Court, 20 July 1984, *Minshu* 38(8), 1051 ((1985) 28 *JAIL* 221); Sakurada, *Kokusai Shiho* (*Private International Law*) (n 1) 293; Tameike (n 16) 469; Yamada, *Kokusai Shiho* (n 16) 450.

rule in tort (AGRAL article 17 ff),[275] whereas other authors contend subjecting it to the choice of law rule in divorce, considering that it is based on conduct within the marital relationship.[276]

While earlier court decisions tended to characterise both types of damages claim as a tort,[277] in 1984 the Supreme Court subjected a claim for solatium to Korean law that governed the divorce at hand.[278] Since then, most inferior courts have followed the decision to classify damages claims in general as seeking financial relief resulting from divorce. Thus, courts have referred damages claims to the law applicable to divorce, without distinguishing between the two types of claim.[279]

While it is not always easy to discern the two types of claim, it ought to be noted that the second category of claims may be enforced independently of divorce. Suppose, for example, that a wife has incurred severe injury due to her husband's domestic violence and been hospitalised for a while. She can remain married and still petition for damages against her husband to the courts as an independent tortious claim. Even if this type of claim is brought on the occasion of divorce, characterisation as a tort ought to always apply. The necessary harmony and consistency with the law governing the divorce can be achieved by accessorily referring to it under the escape clause in AGRAL article 20. Thus, all claims for financial relief can principally be governed by the law applicable to divorce.[280]

D. Children

Various choice of law issues arise in relation to children. One needs to consider, (1) first, the requirements and direct effects of constituting legal parentage, and (2) second, the parent–child relationship resulting from a validly formed legal parentage, which includes issues on parental responsibility, custody, access and parenting orders.

(1) Legal parentage can be constituted either by (i) the birth of the child, or (ii) the adoption of the child. For category (i), Japanese private international law still distinguishes, like its domestic substantive law, the status of legitimate and illegitimate children. Thus, AGRAL contains different choice of law rules for the formation of (a) legitimate legal parentage (article 28) and (b) illegitimate legal parentage (article 29), and for (c) legitimation (article 30) (see section V.D.i).[281] For category (ii), AGRAL article 31 determines the law applicable to the requirements and direct effects of adoptive legal parentage (see section V.D.ii).

[275] eg, Judgment of Kyoto District Court, 7 July 1956, *Kagetsu* 8(7), 59; Sawaki=Dogauchi (n 1) 107; Yamada, *Kokusai Shiho* (n 16) 450.

[276] Tameike (n 16) 460.

[277] eg, Judgment of Kyoto District Court, 7 July 1956, *Kagetsu* 8(7), 59; Judgment of Kobe District Court, 27 April 1957, *Kaminshu* 8(4), 844.

[278] Judgment of Supreme Court, 20 July 1984, *Minshu* 38(8), 1051 ((1985) 28 *JAIL* 221).

[279] As an exception, there have been decisions in which a court discerned the former type of claim from the latter and referred the former to the law governing the divorce, while the latter was referred to the law governing torts. See Judgment of Kobe District Court, 22 February 1994, HT 851, 282.

[280] For a uniform characterisation as divorce, see Aoki, 'Article 27 (RIkon)' (n 267) 60.

[281] For a comparative overview, see Yuko Nishitani, 'Kinship and Legitimation' in Jürgen Basedow, Giesela Rühl, Franco Ferrari and Pedro De Miguel Asensio (eds), *Encyclopedia of Private International Law* (Elgar Publishing, 2017).

(2) Once a legal parentage has validly been established, the legal relationship between parents and children (parental responsibility, custody, access etc) is subject to the law designated by AGRAL article 32 (see section V.D.iii).

i. Legal Parentage and Legitimation

a. Introduction

AGRAL differentiates the law applicable to the formation of legal parentage, depending on whether a child is born in or out of wedlock. AGRAL article 28 deals with legitimate parentage, and AGRAL article 29 with illegitimate parentage.

b. Legitimate Legal Parentage

AGRAL article 28 adopts the *lex personalis* principle and refers the formation of legitimate parentage alternatively either to the national law of the husband or that of the wife. Pursuant to article 28(1), the child is a legitimate child, if the child is held to be born in wedlock under the national law of either parent at the time of the child's birth. If a husband has died before the child's birth, the husband's national law at the time of death decides. In a rare case where a wife (ie, the child's mother) has died before the child's birth,[282] article 28(2) will apply *mutatis mutandis*.[283]

Apparently, this provision favours the legitimacy of the child (*favor legitimitatis*) by employing alternative connecting factors, that is, the nationality of the husband and nationality of the wife. It is sufficient that either law grants legitimacy of the child. Thus, to rebut the presumption of legitimacy, both the national law of the husband and that of the wife need to accept it.[284] As AGRAL article 28 refers to the national law of either spouse, *renvoi* under article 41 may come into play.[285]

As for the scope of application, the law governing the legitimate parentage determines all issues arising from it, particularly the questions surrounding the presumption of legitimacy and the rebuttal of legitimacy (ie, whether it is possible to rebut the presumption at all, and (if so) how, under what conditions, until when, and by whom).[286] In a case concerning the legal parentage of a twin born from a surrogate mother in the US State of Nevada by using gametes of Japanese intending parents as a married couple, the Supreme Court refused to recognise a Nevada court decree confirming legal parentage of the Japanese intending parents on grounds of public policy violation (CCP article 118(3)).[287]

[282] *cf* Macduff in Shakespeare's *Macbeth*.

[283] Sakurada, *Kokusai Shiho* (*Private International* Law) (n 1) 302.

[284] Decision of Mito Family Court, 12 January 1998, *Kagetsu* 50(7), 100.

[285] Decision of Nagoya Family Court, Toyohashi Branch, 2 October 2018, 2018WLJPCA10026002. Sakurada, *Kokusai Shiho* (*Private International Law*) (n 1) 118; Sawaki=Dogauchi (n 1) 47. Some commentators have suggested that whether *renvoi* is permissible should be determined in light of the results of a hypothetical application of relevant laws, with a view to favouring the formation of a legitimate legal parentage to the extent possible.

[286] Sakurada, *Kokusai Shiho* (*Private International Law*) (n 1) 302; Sawaki=Dogauchi (n 1) 110.

[287] Decision of the Supreme Court, 23 March 2007, *Minshu* 61(2), 619 ((2008) 51 *JYIL* 552).

c. Illegitimate Legal Parentage

General Remarks

AGRAL article 29 deals with illegitimate legal parentage, which can be constituted either (a) by birth (eg, establishment of maternity by birth of the child under Japanese law), or (b) by acknowledgement[288] or any other grounds occurring subsequently to birth (eg, paternity or maternity registration, or *possession d'état* under French law).[289] AGRAL article 29 is applied when legitimate parentage has not been established under the law designated by AGRAL article 28. The structure of AGRAL article 29 distinguishes between (a) and (b). Furthermore, (c) AGRAL article 29 also provides for safeguards for the child.

Choice of Law Rules

(a) In the case of illegitimate legal parentage by birth, AGRAL article 29(1) designates the national law of the father for the establishment of paternity, and the national law of the mother for the establishment of maternity. The relevant time is fixed at the time of the child's birth.[290] Since this type of illegitimate parentage is automatically constituted on legal grounds, there is no need to refer to the national law of the child.

(b) In the case of illegitimate legal parentage established by acknowledgement or any other grounds occurring subsequently to birth, AGRAL article 29(1), first sentence, and article 29(2), first sentence, provide for alternative connecting factors. According to these rules, for the establishment of paternity the national law of the father at the time of the child's birth (article 29(1), first sentence) or at the time of the act (article 29(2), first sentence) applies, and for the establishment of maternity the national law of the mother at the time of the child's birth (article 29(1), first sentence) or at the time of the act (article 29(2), first sentence) applies.[291] These two time frames are relevant if meanwhile the father or the mother obtains a different nationality.

[288] It ought to be noted that the term 'acknowledgement' under Japanese substantive law as well as private international law encompasses both 'voluntary acknowledgement' which is carried out as a juristic act, and 'compulsory acknowledgment' which means the establishment of legal parentage by the courts.

[289] AGRAL article 29 reads:

> '(1) In the case of a child born out of wedlock, the formation of a parent–child relationship with regard to the father and the child shall be governed by the father's national law at the time of the child's birth, and with regard to the mother and the child by the mother's national law at said time. In this case, when establishing a parent–child relationship by acknowledgment of parentage of a child, if obtaining the acceptance or consent from the child or a third party is required for acknowledgement under the child's national law at the time of the acknowledgement, such requirement shall also be satisfied.
>
> (2) Acknowledgement of parentage of a child shall be governed by the law designated in the first sentence of the preceding paragraph, or by the national law of the acknowledging person or of the child at the time of the acknowledgement. In this case, if the acknowledging person's national law is to govern, the second sentence of the preceding paragraph shall apply mutatis mutandis.
>
> (3) If a father has died before his child's birth, the father's national law at the time of his death shall be deemed to be the father's national law set forth in paragraph (1). If the person referred to in the preceding paragraph has died before the acknowledgment, the person's national law at the time of his/her death shall be deemed to be the person's national law set forth in said paragraph.'

[290] If a child's father has died before the child's birth, the father's national law at the time of his death applies instead (AGRAL article 29(3)).

[291] If the father or the mother has died prior to the acknowledgement, their national law 'at the time of the act' is understood to be the national law 'at the time of death' (AGRAL article 29(3)).

In addition to these connecting factors, the national law of the child at the time of the act may also apply alternatively (article 29(2), first sentence). In the case of acknowledgment of an embryo prior to birth, the mother's national law should apply in the capacity of the child's national law,[292] as is advocated by authors and practised at the family registry.[293] When acknowledgement of the child is declared in a will (or testament), the national law of the child 'at the time of the act' ought to be understood as indicating the time when the will comes into effect with the commencement of the succession.

Under these choice of law rules, illegitimate legal parentage can be constituted when the requirements under one of the eligible laws are fulfilled. They favour the establishment of legal parentage in the best interests of the child (*favor filiationis*). Conversely, to contest the paternity or the maternity that has once been established, all the requirements under the relevant laws need to be fulfilled cumulatively.

(c) In the case of (b), when illegitimate paternity is established pursuant to the national law of the father, or illegitimate maternity pursuant to the national law of the mother, there may be a risk of disregarding the interests of the child protected under the child's national law. Typically, a father, who has not been in touch with the child for years, may decide to acknowledge the child, who has meanwhile reached majority, to obtain maintenance or financial support from the child. In Japan, in such a case the consent of the child is required to protect the child's interests (CC article 782). With a view to ensuring comparable safeguards at the level of choice of law, AGRAL article 29(1), second sentence, and article 29(2), second sentence, set forth that the requirement of an acceptance or consent of the child or a third party, which is provided by the child's national law at the time of the act, needs to be fulfilled as well (so-called 'safeguard clause').[294]

Other Issues

As AGRAL article 29 refers to the national law of either parent or the child, *renvoi* may come into play (AGRAL article 41).[295] As for the scope of application, the law governing the illegitimate legal parentage designated by AGRAL article 29 determines all related matters, such as the requirements for and effects of acknowledgement, as well as the establishment or contestation of illegitimate legal parentage. The formal requirements of acknowledgment as a legal act are subject to AGRAL article 34, which designates either the law governing the acknowledgement (*lex causae*) (article 34(1)) or the law of the place where the act takes place (article 34(2)).

Legitimation

Legitimation is a legal construct providing legitimacy for a child born out of wedlock. Under Japanese substantive law, legitimation is granted in the following two situations: (1) a child born out of wedlock has been acknowledged by the father, and the parents

[292] Sawaki=Dogauchi (n 1) 114.

[293] Minami (n 255) 126–27; Sawaki=Dogauchi (n 1) 114; Yamada, *Kokusai Shiho* (n 16) 485.

[294] Sakurada, *Kokusai Shiho* (*Private International Law*) (n 1) 304.

[295] Minami (n 255) 207; Sakurada, *Kokusai Shiho* (*Private International Law*) (n 1) 118; Sawaki=Dogauchi (n 1) 47. Some commentators have argued that *renvoi* should be excluded in favour of the best interest of the child. Yokoyama/PIL (n 1) 81.

celebrate their marriage subsequently (CC article 789(1)); (2) the parents celebrate their marriage, and the father subsequently acknowledges the child who had been born out of wedlock (CC article 789(2)). Depending on the legal system, legitimation may also be declared by the authority.

As a matter of choice of law rules, AGRAL article 30 provides that a child acquires the status of a legitimate child when it is so provided by the national law of the father, of the mother, or of the child at the time when the relevant facts are completed.[296] This choice of law rule, which sets forth three alternative connecting factors, is meant to facilitate the child to acquire the status as a legitimate child (*favor legitimitatis*).

As AGRAL article 30 refers legitimation to the national law of the father, of the mother or of the child, *renvoi* may come into play (AGRAL article 41).[297] As for the scope of application, the law applicable to legitimation determines the admissibility, requirements and effects of legitimation. When the designated law applicable to legitimation requires that, like Japanese substantive law, the acknowledgment of the father and marriage celebration by the parents have taken place, the substantive and formal validity of the acknowledgement is determined by the law designated under AGRAL articles 29 and 34, and the substantive and formal validity of the marriage is determined by the law designated under AGRAL article 24(1)–(3).

ii. Adoption

a. General Remarks

Comparatively speaking, legal parentage can generally be established by adoption, except in those jurisdictions that prohibit adoption on religious grounds (eg, Islamic legal systems in general) or for other reasons. As a matter of substantive law, the form of adoption largely differs throughout various jurisdictions. Some jurisdictions allow adoption by agreement between the adoptive and natural parents, others require adoption to be approved by the court or other public bodies. Furthermore, the effects of adoption also vary among jurisdictions. Some jurisdictions are familiar with full adoption that terminates the pre-existing parent–child relationship, whereas others accept simple adoption that upholds the natural legal parentage of the child.

As a matter of Japanese substantive law, both simple adoption grounded on the parties' agreement (CC article 792 ff) and full adoption carried out by the Family Court (CC article 817-2 ff) are provided for. While full adoption is subject to strict conditions and, once ordered, terminates the natural parent–child relationship, simple adoption can readily be effectuated by declaring at the family registry. As will be discussed below, the particularities of Japanese adoption law play a role in cross-border cases.[298]

[296] If a person concerned with the legitimation has passed away before the requirements are completed, article 30(2) stipulates that the national law of that person at the time of death shall apply instead.

[297] Minami (n 255) 209; Sakurada, *Kokusai Shiho* (*Private International Law*) (n 1) 118; Sawaki=Dogauchi (n 1) 47.

[298] (a) Simple adoption under Japanese law is carried out by the parties making an adoption declaration at the family registrar with constitutive effects (CC article 800). The adoptive parent intending to adopt a minor is required to obtain a permission from the Family Court, unless the child is an offspring of the adoptive parent or his or her spouse (CC article 798). Simple adoption is only subject to requirements and often used between adults to change their family name and hide their identity, succeed to a family line, or constitute a family relationship

b. Principal Choice of Law Rules

AGRAL article 30(1), first sentence, deals with the formation of adoption and refers it to the national law of the adoptive parent at the time of adoption. Because the child will usually live in the same environment as the adoptive parents following adoption, it was held appropriate to point to the national law of the adoptive parent.[299] If the adoptive parents have a different nationality, the respective national law is applied to the admissibility and requirements of adoption.[300] This means that each adoptive parentage is established by the national law of each parent. When, for example, a Japanese husband married to a Philippine woman intends to adopt her child born out of wedlock as a simple adoption by agreement. The Japanese law requires a joint adoption in such a case (CC article 795) to avoid a situation that the child remains an illegitimate child for the mother but obtains the status of legitimate child after being adopted by the father (CC article 809). Although Philippine law does not require a joint adoption in such a case (Family Code of the Philippines, article 185), the Japanese authority would require it.

Since AGRAL article 31(1), first sentence, refers adoption to the national law of the adoptive parent, *renvoi* may come into play (AGRAL article 41).[301] The law governing the adoption under AGRAL article 31(1), first sentence, determines the admissibility, requirements (age, eligibility, consent of the child or a third person, etc) and methods of adoption (role of the court). Furthermore, the same governing law determines the direct effects of adoption, that is, whether the natural parent–child relationship and family relationship terminates (AGRAL article 31(2)), as well as whether the adopted child acquires the status of a legitimate child, and whether a family relationship is created between the child and the relatives of the adoptive parents.

Depending on the case, the application of foreign law prohibiting adoption can be deemed as contravening public policy. In a case involving the adoption of an Iranian child by a Japanese–Iranian couple, the Utsunomiya Family Court held in 2007 that the application of Iranian law prohibiting adoption ran counter to public policy pursuant to AGRAL article 42 and allowed a simple adoption, on the grounds that the child had been living with the prospective adoptive parents for a while and settled in the social and family environment in Japan, that the natural mother had consented to adoption, and that there was a risk of the child being abducted by the natural father once returned to Iran.[302]

between a same-sex couple. Simple adoption does not terminate the natural parent–child relationship. (b) On the other hand, full adoption is carried out by a Family Court decree (CC article 817-2). It is subject to strict conditions, ie, the adoptive parents are over 25 years and married, the child is under 15 years in principle, the natural parents consent, full adoption is necessary in the best interests of the child, and the adoptive parents prove to be eligible after caring for the child for more than six months (CC articles 817-3 ff). If one of the adoptive parent or child is a Japanese national, full adoption needs to be reported to the family registrar afterwards, which only has declaratory effects. Once full adoption is ordered by the Family Court, it has the effect of terminating the natural parent–child relationship (CC article 817-9). See Yuko Nishitani, 'Kindschaftsrecht in Japan – Geschichte, Gegenwart und Zukunft' (2014) 37 *JJL* 87. Notably, the requirements for full adoption have been alleviated by the Act of 14 June 2019 (No 34), raising the minimum age of the child from six years to 15 years and introducing two-tier proceedings at the Family Court to facilitate adoptive parents to obtain a full adoption decree.

[299] Sakurada, *Kokusai Shiho* (*Private International Law*) (n 1) 310; Sawaki=Dogauchi (n 1) 118.

[300] Decision of Morioka Family Court, 16 December 1991, *Kagetsu* 44(9), 89.

[301] Sakurada, *Kokusai Shiho* (*Private International Law*) (n 1) 118; Sawaki=Dogauchi (n 1) 47.

[302] Decision of Utsunomiya Family Court, 20 July 2007, *Kagetsu* 59(12), 106. For further discussion, see Yuko Nishitani, 'Identité culturelle en droit international privé de la famille' (2019) 401 *Recueil des cours de l'Académie de droit international de La Haye* 362.

c. Safeguard Clause

Notably, adoption often requires the consent of the child or a third person, or a decision of the authority. To protect the child at the level of choice of law, AGRAL article 31(1), second sentence, provides for a so-called 'safeguard clause'. It requires that the adoptive parents obtain an acquiescence or consent from the child or a third person, or a permission or decision from the authority, insofar as the national law of the child makes it a condition for the adoption. To this extent, the national law of the child is cumulatively applied, in addition to the national law of the adoptive parents.

Notably, in a Japanese–Philippine adoption case, the Mito Family Court excluded the application of the Philippine law designated by AGRAL article 31(1), second sentence, due to public policy violation (AGRAL article 42). Although the Philippine law (Family Code of the Philippines article 188) requires the consent of the elder legitimate children of the adoptive parents, it could not have been obtained in the underlying case as the prospective Japanese adoptive father had lost contact with his children from his previous marriage. Thus, the judge excluded its application on grounds of public policy to pave the way for the adoption.[303]

d. Formality and Procedure of Adoption

Public authorities are engaged in adoption in various ways. For simple adoption under Japanese substantive law, the adoptive parent seeking to adopt a minor is required to obtain permission from the Family Court, unless the child is an offspring of the adoptive parent or his or her spouse (CC article 798). Since simple adoption is effectuated by the parties' declaration at the family registry with constitutive effects, the role played by the Family Court is merely supportive and supervisory. On the other hand, full adoption under Japanese substantive law is carried out by a Family Court decree that has constitutive effects, after determining that the strict conditions provided in CC are all fulfilled.[304]

As a matter of choice of law issues, insofar as the adoption is effectuated by the parties' agreement pursuant to the law governing the adoption (AGRAL article 31), the formality of adoption is either subject to the law governing the adoption or the law of the place where the adoption is carried out (AGRAL article 34).[305] On the other hand, insofar as the adoption needs to be ordered by the court with constitutive effects under the law governing the adoption (AGRAL article 31), the Japanese Family Courts, once seised, need to ascertain whether international jurisdiction is provided. Pursuant to the Domestic Relations Case Procedure Act article 3-5, the Japanese Family Courts have jurisdiction, when either the prospective adoptive parents or the child is domiciled in Japan.

[303] Decision of Mito Family Court, 15 February 1999, *Kagetsu* 51(7), 93.

[304] See above (n 298).

[305] Insofar as a simple adoption should take place between Japanese nationals in a foreign country, CC article 801 allows that the parties make a notification to the Japanese ambassador, minister or consul acting in that country. CC article 801 reads: 'If a Japanese national in a foreign country intends to adopt, or to be adopted by, another Japanese national in that country, notification of adoption may be made to the Japanese ambassador, minister or consul acting in that country. In this case, the provisions of article 739 applied mutatis mutandis to article 799 and the provision of the preceding article shall apply mutatis mutandis'.

There are intertwined issues in cross-border cases. Suppose a Japanese spouse and his or her foreign spouse intend to adopt a Japanese child in a 'simple adoption', but the national law of the foreign spouse only knows full adoption and requires a Family Court decree to carry out adoption. It is debatable what kind of procedure ought to be taken in Japan. From a theoretical viewpoint, it would be desirable to follow the full adoption proceedings under Japanese law, which are suitable to examine the strict requirements for full adoption under the foreign law. However, insofar as the adoption is conceived as a 'simple adoption' pursuant to Japanese substantive law, the practice prefers to employ and adjust the procedure for simple adoption in Japan. Thus, the Family Court will solely approve the 'simple adoption', which will ultimately come into effect by the parties' declaration at the family registry. The requirements under the foreign law grounded on full adoption are understood to be divided into two parts: (a) a thorough examination of the requirements by the Family Court, which is carried out by Family Court approval in Japan, and (b) a Family Court decree ordering full adoption, which is substituted by the parties' declaration at the family registry with constitutive effects in Japan.[306]

e. Dissolution of Adoption

Dissolution of legal parentage created by adoption is also determined by the same applicable law as under AGRAL article 31(1), first sentence, that is, the national law of the adoptive parents (AGRAL article 31(2)). The law governing the dissolution of the adoptive family relationship determines the admissibility, requirements and methods of dissolution, as well as the effects of dissolution. Notably, the Mito Family Court has held that the application of foreign law prohibiting the dissolution of the adoptive family relationship ran counter to public policy under AGRAL article 42.[307]

iii. Parental Responsibility and Guardianship

a. General Remarks

As has been discussed, the formation of legal parentage is covered by AGRAL articles 28–31. On the other hand, the attributes of the legal relationship between parents and children, such as parental responsibility, custody, access (or visitation) and parenting are subject to AGRAL article 32. AGRAL article 32 follows the approach under *Horei* article 21[308] and refers the legal relationship between parents and children, as a whole, to (a) the national law of the child if it is the same as the national law of either parent;[309] (b) in its absence, the law of the child's habitual residence applies. Since AGRAL article 32 seeks the closest connection with child-centred connecting factors, it should not be thwarted by *renvoi*. Thus, AGRAL article 41 explicitly excludes *renvoi* in the case of AGRAL article 32.

[306] Sakurada, *Kokusai Shiho* (*Private International Law*) (n 1) 310–11; Sawaki=Dogauchi (n 1) 118–19.

[307] Decision of Mito Family Court, 8 November 1973, *Kagetsu* 26(6), 56.

[308] For details of the amendments of choice of law rules from *Horei* to AGRAL in this regard, see Minami (n 255) 157–63; Toshiyuki Kono, 'Article 32 (Oyako kan no Horitsu Kankei)' in Yoshiaki Sakurada and Masato Dogauchi (eds), *Chushaku Kokusai Shiho: Dai 2 kan* (*Commentary on Private International Law: Volume 2*) (Yuhikaku, 2011) 127–32.

[309] In cases where one parent has died or has gone missing, the national law of the other parent decides.

b. Scope of Application

The law governing the relationship between parents and child determines all related matters, especially the attribution, exercise, scope and termination of parental responsibility, custody rights, access (or visitation) and parenting. As for the attribution of parental responsibility at divorce, opinion used to be divided prior to the 1989 *Horei* reform whether to characterise it as 'divorce' or 'relationship between parents and child'. Some commentators took the former position to have all the issues consequential to divorce uniformly governed by the law applicable to divorce. The prevailing view, however, took the latter position, considering that custody or parenting is a separate issue and should ensure the best interests of the child also at the choice of law level. Since the 1989 *Horei* reform, the legislator acquiesced to the latter position. The primary reason was that the legislator adopted a child-centred approach in the new *Horei* article 21 (now AGRAL article 32) for the relationship between parents and child, pointing to the law most closely related to the child, whereas *Horei* article 16 (now AGRAL article 27) for divorce concentrated on the closest connection between the spouses. Since then, the practice of family registrars[310] and the court[311] have been consistently applying the law governing the relationship between parents and child[312] (see section V.D.i).

AGRAL article 32 encompasses parental responsibility, which covers various rights and duties. They include, in particular, the right and duty to care for and educate the child; the right to determine the child's residence; the right to administer the child's property and represent the child; the right to provide, limit or revoke permission for the child to exercise profession; and the right to seek handover of the child.[313] The right to access (or visitation) to the child also falls within the scope of AGRAL article 32,[314] as does the suspension and termination of parental responsibility.[315]

Once the child reaches the age of majority under the law designated by AGRAL article 4 (ie, his or her national law), the child obtains full capacity and parental responsibility is terminated automatically, regardless of the law governing the parental responsibility under AGRAL article 32.[316] As for the name of the child, a similar analysis as to the name in general applies. Court decisions are split over the issue. Some courts have characterised naming as a matter of personality right and referred to the child's national law,[317] whereas others characterised it as a matter of legal relationship between parents and child.[318] The practice of family registrars follows the public law approach for name and applies Japanese law unilaterally to Japanese nationals (see section I.A).

[310] Circular Notice No 3900 (n 242).

[311] eg, Judgment of Yokohama District Court, 29 May 1998, HT 1002, 249; Decision of Tokyo High Court, 24 November 2005, *Kagetsu* 58(11), 40 ((2007) 50 *JAIL* 230.

[312] eg, Decision of Maebashi Family Court, 13 May 2009, *Kagetsu* 62(1), 111.

[313] Decision of Kyoto Family Court, 22 February 1993, *Kagetsu* 46(2), 174.

[314] Decision of Kyoto Family Court, 31 March 1994, HJ 1545, 81 ((1996) 39 *JAIL* 275); Decision of Tokyo Family Court, 9 October 1995, *Kagetsu* 48(3), 69.

[315] Decision of Osaka High Court, 12 May 2004, *Kagetsu* 56(10), 56.

[316] Minami (n 255) 165.

[317] Decision of Tokyo Family Court, 17 August 1970, *Kagetsu* 23(4), 84; Decision of Tokyo Family Court, 21 July 1971, *Kagetsu* 24(3), 82.

[318] Decision of Tottori Family Court, 18 September 1975, 1975WLJPCA09180008.

As to guardianship of a minor child, AGRAL article 35 applies, as mentioned above (see sections I.A and V.E). Yet, insofar as there is a person bearing parental responsibility under AGRAL article 32, that person should be given priority and ought to exercise, in respect of the child, the rights and duties that include parental responsibility. This means that, even if the law governing guardianship under AGRAL article 35 orders appointing a guardian in the case at hand, the application of AGRAL article 32 is given precedence to determine parental responsibility in the best interests of the child. This is a method of adjusting two conflicting choice of law rules through characterisation.

iv. Child Support

As for child support and maintenance obligations in general, *Horei* article 21 used to designate the national law of the maintenance obligor. This provision was, however, abolished in 1986 when the Convention of 2 October 1973 on the Law Applicable to Maintenance Obligations (HMOC) entered into force and was implemented by ALAOS in Japan.

Japan is also a Member State of the Convention of 24 October 1956 on the Law Applicable to Maintenance Obligations towards Children (HMCC), which principally designates the law of the habitual residence of the child for child support.[319] The scope of application of HMCC is, however, very limited, as it only designates the applicable law of the Member States of HMCC and is replaced by HMOC between the latter's Member States.[320] Thus, in practice, Japan would apply HMCC only in relation to Austria, Belgium, Lichtenstein and Macau. Notably, after the EU enacted the 2008 Maintenance Regulation and joined Protocol of 23 November 2007 on the Law Applicable to Maintenance Obligations (the 2007 HCCH Maintenance Protocol), EU Member States no longer apply HMCC. For Austria and Belgium, therefore, they only apply the 2008 Maintenance Regulation, which refers to the 2007 HCCH Maintenance Protocol also in relation to Japan.

In Japan, child support that does not fall within the scope of HMCC are subject to ALAOS. Pursuant to ALAOS article 2(1) and (2), maintenance obligations including child support are governed by the law of habitual residence of the obligee; if the obligee cannot obtain maintenance from the obligor under that law, the common national law of the parties applies; if the obligee cannot obtain maintenance from the obligor under that law either, the Japanese law as the *lex fori* applies.[321]

A particular reflection will be necessary in the case of child support being claimed by the custodial parent against the other parent after divorce or separation. Under Japanese law, such a claim for child support is brought in the name of the custodial parent as a matter of expenses for custody as in the US, not in the name of the child as is the case in European

[319] Pursuant to HMCC article 1, a claim for maintenance by an unmarried child (whether legitimate, illegitimate or adopted), who is under 21 years of age and has a habitual residence in any States Party to HMCC, is governed by the law of his or her habitual residence.

[320] According to HMCC article 6, the law governing child maintenance must be the law of the Member States.

[321] Decision of Tokyo High Court, 30 October 2006, HJ 1965, 70 ((2007) 51 *JYIL* 556). ALAOS article 3 allows a defence of the obligor pursuant to the parties' common national law (in its absence, the law of the obligee's habitual residence) in relation to maintenance obligations between persons related collaterally or by affinity. Notably, spousal maintenance obligations after divorce, legal separation or revocation of marriage are governed by the law that has been applied to divorce, instead of ALAOS article 2(1)(2) (ALAOS article 4(1)(2)) (see section V.C.i).

countries in general. Thus, when Japanese law is applicable, the law of the habitual residence of the 'obligee' ought to be understood as that of the custodial parent, and not the child. As an exception to the usual method of characterisation, its criteria should lie in the applicable law itself to be designated by the choice of law rules.

v. Child Abduction

a. 1980 Hague Child Abduction Convention (HCAC)

On 1 April 2014, HCAC took effect in Japan[322] and the Act for Implementation of the Convention on the Civil Aspects of International Child Abduction (AIHCAC), which was enacted for the implementation of HCAC in Japan, entered into force.[323] To tackle cross-border child abduction, HCAC has established an effective mechanism of administrative and judicial cooperation. As HCAH article 1 states, the objects of HCAC are 'to secure the prompt return of children wrongfully removed to or retained in any Contracting State' and 'to ensure that rights of custody and of access under the law of one Contracting State are effectively respected in the other Contracting States'.

Child abduction is defined as a wrongful removal to or retention in a Contracting State ('state of refuge') of a child habitually resident in another Contracting State ('state of origin') in breach of rights of custody provided under the law of the state of origin and actually exercised at the time of removal or retention (HCAC article 3). The child must be under the age of 16 years (HCAC article 4). Once abducted, the child ought to be returned forthwith to the state of origin, unless one of the limited grounds for refusal exists (HCAC articles 12, 13 and 20). The Convention also supports access to the child across borders (HCAC article 21).

The operation of the Convention is warranted by administrative and judicial cooperation (HCAC articles 7–10). Central authorities of the Contracting States are expected to 'co-operate with each other and promote co-operation amongst the competent authorities in their respective States to secure the prompt return of children and to achieve the other objects of HCAC' (article 7), giving priority to a voluntary return of the child (article 10). Since children grow up quickly and become readily accustomed to new surroundings, a swift return to the state of origin, where the child was integrated into his or her family and social environment, is held to be in the best interests of the child. This will in fact duly prevent their alienation from the left behind parent and preclude that an illicit abduction by the taking parent be *de facto* confirmed.[324]

[322] For details of Japan's acceptance of the HCAC, see Tatsushi Nishioka and Takako Tsujisaka, 'Introductory Note: Japan's Conclusion of the Hague Convention on the Civil Aspect of International Child Abduction' (2014) 57 *JYIL* 7; Yuko Nishitani, 'The HCCH's Development in the Asia-Pacific Region' in Rishi Gulati, Thomas John and Ben Köhler (eds), *Elgar Companion to the Hague Conference on Private International Law* (Elgar Publishing, 2020); Masayuki Tanamura, 'International Child Abduction Cases and the Act for Implementation of the Hague Convention – Impact on Domestic Cases and Family Law' (2014) 57 *JYIL* 24.

[323] For an English translation of AIHCAC, see: www.mofa.go.jp/fp/hr_ha/page22e_000250.html.

[324] Elisa Pérez-Vera, 'Explanatory Report' para 9 ff; Paul Beaumont and Peter McEleavy, *The Hague Convention on International Child Abduction* (Oxford University Press, 1999) 28 ff; NV Lowe, Mark Everall and Michael Nicholls, *International Movement of Children: Law, Practice and Procedure*, 2nd edn (LexisNexis, 2016) para 17.4 ff; Rhona Schuz, *The Hague Child Abduction Convention. A Critical Analysis* (Hart Publishing, 2013) 9 ff.

Pursuant to this framework, the state of refuge solely renders a return order without going into the substance of the underlying custody dispute (HCAC articles 16 and 19), whereas the state of origin maintains the jurisdiction to determine custody issues on the merits. Hence, the child is returned, so the authorities of the state of origin as the natural forum render a decision on the merits of the custody dispute. In this respect, the 1980 Convention properly allocates jurisdiction between contracting states and prevents the taking parent from unilaterally finding a favourable forum in the state of refuge.[325]

b. Implementation of HCAC in Japan

In implementing HCAC in Japan, AIHCAC has been enacted, as mentioned above. AIHCAC designates the Minister of Foreign Affairs as the Central Authority of Japan (JCA) and defines its competences, and provides for necessary details on return proceedings and the enforcement of return orders by the Tokyo Family Court and Osaka Family Court.[326]

c. Central Authority of Japan (JCA)

The JCA is equipped with various experts, including (i) diplomats, (ii) former judges, Family Court investigators and attorneys, and (iii) social workers specialising in child psychology or domestic violence. Pursuant to HCAC and AIHCAC, the JCA fulfils the task of finding the whereabouts of the abducted child with the help of various central or regional government bodies and other entities. The JCA also encourages the taking parent to voluntarily return the child, enhances mediation between the parties, and makes necessary arrangements for an access by the left behind parent. Costs for mediation or access arrangement can be borne by the JCA up to four sessions. For judicial proceedings, the JCA assists the parties by providing information on eligible attorneys, supports translation of documents and sustains the enforcement by substitute of a return order.[327]

Both in incoming and outgoing cases, the left behind parent can petition for assistance to the JCA for return of and access to the child. The JCA examines the grounds for return and decides to assist when they are prima facie satisfied. Since HCAC entered into force for Japan on 1 April 2014, there have been 131 approved return applications in incoming cases (36 US, 15 Australia, 8 France, 7 Germany, 7 UK etc) and 108 approved return applications in outgoing cases (23 US, 12 Philippines, 11 Thailand, 7 Korea, 7 Brazil etc). As for access, there have been 101 approved access applications in incoming cases (47 US, 9 UK, 9 Australia etc) and 33 approved access applications in outgoing cases (6 US, 3 Russia, 3 Canada, 3 Germany etc).[328] It is notable that the US outnumbers other countries both in

[325] Pérez-Vera (n 324) para 16 ff; Schuz (n 324) 12.

[326] Hajime Kaneko (ed), *Ichimon Itto: Kokusaiteki na Ko no Tsuresari heno Seidoteki Taio* (*Q&A on Institutional Settings to tackle Cross-border Child Abduction*) (Shojihomu, 2015) 3 ff.

[327] Gaimusho Ryojikyoku Hague Joyakushitsu [Hague Convention Division, Consular Affairs Bureau, Ministry of Foreign Affairs], 'Chuo Tokyoku no Yakuwari' in Mikiko Otani and Yuko Nishitani (eds), *Hague Joyaku no Riron to Jitsumu – Kokkyo wo koeta Ko no Ubaiai Funso no Kaiketsu no tameni* (Horitsu Bunkasha, 2021) 71 ff.

[328] See the statistics as of 1 January 2021, available at: www.mofa.go.jp/mofaj/files/100012143.pdf. There were 55 access applications in incoming cases in 2014. This large number is presumably explained by the fact that HCAC also applies to pre-convention cases in relation to access, so left behind parents, who had been waiting for HCAC to take effect in Japan, rushed to petition for access to the JCA.

incoming and outgoing cases, and that the other countries are diverse, ranging from North and South America and Europe to Asia. As a particularity of the practice in Japan, almost two-thirds of the incoming cases have been amicably settled between the parties, which shows the role played by in-court conciliation and out-of-court mediation.[329]

d. Return Proceedings

In incoming cases, the left behind parent seeking return of the child can either apply for assistance to the JCA or directly file a petition to the courts in Japan. Return proceedings in incoming cases are regulated by AIHCAC.[330] The subject matter jurisdiction and territorial jurisdiction for return proceedings is concentrated on Tokyo Family Court and Osaka Family Court, with a view to facilitating the case management and enhancing the expertise of judges.[331]

The return proceedings are conceived as summary proceedings in non-contentious matters, whereby the judge has the authority of conducting investigation *ex officio*. The Tokyo Family Court and Osaka Family Court generally follow the 'six-week-model' of hearings to abide by the time frame indirectly set out by HCAC article 11(2). According to this 'six-week-model' of hearings, the first hearing is scheduled two weeks after the seisure of the court, where both parties are summoned to clarify disputed points and envision the possibility of in-court conciliation. In the following couple of weeks, the Family Court further examines the case and organises a hearing of the child by the Family Court investigator, who has expertise in law and child psychology. The Family Court investigator reports back to the judge about the child's degree of maturity, mental status, needs and desires, and particularly whether the child objects to being returned to the state of origin. About five weeks after the seisure of the court, the judge summons both parties once again and investigates the parties' allegations and submitted evidence and conduct their personal hearings, when the parties

[329] Out of 98 decided cases, 29 cases were resolved by an out-of-court agreement; 30 cases by in-court conciliation; and 4 cases by judicial settlement grounded of an out-of-court mediation. See the statistics (n 328). See also Shuji Zushi, 'Japan's 5-year Experience in Implementing the 1980 Hague Abduction Convention' (2019) 2 *International Family Law Journal* 80, particularly 83 f.

[330] For details, see Masako Murakami, 'Case Proceedings for the Return of An Abducted Child and the Compulsory Execution in Japan' (2014) 57 *JYIL* 33.

[331] Depending on the child's domicile, either the Tokyo Family Court or Osaka Family Court has jurisdiction. AIHCAC article 32 provides:

'(1) In the cases listed in the following items, the case seeking the return of a child (which means the case pertaining to the petition for the return of a child under the provision of article 26; the same shall apply hereinafter) shall be subject to the jurisdiction of the respective family courts specified in each of said items:

(i) In cases where the place of domicile of the child (when the child has no domicile in Japan or his/her domicile is unknown, his/her residence; the same shall apply in the following item) is located within the jurisdictional district of the Tokyo High Court, the Nagoya High Court, the Sendai High Court, or the Sapporo High Court: The Tokyo Family Court;

(ii) In cases where the place of domicile of the child is located within the jurisdictional district of the Osaka High Court, the Hiroshima High Court, the Fukuoka High Court, or the Takamatsu High Court: The Osaka Family Court.

(2) A case seeking the return of a child shall be subject to the jurisdiction of the Tokyo Family Court where the child has no domicile in Japan or his/her domicile is unknown, and when he/she has no residence in Japan or his/her residence is unknown'.

are present. About one week later, the judge renders a final decision either to order return of the child or dismiss the petition. So far, the Tokyo Family Court and Osaka Family Court have largely followed this 'six-week-model' and carried out return proceedings in a swift and expeditious manner.[332]

Once the parties agree to attempt in-court conciliation, it is conducted by the Family Court judge and two conciliators.[333] However, what is discussed in in-court conciliation remains confidential and cannot be invoked in later return proceedings. To abide by the 'six-week-model', the parties, attorneys and conciliators meet in up to three sessions within a week. In in-court conciliation, a 'caucus' style is normally used to summon the parties separately, with a view to avoiding an escalation of parental conflict and ensure the best interests of the child. On average, the parties reach an agreement in in-court conciliation in almost one-third of the decided cases.[334] The in-court conciliation has the advantage of causing no additional cost and providing binding legal effects, which can possibly substitute a 'mirror order' to be obtained in the state of origin. Out-of-court mediation, on the other hand, is a method of alternative dispute resolution (ADR) and has the advantage of being flexible, expeditious and professional. ADR sessions can be arranged by Zoom or Skype via the internet, unlike in-court conciliation, and is conducted by professional mediators fluent in foreign languages and knowledgeable about HCAC and the particularities of cross-border cases.[335]

Prior to or during the return proceedings, when there is risk that a party abducts the child out of Japan, the judge can render, upon petition by either party, a *ne exeat* order to enjoin the departure of the child from Japan (AIHCAC article 122(1)). Where necessary, such a *ne exeat* order can be combined with an order to surrender the child's passport (AIHCAC article 122(2)).

e. Grounds for Return

To order return of the child, all the grounds for return under AIHCAC article 27 need to be satisfied: (a) the child has not attained the age of 16 years (AIHCAC article 27 no 1); (b) the child is staying in Japan (no 2); (c) the removal or retention of the child violated the applicant's rights of custody pursuant to the laws and regulations of the state of the child's habitual residence (no 3); and (d) at the time of removal or retention, the state of the child's habitual residence was a Contracting State (no 4).

[332] Tomoko Sawamura, 'Katei Saibansho ni yoru "Kokusaiteki na Ko no Dasshu no Minjijo no Sokumen ni kansuru Joyaku no Jisshi ni kansuru Horitsu" no Un-yo Jokyo ni tsuite' (2018) 191 *Ho no Shihai* 89; Ai Kuroda, 'Hague Anken ni kansuru Osaka Katei Saibansho ni okeru Jitsumu – ADR no Riyo: Bengoshi no Tachiba kara' (2019) 20 *Katei no Ho to Saiban* 12; Toshiteru Shibaike, 'Hague Joyaku no Jitsumu – Dairinin no shiten kara' in Mikiko Otani and Yuko Nishitani (eds), *Hague Joyaku no Riron to Jitsumu: Kokkyo wo koeta Ko no Ubaiai Funso no Kaiketsu no tameni* (Horitsu Bunkasha, 2021) 133.

[333] Conciliators are appointed by the Supreme Court among learned and decent persons experienced as a lawyer, academic, corporate manager or any other profession.

[334] See above (n 328).

[335] Ai Kuroda, 'Shiteki Chotei (ADR) nado Saibangai no Kaiketsu Tetsuzuki' in Mikiko Otani and Yuko Nishitani (eds), *Hague Joyaku no Riron to Jitsumu: Kokkyo wo koeta Ko no Ubaiai Funso no Kaiketsu no tameni* (Horitsu Bunkasha, 2021) 301.

The practice in Japan has revealed challenges in locating the habitual residence of the child. The judges have so far reiterated the general criteria in Japanese private international law to define habitual residence as a place where the person lives for a certain period of time, which is determined according to the purpose, period and circumstances of stay (see section V.D.v). In the case of infants, the courts also take into account the common intent of the parents to give up their previous habitual residence and settle in a new place.[336] In further refining these criteria, it would be desirable for the Japanese courts to follow the recent worldwide trend to adopt the so-called 'hybrid approach', established in the EU through the interpretation of the Brussels II*bis* Regulation,[337] as well as in the UK, the US, Canada, Australia and other major jurisdictions.[338] According to the 'hybrid approach', primary focus will be placed on the integration of the child into the social or family environment, or that of the primary caregiver in the case of infants. One of the most recent decisions in Japan alludes to some possible changes in this direction.[339]

f. Grounds for Refusal

Even though grounds for return under AIHCAC are all satisfied, AIHCAC article 28(1) allows the courts to dismiss a petition for return of the child when it appears appropriate in the best interests of the child. The grounds for refusal stipulated in AIHCAC article 28(1) implement HCAC articles 12, 13 and 20.

The grounds for refusal cover cases, where: (a) the application for the return of the child was filed after the lapse of one year from the time of removal or commencement of retention of the child and the child is now settled in his or her new environment (AIHCAC article 28(1) no 1); (b) the applicant was not exercising rights of custody at the time of the removal or commencement of the retention (no 2); (c) the applicant had consented to the removal or retention or subsequently acquiesced to the same (no 3); (d) there is a grave risk that the return would expose the child to physical or psychological harm or otherwise place the child in an intolerable situation (no 4); (e) the child objects to being returned, in a case where it is appropriate to take account of the child's views in light of the child's age and degree of development (no 5); or (f) it would be contrary to the fundamental principles of Japan relating to the protection of human rights and fundamental freedoms (no 6).

[336] See, inter alia, Decision of Osaka High Court, 17 August 2015 (INCADAT: HC/E/JP 1427); Decision of Osaka High Court, 7 July 2016 (INCADAT: HC/E/JP 1429); Decision of Osaka High Court, 24 February 2017 (to be reported in INCADAT); Decision of Osaka High Court, 12 July 2017 (INCADAT: HC/E/JP 1430).

[337] CJEU, 2 April 2009, Case C-523/07 [*A*]; CJEU, 22 December 2010, C-497/10 PPU [*Mercredi*], Rep 2010, I-14309; CJEU, 8 June 2017, C-111/17 PPU [*OL v PQ*]; CJUE, 10 April 2018, C-85/18 PPU [*CV v DU*]; CJEU, 28 June 2018, C-512/17 [*HR v KO*]; CJEU, 17 October 2018, C-393/18 PPU [*UD v XB*]; *cf* also CJEU, 5 September 2019, C-468/18 [*C v P*] (electronic database available at: curia.europa.eu/).

[338] For the UK, UK Supreme Court, *A v A and another (Children: Habitual Residence)* [2013] UKSC 60; *Re L (A Child) (Habitual Residence)* [2013] UKSC 75; *AR v RN* [2015] UKSC 35; for the US, US Supreme Court, 25 February 2020, *Monasky v Taglieri*; for Canada, Supreme Court of Canada, *Office of the Children's Lawyer v Balev*, 2018 SCC 16; for Austraila, High Court of Australia, *LK v Director-General, Department of Community Services* [2009] HCA 9; Family Court of Australia, *Commonwealth Central Authority v Cavanaugh* [2015 FamCAFC 233]; for further details, see Yuko Nishitani, 'Child Protection in Private International Law – An HCCH Success Story?' in Rishi Gulati, Thomas John and Ben Köhler (eds), *Elgar Companion to the Hague Conference on Private International Law* (Elgar Publishing, 2020).

[339] Decision of Tokyo High Court, 15 May 2020 (to be reported in INCADAT).

While in the case of AIHCAC article 28(1) nos 1, 2, 3 and 5, the judge has discretion to overturn fulfilled grounds for refusal and order the return of the child, it is not allowed in the case of AIHCAC article 28(1) nos 4 and 6 (AIHCAC article 28(1), second sentence). This is because the latter grounds for refusal based on 'grave risk' and 'human rights violation' have serious causes, which may not be thwarted through the exercise of discretion by the judge.

AIHCAC article 28(1) no 4 sets out the 'grave risk' exception, which corresponds to HCAC article 13(1)(b).[340] Like other jurisdictions, to secure a safe return of the child to the state of origin, this ground for refusal also plays an important role in Japan. When deliberation was going on whether to join the HCAC in Japan, there was a strong opposing view contending that the HCAC would endanger Japanese mothers living in a foreign country, who fled to Japan with the child after suffering from domestic violence or any other hardships. To ease the opponents and set out necessary safeguards, the legislator ultimately decided to insert a particular provision in AIHCAC article 28(2) to define the circumstances to be considered in determining the 'grave risk' exception.[341]

Pursuant to AIHCAC article 28(2),[342] the judge contemplates the following factors in assessing the 'grave risk' exception: (i) whether return would expose the child to the petitioner's words and deeds which may cause physical or psychological harm to the child (no 1) (eg, violence, sexual abuse, neglect, verbal threatening etc against the child); (ii) whether return would expose the respondent to violence etc by the petitioner in such a manner as to cause psychological harm to the child (no 2) (eg, domestic violence against the respondent in front of the child, or mental instability of the respondent affecting the child); (iii) whether there are circumstances that make it difficult for the petitioner or the respondent to provide care for the child in the state of origin (no 3) (eg, alcohol or drug addiction or any other serious grounds making it impossible for the petitioner to care for the child; lack of permission to stay, or a warrant or any other serious grounds making it impossible for the respondent to re-enter the state of origin and care for the child there).[343]

Like the 2007 federal statute (article 5) in Switzerland,[344] there was concern that such detailed rules defining 'grave risk' in AIHCAC article 28(2) would allow the judges to extend

[340] For further details, see Hague Conference on Private International Law, 'Guide to Good Practice Child Abduction Convention: Part VI: Article 13(1)(b)' (2020), available at: www.hcch.net/en/publications-and-studies/details4/?pid=6740&dtid=3).

[341] Kaneko (ed) (n 326) 141 ff.

[342] Article 28(2) reads: 'The court, when judging whether or not the grounds listed in item (iv) of the preceding paragraph exist, shall consider all circumstances such as those listed below:

(i) Whether or not there is a risk that the child would be subject to physical violence or any other words and deeds which would cause physical or psychological harm (referred to as "violence, etc" in the following item) by the petitioner, in the state of habitual residence;

(ii) Whether or not there is a risk that the respondent would be subject to violence, etc by the petitioner in such a manner as to cause psychological harm to the child, if the respondent and the child entered the State of habitual residence;

(iii) Whether or not there are circumstances that make it difficult for the petitioner or the respondent to provide care for the child in the state of habitual residence'.

[343] Kaneko (ed) (n 326) 145 ff.

[344] Bundesgesetz über internationale Kindesentführung und die Haager Übereinkommen zum Schutz von Kindern und Erwachsenen (BG-KKE) of 21 December 2007, article 5.

the scope of 'grave risk' and readily dismiss a petition for the return of a child. Against such prediction, however, the practice in Japan has demonstrated a restrictive interpretation of the 'grave risk' exception. As for AIHCAC article 28(2) items (i) and (ii), the judges first ascertains whether there was violence etc against the child or respondent in the past and assesses the risk that the petitioner may exercise serious violence etc as to cause 'grave risk' to the child after return in the future.[345] The judges never solely rely on the respondent's allegations, but require the respondent to submit objective evidence and prove the existence of concrete acts of the petitioner, conducting meticulous and detailed examination of the case at hand. It generally does not suffice to prove sporadic violent acts etc (scolding the respondent, use of cannabis, shouting while drinking etc). Rather, certain strong violent acts etc usually need to have been carried out repeatedly or continuously to constitute 'grave risk'.[346] As for AIHCAC article 28(2) item (iii), mere financial difficulties or insufficient means of covering the cost of living do not suffice, but serious grounds, such as potential risk of criminal prosecution, risk of committing suicide and lack of any means for surviving for the respondent are held to be necessary to constitute 'grave risk'.[347]

Even though there is an immanent risk of violent acts by the petitioner, the judge can render a return order, insofar as appropriate protective measures are available in the state of origin (restriction order for domestic violence, provision of shelter or housing, maintenance order etc). Despite the absence of an explicit provision in AIHCAC comparable to the EU Brussels II*bis* Regulation article 11(4), judges in Japan generally follow the same interpretation to restrict the scope of the 'grave risk' exception.[348] Needless to say, it poses another challenge for Japanese judges to ascertain the actual practice of the state of origin and evaluate the effectiveness of protective measures available there.[349] To obtain accurate information, it would be desirable to seek the assistance of the foreign central authority or make use of foreign network judges *de lege ferenda*, even though at present Japanese network judges are not allowed to exchange concrete information on the case at hand for fear of infringing upon the neutrality and independence of judges.[350] In any case, a promise of voluntary cooperation by the petitioner (abiding by a restriction order, providing housing and maintenance etc) is not relied on when determining the petition for return of the child, insofar as there is no means to ensure its enforcement in the state of origin.[351]

[345] Decision of Tokyo High Court, 14 July 2015 (INCADAT: HC/E/JP 1439); Decision of Tokyo High Court, 18 May 2018 (to be reported in INCADAT); see also Yoshihito Yoda, 'Hague Joyaku Jisshiho ni motozuku Ko no Henkan Moshitate Jiken no Shukyoku Ketteirei no Keiko ni tsuite' (2018) 12 *Katei no Ho to Saiban* 32.

[346] Decision of Tokyo High Court, 14 July 2015 (n 345); Decision of Osaka High Court, 29 August 2016 (INCADAT: HC/E/JP 1440); Decision of Osaka High Court, 12 July 2017 (n 336); Decision of Osaka High Court, 15 September 2017 (INCADAT: HC/E/JP 1390); Decision of Tokyo High Court, 28 February 2019 (to be reported in INCADAT); Tokyo High Court, 27 March 2019 (to be reported in INCADAT); see also Yoda (n 345) 32 f. As an exception, one-time violence was held sufficient to constitute 'grave risk' due to the serious injury caused to the respondent. Decision of Tokyo High Court, 18 May 2018 (to be reported in INCADAT).

[347] Decision of Tokyo High Court, 31 March 2015 (INCADAT: HC/E/JP 1437); Yoda (n 345) 34.

[348] Decision of Tokyo High Court, 31 March 2015 (INCADAT: HC/E/JP 1437); Decision of Tokyo High Court, 14 July 2015, 14 July 2015 (INCADAT: HC/E/JP 1439); Decision of Osaka High Court, 15 September 2017 (n 346); Yoda (n 345) 33.

[349] Notably, in a case of child abduction from Turkey to Japan, the Tokyo High Court dismissed in its decision of 14 July 2015 (n 345) the petition for return of the child due to 'grave risk', although the first instance, Tokyo Family Court, had relied on the protective orders and provision of shelters in Turkey and rendered a return order. This case shows how difficult it is to exactly assess the effectiveness of protective measures in the state of origin.

[350] Nishitani, 'Child Protection in Private International Law (n 338) 263, fn 22.

[351] Yoda (n 345) 34.

g. Enforcement of a Return Order

When the respondent does not abide by a court order (or conciliation) to return the child, the petitioner can further have recourse to compulsory enforcement measures under AIHCAC.[352] Pursuant to the original AIHCAC article 136, it was obligatory to follow two-step execution measures for the enforcement of a return order. Under this system, it was first necessary to institute an 'indirect enforcement', ordering the respondent to pay a certain amount of money per day. Only when it remains unsuccessful, was it possible after the lapse of two weeks to move to 'execution by substitute', ordering an enforcement officer to release the child from the respondent and hand the child over to a return implementer tasked with the child's return to the state of origin (AIHCAC article 137 ff). For the 'execution by substitute', it was required to take place at a venue, which is a place of living or any other place occupied by the respondent, while the respondent was staying with the child ('simultaneous presence'). Moreover, the enforcement officer was supposed to primarily persuade the respondent to seek a voluntary release of the child (AIHCAC article 140(1)–(3)).

This enforcement system under the original AIHCAC was meant to avoid or alleviate damage to the child and enhance an amicable solution. In practice, however, the two-step execution measures turned out to be ineffective, cumbersome and time-consuming. Furthermore, the requirement of 'simultaneous presence' of the child and taking parent frequently resulted in escalating resistance against the enforcement officer and even allowing *de facto* the taking parent to hide with the child or entrust the child to a third person to circumvent execution.

To complement the insufficient enforcement measures, the left behind parent sometimes petitioned for a habeas corpus order. Habeas corpus, which originates in a common law system, is conceived as an administrative summary procedure and is meant to restore the freedom of an illegally retained person ('retention'), insofar as the illegality is conspicuous ('conspicuously illegal') and there is no other viable means ('subsidiarity').[353] In a case where Japanese parents were living in the US and the mother wrongfully removed the youngest son to Japan, the mother continuously refused to return the child to the US, ignored a return order rendered by the Tokyo Family Court which had become final and conclusive, and the two-step execution measures remained unsuccessful because of forceful resistance by the mother. Upon the father's petition for a habeas corpus order, the Supreme Court held that the retention of the child by the mother was 'conspicuously illegal' and there were no justifying grounds.[354] After the case was remanded to the Nagoya High Court, a habeas corpus order was ultimately rendered.[355]

[352] See also, Hajime Sakai, 'Enforcing the Obligation to Return A Child in Japan: With Insight into the Recognition and Enforcement of Foreign Judgments in Cross-border Child Abduction Cases' (2010) 53 *JYIL* 438.

[353] See Hiroshi Mitsuoka (2019) 71(10) *Hoso Jiho* 197 ff (comment on the Supreme Court judgment, below (n 354).

[354] Judgment of Supreme Court, 15 March 2018, *Minshu* 72(1), 17 ((2019) 62 *JYIL* 452; INCADAT: HC/E/JP 1388). Although the child was over 13 years of age, his intention to stay with the mother was not respected on the grounds that he was taken to Japan at 11 years and 3 months and had been since then deprived of opportunities to obtain objective information, have access to the father and understand his situation.

[355] Judgment of Nagoya High Court, 17 July 2018, HJ 2398, 87.

While a habeas corpus order could be a viable solution to some extent in complementing the execution measures under AIHCAC, as in domestic child abduction cases,[356] it also entails several drawbacks. First, a habeas corpus order establishes an obligation to 'release and hand over the child to the petitioner', instead of an obligation to 'return the child to the state of origin' as under AIHCAC. Thus, once a habeas corpus order is rendered, the taking parent is immediately deprived of his or her custody and can no longer decide to voluntarily go back to the state of origin with the child. Second, habeas corpus proceedings belong to the subject-matter jurisdiction of District Courts and High Courts,[357] which do not have the means or expertise to thoroughly examine the child, nor are they assisted by Family Court investigators. Third, a habeas corpus order does not have the civil law effects of enforceability, and sanctions for its breach by subpoena, detention, non-criminal fine or criminal charges are seldom employed.[358] Considering that habeas corpus also has limitations to complement compulsory execution of a return order, it was held more desirable to strengthen the enforcement measures pursuant to AIHCAC.[359]

In 2019, the legislator eventually amended AIHCAC, together with the reform of the CEA, to rationalise and facilitate execution measures for the return of a child.[360] The current AIHCAC creates an exception to the two-step execution measures and allows for immediately instituting 'execution by substitute' when indirect execution is likely to be unsuccessful or there is imminent danger to the child (AIHCAC article 136, nos 2 and 3). Furthermore, the requirement of 'simultaneous presence' of the child and taking parent has been abolished and substituted by the presence of the left behind parent or his or her agent, with a view to creating a familiar and peaceful environment for the child (AIHCAC article 140(1) and the Civil Execution Act (CEA) article 175(5) and (6) *mutatis mutandis*). Under strict conditions, release of the child can now also take place in a public place (eg, on the street or in a park), at school or hospital with permission of a representative, or at the residence of a third person where the child also resides[361] (AIHCAC article 140(1) and CEA article 175(2) and (3) *mutatis mutandis*). It is expected that the practice of enforcing return orders will ameliorate with the reform of AIHCAC in Japan.

h. Change of Circumstances

After a return order has become final and binding, circumstances may change and make it inappropriate to uphold the order for the sake of the best interests of the child. In such

[356] Judgment of Supreme Court, 18 January 1949, *Minshu* 3(1), 10; Judgment of Supreme Court, 28 May 1958, *Minshu* 12(8), 1224; Judgment of Supreme Court, 4 July 1968, *Minshu* 22(7), 1441.

[357] Habeas Corpus Act article 4.

[358] Habeas Corpus Act articles 18 and 26.

[359] Yuko Nishitani, 'Nihon ni okeru Kodasshu Joyaku no Un-yo to Kinji no Doko ni tsuite' (2020) 26 *Katei no Ho to Saiban* 55.

[360] Act of 17 May 2019 (Act 2019, No 2; entry into force on 1 April 2000). For a detailed explanation by the officers of the Ministry of Justice, see Muneki Uchino (ed), *Q & A: Reiwa Gannen Kaisei Minji Shikko Hosei* (Kin-yu Zaisei Jijo Kenkyukai, 2020) 304 ff; for academic opinions, see Yukiko Oda, 'Hague Kodassyu Joyaku no Riko Kakuho no Ichi sokumen – Joyaku Jisshi Ho Kaisei wo chu shin'ni' (2020) 119(3) *Kokusai Ho Gaiko Zasshi* 1.

[361] When releasing the child at the residence of a third person (eg, the child's grandparents), where the child also resides, a permission of the third person can now be replaced by a Family Court order. Unlike the original AIHCAC, this will prevent the taking parent from circumventing the execution by entrusting the child to a third person.

exceptional cases, AIHCAC article 117 allows the judge to modify the return order. This would be the case, for example, when (i) the child has fallen seriously ill and needs to be hospitalised in Japan; (ii) the petitioner has been imprisoned for a long period of time and there is nobody else in the state of origin who could take care of the child; or (iii) a civil war has occurred in the state of origin, seriously deteriorating public security there. It goes without saying that a modification of a final and conclusive return order needs to be strictly limited to those exceptional cases, where such modification becomes necessary due to circumstances that changed subsequent to the return order.[362]

In 2017, the Supreme Court rendered a controversial decision, dismissing the father's petition for return of the children by modifying a return order pursuant to AIHCAC article 117(1).[363] The Supreme Court reasoned that the father's living conditions had seriously deteriorated after the return order had become final and binding, so as not to allow the father to duly care for his two pairs of twins should the children be returned to the US. Thus, the petition for return was dismissed, on the grounds that the elder twins, who had consistently been opposed to being retuned, could no longer be subject to a return order by discretion of the judge (AIHCAC article 28(1) no 5), and the younger twins would be exposed to 'grave risk' if they were separated from their elder siblings (AIHCAC article 28(1) no 4). While the final outcome of this Supreme Court decision appears reasonable, it is rather questionable that this case satisfied the exceptional circumstances test under AIHCAC article 117. Under the circumstances of this case, the Osaka Family Court and Osaka High Court arguably should have dismissed the petition for return of the child from the outset. Japanese authors rightly point out that AIHCAC article 117 should not be used as a backdoor solution to deny return of the child. Rather, its application needs to be limited to truly exceptional cases, where the modification becomes indispensable because of changed circumstance.[364]

i. Non-Convention Cases

In non-convention cases, where a child is abducted from a non-Member State of the HCAC to Japan, the left behind parent can only seek remedies under domestic law. First, the left behind parent can obtain a custody decision on the merits before the Japanese family courts, ordering the handover of the child, and have it enforced in Japan. The execution measures under CEA are now largely in line with those of AIHCAC after its 2019 reform. Second, the left behind parent can also obtain a custody decision in the foreign country where the child used to habitually reside and have it recognised and enforced in Japan. However, this avenue is cumbersome and may well be hindered on grounds of public policy, after a certain

[362] Kaneko (ed) (n 326) 246 ff.

[363] Decision of Supreme Court, 21 December 2017, *Saiji* 1691, 10.

[364] Shin'ichiro Hayakawa (2019–20) 59 *Shiho Hanrei Remarks* 136 f; Yuko Nishitani (2018) 770 *Koseki Jiho* 50 ff; for authors who affirm modifying a return order more broadly for the best interests of the child, see Masako Murakami (2018) *Hanrei Hisho* (HJ 100036) 5–9; Shinobu Ohama 154(6) *Minshoho Zasshi* 106. In 2020, the Supreme Court allowed applying AIHCAC article 117 mutatis mutandis to a case, where the parents had reached an agreement in in-court conciliation to return the child to Russia, but the circumstances changed afterwards. Decision of Supreme Court, 16 April 2020, *Minshu* 74(3), 737. It remains to be seen to what extent AIHCAC article 117 finds application in the future. For a reserved view, see Shin'ichiro Hayakawa (2021) 1557 *Jurist* 247.

amount of time has lapsed and the child has become accustomed to the new environment in Japan.[365]

E. Protection of Adults and Minors

i. General Remarks

Japan has certain legal institutions to protect mentally incapacitated adults due to impaired intelligence or age-related illnesses such as Alzheimer's disease (see section I.A). Japanese law offers, for instance, guardianship, curatorship or assistance, as other jurisdictions do. At the substantive law level, the available protective institutions vary in accordance with the severity of a person's mental incapacity and so is governed by different provisions. At the private international law level, those protective institutions are subject to the same choice of law rule. AGRAL divides the protective measures into two steps (ie, those that trigger the commencement of a measure and the appointment of guardians etc) and regulates them separately. The commencement of protective measures is subject to AGRAL article 5 (see section I.A), while other aspects (such as the appointment or dismissal of a guardian, the rights and obligations of a guardian, and the termination of guardianship) are subject to AGRAL article 35. AGRAL article 35 also covers the protection of a minor child. It has been left to the courts to interpret whether article 35 extends to a voluntary guardianship contract.[366]

ii. Guardianship etc of Adults

AGRAL article 35(1) adopts the nationality principle and refers the matter of guardianship, curatorship or assistance to the national law of a ward, person under curatorship or person under assistance. As AGRAL article 35(1) adopts a person's nationality as a connecting factor, *renvoi* under AGRAL article 41 may come into play.

AGRAL article 35(2) contains an exceptional choice of law rule, according to which, where a foreign national is a protected person, the Japanese courts may appoint a guardian, curator or assistant and may make related rulings according to Japanese law, (a) if the grounds of commencement of protective measures exist under the person's national law and there is no person to carry out guardianship in Japan, or (b) if a ruling for the commencement of guardianship has been made in Japan pursuant to AGRAL article 5. As is evident from the wording, Japanese law is always applied. Furthermore, pursuant to item (i), a guardian can only be appointed when there is no one (including a foreign guardian) to carry out guardianship in Japan. The decisive factor is whether there is anyone who can deal with a protected person's affairs in Japan, so it does not matter whether a

[365] Judgment of Tokyo High Court, 15 November 1993, *Komin* 46(3), 98 ((1994) 37 *JAIL* 158). In this case, there was a custody decision of a Texas court (US) ordering the handover of a child. The Tokyo High Court, however, refused to render an *exequatur* for the enforcement of this court order on grounds of public policy, considering the circumstances that occurred subsequently to the Texan court decision, namely the fact that the child had been accustomed to the new social and family environment in Japan.

[366] Koide (n 31) 340–41.

guardian has been appointed and is active in carrying out his or her duties abroad.[367] The provision is concerned with implementing an effective guardianship in Japan,[368] authorising the Japanese courts to complement a foreign guardianship and cater for the necessary protection for a person in need. This exception would not apply insofar as a foreign guardian could care for a ward in Japan, which would however seldom be the case.

The governing law of guardianship, curatorship or assistance determines matters arising from these relationships. They cover, in particular, the grounds for commencing these protective measures, the appointment or removal of a guardian, the rights and obligations of a guardian, the nomination or appointment of a supervisor of a guardian and the duties of such supervisor, and the termination of guardianship.

iii. Guardianship etc of Minors

As to the guardianship of a minor, the preliminary question of whether that person has not yet attained the age of majority is determined by the national law of that person under AGRAL article 4 (see section I.A).[369]

For the protection of a minor, guardianship can be ordered pursuant to (b) the law designated by AGRAL article 35. Yet, in a usual case, one or both parents have and exercise rights and obligations to care for the child, whereby the attribution of and rights and obligations arising out of parental responsibility are determined by (a) the law designated by AGRAL article 32 (see section V.D.iii). Law (a) governs the preliminary question of parental responsibility, and only in those cases where there is no parent or custodian caring for the child under law (a), a guardian ought to be appointed pursuant to law (b). Thus, when both applicable laws contradict and law (b) orders commencement of guardianship, whereas law (a) considers a parent as a custodian, the application of law (a) ought to be given priority for the sake of assuring the parent–child relationship in the best interests of the child. Conversely, when law (a) holds parental responsibility to be terminated, but law (b) does not order the commencement of guardianship, an adjustment would be necessary for the Japanese judge to appoint a guardian nonetheless.[370]

F. Succession

i. Choice of Law Rule

AGRAL contains only one choice of law rule on succession in article 36, while the validity and effect of a will is subject to AGRAL article 37 and the formal validity of a will to the Act on the Law Applicable to the Form of Wills (ALAFW). AGRAL article 36 is based on the principle of unity of an estate (in contrast to the principle of separation of an estate, typically, followed in common law jurisdictions and some other countries).

[367] ibid 334.
[368] ibid.
[369] Sakurada, *Kokusai Shiho* (*Private International Law*) (n 1) 333.
[370] ibid 334.

AGRAL article 36 is simply worded and refers all matters of succession to the national law of the deceased. Accordingly, even if the deceased has movable and immovable property in several jurisdictions, they are all subject to the single law designated by AGRAL article 36.

Notably, however, because this provision refers to the national law of the deceased, *renvoi* under AGRAL article 41 may come into play. This is especially the case, when the choice of law rules of the applicable foreign law designated by AGRAL article 36 follow the principle of separation of estate, subjecting immovable property to the *lex rei sitae* and movable property to the law of domicile or habitual residence of the deceased, as in the case of common law jurisdictions and China. Indeed, Japanese courts have recognised such a *renvoi* from Chinese law,[371] English law,[372] Indian law[373] and New Zealand law,[374] either because the immovable property of the deceased was situated in Japan, or because the deceased was last domiciled in Japan and bequeathed movable property. A 'partial *renvoi*' concerning only a part of an estate is held admissible by case law and authors, even though it may breach the unity of succession and complicate the law application.[375]

ii. Scope of Application

The law governing the succession under AGRAL article 36 determines all matters arising from the succession. The questions include, in particular, (i) when, how and where the inheritance commences; (ii) who are heirs;[376] (iii) portion of inheritance; (iv) range of estates; and (v) the availability of qualified acceptance or renunciation.[377] When the Japanese judge declares a person's disappearance in accordance with AGRAL article 6, only the direct effect of such declaration (ie, presumption of death) is governed by Japanese law, whereas the law governing the succession, that is, the national law of the deceased (AGRAL article 36), determines whether and when the inheritance commences.[378]

iii. Range of Estates

Concerning the range of assets belonging to estates, it needs to be determined, for instance, whether a claim, which does not fall within estates under the law governing the claim, can nonetheless constitute a part of estates if the law governing the succession provides so. In other words, the question is whether the law governing the succession or the law governing the claim prevails. The traditional academic view favours the German principle of '*Einzelstatut bricht Gesamtstatut*'. This means that, while the law governing the succession

[371] Judgment of Supreme Court, 8 March 1994, *Shumin* 172, 1 ((1995) 38 *JAIL* 142).
[372] Judgment of Tokyo High Court, 5 October 1988, HT 703, 215.
[373] Decision of Kobe Family Court, 27 July 1994, *Kagetsu* 47(5), 60 ((1996) 39 *JAIL* 277).
[374] Decision of Tokyo Family Court, 15 October 1999, *Kagetsu* 52(3), 60.
[375] Kitazawa, 'Uji' (n 9) 326 f. Only a minor opinion used to contend denying a 'partial *renvoi*' to maintain the unity of succession. See Ryoichi Yamada, *Kokusaishiho* (Chikuma Shobo, 1982) 459 f (old view).
[376] Decision of Tokyo High Court, 9 May 2011, *Kagetsu* 63(11), 60.
[377] eg, Decision of Tokyo High Court, 29 October 1987, *Kagetsu* 40(2), 190.
[378] Sakurada, *Kokusai Shiho* (*Private International Law*) (n 1) 339; Sawaki=Dogauchi (n 1) 133.

principally determines the range of estate in principle, the law governing the claim regulating differently and denying inheritability is respected. As a result, both governing laws apply cumulatively.[379]

In a notable case, a Japanese student A had died in a car accident in California, and his Japanese fellow student X, who was a passenger in the car, suffered a serious injury. X brought a claim for damages against A's parents Y1 and Y2 before the Osaka District Court, contending that Y1 and Y2 inherited A's debt to pay damages to X. To determine the inheritability of the debt, the judge applied cumulatively (a) the law governing the succession as a matter of the entire estate, that is, Japanese law as A's national law (*Horei* article 25 prior to the 1989 amendment), and (b) the law governing the tort to define the individual character of the debt, that is, the law of the State of California (*Horei* article 11(1)). The judge dismissed X's claim by denying the inheritability of the debt, on the ground that under California law assets belonging to estates are first subject to liquidation before being distributed to heirs, so heirs can never inherit debts.[380] Arguably, however, even by following the traditional view of cumulative application, the judge could have granted inheritability of the debt in the underlying case, considering that debts are also subject to liquidation in California, which presupposes the inheritability in the sense of 'transferability' of debts.[381]

After this judgment, commentators started to argue instead to apply (a) the law governing the succession and (b) the law governing the debt in a distributive manner. According to this distributive approach, (a) solely determines the general framework of 'inheritability', whereas the law governing the individual assets or debts determines their characteristics, including their 'inheritability'.[382] Today, a majority of authors endorse this distributive approach to clearly discern the scope of application of the respective governing laws and avoid dual characterisation.[383] Other scholars opine that only the law governing each asset or debt ought to be applied, without considering the law applicable to succession.[384]

iv. Transfer of Estates

A similar question arises in relation to the transfer of an estate. For instance, the law governing the succession may provide that the entire estate including movable and immovable property is transferred to the heirs at the time of death of the deceased, while the *lex situs* of such property may require registration or delivery for their transfer.

In a case of a Taiwanese deceased bequeathing several immovable properties situated in Japan, the question arose whether some of the heirs could validly transfer their portion

[379] eg, Tameike (n 16) 542; Yamada, *Kokusai Shiho* (n 16) 575.

[380] Judgment of Osaka District Court, 27 February 1987, HJ 1263, 32.

[381] Sakurada, *Kokusai Shiho* (*Private International Law*) (n 1) 339.

[382] eg, Takami Hayashi, 'Article 36 (Sozoku)' in Yoshiaki Sakurada and Masato Dogauchi (eds), *Chushaku Kokusai Shiho: Dai 2 kan* (*Commentary on Private International Law: Volume 2*) (Yuhikaku, 2011) 198; Sawaki=Dogauchi (n 1) 134–35; Shin'ichiro Hayakawa, '*"Souzoku Zaisan no Kousei" no Junkyo ho ni tsuite*' 38(2–3) *Kandai Hogaku* 707.

[383] For details, see Hayashi (n 382) 198–200.

[384] Kazunori Ishiguro, *Kokusaishiho*, 2nd edn (Shinseisha, 2007) 407 ff.

of inheritance to a third party prior to the division of the estate. While such a disposition was valid under Japanese law, it was not under Taiwanese law, which required the consent of all the other heirs. The Supreme Court divided the issue into two questions: (a) the form of co-ownership between the heirs and the admissibility of disposing of their own portion of inheritance in immovable property prior to the division of the estate, and (b) the proprietary effects of disposing of their portion of inheritance. The first question (a) concerning the effects of succession was referred to the law governing the succession, which was Taiwanese law as the national law of the deceased (*Horei* article 25 prior to the 1989 amendment [now AGRAL article 36]). The second question (b) concerning property rights was referred to the *lex rei sitae*, which was Japanese law (*Horei* article 10 [now AGRAL article 13]).[385] In the underlying case, for lack of consent of the other heirs, the respective portion of inheritance would not have been transferrable to a third party under Taiwanese law. The Supreme Court, however, opined that the proprietary effects need to be determined by Japanese law as the *lex rei sitae*, and that the restriction of transfer of estates under Taiwanese law could not have been entered into the registry of immovables in Japan. Ultimately, for the sake of security of transactions, the Supreme Court applied Japanese law by giving priority to the characterisation as a proprietary issue and validated this transaction.[386]

v. *Administration of Estates*

Under Japanese substantive law, as in most civil law jurisdictions, it is not necessary to appoint an administrator of estates at the commencement of inheritance, because estates are automatically transferred to the heirs. Only in cases where there is obviously no heir or no heir has been identified, will the Family Court appoint an administrator upon request of the parties concerned. By contrast, in common law jurisdictions, an estate administrator needs to be appointed, who first winds up the entire estate of the deceased (including assets and debts), before transferring the remaining assets to the heirs. When, for instance, English law is applicable under AGRAL article 36 and the estate of the deceased is situated in Japan, an adaptation becomes necessary to accommodate the process of administration under the *lex fori*.

vi. *Absence of Heirs*

If there exists no heir, the estate will normally be attributed to the national treasury. Depending on the substantive law, however, the 'attribution of estates' is either conceived as a succession by the state as the last heir (eg, in Germany) or acquisition of ownerless property by the state (*bona vacantia*) (eg, in Japan [CC article 959] or France). According

[385] Judgment of Supreme Court, 8 March 1994, *Shumin* 172, 1 ((1995) 38 *JAIL* 142).

[386] For further details and criticism against this Supreme Court judgment, see Yoshiaki Sakurada, 'Horitsu-Kankei no Seishshitsu-Kettei' in Yoshiaki Sakurada and Masato Dogauchi (eds), *Kokusaishiho Hanrei Hyakusen*, 2nd edn (Yuhikaku, 2012) 5; Shin'ichiro Hayakawa, 'Kokusaiteki na Sozoku/Isankanri no Ichidanmen: Gaikokujin no Isan taru Wagakuni no Fudosan no Torihiki wo megutte (1)–(2)' (1993) 1019 *Jurist* 126; (1993) 1020 *Jurist* 131.

to court decisions and the majority academic view, this question is governed by the law of the state where the property is situated, because it simply concerns the disposition of estates in the absence of heirs, which is an avenue different from the usual succession.[387]

Even in cases where there are no heirs, a person may have shared a livelihood with the deceased, contributed to the deceased's medical treatment and nursing, or had a special connection with the deceased. Under Japanese substantive law (CC article 958-3), such a person can claim the deceased's estate. A majority of authors regard this matter as a particular attribution of property, not the division of estates, to fall within the scope of the law of the place where the property is situated.[388] Court decisions, however, are split on this point. While some lower courts, based on *jori*, referred this question to the *lex rei sitae*,[389] others characterised the issue as an aspect of succession and referred it to the law governing the succession.[390]

Insofar as the deceased was married, matrimonial property claims also come into play. Since the law governing the matrimonial property regime (AGRAL article 26) defines the ownership of assets between the spouses, it ought to first apply to ascertain the range of estates belonging to the deceased, before moving on to the division of the estate among the heirs under the law governing the succession (AGRAL article 36). Depending on the case, some adaptation of both applicable laws may become necessary (see section V.B.ii).[391]

G. Wills

i. *Substantive Validity and Effects of Wills*

A will (or testament) is a unilateral juristic act to express a testator's intention. As part of a will, the testator may determine the division or legacy of his or her estate, establish a trust by appointing a trustee, or acknowledge a child. In determining the applicable law, the majority of Japanese authors distinguish the following two questions: (i) the validity and effects of a will itself, and (ii) the validity and effects of the individual juristic acts (eg, legacy or appointment of a trustee or guardian) that constitute the content of a will.[392]

As for (ii), it is a matter of individual juristic acts. Since the question as to the admissibility of undertaking such act in a will and its validity and effects are specific to those acts, the *lex cause* ought to apply. Thus, legacy and testamentary trust are subject to the law applicable to succession (AGRAL article 36), acknowledgment of the child to the law applicable to

[387] Decision of Osaka District Court, 7 August 1965, HT 185, 154; Decision of Osaka High Court 30 November 1965, *Kagetsu* 18(7), 45; Decision of Tokyo Family Court, 26 September 1966, *Kagetsu* 19(5), 112; Yamada, *Kokusai Shiho* (n 16) 581; Tameike (n 16) 543–44; *cf* Sawaki=Dogauchi (n 1) 137.

[388] eg, Tameike (n 16) 544; Yamada, *Kokusai Shiho* (n 16) 582; *cf* Hayashi (n 382) 207–08.

[389] Decision of Osaka Family Court, 12 August 1977, *Kagetsu* 30(11), 67; Decision of Nagoya Family Court, 25 March 1994, *Kagetsu* 47(3), 79 ((1997) 40 *JAIL* 13).

[390] Decision of Sendai Family Court, 25 January 1972, *Kagetsu* 25(2), 112.

[391] Sakurada, *Kokusai Shiho* (*Private International Law*) (n 1) 285; Hayashi (n 382) 209.

[392] Hayashi (n 382) 213–14; Orimo, *Kokusai Shiho* (n 38) 444; Sakurada, *Kokusai Shiho* (*Private International Law*) (n 1) 341; Masao Sanekata, *Kokusaishiho Gairon* (Yuhikaku, 1952) 388–89; Sawaki/Dogauchi (n 1) 141; Tameike (n 16) 546. As a minority view, Shoichi Kidana, *Kokusai Sozokuho no Kenkyu* (Yuhikaku, 1995) 387–88 contends always applying the law governing the succession, no matter what juristic acts constitute the content of the will.

illegitimate legal parentage (AGRAL article 29), and appointment of a guardian to the law applicable to guardianship (AGRAL article 35).

As for (i) concerning the formation, substantive validity and effects of a will, AGRAL article 37(1) follows the nationality principle and designates the national law of a testator at the time of drawing up the will. *Renvoi* under AGRAL article 41 may come into play.[393] The formal validity of a will is subject to ALAFW, as discussed below.

The law designated by AGRAL article 37(1) applies, in particular, to testamentary capacity, a testator's vitiated intention, and the time of coming into effect of a will. Since AGRAL article 37(1) covers testamentary dispositions in general, the legal institution of succession contracts (eg, in German law) ought to fall within the scope of this provision as well. On the other hand, the admissibility of joint wills requires further consideration. As a matter of substantive law, joint wills are often used in Germany as '*Berliner Testaments*' between spouses, whereas joint wills are prohibited in Japan (CC article 975) and prohibited or restricted in other countries including France and Italy, in order not to bind subsequent dispositions of assets by the surviving party (spouse) and to avoid contradictory content and effect of the will between more than one testator. Against this background, some authors contend always applying the *lex causae* to the admissibility of joint wills as under (ii), characterising this issue as the validity of juristic acts constituting the content of a will.[394] Other authors characterise this issue as primarily falling within AGRAL article 37(1), on the ground that it is closely related to the questions of whether the revocation of a will is restricted and how the testator's free expression of his or her intention ought to be ensured.[395]

ii. Revocation of Wills

Revocation of a will is subject to AGRAL article 37(2), which refers to the national law of a testator at the time of the revocation. *Renvoi* under AGRAL article 41 may come into play. The law applicable to revocation of a will determines capacity to revoke a will, a testator's vitiated intention to revoke a will, and the time of coming into effect of a will. Notably, however, the question of whether a will can be voluntarily revoked by the testator concerns the binding effects of the relevant will, which ought to be governed by the law designated under AGRAL article 37(1), and not under AGRAL article 37(2). When there are several contradictory wills, a majority of authors support applying the *lex cause*, considering that it primarily concerns the validity of juristic acts constituting the content of the wills.[396]

iii. Probate

A will is normally subject to probate by the court prior to the administration of the deceased's estate, although the purpose, method and effects of probate vary from one

[393] Judgment of Tokyo District Court, 24 April 1988, *Kagetsu* 40(9), 77 ((1989) 32 *JAIL* 151).

[394] Sanekata (n 392) 396–97; Orimo, *Kokusai Shiho* (n 38) 446.

[395] Hayashi (n 382) 216; similarly, Jun-ichi Akiba, 'Horei 26: Igon' in Ichiro Shimazu (ed), *Hanrei Kommentar Minpo: Sozoku (Dai 882jo-Dai 1044jo)/Shogai Kazokuho*, enlarged edn (Sanseido, 1983) 884 (Akiba though allows applying the law governing the individual juristic acts constituting the content of a will, insofar as the relevant regulation on joint wills is closely related to the content of the will).

[396] Hayashi (n 382) 215 and 217; Tameike (n 16) 547.

jurisdiction to another. Under Japanese law, probate is intended to archive the will as evidence and prevent it from being forged or falsified. In some jurisdictions (typically, common law jurisdictions), a will must be proved in court before an administrator or executor can distribute or dispose of the deceased's estate in accordance with the will. It is generally accepted that probate, being a matter of procedure, is governed by the *lex fori*. Japanese courts will carry out probate in accordance with local rules, taking the law governing the individual juristic acts constituting the will into account. Although it is usually non-contentious, the judge may need to give special consideration to the substantive or formal validity of the will or other related matters in the course of granting probate.[397]

iv. Formal Requirements

On the form of a will (or testament), Japan is a Contracting State of the Convention of 5 October 1961 on the Conflicts of Laws Relating to the Form of Testamentary Dispositions and enacted ALAFW to implement the Convention. The form of a will is, therefore, subject to ALAFW.

ALAFW article 2 is grounded on the principle of *favor testament* by setting out a series of alternative connecting factors. It was held appropriate to favour the formal validity of a will, as the testator cannot remake a will when its defects are discovered after his or her decease. Under ALAFW article 2, therefore, a will is held formally valid, insofar as formal requirements of any of the following laws are satisfied: (a) the law of the place where the act was performed (*lex loci actus*); (b) the law of the country where the testator had his or her nationality either at the time of making the will or at the time of death; (c) the law of the place where the testator was domiciled at the time of making the will or at the time of death; (d) the law of the place where the testator had his or her habitual residence at the time of making the will or at the time of death; or (e) in the case of a will concerning real property, the law of the place where the real property is situated. Since AGRAL article 41 does not apply to the form of will according to AGRAL article 43, *renvoi* does not come into play.

As to the form of a will revoking an earlier will, ALAFW contains a special choice of law rule in article 3. Pursuant to this provision, the form of a will revoking an earlier will is subject to the law according to which the earlier will was valid or one of the laws listed in article 2. Pursuant to ALAFW article 4, articles 2 and 3 apply to the form of a joint will, insofar as a joint will is admissible under its applicable law, as discussed above. ALAFW article 5 explicitly defines the scope of application of the law governing the form, which extends to limitations due to age, nationality or other personal status of the testator, as well as the qualification of witnesses. Articles 6 and 7 contain supplemental rules to define the testator's national law in the case of a multi-unit state, and the testator's domicile subject to the law of the state where domicile is allegedly located. Article 8 provides for public policy

[397] See Hayashi (n 382) 217–19. To decide whether probate was necessary for the will of a French national, one lower court applied the law governing the formation of a will and the *lex fori* cumulatively without giving any reasons. Decision of Kobe Family Court, 28 November 1958, *Kagetsu* 11(2), 85. On the other hand, there have been some judgments, in which the judges seem to have granted probate simply in accordance with the *lex fori*, that is, Japanese law. For example, Decision of Kobe Family Court, 28 November 1958, *Kagetsu* 11(2), 85.

as a safety valve, although it would seldom occur that applying a foreign law to the form of a will ran counter to public policy in Japan.

VI. Insolvency Law

Questions of insolvency proceedings are subject to the *lex fori concursus*, that is, the law of the place where insolvency proceedings have been opened. That law covers various questions, including the commencement and termination of insolvency proceedings, the extent of assets subject to bankruptcy or rehabilitation, the powers of creditors and liquidators, and the effects of insolvency proceedings.[398] Moreover, several insolvency laws in Japan (namely, the Bankruptcy Act, the Civil Rehabilitation Act and the Corporate Reorganisation Act) deal with particular substantive law issues, such as cancellation by the liquidator of a not yet performed contract between the bankrupt and a counterparty,[399] restriction on a creditor's right of set-off,[400] the right of avoidance exercised by the liquidators, and the invalidity of certain activities by liquidator without permission of the courts.[401] It is still an open question how a Japanese court should deal with these substantive law matters.[402]

Insolvency proceedings aim to secure, among others, an appropriate adjustment of the interests of all the concerned parties (including secured and unsecured creditors) and the rehabilitation of a debtor's economic activities. For the proceedings of a liquidation to be fair, it would be reasonable to follow a packaged framework so that the management of the debtor's affairs can be dealt with uniformly in accordance with a single law, that is, the *lex fori concursus*.[403] Nonetheless, the expectation of the parties concerned (especially creditors) should not be disregarded. Instead, certainty and predictability should be respected to the extent possible, as otherwise safety in transactions would be severely distorted. For instance, where a creditor exercises a right of set-off or right *in rem*, the applicable law of his or her underlying legal relationship should continue to apply either cumulatively or alternatively.[404]

Under Japanese insolvency law, some security rights including a special statutory lien, pledge and mortgage are preferentially treated as rights of separate satisfaction which

[398] Yukio Kaise, 'Tosan Kokusai Shiho' in Akira Takakuwa and Masato Dogauchi (eds), *Shin Saiban Jitsumu Taikei (3): Kokusai Minji Soshoho (Zaisanho Kankei) (International Civil Litigation Law (Proprietary Matters))* (Seirinshoin, 2002) 526–27.

[399] If the bankrupt and his or her counterparty under a bilateral contract have not yet completely performed their obligations by the time of commencement of bankruptcy proceedings, a trustee-in-bankruptcy may cancel the contract or may perform the bankrupt's obligation and request the counterparty to perform the corresponding obligation in accordance with BA article 53(1) (CIRA article 49(1) and CORA article 61(1)).

[400] BA articles 67–73; CIRA articles 92 and 93; and CORA articles 47-2–49.

[401] BA articles 78(5) and 93(2); CIRA articles 41(2), 54(4) and 81(2); and CORA articles 32(2), 35(3), 46(9) and 72(3).

[402] For developments in Japan, see Yoshihisa Hayakawa, 'Tosan Kokusai Shiho' in Yoshiaki Sakurada and Masato Dogauchi (eds), *Chushaku Kokusai Shiho: Dai 1 kan (Commentary on Private International Law: Volume 1)* (Yuhikaku, 2011) 591–97.

[403] Some commentators take the view that as the insolvency law provisions regulating these substantive law matters strongly reflect the public interest, the provisions should be regarded as overriding mandatory rules and applied so long as they require application. Sawaki=Dogauchi (n 1) 396.

[404] *cf* article 7 of the Regulation (EU) 2015/848 of the European Parliament and of the Council of 20 May 2015 on insolvency proceedings (recast) [2015] OL L141/19.

can be exercised without going through insolvency proceedings.[405] Issues that the *lex fori concursus* does not cover (such as the capacity of a bankrupt to conclude a contract and the formation and effects of security rights) should be governed by the law applicable to the relevant legal relationship.

VII. Competition Law

Competition (antitrust) law concerns a broad range of areas, giving rise to various legal relationships (see chapter three, section III.B). Depending on their nature, those relationships can be categorised into two groups: (1) contractual relationships, and (2) tortious relationships. For these relationships, the relevant choice of law rules in contract or tort will apply respectively (for contractual relationships, see section II.A; for tortious relationships, see section II.C).

A. Contracts

The first group covers situations such as, for instance, where a party to a contract sues the other party to seek a declaration of the nullity of allegedly unfair contractual terms, contending the defendant infringing competition law. Such issue would be subject to the law applicable to the contract: (a) the applicable law that the parties had designated in accordance with AGRAL article 7 or (b), in the absence of such choice of law, the law that has the closest connection with the contract pursuant to AGRAL article 8.

Competition law rules that regulate anti-competitive activities (such as abuse of dominant position) to maintain and promote the market order in Japan and thereby nullify the contract may be regarded as overriding mandatory rules of Japan.[406] When such rule requires its unilateral application to the case at hand, it would interfere in specific issues (eg, the validity of a whole contract or some particular contractual terms), irrespective of the applicable law designated under the general choice of law rules for contract in AGRAL articles 7–9 (see section II.A.vi). As a result, Japanese overriding mandatory rules literally will 'override' relevant provisions of otherwise applicable foreign law.

B. Torts

The second group covers situations such as, for instance, where a victim of a cartel sues cartel participants to seek damages or an injunction based on the infringement of competition law or where a party to a contract sues the other party for damages in respect of an abuse of a dominant market position contrary to competition law. It remains unclear how Japanese courts will approach these issues for the choice of law purpose.

[405] eg, BA article 65 and CIRA article 53.

[406] eg, Decision of Tokyo District Court, 28 August 2007, HJ 1991, 89.

During the drafting of AGRAL, there were concerns about the application by the Japanese courts of foreign competition law as such law was regarded as being of a public law nature.[407] It is true that competition law civil claims contribute to the market order, that is, serve the public interest. Those claims simply seek private law remedies and are of a strictly private law nature. Victims are free to dispose of their own claims and they are not compelled by competition authority or courts to bring competition law claims. They can even settle their claims. In this sense, competition law civil claims have a nature similar to tortious claims (including product liability) that further public interest to a certain extent. There seems to be no good reason to treat these claims differently from other tortious claims. Accordingly, the applicability of foreign competition law should not be denied, as far as civil aspects of competition law are concerned.[408]

Considering that claims based on competition law infringement are in nature tortious, Japanese courts will likely rely on the general choice of law rules for tort (in particular, AGRAL article 17).[409] If so, the place of the relevant competition law wrong must be identified. The place of injury within the meaning of AGRAL article 17, first sentence, could be interpreted as the place where the market is (or is likely to be) affected by the anti-competitive activity. This is because competition law aims to promote the development and maintenance of market order by regulating anti-competitive activities, thereby protecting the interests of private parties in having a level playing field within the market. This understanding of the place of injury should apply to competition law infringement by means of cartel agreements and an abuse of dominant position. Note, however, that the law of the place of injury can be excluded if the occurrence of injury at that place would be unpredictable (AGRAL article 17, second sentence). That said, the harm should normally be predictable because anti-competitive activities such as a cartel and an abuse of dominant position target specific markets or competitors in specific markets. Therefore, the law of the place where the harmful act originates is unlikely to come into play. In addition, the law of the place of the harmful act may not have the closest connection with the case. This is because it is widely accepted that each state applies its competition law based on

[407] Minutes of 6th and 17th Meetings (AGRAL); Koide (n 31) 228–29.

[408] If the applicability of foreign competition law was denied, in cases of cross-border competition law claims, Japanese courts would apply only Japanese competition law, with the result that they could deal with competition law claims based solely on Japanese law. In this case, the critical question is the international scope of Japanese competition law, that is, how far that law can reach. As to the international scope of Japanese competition law in cartel cases, the Supreme Court has adopted the effects doctrine and clarified that Japanese competition law can be applied to a case having foreign elements insofar as the requirements of relevant substantive law provisions were satisfied (namely, evidence that an anti-competitive activity (wherever it may take place) runs counter to some substantive provision of Japanese competition law). Decision of Supreme Court, 12 December 2017, *Minshu* 71(10), 1958 ((2018) 61 *JYIL* 399). See Kazuaki Nishioka, 'International Scope of the Japanese Anti-Monopoly Act in Cross-Border Cartel Cases: A Japanese Approach to "Extraterritorial Application"' (2020) 8 *Journal of Antitrust Enforcement* 590.

[409] As to abuse of dominant power, Judgment of Tokyo District Court, 4 September 2019, 2019WLJPCA09048001. See also Kazuaki Nishioka, 'Kyoso Seigen Koi no Junkyoho: EU oyobi Switzerland ni okeru Giron karano Shisa' (2015) 17 *JYPIL* 157; Kanzaki, *Kaisetsu Ho no Tekiyou ni kansuru Tsuusokuho* (*Commentary on the Act on General Rules for Application of Law*) (n 123) 122–23. *cf* Nishitani, 'Article 17 (Fuho Koi)' (n 219) 452–53. Given that an anti-competitive activity is a market-based tort, one may argue that claims for competition law infringement should be governed, based on *jori*, exclusively by the law of the market which is (or is likely to be) affected. As *de lege ferenda* it would be reasonable to set out a choice of law rule referring tortious claims based on competition law infringement to the law of the market with only the limited party autonomy described in the main text.

the effects of a cartel agreement or the abuse of dominant position on its market. Only a state, whose market is affected, will have a genuine interest in applying its law and regulating anti-competitive activities. For instance, when it comes to the effects of a cartel on the Swiss market, Japanese law does not have an interest in regulating such conduct, even if the cartel agreement had been concluded in Japan. In this regard, the application of the place of harmful act should be excluded.

Under AGRAL article 20, another law that is obviously more closely connected with the case may be applied in the alternative. In a case involving the abuse of dominant power, the Tokyo District Court referred tortious claims based on an abuse of dominant power to the governing law of the contract via AGRAL article 20. This was done on the basis that, as the abuse was in relation to contractual obligations, it was necessary to ascertain the exact scope of the wrongdoer's contractual obligations in order to determine whether the alleged wrongs constituted torts. The claims were thus more closely connected with the state whose law governed the contract.[410] However, in the context of competition law, such an exceptional reference should not be granted. First, as mentioned earlier, the state whose market is (or likely to be) affected should have the closest connection with the case and no other state can be more plainly closely connected. Anti-competitive activities can only have any meaning in the context of a specific market (a market-based tort). In other words, without an effect on competition in a specific market, there could be no anti-competitive activity at all. In this way, the relationship between the wrongful activities and the specific market is inseparable. Indeed, each market has its own market rule to regulate and maintain order. If different laws apply to a single market as a result of the resort to different choice of law rules, the same activity may be legal or illegal, depending on the applicable market rules. Such a situation could distort the market order and result in increasing legal uncertainty.

Parties can agree on the applicable law subsequent to a tort in accordance with AGRAL article 21. This should be the case in the competition law context as well, as competition law civil claims simply seek private law remedies such as damages. Victims are free to dispose of their own claims. The parties' choice should, however, be confined to the purely civil aspects of competition law claims, that is, provisions regarding private law remedies (in particular, what remedies are available and to what extent damages can be awarded). This is because market rules embody the national policy of competition and their applicability should not be left to private parties. If the parties were free to choose any market rules other than those of the state whose market has been affected, there would again be the risk of different (potentially incompatible) law applying to a single market. This could distort the market order.

In addition, Japanese law is always cumulatively applied pursuant to the double actionability rule (AGRAL article 22). However, article 22 ought to be abolished *de lege ferenda*, and at least be subject to a strictly narrow interpretation, restricting its scope of application (see section II.C.i).

[410] Judgment of Tokyo District Court, 4 September 2019, 2019WLJPCA09048001.

4

Recognition and Enforcement of Foreign Judgments

I. Recognition

A. General Principles and Overview

With regard to the recognition and enforcement of foreign judgments,[1] Japan has concluded some international conventions in specific legal areas (see section I.B). It has not ratified relevant Hague Conventions: the Convention on the Recognition and Enforcement of Foreign Judgments in Civil and Commercial Matters (HREC, 1971); the Convention on Jurisdiction, Applicable Law, Recognition, Enforcement and Co-operation in Respect of Parental Responsibility and Measures for the Protection of Children (HPRC, 1996); the Convention on Choice of Court Agreements (Hague Choice of Court Convention) (HCC, 2005); the Convention on the International Recovery of Child Support and Other Forms of Family Maintenance (HIRC, 2007); or Convention of 2 July 2019 on the Recognition and Enforcement of Foreign Judgments in Civil or Commercial Matters (Hague Judgments Convention) (HJC, 2019). Recognition of foreign judgments in Japan is thus to a large extent subject to domestic laws. Recognition of foreign judgments in civil and commercial matters is largely governed by the Code of Civil Procedure (CCP) article 118. Recognition of foreign judgments in family law matters is subject to different laws, depending on the nature of relevant matters[2] (see chapter two, section III.A.i).[3] Recognition of foreign judgments on matters that come under the Personal Status Litigation Act (PSLA) is subject to CCP article 118, while judgments on matters that come under the Domestic Relations Case Procedure Act (DRCPA) are governed by DRCPA article 79-2. Having said that, the requirements under DRCPA are principally identical to those under CCP article 118. This is because DRCPA article 79-2 refers to CCP article 118, applying *mutatis mutandis* the requirements

[1] For recognition and enforcement of foreign arbitral awards, see ch 5.

[2] As to recognition of foreign judgments in family law matters, some commentators once took the view that recognition of judgments determining a legal right or status (in particular, divorce decrees) and judgments on non-contentious matters were subject to relevant choice of law rules in *Horei* (for instance, Hidefumi Egawa, 'Gaikoku Hanketsu no Shonin' (1932) 50(11) *Hogaku Kyokai Zasshi* 2054, 2082; Shoichi Kidana, 'Gaikoku Rikon Hanketsu no Shonin ni kansuru ichi Kosatsu – Shonin Kisoku to Teishoku Kisoku no Kankei ni tsuite' (1978) 137 *Ritsumeikan Hogaku* 31). Today, it is widely acknowledged that recognition of foreign judgments on those matters is governed by the recognition scheme of CCP. See, eg, Takaki Tokuoka, 'Mibun Kankei Jiken nikansuru Gaikoku Saiban no Shonin' in Takao Sawaki and Yoshimitsu Aoayama (eds), *Kokusai Minji Soshoho no Riron* (Yuhikaku, 1987); Morio Takeshita, 'Article 118' in Hajime Kaneko et al, *Jokai Minji Soshoho*, 2nd edn (Kobundo, 2011).

[3] Where a family relationship is formed by reason of a factual act abroad such as voluntary recognition by a father or delivering a baby, such relationship to be legally binding in Japan, must fulfil the requirements of designated applicable laws under relevant choice of law rules (choice of law approach).

of the latter. Accordingly, to be recognised in Japan, foreign judgments or decisions must principally satisfy the requirements under CCP article 118. An exception is the recognition of foreign insolvency proceedings, which is subject to the Act on Recognition and Assistance for Foreign Insolvency Proceedings (ARAFIP) (see section III). This chapter mainly deals with the recognition scheme under article CCP 118 for the sake of convenience.

Foreign judgments are automatically recognised in Japan as long as the requirements in CCP article 118 are satisfied (see section I.C). It is not necessary to apply to the Japanese court for a decision recognising a foreign judgment. Article 118 sets out five requirements for recognition: (a) a final and binding judgment rendered by a foreign court; (b) indirect jurisdiction of the foreign court; (c) proper service of process; (d) conformity with public policy in Japan; and (e) reciprocity. Article 118 does not explicitly rule out the possibility of a review of the merits (*révision au fond*) of the foreign judgment. However, in light of the Civil Execution Act (CEA) article 24 stipulating that there is no review of the merits in rendering an *exequatur* (see section II.B), it is generally acknowledged that such review is not admissible for recognising foreign judgments.[4] Since a foreign judgment is automatically recognised, the parties do not need to go through any formal procedure.[5] In practical terms, nevertheless, parties can seek a judicial confirmation that foreign judgments do or do not fulfil the requirements of recognition, insofar as they can prove their legitimate interests in such a decision. Furthermore, the parties can invoke the effects of a foreign judgment when a Japanese court has actually recognised it incidentally as a *res judicata* in different court proceedings. In theory, foreign judgments have effect unless their validity is contested.[6]

Conceptually, Japanese law distinguishes recognition from enforcement. Recognition involves admitting in Japan the effects of foreign decisions (for instance, declaratory judgments, judgments determining a legal right or status, and judgments ordering the defendant to perform or refrain from a certain action).[7] It is governed by CCP article 118. Enforcement, on the other hand, concerns the exercise of state power in Japan to execute foreign judgments. It is governed by CEA article 22(6) and 24. Only judgments ordering the defendant to perform or refrain from a specific action can be enforced.[8] To enforce such judgments, a successful party needs to obtain an enforcement judgment or *exequatur* (*shikko hanketsu*) from a competent court in Japan. However, since the court is prohibited to conduct a review of the merits (CEA article 24(4)), its examination is limited to whether the foreign judgment fulfils the requirements for recognition in CCP article 118. In other words, a foreign

[4] Yoshiaki Sakurada, *Kokusai Shiho* (*Private International Law*), 7th edn (Yuhikaku, 2020) 395 (Sakurada).

[5] Yuko Nishitani, 'Jinji Sosho Jiken oyobi Kaji Jiken no Kokusai Saibankankatsu tou ni kansuru Shin Hosei (2)' (2019) 71 *Hoso Jiho* 715, 748 (Nishitani (2)).

[6] See Judgment of Tokyo District Court, 17 December 1971, HJ 665, 72; Judgment of Tokyo District Court, 30 November 1973, *Kagetsu* 26(10), 83; Judgment of Tokyo District Court 19 September 1980, HT 435, 155; Judgment of Yokohama District Court, 19 October 1982, *Kagetsu* 36(2), 101; Judgment of Tokyo District Court, 11 November 1988, HJ 1315, 96; Judgment of Yokohama District Court, 30 March 1999, HJ 1696, 120; Judgment of Tokyo Family Court, 11 September 2007, *Kagetsu* 60(1), 108.

[7] It is still an open question whether Japan assumes the effects of foreign judgments under the law of the rendering state or gives effect to the foreign judgment under Japanese law. See Akira Takakuwa, 'Gaikoku Saiban no Shonin' in Akira Takakuwa and Masato Dogauchi (eds), *Shin Saiban Jitsumu Taikei (3): Kokusai Minji Soshoho (Zaisanho Kankei)* (*International Civil Litigation Law* (*Proprietary Matters*)) (Seirinshoin, 2002) 311.

[8] This includes foreign decisions ordering delivery of a child. On the other hand, other types of foreign judgments, ie, declaratory judgments (eg, negative declaration of obligations to pay damages) and constitutive judgments (eg, divorce decree), do not presuppose 'enforcement' under Japanese law. Thus, the registration of a foreign divorce judgment at municipal office does not fall under the category of 'enforcement' in Japan.

judgment ordering the defendant to perform or refrain from a specific action is basically enforceable insofar as it can be recognised in Japan.

B. Recognition under Bilateral, Multilateral Treaties and Conventions

Japan has not entered into any bilateral treaties with other countries for the mutual recognition and enforcement of judgments. As stated earlier, Japan has concluded some international (multilateral) conventions which provide for the mutual recognition and enforcement of judgments. These are: the International Convention on Civil Liability for Oil Pollution Damage (CLC); the Protocol of 1992 to the International Convention on the Establishment of an International Fund for Compensation for Oil Pollution Damage (FUND 1992); the Protocol of 2003 to the International Convention on the Establishment of an International Fund for Compensation for Oil Pollution Damage (FUND 2003); and the Convention on Supplementary Compensation for Nuclear Damage (CSC). Typically, under these conventions, a foreign judgment is recognised as long as the rendering court has jurisdiction in accordance with the relevant provisions of a convention and a judgment is no longer subject to ordinary forms of review in the rendering state (CLC article 10(1); FUND 1992 article 8; FUND 2003 article 8(1); and CSC article 13(5)). However, the recognition of judgments may be refused in exceptional cases, such as where the foreign judgment was obtained by fraud or a defendant was not given reasonable notice or a fair opportunity to present a case (CLC article 10(1); FUND 1992 article 8; FUND 2003 article 8(1); and CSC article 13(5)). In addition, under the CSC, the recognition of judgments may be refused where it would be contrary to public policy or it would not accord with fundamental standards of justice (article 13(5)(c)). FUND 2003 article 8(2) authorises a contracting state to 'apply other rules for the recognition and enforcement of judgments, provided that their effect is to ensure that judgments are recognised and enforced at least to the same extent as under paragraph 1'. Once recognised pursuant to one of these conventions, a judgment is enforceable in a contracting state as long as the requisite formalities have been complied with (CLC article 10(2); FUND 1992 article 8; FUND 2003 article 8(1); and CSC article 13(6)). The enforcing state cannot reopen the merits of the case (CLC article 10(2); FUND 1992 article 8; FUND 2003 article 8(1); and CSC article 13(6)). Japan has enacted the Act on Liability for Oil Pollution Damage (ALOPD) to implement CLC, FUND 1992 and FUND 2003. Therefore, recognition of foreign judgments relating to matters falling under any of those conventions is subject to the recognition scheme therein.[9]

C. Recognition under National Laws

i. *Final and Binding Judgment*

To be recognised in Japan, a foreign judgment must be 'a final and binding judgment rendered by a foreign court' within the meaning of CCP article 118. CCP and CEA do not

[9] See ALOPD articles 12, 27 and 30-3.

define 'a final and binding judgment rendered by a foreign court'. The Supreme Court has defined this term as follows:

> A final judgment rendered by a foreign court on private law relations by providing procedural guarantee to both parties, regardless of the name, procedure, or form of judgment. Even if the judgment is called a decision or order, insofar as it possesses the characteristics of the above, it should be regarded as a judgment of a foreign court.[10]

It follows from the holding that the term 'court' may include any authority that regularly exercises judicial functions and is empowered to issue binding decisions on the parties.[11] As regards the types of judgment to be recognised, Japanese courts have held that default judgments,[12] summary judgments[13] and decisions on procedural costs[14] also fall within the notion of a 'judgment'. The Supreme Court in 2014 held that a permanent injunctive order can also be recognised.[15] Accordingly, both monetary and non-monetary judgments are recognisable in Japan. The prevailing view is that admissions, waiver of claims, authentic instruments or judicial settlements do not fall under the notion of a 'judgment', and therefore they are not recognisable in Japan, even if they have the same effect as a final and binding judgment in the rendering state.[16] On the other hand, a judgment by a foreign court based on a settlement agreement, or consent order, is recognisable and enforceable as a foreign judgment.[17]

The Supreme Court has stressed that a foreign judgment pertaining to 'private law relations' is capable of being recognised under CCP article 118.[18] It is generally understood in Japan that the term 'private law relations' refers to 'civil and commercial matters' including personal status matters.[19] Decisions relating to administrative, criminal or tax matters do not fall within the notion of 'civil and commercial matters' and therefore are not recognisable under CCP. A much-debated question is whether judgments awarding punitive damages can be considered as a 'foreign judgment on private law relations'. The Supreme Court and

[10] Judgment of Supreme Court, 28 April 1998, *Minshu* 52(3), 853 ((1999) 42 *JAIL* 155). This should also be the case in the family law context, as long as procedural guarantee is provided to the parties. Nishitani (2) (n 5) 750; Manabu Iwamoto, 'Recognition and Enforcement of Foreign Decisions on Personal Status Litigation and Family Relations Cases' (2019) 62 *JYIL* 226, 229–30 and 240–41.

[11] Nozomi Tada, 'Enforcement of Foreign Judgments in Japan regarding Business Activities' (2003) 46 *JAIL* 75, 82; Muneki Uchino (ed), *Ichimon Itto Heisei 30 Nen Jinji Soshoho Kaji Jiken Tetsuzukiho to Kaisei: Kokusai Saiban Kankatsu Hosei no Seibi* (*Explanatory Note on the 2018 Reform of the Personal Status Litigation Act, Domestic Relations Case Procedure Act: Improvement of the institution on International Adjudicative Jurisdiction*) (Shojihomu, 2019) 164 (Uchino).

[12] Judgment of Nagoya District Court, 6 February 1987, HJ 1236, 113 ((1990) 33 *JAIL* 189); Judgment of Tokyo District Court, 14 January 1994, HJ 1509, 96; Judgment of Tokyo District Court, 31 January 1994, HJ 1509, 101.

[13] Judgment of Tokyo District Court, 25 February 1998, HT 972, 258.

[14] Judgment of Supreme Court, 28 April 1998, *Minshu* 52(3), 853 ((1999) 42 *JAIL* 155).

[15] Judgment of Supreme Court, 24 April 2014, *Minshu* 68(4), 329 ((2015) 58 *JYIL* 463). On this decision, see Béligh Elbalti, 'The Jurisdiction of Foreign Courts and the Recognition of Judgments Ordering Injunction – The Supreme Court Judgment of April 24, 2014' (2016) 59 *JYIL* 395.

[16] Takakuwa, 'Gaikoku Saiban no Shonin' (n 7) 308; Yasunori Honma, Shun'ichiro Nakano and Hajime Sakai, *Kokusai Minji Tetsuzuki-ho* (*International Procedure Law*), 2nd edn (Yuhikaku, 2012) 181 (Honma/Nakano/Sakai). *cf* Eiji Adachi, 'Wagakuni ni okeru Beikoku Kurasu Akushion jouno Wakai no Shounin Tekikaku' in Yoshimitsu Aoayama et al (eds), *Gendai Shakai ni okeru Minji Tetsuduki-ho no Tenkai* (Shoji Homu, 2002).

[17] Takakuwa, 'Gaikoku Saiban no Shonin' (n 7) 308.

[18] Judgment of Supreme Court, 28 April 1998, *Minshu* 52(3), 853 ((1999) 42 *JAIL* 155).

[19] Yasuhiro Okuda, 'Recognition and Enforcement of Foreign Judgments in Japan' (2013/14) 15 *YPIL* 413 (Okuda/REJ) 413; Jun Yokoyama, *Private International Law in Japan*, 2nd edn (Kluwer Law International, 2019) 151.

the prevailing view are that foreign judgments awarding punitive damages generally qualify as civil and commercial matters, although their recognition and enforcement may well be refused for breaching public policy (see section I.C.iv).[20]

The expression 'final and binding' means that a foreign court judgment is no longer subject to ordinary forms of review in the rendering state.[21] Therefore, judgments that are not final and binding, such as interlocutory judgments,[22] cannot be recognised under CCP article 118.[23] By a similar token, according to the prevailing view and case law, provisional measures and judicial settlements do not qualify as 'final and binding' judgments under CCP article 118.[24]

The fact that the rendering state has not been diplomatically recognised by the Japanese government in terms of public international law does not affect the eligibility of judgments of that state to be recognised in Japan.[25] Furthermore, there are various 'common courts' in the world, such as the BENELUX Court and the envisaged European Patent Court, to which the participating sovereign states have transferred judicial authority to render a binding judgment. Insofar as such common courts exercise judicial power and render judgments in civil and commercial matters, they are capable of being recognised and enforced in Japan.[26]

In the family law context, DRCPA article 79-2 not only refers to 'final and binding decisions by a foreign court', but also to 'decisions by equivalent public authorities'. The latter wording clarifies that that the article covers decisions by a foreign legislative or administrative body concerning, for instance, divorce or payment of child support decrees.[27]

ii. Indirect Jurisdiction

CCP article 118(1) requires a foreign court to have jurisdiction (so-called 'indirect jurisdiction') to render a judgment under Japanese law or treaties.[28] However, there are

[20] Judgment of Supreme Court, 11 July 1997, *Minshu* 51(6), 2573 ((1998) 41 *JAIL* 104); Takakuwa, 'Gaikoku Saiban no Shonin' (n 7) 308–09. *Contra*, eg, Judgment of Tokyo High Court, 28 June 1993, HJ 1471, 89 ((1994) 37 *JAIL* 155).

[21] Judgment of Tokyo District Court, 19 March 2008, 2008WLJPCA03198003. Honma/Nakano/Sakai (n 16) 180; Takao Sawaki and Masato Dogauchi, *Kokusai Shiho Nyumon* (*Introduction to Private International Law*), 8th edn (Yuhikaku, 2018) 345 (Sawaki=Dogauchi); Uchino (n 11) 162.

[22] Toshiyuki Kono, 'Japan' in Adeline Chong (ed), *Recognition and Enforcement of Foreign Judgments in Asia* (Asian Business Law Institute, 2017) 106–07 [4] (Kono/Report); Yokoyama (n 19) 151.

[23] Kono/Report (n 22) 106–07 [4]; Yokoyama (n 19) 429.

[24] Judgment of the Supreme Court, 26 February 1985, *Kagetsu* 37(6), 25 ((1985) 28 *JAIL* 225). Some commentators take the view that foreign provisional measures should be recognised in exceptional cases. See, eg, Shun'ichiro Nakano, 'Gaikoku Hozen Meirei no Koryoku' in Akira Takakuwa and Masato Dogauchi (eds), *Shin Saiban Jitsumu Taikei (3): Kokusai Minji Soshoho (Zaisanho Kankei)* (*International Civil Litigation Law (Proprietary Matters)*) (Seirinshoin, 2002) 414.

[25] Takakuwa, 'Gaikoku Saiban no Shonin' (n 7) 307; Toshiyuki Kono, 'Gaikoku Saibansho' in Akira Takakuwa and Masato Dogauchi (eds), *Shin Saiban Jitsumu Taikei (3): Kokusai Minji Soshoho (Zaisanho Kankei)* (*International Civil Litigation Law (Proprietary Matters)*) (Seirinshoin, 2002) 318–21; Shun'ichiro Nakano, 'Gaikoku Hanketsu no Shikko' in Hiroshi Takahashi and Shintaro Kato (eds), *Jitsumu Minji Sosho Koza (Dai San Ki) Dai Roku Kan: Joso, Saishin, Shogaku Sosho to Kokusai Minji Sosho* (Nippon Hyoron Sha, 2013) 445. As for recognition of judgments by international courts such as the Court of Justice of the EU (CJEU) and the International Court of Justice (ICJ), see Honma/Nakano/Sakai (n 16) 180; Kono, ibid, 322–24; Nakano, ibid, 445.

[26] See discussions in relation to HJC, in particular, Preliminary Document No 7 of April 2019 – Note on 'common courts' in article 4(5), (6) of the 2018 draft Convention.

[27] Uchino (n 11) 164; Minutes of 5th Meeting (PSLA and DRCPA).

[28] Judgment of Supreme Court, 28 April 1998, *Minshu* 52(3), 853 ((1999) 42 *JAIL* 155).

no provisions setting out grounds for indirect jurisdiction. Nor has Japan ratified any bilateral or multilateral treaties on the mutual recognition and enforcement of judgments (except for CLC; FUND; and CSC). In the absence of specific rules for indirect jurisdiction, the Supreme Court held in 1998 that indirect jurisdiction should be examined in light of *jori* (reasonableness), principally in accordance with the rules on local jurisdiction from the viewpoint of whether it is appropriate to recognise a given foreign judgment, taking into consideration the specific circumstances of each case (ie. the criteria used by the foreign court to establish its direct jurisdiction over a case). While the Supreme Court decision has been explained by a Supreme Court Judicial Research Officer (*saiko saibansho chosakan*) as not adopting the 'mirror-image' approach that dictates application of identical rules to direct and indirect jurisdiction,[29] this has remained controversial among academics,[30] and lower courts have simply reiterated the formulation of the Supreme Court.[31] Even after the 2012 amendment of CCP introducing direct jurisdiction rules, the position under case law remained unclear. In 2014, the Supreme Court opined:

> It is appropriate to construe that in an action other than those relating to personal status matters, indirect jurisdiction of the foreign rendering court should be determined in light of *jori* (reasonableness), considering whether it is appropriate for Japan to recognise a judgment rendered by the foreign court in light of specific circumstances of the individual case, principally following the provisions on international jurisdiction under the CCP.[32]

The Supreme Court Judicial Research Officer again explained the decision as not adhering to the mirror-image approach,[33] while academic opinion remains divided on how to assess the Supreme Court's position.[34] Despite these uncertainties, the Supreme Court at least has made it clear that direct jurisdiction grounds under CCP are relevant. Thus, foreign judgments satisfy the requirement of indirect jurisdiction in principle, insofar as the foreign rendering court fulfilled one of the direct jurisdiction grounds under CCP, such as the defendant's domicile[35] or principal place of business,[36] place of performance of the contractual obligation,[37] place of tort[38] and the defendant's submission.[39]

[29] Yoshinori Kawabe, 'Saiko Saibansho Chosakan Kaisetsu' in Hoso Kai (ed), *Saiko Saibansho Hanrei Kaisetsu Heisei 10 (1998) Nendo (Jo)* (Hoso Kai, 1998) 339.

[30] Some commentators take the view that the Supreme Court adopted the mirror-image approach (eg, Kazuhiko Yamamoto, 'Case Notes' (1999) 1157 *Juristo* 299; Yasushi Nakanishi, 'Case Notes' (2003) 169 *Bessatsu Juristo* 253), while others advocate that it did not do so (eg, Kono, 'Gaikoku Saibansho' (n 25) 337; Eiji Adachi, 'Case Notes' (1999) 678 *NBL* 65).

[31] Mari Nagata, 'Kokusai Saibankankatsu Kitei no Rippo to Kokusai Torihiki he no Eikyo' (2012) 13 *Kokusai Shotorihiki Gakkai Nenpo* 205, 219.

[32] Judgment of Supreme Court, 24 April 2014, *Minshu* 68(4), 329 ((2015) 58 *JYIL* 463).

[33] Takashi Hirose, '*Saiko Saibansho Chosakan Kaisetsu*' (2015) 67(9) *Hoso Jiho* 339.

[34] For the view that the Supreme Court adopted a mirror-image approach, see Yokoyama (n 19) 151–52. For the view that the criteria for direct and indirect jurisdiction are not necessarily identical, see, eg, Naoshi Takasugi, 'Nihon Kokunai deno Shingai Koui no Sashitome wo meijita Gaikoku Hanketsu no Nihon deno Shikko' (2014) 1032 *NBL* 18, 21–22.

[35] Judgment of Supreme Court, 28 April 1998, *Minshu* 52(3), 853 ((1999) 42 *JAIL* 155).

[36] Judgment of Supreme Court, 26 September 2002, *Minshu* 56(7), 1551 ((2002) 45 *JAIL* 175).

[37] Judgment of Tokyo District Court, 14 January 1994, HJ, 1509, 96.

[38] Judgment of Tokyo District Court, Hachioji Branch, 13 February 1998, HT 987, 282.

[39] Judgment of Nagoya District Court, 6 February 1987, HJ 1236, 113 ((1990) 33 *JAIL* 189).

A further question is whether the special circumstances test under CCP article 3-9 applies when assessing indirect jurisdiction. There has been no case law in this respect and academic opinions are divergent.[40] Some authors support its applicability, while others are opposed, on the grounds that this provision solely serves as a basis for refusing jurisdiction, instead of establishing jurisdiction. According to the Supreme Court, however, indirect jurisdiction is determined in light of *jori*, allowing use of criteria different from direct jurisdiction rules. It would be reasonable to assume that the judge may consider the specific circumstances of an individual case within the framework of *jori*, irrespective of whether CCP article 3-9 applies.

PSLA and DRCPA provide relatively narrow jurisdictional grounds, compared with foreign legal systems (see chapter two, section III). For instance, Japanese courts may not take jurisdiction in divorce cases merely upon the plaintiff's domicile or habitual residence in Japan, as opposed to a large number of foreign jurisdictions.[41] As a result, foreign judgments or decisions (particularly in matrimonial matters) will be refused recognition for lack of indirect jurisdiction, if the same criteria as those for direct jurisdiction are applied. This outcome would run counter to some basic principles such as maintaining the stability of family relationships, deterrence of limping family relations and fulfilment of a child's best interests. In this respect, indirect jurisdiction ought to be granted in accordance with a different, more generous standard than direct jurisdiction.[42] Specifically, courts should promote the test of foreseeability and legal certainty, such as, for instance, whether a foreign rendering state had a sufficiently close connection with a case justifying summonsing the other party before the court of that state.[43]

iii. Proper Service of Process

The requirement of proper service under CCP article 118(2) aims to ensure the defendant's right to be heard at the commencement of proceedings. Japanese courts are required to examine whether the defendant has duly been served with necessary documents to institute proceedings. The Supreme Court has held that:

> [T]he serving of process necessary to commence an action against defendants mentioned in CCP article 118(2) does not have to comply with the laws and rules of our civil procedure. But it is required that the service provide the defendant with actual knowledge of the commencement of an action and not hinder the exercise of his or her right to be heard.[44]

CCP article 118(2) explicitly excludes service by public notice and other similar types of service. In such a case, even if service by public notice was admissible under the law of

[40] See Eiji Adachi, 'Gaikoku Hanketsu no Shonin Shikko ni okeru Kokusai Saiban Kankatsu' in Hideyuki Kobayashi (ed), *Kokusai Saiban Kankatsu no Riron to Jitsumu* (Shinnippon Hoki, 2017) 352.

[41] For instance, in the EU, article 3(a) of the 2003 Brussels II*bis* Regulation (Council Regulation (EC) No 2201/2003) and 2019 Brussels II*bis* Regulation (Recast) (Council Regulation (EU) 2019/1111); in the UK, article 5(2)(b) of the Domicile and Matrimonial Proceedings Act (DMPA) 1973; in the US, *Williams et al v North Carolina* 317 US 287 (1942); in Australia, article 39(3)(b) of the Family Law Act 1975.

[42] Nishitani (2) (n 5) 754.

[43] Nishitani (2) (n 5) 754; Masako Murakami, 'Gaikoku Saiban no Shounin, Shikko' (2018) 27 *Ronkyu Juristo* 47, 49.

[44] Judgment of Supreme Court, 28 April 1998, *Minshu* 52(3), 853 ((1999) 42 *JAIL* 155).

the rendering state, the foreign judgment is refused recognition.[45] Moreover, the Supreme Court held:

> [F]rom the viewpoint of ensuring clarity and stability of the procedure of litigation, if there is a treaty of judicial cooperation between the country of judgment and Japan and if this treaty provides that the service of the document required for the commencement of litigation must be effected in a manner set out in this treaty, service of documents not in accordance with the manner set out in the treaty should not be regarded as service which fulfils the requirement of the above provision of the CCP.[46]

In addition to bilateral treaties with the US and UK and some judicial assistance agreements or arrangements,[47] Japan has ratified the Convention of 15 November 1965 on the Service Abroad of Judicial and Extrajudicial Documents in Civil or Commercial Matters (HSC)[48] and Convention of 1 March 1954 on Civil Procedure (see chapter two, section I.C). Where one of these instruments applies, service must have been conducted accordingly when initiating the foreign proceedings.[49] Japan has made reservation to HSC article 8 and 10(a)(b)(c), so postal service to and direct consulate service in Japan, among others, are excluded. A defendant's voluntary submission before the foreign court would cure the absence of proper service. It is sufficient that the defendant appeared only to object to the jurisdiction of the court seised.[50]

DRCPA article 79-2 stipulates with regard to recognition of judgments or decisions by a foreign court on family law matters that the provisions of CCP article 118 shall apply *mutatis mutandis*, unless it is contrary to the nature of the case in question. With a view to properly guaranteeing the parties' right to be heard and due process, special consideration is necessary for non-contentious family matters under DRCPA.[51] When there is no opposing party, the requirement of proper service of process is not necessary (eg, in the case of a declaration of disappearance or appointment of a guardian). However, there are exceptional cases in which proper service of process on parties concerned needs to be carried out to ensure access to justice. For instance, in the case of a decree to permit a simple contractual adoption, approval by the natural parents of an adoptive child is required to be shown in the proceedings.[52]

iv. Public Policy

The public policy requirement is in CCP article 118(3). Japanese courts examine on their own motion whether the recognition of foreign judgments would run counter to

[45] Service by public notice to a foreign defendant is not prohibited under CCP article 110(1)(3).
[46] Judgment of Supreme Court, 28 April 1998, *Minshu* 52(3), 853 ((1999) 42 *JAIL* 155).
[47] For details, see: www.hcch.net/en/states/authorities/details3/?aid=261.
[48] On the operation of HSC from a Japanese perspective, see Yuko Nishitani, 'The Operation of the 1965 Hague Service Convention in Japan' (2004) 9 *JJL* 215; Keisuke Takeshita, 'Sovereignty and National Civil Procedure: An Analysis of State Practice in Japan' (2016) 9 *Journal of East Asia and International Law* 361.
[49] Judgment of Supreme Court, 28 April 1998, *Minshu* 52(3), 853 ((1999) 42 *JAIL* 155). The Supreme Court held that personal service in Japan (service of documents through direct delivery to the recipient by a person who had personally been asked by the plaintiff) did not fulfil the requirement of CCP article 118(2), as it did not conform to HSC or the UK Consular Convention.
[50] Judgment of Supreme Court, 28 April 1998, *Minshu* 52(3), 853 ((1999) 42 *JAIL* 155). It is different from submission under article CCP 3-8, which requires that the defendant argue on the merits of a case.
[51] Nishitani (2) (n 5) 754–55; Murakami (n 43) 50.
[52] *cf* Sawaki=Dogauchi (n 21) 353.

ordre public (public policy) (ie, public order or the good morals of Japan).[53] Public policy at the stage of recognition and enforcement of foreign judgments is two-pronged: substantive and procedural public policy.[54] Substantive public policy concerns the substance and contents of the judgment, while procedural public policy concerns the proceedings before the foreign rendering court. The criteria for determining whether the recognition would be contrary to public policy are also two-pronged: (a) incompatibility of the effects of the foreign judgment with the Japanese legal order (the impact of recognising and enforcing the foreign judgment); and (2) close connection of the case with Japan (strength of domestic nexus).

As in most jurisdictions, a typical question of substantive public policy[55] concerns a foreign judgment awarding punitive damages, in addition to compensatory damages and costs. The Supreme Court excluded the punitive parts of a Californian judgment, while recognising and enforcing the compensatory parts (partial recognition).[56] The Court reasoned as follows:

> [T]he system in which in tort cases, the victim is paid damages for the purpose of imposing sanction on the culprit and general deterrence in addition to damages for the actual loss should be regarded as against the basic principles or basic ideas of the system of compensation based upon tort in Japan.

This has become established case law in Japan.[57] Foreign judgments ordering the payment of debts may be refused recognition if the debts arise from, for instance, drug dealing, gambling or human trafficking.[58] In civil and commercial matters, lower courts have granted recognition of the following judgments as not being contrary to public policy: a Korean money judgment calculated on the basis of an agreed interest rate between two individuals (48 per cent per year in contrast to a maximum of 20 per cent per year permitted by Japanese law);[59] a Korean judgment awarding damages on the basis of the

[53] In this regard, the Supreme Court held that '[o]ne may not conclude that this requirement is not fulfilled solely by the fact that the foreign judgment contains an institution which does not exist in Japan, but if the given institution is against the basic principles or basic ideas of the legal order in Japan, the judgment should be regarded as being against public order in the above-cited provision'. Judgment of Supreme Court, 11 July 1997, *Minshu* 51(6), 2573 ((1998) 41 *JAIL* 104). Also, Decision of Supreme Court, 23 March 2007, *Minshu* 61(2), 619 ((2008) 51 *JYIL* 552).

[54] Prior to the 1996 amendment of CCP, the Supreme Court held that public policy at the stage of recognition 'may reasonably be interpreted as requiring that neither the contents nor the formation of the judgment rendered by a foreign court be adverse to "public order or standards of decency" in Japan'. Judgment of Supreme Court, 7 June 1983, *Minshu* 37(5), 611 ((1984) 27 *JAIL* 119).

[55] Another typical example in Japan is that recognition of a foreign judgment ordering a registration of the mother–child relationship between a mother and twins whom a foreign surrogate mother bore. See Judgment of Supreme Court, 23 March 2007, *Minshu* 61(2), 619 ((2008) 51 *JYIL* 552).

[56] Judgment of Supreme Court, 11 July 1997, *Minshu* 51(6), 2573 ((1998) 41 *JAIL* 104). As for punitive damages judgments, some commentators take the view that such judgments do not fall within the notion of a 'judgment' in CCP article 118 due to their penal nature, while others consider that even punitive parts are recognisable and enforceable unless they were rendered on discriminatory grounds or the amount is excessive. For the former view, see, eg, Masato Dogauchi, 'Amerika no Choubatasu teki Songai Baisho Hanketsu no Nihon ni okeru Shikko' in Teiichiro Nakano et al (eds), *Minji Tetsuduki Ho-gaku no Kakushin (jou)* (Yuuhikaku, 1991) 423. For the latter view, see, eg, Kazuaki Nishioka, 'Kyouso Seikyu'u ni kansuru Gaikoku Hanketsu no Shounin oyobi Shikko' (2015) 25 *Nihon Kokusai Keizaiho Gakkai Nenpo* 105; for an overview, see Yuko Nishitani, 'Anerkennung und Vollstreckung US-amerikanischer punitive damages-Urteile in Japan – anhand des Mansei Kogyo-Falls' (2001) *IPRax* 365–67.

[57] For instance, Judgment of Tokyo District Court, 19 February 2008, 2008WLJPCA02198003.

[58] Honma/Nakano/Sakai (n 16) 192.

[59] Judgment of Tokyo District Court, 13 December 2013, 2013WLJPCA12138015.

statutory rate (20 per cent per year, in contrast to 5 per cent or 6 per cent per year in Japan);[60] and a Californian judgment ordering the payment of an attorney's fee (approximately 1.7 times higher than what would have been payable in Japan).[61]

Procedural public policy aims to safeguard fair trials and the party's right to be heard before the foreign court. In family law matters, it should also be examined, where appropriate, whether a mature child was given opportunities to express his or her opinions that ought to be duly reflected in the foreign decision.[62] In some cases, Japanese courts have refused the recognition and enforcement of a foreign judgment as against procedural public policy. In 2019, the Supreme Court refused to recognise a Californian judgment, which had failed to provide the litigants, through the lack of proper notification of the judgment, with an opportunity to file an appeal before the judgment became final and binding.[63] The Court reasoned as follows:

> [T]aking into account that it is obvious that the procedural rules on service of a judgment document ... are different for each country or jurisdiction, it cannot be immediately construed that the foreign judgment is contrary to public policy under CCP article 118(3) due to the mere failure of serving a judgment document in the foreign proceedings.

Yet, the CCP can be construed to be securing the act of giving an opportunity to file an appeal against a judgment by notifying the litigants of the judgment's content or substantially giving them an opportunity to know the judgment's content, except in the case where there are circumstances where the above-mentioned principle serving methods cannot be used, as an important procedure constituting the basis of the legal order in litigations.

Accordingly, if a foreign judgment becomes final and binding without an opportunity to file an appeal being given due to the actual failure of notifying the litigants of the judgment's content or substantial failure in giving them an opportunity to know the judgment's content even though it was possible to notify them of the judgment's content, the litigation proceedings of such a foreign judgment can be said to be incompatible with the fundamental principle or fundamental idea of the legal order in Japan and contrary to public policy in CCP article 118(3).

As evident from the judgment, the mere facts that foreign rules on service of a judgment document are different from those of Japan and that a judgment was not delivered to the litigants do not automatically run counter to the procedural public policy of Japan. One must examine in light of the specific circumstances of individual cases whether litigants were notified or given a fair opportunity to know about the judgment's content. In addition, procedural public policy intervenes when a foreign judgment has been obtained fraudulently (eg, by falsification of documents)[64] or there are procedural defects other than the lack of

[60] Judgment of Tokyo District Court, 12 February 2009, HJ 2068, 95.

[61] Judgment of Tokyo District Court, 9 September 2003, 2003WLJPCA09090007. For other reported cases in which foreign judgments were found not to be contrary to public policy, see Masaaki Haga, *Gaikoku Hanketsu no Shounin* (*Recognition of Foreign Judgments*) (Keio University Press, 2018) 203–06; Tada (n 11) 89–90.

[62] Murakami (n 43) 51.

[63] Judgment of Supreme Court, 18 January 2019, *Minshu* 73(1), 1. Also, Judgment of Tokyo District Court, 29 January 2008, 2008WLJPCA01298006; Judgment of Tokyo High Court, 16 September 2009, unpublished.

[64] Judgment of Yokohama District Court, 24 March 1989, *Kagetsu* 42(12), 37; Judgment of Tokyo High Court, 27 February 1990, HJ 1344, 139 ((1991) 34 *JAIL* 166). For cases in which the fraud defence was not accepted, Judgment of Tokyo District Court, 14 January 1994, HJ 1509, 96; Judgment of Tokyo District Court, Hachioji Branch, 13 February 1998, HT 987, 282.

proper service, such as the unfair conduct of proceedings by a judge.[65] Moreover, as the Osaka District Court noted when refusing to recognise a US judgment, the fact that there is 'a conflicting final Japanese judgment between the same parties on the same dispute or cause of action' can trigger the procedural public policy control.[66] This also means that an existing final and conclusive Japanese judgment always prevails over a foreign judgment on the same subject matter, irrespective of which judgment was rendered first.[67] There is a debate as to what the decisive moment is for determining the compatibility of a foreign judgment with (in particular, substantive) public policy. In one case, a lower court examined the public policy requirement, taking into consideration circumstances which occurred after the foreign judgment had become final and conclusive in the rendering state.[68] In light of the Japanese recognition system under which foreign judgments are automatically recognised provided that the requirements of CCP article 118 are fulfilled, one may argue that the relevant time should be when the foreign judgment becomes final and conclusive in the rendering state.[69] However, the function of the public policy requirement is to protect the legal order of Japan when deciding on the recognition of the foreign judgment. In this respect, subsequent circumstances should also be considered within the framework of public policy.

v. Reciprocity

CCP article 118(4) sets out the reciprocity requirement. The theoretical ground for this requirement lies in the equality of sovereign states.[70] This principle, however, does not necessarily apply to private law relations, where private parties are most affected but cannot influence states reciprocally to recognise judgments.[71] While reciprocity allegedly enhances the recognition of Japanese judgments in foreign states, it is difficult to ascertain and could even have the reverse effects when the foreign state does not recognise Japanese judgments unless Japan reciprocates.[72] Thus, reciprocity has been heavily criticised for its insufficient theoretical and practical foundations and suggestions have been made for the requirement of reciprocity to be abolished *de lege ferenda*.[73] Nevertheless, CCP article 118(4) has upheld this requirement until today.

The criteria for reciprocity were materialised by two landmark decisions of the highest judicial authority in 1933 and 1983. In the Great Court of Cassation precedent

[65] Kono/Report (n 22) 112, [13].

[66] Judgment of Osaka District Court, 22 December 1977, HT 361, 127.

[67] Masato Dogauchi, 'Naikoku Hanketsu tono Teishoku' in Akira Takakuwa and Masato Dogauchi (eds), *Shin Saiban Jitsumu Taikei (3): Kokusai Minji Soshoho (Zaisanho Kankei)* (*International Civil Litigation Law* (*Proprietary Matters*)) (Seirinshoin, 2002) 370. *cf* Akira Takakuwa, 'Wagakuni ni okeru Gaikoku Hanketsu no Shonin ni tsuite no Sairon' (2010) 72 *Seikei Hogaku* 95, 101.

[68] Judgment of Tokyo High Court, 15 November 1993, *Kominshu* 46(3), 98 ((1994) 37 *JAIL* 158). Some academics also take this view, see, eg, Hiroshige Takata, 'Article 200 CCP' in Masahiro Suzuki and Yoshimitsu Aoyama (eds), *Chu'u Shaku Minji Soshoho (4)* (Yuuhikaku, 1997) 384.

[69] For instance, Mafumi Kamatani, 'Gaikoku Hanketsu Shonin Shikko Seido to Gaikoku Hanketsu go no Jijo no Koryo ni tsuite – Ko no Hikiwatashi ni kansuru Heisei 5 nen Tokyo Kosai Hanketsu wo Keiki ni' (2002) 83 *Kyudai Hogaku* 131; Murakami (n 43) 50.

[70] Takakuwa, 'Gaikoku Saiban no Shonin' (n 7) 377.

[71] Nishitani (2) (n 5) 758.

[72] It is hard for parties to ascertain whether there exists reciprocity with a foreign state.

[73] See, eg, Yoshimitsu Aoyama, 'Article 24 CEA' in Chu'uichi Suzuki and Akira Mikazuki (eds), *Chu'ukai Minji Shikko-ho (1)* (*Annotation on Civil Execution Act*) (Daiichi Hoki Shuppan, 1984) 367; Yoshihisa Hayakawa, 'Gaikoku Hanketsu Shonin Shikko Seido ni okeru "Sogo no Hosho no Youhi"' (2002) 1232 *Juristo* 144.

of 5 December 1933,[74] an *exequatur* was petitioned in the Japanese courts for a judgment rendered by a California state court. The defendants moved to dismiss the claim for lack of reciprocity but were unsuccessful. The Great Court of Cassation reasoned that the reciprocity requirement was fulfilled, insofar as the state of origin recognised Japanese judgments pursuant to an international treaty or domestic law, without reopening the same on the merits, under identical or more lenient conditions than those provided by Japanese law. By applying these criteria, reciprocity was established between Japan and the State of California.

While the standard set by the Supreme Court in 1933 was first supported by leading authors and lower court decisions in Japan, critical voices gradually increased. It was primarily maintained that the reciprocity requirement ought to be abolished, as it would unduly hamper the recognition and enforcement of foreign judgments and risk causing re-litigation or conflicting judgments.[75] It was argued *de lege lata* that the requirements for recognising and enforcing foreign judgments largely differ throughout various jurisdictions, so that the relevant foreign and Japanese laws can hardly have 'identical' conditions. Nor could it be readily ascertained which of them provides for 'more lenient' conditions. Rather, it should be sufficient that the requirements for recognition under Japanese and foreign law are essentially equivalent.[76] This more generous understanding of reciprocity was later followed by a lower court and eventually adopted by the Supreme Court on 7 June 1983. In 1983, the Supreme Court held that reciprocity exists

> if in the rendering state, judgments of the courts of Japan that are of the same type as the judgment at issue are capable of being recognised in accordance with conditions that are not different in any material respect from those in CCP article 118.[77]

Japanese courts have taken a liberal approach and recognised judgments from a wide range of jurisdictions, including Australia (New South Wales[78] and Queensland),[79] Canada (British Columbia),[80] France,[81] Germany,[82] Hong Kong,[83] the Republic of Korea,[84] Singapore,[85] Switzerland (Canton of Zurich),[86] the UK (England and Wales)[87] and the US (California,[88]

[74] Judgment of Great Court of Cassation (Highest Judiciary of Japan until 1947), 5 December 1933, *Shinbun* 3670, 16.

[75] Sueo Ikehara, 'Kokusai Shiho' in Teruhisa Ishii, Toru Ariizumi and Yoshio Kanazawa, *Keiei Hogaku Zenshu (20): Kokusai Torihiki* (*Daiyamondo sha*, 1967) 339.

[76] Egawa (n 2).

[77] Judgment of Supreme Court, 7 June 1983, *Minshu* 37(5), 611 ((1984) 27 *JAIL* 119).

[78] Judgment of Tokyo Family Court, 11 September 2007, *Kagetsu* 60(1), 108.

[79] Judgment of Tokyo District Court, 25 February 1998, HT 972, 258.

[80] Judgment of Tokyo District Court, 25 May 2017, 2017WLJPCA05258005.

[81] Decision of Kyoto Family Court, 31 March 1994, HJ 1545, 81 ((1996) 39 *JAIL* 275); Judgment of Intellectual Property High Court, 22 June 2016, HJ 2318, 79.

[82] Judgment of Nagoya District Court, 6 February 1987, HJ 1236, 113 ((1990) 33 *JAIL* 189); Judgment of Tokyo District Court, 24 February 1998, HT 995, 271.

[83] Judgment of Supreme Court, 28 April 1998, *Minshu* 52(3), 853 ((1999) 42 *JAIL* 155).

[84] For instance, Judgment of Yokohama District Court, 30 March 1999, HJ 1696, 120; Judgment of Tokyo District Court, 10 December 2018, 2018WLJPCA12108008; Judgment of Tokyo District Court, 5 October 2018, 2018WLJPCA10058007; Judgment of Tokyo District Court, 29 May 2018, 2018WLJPCA05298002.

[85] Judgment of Tokyo District Court, 19 January 2006, HT 1229, 334 ((2007) 50 *JAIL* 240).

[86] Judgment of Tokyo District Court, 13 November 1967, HT 215, 173.

[87] Judgment of Tokyo District Court, 31 January 1994, HJ 1509, 101; Judgment of Tokyo District Court, 26 January 2017, 2017WLJPCA01268002.

[88] Judgment of Tokyo District Court, 6 September 1968, HT 242, 263; Judgment of Tokyo District Court, 18 February 1991, HT 760, 250 ((1992) 35 *JAIL* 177); Judgment of Tokyo District Court, Hachioji Branch,

District of Columbia,[89] Hawaii,[90] Illinois,[91] Maryland,[92] Minnesota,[93] Nevada,[94] New York,[95] Oregon,[96] Texas,[97] Virginia[98] and Wisconsin).[99]

In contrast, Japanese courts have refused to recognise judgments of the Belgian[100] and Mainland Chinese[101] courts for lack of reciprocity.[102] In addition, judgments from states requiring 'treaty-based' reciprocity may be refused recognition.[103] The Belgian judgment was refused recognition because Belgium at that time allowed *révision au fond* (review of the merits). Nevertheless, since Belgium abolished *révision au fond* in 2004, Belgian judgments should be eligible for recognition and enforcement in Japan.[104] As for Mainland China, according to case precedents, it is in practical terms impossible for its judgments over pecuniary disputes to be recognised in Japan due to the reciprocity requirement. So far Japanese courts have recognised Chinese judgments only in respect of divorce and orders for ancillary support.[105] In light of current practice in Japan, Chinese judgments on other family matters are likely to be refused recognition for lack of reciprocity.

In family matters, there were deliberations in 2018, in the context of discussions to reform PSLA and DRCPA, whether to abolish the reciprocity requirement.[106] Despite some support from practitioners and commentators on that front, the legislator eventually upheld

13 February 1998, HT 987, 282; Judgment of Tokyo District Court, 19 February 2008, 2008WLJPCA02198003; Judgment of Tokyo District Court, 28 March 2011, HT 1351, 241.

[89] Judgment of Supreme Court, 7 June 1983, *Minshu* 37(5), 611 ((1984) 27 *JAIL* 119).

[90] Judgment of Tokyo District Court, 24 October 1970, HT 259, 254; Judgment of Mito District Court, Ryuugasaki Branch, 29 October 1999, HT 1034, 270.

[91] Judgment of Tokyo District Court, 29 January 2016, HJ 2313, 67.

[92] Judgment of Osaka District Court, 17 January 1996, HT 956, 286.

[93] Judgment of Tokyo District Court, 2 September 1996, HJ 1608, 130.

[94] Judgment of Tokyo District Court, 16 December 1991, HT 794, 246.

[95] Judgment of Tokyo District Court, 14 January 1994, HJ 1509, 96; Judgment of Tokyo District Court, Hachioji Branch, 8 December 1997, HT 976, 235; Judgment of Tokyo District Court, 29 January 2008, 2008WLJPCA01298006; Judgment of Tokyo District Court, 8 January 2014, 2014WLJPCA01088001; Judgment of Tokyo District Court, 25 April 2017, 2017WLJPCA04256012.

[96] Judgment of Nagoya District Court, 24 November 1999, HJ 1728, 58.

[97] Judgment of Tokyo District Court, 30 January 1992, *Kagetsu* 45(9), 45; Judgment of Tokyo High Court, 15 November 1993, *Kominshu* 46(3), 98 ((1994) 37 *JAIL* 158).

[98] Judgment of Tokyo District Court, 29 May 1995, HT 904, 202.

[99] Decision of Osaka High Court, 18 February 2010, *Kagetsu* 63(1), 99.

[100] Judgment of Tokyo District Court, 20 July 1960, *Kaminshu* 11(7), 1522.

[101] Judgment of Osaka High Court, 9 April 2003, HT 1141, 270 ((2005) 48 *JAIL* 171); Judgment of Tokyo District Court, 20 March 2015, HT 1422, 348 (affirmed by the Tokyo High Court Judgment (25 November 2015, 2015WLJPCA11256007)). See Satoshi Watanabe, 'A Study of a Series of Cases Caused Non-Recognition of a Judicial Judgment between Japan and Mainland China – A Cross-border Garnishment Order of the Japanese Court Issued to a Chinese Company as a Third-Party Debtor' (2014) 57 *JYIL* 287. The Tokyo High Court judgment was appealed to the Supreme Court, but the latter rejected the appeal. See also Yuko Nishitani, 'Coordination of Legal Systems by the Recognition of Foreign Judgments – Re-thinking Reciprocity in Sino–Japanese Relationships' 14 *Frontiers of Law in China* (2019) 193.

[102] One commentator pointed out that there was a judgment in which an Indian judgment was refused recognition due to lack of reciprocity (Judgment of Tokyo District Court, 4 July 1960, unreported). But that commentator has suggested that today reciprocity with India would be upheld. Nakano, 'Gaikoku Hanketsu no Shikko' (n 25) 45, fn 74.

[103] Nishitani (2) (n 5) 758.

[104] Nagata (n 31) 227.

[105] Decision of Tokyo Family Court, 31 March 2005, LEX/DB 2831220; Judgment of Tokyo High Court, 30 October 2006, HJ 1965, 70 ((2008) 51 *JYIL* 556).

[106] *Zadankai* (PSLA and DRCPA) 25–26 [Comments by Otani].

the reciprocity requirement. However, reciprocity should be generously affirmed as far as possible, for the sake of the stability of family relationships and foreseeability by parties.[107]

vi. *Recognition for the Purpose of Establishing* res judicata *and issue estoppel*

While foreign judgments are automatically recognised in Japan as long as the requirements in CCP article 118 are satisfied, a party can seek a declaratory judgment confirming the recognition or non-recognition of a foreign judgment.[108] When it comes to judgments ordering the defendant to perform a certain action,[109] it is still debatable whether a party may bring a fresh action on the merits in relation to the same cause of action (re-litigation) in order to have the foreign judgment *de facto* 'recognised', instead of seeking an *exequatur* under CEA article 26. Some commentators take the view that a party who has already obtained a foreign judgment in his or her favour may bring such an action, on the grounds that the *exequatur* proceedings are not necessarily more expeditious or less cumbersome, and the foreign judgment may turn out not to fulfil the requirements for recognition.[110] However, other authors opine that such action is not allowed, considering that the party does not have a legitimate interest to do so insofar as an *exequatur* can be sought for the purpose of enforcement and a second claim on the merits would violate the prohibition of *revision au fond*.[111]

vii. *Interlocutory Judgments*

As mentioned above (see section I.C.i), only final and binding judgments are recognisable under CCP article 118. Therefore, judgments that have not yet become final or binding, such as interlocutory judgments, cannot be recognised under CCP article 118.

D. Different Categories of Judgment

There are no special rules for the recognition of foreign judgments tailored to individual categories of subject matter. Foreign judgments are recognised when the requirements set out in CCP article 118 (and DRCPA article 79-2) are satisfied. Each requirement must be examined in light of the specific nature of the case at hand, particularly with regard to indirect jurisdiction. As earlier stated, although it remains unclear whether the criteria of

[107] Nishitani (2) (n 5) 759.

[108] Yuko Nishitani, '§ 26: Internationales Privat- und Zivilverfahrensrecht' in Harald Baum and Moritz Bälz (eds), *Handbuch Japanisches Handels- und Wirtschaftsrecht* (*Handbook on Japanese Commercial law and Economic law*) (Carl Heymanns Verlag, 2011) 1273 [177]; Sakurada (n 4) 397; Takata (n 68) 364–65; Aoyama (n 73) 389–90.

[109] With regard to declaratory and constitutive judgments, settled academic opinion seems to deny the possibility of a successful party bringing a fresh action on the basis that the latter would have no interest in so doing. See Aoyama (n 73) 389.

[110] Aoyama (n 73) 389; Honma/Nakano/Sakai (n 16) 199; Nakano, 'Gaikoku Hanketsu no Shikko' (n 25) 444; Takata (n 68) 365–66.

[111] Sakurada (n 4) 396–97; Kazunori Ishiguro, *Gendai Kokusai Shiho: Jou* (*Modern Conflict of Laws in Japan: Volume One*) (University of Tokyo Press, 1986) 391–404.

determining indirect jurisdiction of a foreign court should be identical to those of direct jurisdiction of the Japanese courts (ie, the mirror approach), case law at least indicates that Japan's direct jurisdiction rules ought to be taken as a starting point (see section I.C.ii). Thus, indirect jurisdiction of a foreign court is, or is likely to be, upheld when any of the direct jurisdiction grounds in the CCP, PSLA or DRCPA is fulfilled by the rendering state (for the individual jurisdiction grounds, see chapter two).

i. Persons

a. Natural Persons

To be recognised in Japan, foreign judgments or decisions on matters of natural persons must satisfy the requirements under CCP article 118 (via DRCPA article 79-2). In some cases where there exists no opposing party, such as in a declaration of disappearance, there is no need for service of process. Foreign decisions will be recognised as long as other requirements in CCP article 118 are fulfilled (for jurisdiction, see section I.C). Notably, the territorial scope of the effect of such a foreign decision, that is, presumption of death, may vary. For instance, if the court of the rendering state has confined the effect within that country, such decision will not enjoy legally binding effect in Japan, even if it is recognised in Japan (as under the Act on General Rules for Application of Laws (AGRAL) article 6). On the other hand, if the foreign court has issued a decision with legally binding effect around the globe, that decision, once recognised, may have legal effect within the territory of Japan.[112] Furthermore, it should be noted that a declaration of disappearance does not have *res judicata* effect, so the competent court of Japan can rescind a declaration of disappearance, once it turns out that the absentee is alive or that he or she died at a different time from that originally presumed (see chapter two, section III.B).

Japanese law treats the commencement of guardianship, curatorship and assistance (hereinafter guardianship etc) of adults and the appointment of a guardian, curator and assistant of adults as separate categories of cases in determining direct jurisdiction and applicable law (AGRAL articles 5 and 35 respectively). As for the recognition of foreign decisions on the appointment of a guardian etc of adults, the above analysis of non-contentious matters does not necessarily apply as such (for jurisdiction, see chapter two, section III.B). This is because the majority of commentators advocate refusing recognition of the effects of foreign decisions on the commencement of guardianship etc of adults in Japan for lack of a registration system indicating the limited capacity of adults or authority of guardians etc, with a view to securing transactions that third parties might enter into with protected adults or their guardians etc in Japan.[113] The prevailing view during the legislative process turned to favour recognising such foreign decisions, on the basis that registration is not a prerequisite

[112] Sawaki=Dogauchi (n 21) 153.

[113] Some commentators take the view that such decisions should not be recognised on the ground that a ruling for commencement of guardianship is territorial (in particular, closely connected with a public notice system) and foreign rulings on guardianship cannot be made public in Japan, with the result that recognising such decisions would lead to uncertainty (eg, Yoshio Tameike, *Kokusai Shiho Kogi* (*Private International Law Course*), 3rd edn (Yuhikaku, 2005) 287; Ryoichi Yamada, *Kokusai Shiho*, 3rd edn (*Private International Law*) (Yuhikaku, 2014) 221). But, such decisions may come into force without being made public.

for recognition, and recognising such foreign decisions would better protect adults. The legislator, however, ultimately refrained from stipulating any rules in this respect,[114] leaving it to an appropriate interpretation by the Japanese courts. *De lege lata*, with a view to protecting incapacitated adults, it would be preferable to recognise such foreign decisions if the relevant requirements of CCP article 118 via DRCPA article 79-2 are fulfilled.[115]

By the same token, the legislator decided not to take a position as to the recognition of foreign decisions instituting guardianship, curatorship or comparable protective measures for children in the absence of custodial parents. Thus, DRCPA article 3-9 solely sets out jurisdiction rules to appoint a guardian, curator or analogous person for the purpose of protecting a child in Japan, when grounds for commencing guardianship, curatorship or comparable protective measures are fulfilled under the child's national law (AGRAL article 35(1) and (2)(i)). As a matter of interpretation, along the lines of previous case law,[116] foreign decisions appointing a guardian etc for children ought to be recognised in Japan, in order to provide effective child protection and ensure the best interests of the child.

b. Corporations or Legal Persons

The recognition of foreign judgments in matters of corporations or legal persons is subject to CCP article 118 including indirect jurisdiction. Pursuant to CCP article 3-5(1) and (2), certain matters (eg, invalidity of incorporation, liability of CEOs etc) of corporations or legal persons incorporated under Japanese law fall under the exclusive jurisdiction of the Japanese courts. Thus, foreign judgments concerning those matters of Japanese corporations or legal persons cannot be recognised in Japan for lack of indirect jurisdiction, as in the case of intellectual property rights that come into existence by registration (see section I.D.iv). Some other issues relating to corporations or legal persons are governed by ordinary direct jurisdictional rules, as indicated in CCP article 3-3(7) (see chapter two, section II.B.iii). Thus, foreign judgments on those issues relating to Japanese corporations or legal persons are recognised in Japan, provided that the other requirements of CCP article 118 are fulfilled.

ii. *Law of Obligations*

a. Judgments Relating to Specific Contracts

To be recognised in Japan, foreign judgments on contractual disputes must satisfy the requirements of CCP article 118. With regard to judgments relating to contracts, the

[114] Minutes of 5th and 8th Meetings (PSLA and DRCPA). Even with the repeal of *Horei* (by the enactment of AGRAL), the legislator did not adopt any rules on this matter and left it open. See Kunio Koide (ed), *Chikujo Kaisetsu Ho no Tekiyo ni kansuru Tsusokuho* (*Commentary on the Act on General Rules for Application of Law*) (Shojihomu, expanded edn, 2015) 56.

[115] Nishitani (2) (n 5) 735–36; Sawaki=Dogauchi (n 21) 159; Yokoyama (n 19) 127. Also, Sakurada (n 4) 179; Yasuhiro Okuda, *Kokusai Kazokuho* (*International Family Law*) (Akashi Shoten, 2015) 454–55.

[116] *cf* Judgment of Tokyo High Court, 9 July 1958, *Kagetsu* 10(7), 29. The Court upheld the claim by the minor child's guardian who had been appointed in Sweden. The guardian was seeking delivery of the child who had been living in Japan, on the basis that the Swedish decision on the appointment of the guardian was recognised in Japan.

defendant's domicile is the general ground (CCP article 3-2). In addition, some other notable jurisdictional grounds apply as follows. First, parties can select the competent court. Parties to a contract often agree on dispute resolution before a designated court. Where a forum selection clause is valid and the judgment is rendered by the designated court, indirect jurisdiction will be upheld. Notably, however, there are specific conditions in respect of the validity of a choice of court agreement in labour contracts and consumer contracts, which should apply in establishing indirect jurisdiction of the foreign court. Second, the defendant may enter a submission. Indirect jurisdiction will be affirmed when the defendant voluntarily appeared before the foreign court to defend the merits of the case. Further, other specific jurisdictional grounds under CCP article 3-3 (in particular, the place of performance, the situs of assets, the defendants' branch office or constant business activities) may establish the indirect jurisdiction of the foreign court (see chapter two, section II.B.i). This analysis basically applies to any type of contract, including contracts for the sale of goods or immovable property, and insurance contracts. However, if a contract falls within the concept of 'consumer contracts' or 'labour contracts', indirect jurisdiction is subject to special jurisdictional rules, as in the case of direct jurisdiction. In particular, CCP article 3-4(3) stipulates that CCP article 3-3 shall have no application to an action brought by a business operator against a consumer or to an action brought by an employer against an employee. In this case, to the exclusion of specific jurisdictional grounds in CCP article 3-3, indirect jurisdiction can only be grounded on the defendant's domicile, forum selection by the parties, or submission by the defendant. On the other hand, in cases where a consumer brings an action against a business operator or an employee against an employer, there is no such limitation, so all the usual jurisdiction grounds (in addition to the specific protective jurisdictional grounds) are available. This construction leads to a different treatment of the indirect jurisdiction of a foreign court, depending on who has instituted the court proceedings.

b. Judgments Relating to Specific Torts

Foreign judgments on tortious matters are recognised when they satisfy the requirements of CCP article 118. In addition to the defendant's domicile as the general ground (CCP article 3-2), other jurisdictional grounds may also constitute indirect jurisdiction (CCP articles 3-3–3-8). They are, in particular, the defendant's branch office, constant business activities and the place of tort (CCP article 3-3(4), (5) and (8)). In light of the branch office jurisdiction under CCP article 3-3(4), indirect jurisdiction will be granted if an alleged tort arises out of activities (for instance, a business transaction) of the defendant's branch office in the foreign state. The defendant's constant business activities in the foreign state will also constitute a basis for indirect jurisdiction (CCP article 3-3(5)). Under CCP article 3-3(8), indirect jurisdiction will be founded in the place of a tort (*locus delicti*), which includes the place where a harmful act is committed and the place where a result of the act occurred. However, indirect jurisdiction in respect of the place where injury has occurred or is likely to occur (*locus damni*), may be precluded when the occurrence of the injury at that place was not foreseeable. In addition, the *locus damni* jurisdictional ground is not applicable to the place where mere indirect or secondary injury has occurred or is likely to occur (see chapter two, section II.B.i.b).

c. Judgments Relating to Unjust Enrichment

Foreign judgments on unjust enrichment are recognised once they fulfil the conditions of CCP article 118. Unjust enrichment has two categories. The first category is when unjust enrichment arises out of a contractual relationship between the parties (eg, restitution of payment after avoiding a sales contract). In this case, indirect jurisdiction grounds follow those of contractual disputes, particularly the place of performance of the contractual obligation in question under article 3-3(1) (see chapter two, section II.B.i.c). The second category is unjust enrichment which arises without any prior connection between the parties (eg, mistake in a wire-transfer to a bank account). In this case, ordinary jurisdictional grounds will be applied to determine whether the foreign court had indirect jurisdiction, that is, the defendant's domicile (article 3-2), situs of assets (article 3-3 (3)), branch office and business activities (article 3-3(4) and (5)), in addition to submission by the defendant and choice of court agreement by the parties (articles 3-7 and 3-8).

d. Judgments Relating to Trust and Charitable Foundations

Foreign judgments on trust and charitable foundations are subject to the requirements in CCP article 118. As in other types of contractual obligations, the defendant's domicile and other specific jurisdictional grounds constitute indirect jurisdiction of the foreign court (see chapter two, section II.B.i.d).

iii. Law of Property

a. Judgments Relating to Immovable Property

The recognition of foreign judgments in relation to immovable property deserves particular mention in light of CCP article 118. Pursuant to article 3-3(11), the situs jurisdiction of actions relating to immovable property located in Japan, including disputes over rights *in rem*, does not exclude other jurisdictional grounds. Only actions relating to entries in public registers, not limited to the challenges to the validity of such entries, are subject to the exclusive jurisdiction of the Japanese court (see chapter two, section II.B.ii.a). Thus, foreign judgments deciding on entries in Japanese public registers will not be recognised in Japan, whereas foreign judgments relating to disputes over immovable property located in Japan, including rights *in rem*, can be recognised when any of the jurisdictional grounds in articles 3-2–3-10 are fulfilled, such as the defendant's domicile. The same principle applies to foreign judgments relating to immovable property in a third country.

b. Judgments Relating to Intangible Property

The recognition of foreign judgments relating to intangible property is governed by CCP article 118. Intangible property encompasses a wide range of assets, such as contractual debts (claims), shares in companies, securities and other financial instruments, and intellectual property (see chapter two, section II.B.ii.b). Under Japanese law, disputes over intangible property (except for the existence and validity of intellectual property by registration) do not fall under the exclusive jurisdiction of the Japanese courts, so foreign judgments are eligible to be recognised. Insofar as disputes over intangible property are of a contractual nature (eg, disputes over the sales or assignment of contractual debts or securities), relevant jurisdictional rules on contracts apply (see chapter two, section II.B.i.b). In other cases of an extra-contractual nature (eg, claims in tort or rights arising from trusts), the respective jurisdictional rules apply (see chapter two, section II.B.i.b).

iv. Intellectual Property

The recognition of foreign judgments relating to intellectual property is governed by CCP article 118. Pursuant to article 3-5(3), disputes concerning the existence or non-existence and the validity of intellectual property rights (the Intellectual Property Basic Act article 2(2)), whose establishment requires registration – patents, trademarks, plant variety rights etc – fall under the exclusive jurisdiction of the Japanese courts, insofar as registration has been effected in Japan. Thus, foreign judgments concerning these types of disputes cannot be recognised in Japan. Two court decisions are well known in this regard. The Mito District Court refused to recognise a Korean judgment, ordering the Japanese respondent to submit a notification that the name in a Japanese patent application procedure be changed to that of the claimant.[117] Neither did the Nagoya High Court recognise a Korean judgment, ordering the Japanese respondent to complete the transfer registration of a patent registered in Japan and make a payment of costs relating to patents registered in Taiwan and the US.[118] Both courts reasoned that actions relating to the registration (or the transfer of such registration) of a patent should fall under the exclusive jurisdiction of Japan as the state of the registration. Thus, the foreign courts lacked indirect jurisdiction.[119] Consequently, foreign judgments relating to the registration of an intellectual property right – such as a patent – in Japan or a third state cannot be recognised for lack of indirect jurisdiction.[120] But disputes relating to Japanese intellectual property rights that come into existence without registration, such as copyrights and related rights, are not subject to the exclusive jurisdiction of the Japanese courts. The recognition of foreign judgments relating to these types of intellectual property are, therefore, eligible to be recognised in Japan under CCP article 118 (see chapter two, section II.B.ii.c). Contractual disputes over Japanese intellectual property rights that come into existence by registration (*eg*, assignment or licensing of a Japanese patent) and tortious actions seeking remedies for an infringement of such intellectual property rights do not fall under the exclusive jurisdiction of the Japanese courts (see chapter two, section II.B.ii.c). Thus, foreign judgments relating to these matters are recognisable, as long as the requirements of CCP article 118 are fulfilled. This analysis will also apply to judgments relating to intellectual property rights registered in a third state.

v. Family Law

In the field of family law, foreign judgments on personal status matters covered by PSLA (eg, divorce or establishment of parentage) must satisfy all the requirements of

[117] Judgment of Mito District Court, Shimozuma Branch, 5 November 2012, 2012WLJPCA11056005.

[118] Judgment of Nagoya High Court, 17 May 2013, 2013WLJPCA05176005.

[119] In these cases, article 3-5(3) did not apply because the actions had been initiated before such provision was introduced.

[120] As for a legislative proposal on recognition and enforcement of foreign judgments relating to intellectual property rights, see Toshiyuki Kono (ed), *Chiteki Zaisanken to Shougai Minji Sosho* (Kobundo, 2010) 331.

CCP article 118,[121] while foreign decrees in domestic relation matters governed by DRCPA must satisfy the requirements of DRCPA article 79-2 that refers to CCP article 118 *mutatis mutandis* (see section I.A). The recognition requirements both in matters covered by PSLA and DRCPA basically coincide.

A minor difference is as to the requirement of proper service of documents in non-contentious matters under DRCPA that do not have a respondent. Whether a foreign decision belongs to contentious civil and commercial matters (CCP), personal status matters (PSLA), or non-contentious domestic relation matters (DRCPA), is determined pursuant to the criteria of Japanese law.[122] Thus, even if a foreign court judgment ordering the payment of maintenance obligations is characterised as a contentious civil matter by the foreign rendering state, its recognition and enforcement is governed by DRCPA in Japan. Consequently, an *exequatur* ought in principle to be petitioned before the Family Court, not the District Court.

A family relationship can be constituted or dissolved in a foreign state by a simple juristic act, as in the case of a marriage celebration or a consensual divorce, without involving a decision of a foreign judicial authority. The recognition of such family relationship is not governed by CCP article 118 or DRCPA article 79-2. Instead, the substantive requirements provided for by the applicable law, which is determined by AGRAL in Japan, must be fulfilled.

a. Decrees Relating to Maintenance Obligations

The recognition of foreign judgments or decrees on maintenance obligations in marital relationships (ie, maintenance, dispositions on cooperation and mutual assistance, or the sharing of living expenses between spouses), is subject to DRCPA article 79-2 and CCP article 118 *mutatis mutandis*. Although matters on maintenance obligations belong to non-contentious matters under DRCPA in Japanese law, they directly involve the interests of the respondent, who ought to be properly summoned and given an opportunity to submit a defence before the foreign courts. Thus, foreign decisions on maintenance obligations need to satisfy all the requirements in CCP article 118, including its no 2 on proper service of process. Indirect jurisdiction will generally be granted, where a maintenance obligor (ie, a person who is obliged to provide maintenance) or a maintenance obligee is domiciled in the foreign rendering state (*cf* DRCPA article 3-10).

b. Decrees of Divorce, Nullity and Separation

To be recognised in Japan, foreign decrees on divorce, nullity and separation, which belong to contentious matters under PSLA in Japanese law, must satisfy the requirements provided in CCP article 118.[123] As earlier mentioned (see section I.C.ii), PSLA provides relatively

[121] *Zadankai* (PSLA and DRCPA) 25 [Comments by Uchino]; Uchino (n 11) 160.

[122] Uchino (n 11) 174.

[123] Judgment of Tokyo Family Court, 11 September 2007, *Kagetsu* 60(1), 108; Judgment of Yokohama District Court, 30 March 1999, HJ 1696, 120; Judgment of Yokohama District Court, 19 October 1982, *Kagetsu* 36(2), 101. A Circular Notice of the Director General of the Civil Affairs Bureau (No 280 of the Civil Affairs Second Division on 14 January 1976) excluded choice of law control and expressly required that recognition of foreign divorce decrees be examined solely in accordance with CCP article 200 (now article 118). Following this Circular

narrow direct jurisdiction grounds, compared with the EU Brussels II*bis* Regulation and other foreign legal systems, as Japanese courts do not assume direct jurisdiction in divorce cases merely on grounds of the plaintiff's domicile or habitual residence.[124] Thus, if one were to follow the 'mirror image' approach, it would mean refusing recognition of a number of foreign divorce judgments for lack of indirect jurisdiction, which would lead to limping marriages and run counter to the need for stability in personal status matters. With a view to circumventing such inappropriate results, indirect jurisdiction should be established to a broader extent than the direct jurisdiction rules of PSLA article 3-2 would permit (see chapter two, section III.A.i). Thus, it suffices to grant indirect jurisdiction when the foreign courts had a sufficiently close connection with the case,[125] in addition to any jurisdiction grounds stipulated in PSLA article 3-2.

c. Judgments Relating to Parentage and Parental Responsibility

Legal Parentage

The recognition of foreign judgments relating to parentage in personal status cases under PSLA (eg, declaratory judgments confirming the parentage or judgments rebutting the marital paternity presumption) is governed by CCP article 118. Indirect jurisdiction is generally established when any of the jurisdictional grounds in PSLA article 3-2 are fulfilled (see chapter two, section III.A.i).

As for legal parentage arising out of cross-border surrogacy, the Supreme Court rendered a notable decree in 2007.[126] The justices were seised with a dispute over the birth registration of twins born from a US surrogate mother by using the gametes of the Japanese intending parents, a married couple. While the Japanese intending parents sought to have the twins registered as their own children in accordance with a US Nevada court decree confirming their legal parentage, the question arose whether recognition of the Nevada decree would run counter to public policy in Japan. The Supreme Court denied recognition, reasoning as follows:

> That decision is incompatible with the fundamental principles or core values of our country's current personal status order. This is because the [Nevada] decree established parentage between persons, who could not be parents and children under the Civil Code setting forth the personal status order in our country. Thus, we conclude that the decision in question violates public policy in the sense of CCP article 118(3) and has no effects in our country.[127]

Notice, family registration has changed its practice. Japanese courts and most commentators now take the view that recognition of foreign divorce decrees is subject to all the requirements in CCP article 118. Nevertheless, some commentators believe that the reciprocity requirement should not be applied in respect of recognition of judgments determining a legal right or status. For details, see Satoshi Watanabe, 'Gaikoku Keisei Hanketsu no Shonin' in Takao Sawaki and Jun'ichi Akiba, *Kokusai Shiho no Ronten Shinban* (*Points on Private International Law, New Edition*) (Yuhikaku, 1996) 243.

[124] For instance, in the UK, article 5(2)(b) of the Domicile and Matrimonial Proceedings Act (DMPA) 1973; in the US, *Williams et al v North Carolina* 317 US 287 (1942); in Australia: article 39(3)(b) of the Family Law Act 1975.

[125] Murakami (n 43) 49; Nishitani (2) (n 5) 754.

[126] Judgment of Supreme Court, 23 March 2007, *Minshu* 61(2), 619 ((2008) 51 *JYIL* 552).

[127] The Court stressed: 'Although within JCC there is no provision that directly specifies the formation of the mother–child relationship between a mother and her legitimate child, JCC does provide a provision [article 772(1)] that presupposes the natural formation based on the objective fact of conception and delivery. Further, even in the

According to this precedent, foreign decisions establishing the parentage of intending parents in surrogacy cases cannot be recognised as such. To establish legal parentage for the twins, the Japanese intending parents ultimately proceeded to full adoption, which would enable the couple to exercise parental authority, care for the children and pass Japanese nationality to them. Taking the avenue of full adoption has become a usual practice in 'surrogacy tourism' cases in Japan.[128]

Adoption

The recognition of foreign adoption decrees is governed by CCP article 118 *mutatis mutandis* via DRCPA article 79-2 in principle. Indirect jurisdiction is generally founded when either an adoptive parent or the child was domiciled in the foreign rendering state at the time of the foreign court decision (*cf* DRCPA article 3-5).

Notably, however, there is an exception in the practice of Japanese family registrars. In general, the recognition of a family relationship established by a court decision is governed by CCP article 118 (possibly via DRCPA article 79-2), while a family relationship constituted by a juristic act is controlled by the substantive requirements of the applicable law (see section II.D.v). Family registrars deviate from this construct only for adoption and always refer to the substantive conditions of the applicable law designated by AGRAL article 31, both in recognising a foreign adoption established by a juristic act and a court decree. The Japanese authority justifies this in-depth examination by the fact that substantive requirements and effects of adoption largely differ among various jurisdictions (eg, requirements of a contract or a court decree, effects of dissolving or maintaining the native parentage etc).[129] Yet, this explanation is not convincing, as the substantive law control remains toothless and ineffective insofar as the applicable law does not provide for strict conditions. It may be time for the practice of family registrars to turn to applying DRCPA article 79-2, now that this provision for non-contentious matters follows the same recognition scheme as CCP article 118.[130]

Parental Responsibility

The recognition of foreign decisions on parental responsibility, custody or visitation is subject to DRCPA article 79-2, referring analogously to CCP article 118.[131] Japan has not yet ratified HPRC. Thus, such decisions ought to satisfy all the requirements in CCP article 118. The indirect jurisdiction of the foreign court is generally accepted, insofar as the child was

mother–child relationship between a mother and illegitimate child, it is understood that in the same way the mother–child relationship is naturally formed based on the objective fact of delivery (see Judgment of Supreme Court, Second Petty Bench, 27 April 1962, *Minshu* 16(7), 1247). Under a current interpretation of JCC, we must understand a mother as the woman who conceives and delivers the child that is born. This is because, when the Civil Code was enacted, the woman who conceives and delivers the child always had a genetic link with the child. Further, relying on the objective fact of delivery served to establish maternity at the time of birth in the best interests of the child. Thus, we cannot recognize the formation of a mother–child relationship between a child and a woman who did not conceive and deliver that child even where she provided eggs for the child'.

[128] See Yuko Nishitani, 'Identité culturelle en droit international privé de la famille' (2019) 401 *Recueil des cours de l'Académie de droit international de La Haye* 188 ff, 383 ff.

[129] Circular Notice of the Director General of the Civil Affairs Bureau (No 3900 of the Civil Affairs Second Division on 10 July 1989).

[130] *Zadankai* (PSLA and DRCPA) 26 [Comments by Uchino, Takata and Dogauchi].

[131] Judgment of Tokyo High Court, 15 November 1993, *Kominshu* 46(3), 98 ((1994) 37 *JAIL* 158).

domiciled in the rendering state at the time of court decisions (*cf* DRCPA article 3-8). Since these matters concern the best interests of the child, compatibility with public policy needs to be carefully examined (as to cross-border child parental abduction, see chapter three, section III.D.v).

The recognition of foreign child support decrees is governed by DRCPA article 79-2 and CCP article 118 *mutatis mutandis*, as in cases of maintenance obligations arising from matrimonial relationships. Japan has not yet ratified HIRC.[132] Thus, foreign child support decrees ought to satisfy all requirements in CCP article 118. Indirect jurisdiction is generally established, where a maintenance obligor (ie, a person who is obliged to provide maintenance) or a maintenance obligee has a domicile in the foreign rendering state (*cf* DRCPA article 3-10).

d. Judgments Relating to Succession

The recognition of foreign judgments or decisions in succession matters is governed either directly by CCP article 118 or via DRCPA article 79-2. Depending on the nature of the dispute, succession cases may be categorised into contentious civil matters or domestic relation matters (see chapter two, section III.E). In matters coming under DRCPA, the requirement of proper service of process ought to be disregarded when there is no respondent. Indirect jurisdiction is generally established, when the deceased was domiciled in the foreign rendering state at the time of commencement of the succession or, under limited circumstances, when the inherited property was situated in that state or the heirs designated the foreign court for division of estates (see chapter two, section III.E).

vi. Competition Law

To be recognised in Japan, competition-related decisions rendered in a foreign country must satisfy the requirements in CCP article 118.[133] Competition law covers various areas of law. Competition law matters may arise in (a) contractual relationships, and (b) tortious relationships (see chapter two, section IV.B). Since disputes over competition law do not fall under the exclusive jurisdiction of the Japanese courts, indirect jurisdiction is determined in light of the general jurisdiction rules in CCP articles 3-2–3-10 and the nature of the disputes. When the infringement of competition law is claimed to nullify a contract, it is treated as an ordinary contractual dispute (see chapter two, section II.B.i.a). Where a party sues a cartel member for damages or an injunction for breach of competition law, direct jurisdiction rules on tort are applicable (see chapter two, section II.B.i.b).

Foreign judgments relating to competition law claims may be refused recognition on the public policy ground, particularly when recognition would not accord with Japanese competition law and manifestly distort the market order in Japan. This would also be the case with punitive, exemplary, or treble damage judgments (typically granted by the US and other countries' antitrust laws), which would be refused recognition on grounds of public policy.

[132] In addition, Japan is not a contracting state to the UN Convention on the Recovery Abroad of Maintenance (Entry into force 25 May 1957. United Nations, Treaty Series, vol 268 3 and vol 649 330).

[133] See Kazuaki Nishioka, 'Japan' in Anselmo Reyes, *Recognition and Enforcement of Foreign Judgments in Civil and Commercial Matters* (Hart Publishing, 2019) 115.

An additional question may arise in the context of class actions. If class actions follow the opt-out principle as in the US, all members of the class should in theory have been informed of the action, so they would be bound by the outcome unless they opt out of the proceedings. In practice, however, some class members (mainly from outside a relevant state) may have been deprived of their right to opt out for lack of notice (often called 'absent claimants'). Although there is no doubt that the foreign judgment should be recognised and be treated as binding among claimants who participated in the proceedings, this construction would be problematic for absent claimants (eg, as far as *res judicata* effects are concerned). Thus, to protect absent claimants, the recognition of the foreign judgment ought to be denied for violating procedural public policy in light of their right to be heard under CCP article 118(3).[134] On the other hand, if class actions follow an 'opt-in' mechanism, all class members who have opted in would be treated as being legally bound by the outcome. There have been no precedents in this regard in Japan.

II. Enforcement of Judgments

A. Means of Enforcing Judgments in Japan

The enforcement of foreign judgments as an exercise of sovereign judicial power in the territory of Japan is determined by domestic law, that is, the CEA. As to the conditions for recognising foreign judgments, Japan has ratified only a limited number of international conventions on specific subject matters (see chapter four, section I.A). Japan has not ratified HREC, HCC or HJC. Thus, the requirements of recognising foreign judgments are generally governed by domestic law as well. In order to proceed to enforce monetary or non-monetary claims granted in a foreign judgment, the successful party needs to file an action for an enforcement judgment, or *exequatur* (*shikko hanketsu*), before the competent court. An enforcement judgment constitutes, together with the foreign judgment, an enforcement title (*saimu meigi*), which is required to institute compulsory execution in Japan (CEA article 22(6)).

B. Procedures for Enforcing Judgments

The CEA does not expressly provide when the Japanese courts have international jurisdiction to proceed to the execution of foreign judgments. In general understanding, the Japanese courts may exercise their judicial authority when the subject matter of the claim or the seizable assets of the debtor are situated in Japan.[135] Pursuant to CEA article 24(1),

[134] Eiji Adachi, 'Kurasu Akushion Hanketsu/Wakai no Chiriteki Han'i' (2014) 86(2) *Horitsu Jiho* 51; similarly, Eiji Adachi, 'Beikoku Kurasu Akushion Hanketsu/Wakai no Shounin Shikko to Koujo' (2002) 69 *Seijo Law Review* 266; Masato Dogauchi, '*Gaikoku Saibansho niyoru Kurasu Akushion Hanketsu (Wakai) no Nihon deno Koryoku*' (2010) 925 *NBL* 20.

[135] Okuda/REJ (n 19) 418.

an execution judgment is issued by (a) the District Court or Family Court having general jurisdiction over the debtor or, in the debtor's absence, (b) the District Court or Family Court having jurisdiction over the place where the subject matter of the claim or the seizable assets of the debtor are situated.

Since the reform of 2018, competence for rendering an execution judgment for a foreign decision in domestic relation matters has been transferred from the district courts to the family courts. This is because the family courts (with special and technical knowledge in family law matters) are deemed to be in a better position than district courts to examine public policy requirements and the wellbeing of children. District courts remain competent for all other types of case. Pursuant to CEA article 24(2) and (3), however, even when the relevant action partially or entirely comes under jurisdiction of the District (or Family) Court, a Family (or District) court may hear and decide on the action *ex officio* or upon the party's request. The rationale is not to burden the private party who has mistakenly gone to the wrong court. This rule can also deal with difficult situations, where the foreign judgment contains both a contentious claim in civil matters (eg, recovery of arrears in maintenance disputes) and a non-contentious claim in domestic relation matters (eg, future recurring payment of maintenance obligations).[136]

Since CEA article 24(4) explicitly prohibits *révision au fond*, Japanese courts cannot review the merits of a case when rendering an enforcement judgment. The court only examines whether the requirements of CCP article 118 or DRCPA article 79-2 are satisfied (CEA article 24(5)). When those requirements are met, a court issues an enforcement judgment which declares that compulsory execution of the foreign judgment is permitted (article 24(6)). Once an enforcement judgment becomes final and conclusive, it constitutes a title of execution, authorising the successful creditor to file a petition for compulsory execution with the competent court (article 22(6)).

Possible means of enforcement differ between monetary and non-monetary judgments. For monetary judgments, the following means are available: filing a petition for attachment of claims or seizure of assets; seizure and judicial auction of immovable property, semi-immovable property (such as a car) and movable property; attachment and execution of a respondent's rights against a third party; and liquidation of the respondent's assets and distribution of the resultant proceeds (CEA articles 43–167-16). For non-monetary judgments, vacating immovable property to secure a creditor's possession and delivery of movable property are available as a means of enforcement (CEA articles 180–95). Indirect compulsory execution may be available, when the debtor fails to perform his or her obligation. Pursuant to CEA article 172, the executing court may order the debtor to pay money of a certain amount that is found to be reasonable for securing the performance of the obligation according to the period of the delay, or immediately if the obligor fails to perform his or her obligation within a certain period that is found to be reasonable.

In short, to enforce a foreign judgment, a party needs to obtain an enforcement judgment. At that stage, the respondent may object to the enforcement, and the objection may take time to resolve. There are no available statistics on the average time taken to enforce judgments.

[136] *Hosoku Setsumei* (PSLA and DRCPA) 67; Murakami (n 43) 53; Nishitani (2) (n 5) 760.

III. Recognition of Foreign Insolvency Proceedings

Recognition of foreign insolvency proceedings is governed by ARAFIP, which is modelled on the 1997 UNCTIRAL Model Law on Cross-Border Insolvency.[137] Although the term 'recognition' is used in ARAFIP, foreign insolvency proceedings are not automatically 'recognised', in contrast to the position under CCP article 118 or DRCPA article 79-2. Instead, a foreign insolvency trustee or representative[138] (or the debtor if no foreign representative is appointed in the foreign proceedings) must file a petition with the competent court in Japan (ARAFIP article 17). Pursuant to ARAFIP article 17(1), foreign insolvency proceedings can be recognised when the debtor's domicile, residence or office is located in that country, independently of whether the foreign insolvency proceedings are primary or ancillary proceedings. In relation to the recognition of foreign insolvency proceedings, the Tokyo District Court has exclusive jurisdiction (ARAFIP article 4). The Tokyo District Court may, however, transfer the case on its own motion to another District Court where the debtor's domicile, residence, office or assets are located. This may be done on granting recognition or subsequently 'when [the court] finds it necessary in order to avoid substantial harm or delay' (article 5).

There are eight grounds for refusing to recognise foreign insolvency proceedings. First, pursuant to ARAFIP article 21, the competent court 'shall dismiss with prejudice on the merits a petition for recognition of foreign insolvency proceedings' if any of the following requirements are fulfilled: (a) where there has been no advance payment of expenses for recognition and assistance proceedings; (b) where it is obvious that the effects of the foreign insolvency proceedings do not extend to the debtor's assets in Japan; (c) where it would be contrary to public policy to render a disposition of assistance for the foreign insolvency proceedings pursuant to the relevant provisions in ARAFIP chapter 3; (d) where it would obviously be unnecessary to render assistance to the foreign insolvency proceedings pursuant to the relevant provisions in ARAFIP chapter 3; (e) where there has been a serious violation of article 17(3) by the foreign trustee;[139] and (f) where it is obvious that the petition was filed for an unjust purpose or in bad faith. In addition, where it becomes apparent, before deciding on a petition for recognition of foreign insolvency proceedings, that domestic insolvency proceedings are pending, the court shall dismiss the petition, unless all of the following requirements in ARAFIP article 57(1) are fulfilled: (a) the foreign insolvency proceedings are the primary foreign proceedings; (b) rendering assistance to the foreign insolvency proceedings under the provisions of ARAFIP chapter 3 would conform with the common interest of creditors; and (c) rendering assistance to the foreign insolvency proceedings under ARAFIP chapter 3 is not likely unduly to harm the interests of creditors in Japan. When the court decides to recognise foreign insolvency proceedings, it has to order a stay of domestic insolvency proceedings (article 57(2)).

[137] Adopted on 30 May 1997: uncitral.un.org/en/texts/insolvency/modellaw/cross-border_insolvency.

[138] ARAFIP article 2(7) defines 'foreign representative' as a person, other than the debtor, who has a right to administer and dispose of a debtor's property in a foreign insolvency proceeding.

[139] Article 17(3) reads: 'Where a foreign trustee (or the debtor if no foreign trustee is appointed in the foreign insolvency proceedings) has filed a petition set forth in [article 17(1)], he/she shall, as provided for by the court, report to the court progress in the foreign insolvency proceedings to which the petition pertains, and any other matters ordered by the court.'

Pursuant to ARAFIP article 62(1), if it turns out that an order of recognition has already been issued for another foreign insolvency proceeding against the same debtor, the competent court shall dismiss a petition for the recognition of a second foreign insolvency proceeding, (a) where the earlier foreign insolvency proceeding recognised is the 'primary foreign proceeding',[140] or (b) where the earlier foreign insolvency proceeding recognised is an ancillary foreign proceeding and rendering assistance would not cater for the common interests of creditors. ARAFIP does not explicitly provide for the 'decisive moment' in determining which of concurrent foreign insolvency proceedings over the same debtor should be given priority. In a case where the debtor's principal place of business was transferred from Italy to Delaware, insolvency proceedings were first opened in Italy and later in the US. The US trustee first petitioned for the recognition of the US insolvency proceedings at the Tokyo District Court and subsequently the Italian trustee for the recognition of the Italian insolvency proceedings. Following a comparative study and interpretation of the UNCITRAL Model Law with a view to applying clear and objective criteria, the Tokyo District Court and Tokyo High Court opined that the critical moment was when the first insolvency proceedings over the same debtor were opened in Italy.[141] When foreign insolvency proceedings are recognised, the competent court in Japan issues an order of recognition, which immediately becomes effective (ARAFIP article 22). If necessary, the competent court can also render a disposition of assistance under ARAFIP chapter 3, whereby different kinds of assistance are available.

Pursuant to ARAFIP article 24, an immediate appeal may be filed against a decision by the competent court on whether or not to recognise foreign insolvency proceedings. Moreover, upon request of an interested person or *ex officio*, the court may revoke the recognition order under the conditions set out in article 56.[142] Where it becomes obvious,

[140] Article 2(2) defines primary foreign proceedings as: '[I]n the case of a debtor who engages in a commercial business, foreign insolvency proceedings petitioned for in the country where the debtor's principal business office is located; in the case of a debtor who does not engage in commercial business or who engages in commercial business but does not have any business offices, foreign insolvency proceedings petitioned for in the country where the debtor, if an individual, has a domicile, or petitioned for in the country where the debtor, if a juridical person or any other association or foundation, has its principal office'.

[141] Decision of Tokyo District Court, 31 July 2012, HJ 2174, 61 (this case was appealed to the Tokyo High Court: Decision of Tokyo District Court, 2 November 2012, HJ 2174, 55).

[142] Article 56(1) and (2) read:

(1) 'If any of the following items applies, the court, upon the petition of an interested person or by its own authority, shall issue an order of rescission of recognition of foreign insolvency proceedings:
   - (i) where it has become obvious that the petition for recognition of the foreign insolvency proceedings fails to meet the requirements prescribed in article 17(1);
   - (ii) where it has become obvious that any of the grounds prescribed in article 21(2) to (6) exist with regard to the foreign insolvency proceedings;
   - (iii) where the foreign insolvency proceedings are closed with a decision equivalent to an order of termination of bankruptcy proceedings, order of confirmation of the rehabilitation plan, order of confirmation of the reorganisation plan, or order of termination of special liquidation proceedings being issued; or
   - (iv) where the foreign insolvency proceedings are closed for reasons other than those prescribed in the preceding item.

(2) If any of the following items applies, the court, upon the petition of an interested person or by its own authority, may issue an order of rescission of recognition of the foreign insolvency proceedings:
   - (i) where the debtor has violated article 31(1)
   - (ii) where a foreign trustee who is a recognition trustee has violated article 35(1) or article 46; or
   - (iii) where a foreign trustee who is not a recognition trustee has disposed of the debtor's property in Japan or has taken it out of Japan.'

after the court has issued an order of recognition of foreign insolvency proceedings, that an order of commencement of domestic insolvency proceedings has been issued against the same debtor prior to or after the recognition order, the court shall either stay the domestic insolvency proceedings (if all the requirements in ARAFIP article 57(1) are satisfied) or stay the recognition and assistance proceedings (if the requirement in ARAFIP article 57(1) is not met) (ARAFIP article 59).

As it is obvious from the foregoing summary of the recognition system Japanese insolvency law assumes that domestic insolvency proceedings are likely to run in parallel with foreign proceedings. Japanese law adopts a 'one running proceeding for one debtor' approach insofar as domestic insolvency proceeds are concerned. This avoids a multiplicity of insolvency proceedings among domestic courts. But the same approach may not hold in respect of cross-border insolvency. Thus, Japanese law sets priorities between domestic or foreign insolvency proceedings. It gives priority to primary foreign insolvency proceedings as between foreign proceedings, but it, in principle, gives priority to local proceedings as between domestic and foreign proceedings.

5

Arbitration and Mediation

I. International Commercial Arbitration

A. Overview in Japan

In international commercial transactions, parties often agree on a specific dispute resolution method to secure predictability in settling possible conflicts arising from or relating to their legal (in particular, contractual) relationship. One of the preferred methods of dispute resolution is arbitration. Arbitration is an alternative and private dispute resolution method based on the parties' agreement.[1] Pursuant to an arbitration agreement, a dispute is referred to a 'private judge', that is, an arbitrator or arbitrators (an arbitral tribunal) for determination.

As is well known, arbitration has the advantages of being flexible, neutral, confidential, professional and expeditious. The readiness of cross-border recognition and enforcement of arbitral awards pursuant to the Convention on the Recognition and Enforcement of Foreign Arbitral Awards of 10 June 1958 (New York Convention, NYC), which has so far attracted 168 contracting states (as of March 2021), renders arbitration preferable to litigation in dealing with international business disputes. In fact, arbitration is particularly important to complement litigation in Asia, considering that quite a few countries still lack a reliable judicial system, and that the recognition and enforcement of judgments encounter major difficulties due to reciprocity requirements. In fact, the recognition and enforcement of foreign judgments is excluded in the absence of treaties in Indonesia and Thailand, and considerably restricted in the People's Republic of China (PRC), Cambodia, Myanmar, the Philippines and Viet Nam (see chapter four).[2]

In the field of international commercial arbitration, the main legal source in Japan is the Arbitration Act (AA)[3] which was modelled on the 1985 UNCITRAL Model Law on

[1] For the use of alternative dispute resolution in Japan, see, eg, Aya Yamada, 'ADR in Japan: Does the New Law Liberalize ADR from Historical Shackles or Legalize it?' (2009) 2 *Contemporary Asia Arbitration Journal* 1.

[2] See national reports in Adeline Chong (ed), *Recognition and Enforcement of Foreign Judgments in Asia* (Asian Business Law Institute, 2017); and Anselmo Reyes (ed), *Recognition and Enforcement of Judgments in Civil and Commercial Matters* (Hart Publishing, 2019); see also Yuko Nishitani, 'Coordination of Legal Systems by the Recognition of Foreign Judgments – Rethinking Reciprocity in Sino–Japanese Relationships' (2019) 14(2) *Frontiers of Law in China* 193.

[3] Arbitration was dealt with as a part of CCP (until 1996) and thereafter as a part of the Act on Public Notice Procedure and Arbitration Procedure. For an overview of AA, see Shun'ichiro Nakano, 'International Commercial Arbitration under the New Arbitration Law of Japan' (2004) 47 *JAIL* 96; Tatsuya Nakamura and Luke Nottage, 'Arbitration in Japan' in Shahla Ali and Tom Ginsburg (eds), *International Commercial Arbitration in Asia*, 3rd edn

International Commercial Arbitration (the Model Law) with a few modifications to adjust to the Japanese legal system.[4] With regard to the recognition and enforcement of foreign arbitral awards, Japan has entered into the following multilateral international conventions: (a) the Protocol on Arbitration Clauses (Geneva Protocol, GP);[5] (b) the Convention on the Execution of Foreign Arbitral Awards of 26 September 1927 (Geneva Convention, GC); and (c) the New York Convention (NYC). Further, it has concluded a number of bilateral agreements with other states, which contain provisions on the reciprocal recognition and enforcement of arbitral awards, for instance, the Treaty of Friendship, Commerce and Navigation between Japan and the US (see section I.E).[6]

In Japan, there are several arbitration institutions,[7] for example: the Japanese Commercial Arbitration Association (JCAA);[8] the Tokyo Maritime Arbitration Commission of the Tokyo Shipping Exchange;[9] the Japan Intellectual Property Arbitration Center;[10] the International Arbitration Centre in Tokyo;[11] and the Japan Sports Arbitration Agency.[12] AA does not prohibit ad hoc arbitration. Therefore, parties may also agree to resolve their disputes by way of ad hoc arbitration. Further, there is a recently established dispute resolution complex, the Japan International Dispute Resolution Centre (JIDRC) with facilities in Tokyo and Osaka.[13] JCAA is the most prestigious arbitration institution administering commercial arbitration in Japan. However, the JCAA's caseload remains low.[14] The JCAA's statistics below show the total number of arbitration cases filed with the JCAA from 2015 to 2019: 74; 82 per cent of these cases were international cases, that is, at least one party was a foreign individual or entity.[15]

(Juris, 2013) 223. Also, see annotations by legislators: Masaaki Kondo, Takeshi Goto, Hirotasu Uchibori, Tomomi Kataoka and Hiroshi Maeda, *Chusai Ho Konmentar* (Shojihomu, 2003).

[4] For comparative research on AA and the Model Law, see Hisashi Harata, '3. Japan: Japanese Arbitration Law and UNCITRAL Model Law' in Gary Bell (ed), *The UNCITRAL Model Law and Asian Arbitration Laws: Implementation and Comparisons* (Cambridge University Press, 2018) 69.

[5] This instrument deals with the recognition of the validity of an arbitration agreement by contracting states and does not directly deal with recognition and enforcement of a foreign arbitral award. Article 3 simply provides: 'Each Contracting State undertakes to ensure the execution by its authorities and in accordance with the provisions of its national laws of arbitral awards made in its own territory under the preceding articles'.

[6] Treaty No 27 of 28 October 1953. Apart from this, there are numerous bilateral agreements with, for instance, the UK, the PRC, Pakistan, Peru, El Salvador, Argentina, Romania, Poland, Bulgaria, Hungry, the former Yugoslavia and the former Soviet Union.

[7] For details on Japanese arbitral institutions and detailed rules of arbitration proceeding under Japanese law, see, eg, Yoshimi Ohara and Shuji Yanase, 'Japan' in Michael Moser and John Choong (eds), *Asia Arbitration Handbook* (Oxford University Press, 2011); Nobumichi Teramura and Luke Nottage, 'Arbitration Reform in Japan: Reluctant Legislature and Institutional Challenges' in Anselmo Reyes and Weixia Gu, *The Developing World of Arbitration: A Comparative Study of Arbitration Reform in the Asia Pacific* (Hart Publishing, 2018).

[8] See: www.jcaa.or.jp/en/. For the new JCAA arbitration rules, Douglas Freeman, 'The New JCAA Arbitration Rules – Japan's Attempt in Innovative Dispute Resolution' (2020) 1 *Japan Commercial Arbitration Journal* 4.

[9] See: www.jseinc.org/en/tomac/index.html.

[10] See: www.ip-adr.gr.jp/eng/.

[11] See: www.iactokyo.com.

[12] See: www.jsaa.jp.

[13] See: idrc.jp/en/. For details, see Yoshihisa Hayakawa, 'An Introduction to Japan International Dispute Resolution Center' (2020) 1 *Japan Commercial Arbitration Journal* 79.

[14] For the situation up to 2017, see Yoshimi Ohara, 'Arbitration in Japan' (2017) 19 *Asian Dispute Review* 197.

[15] See: www.jcaa.or.jp/en/arbitration/performance.html.

Figure 5.1

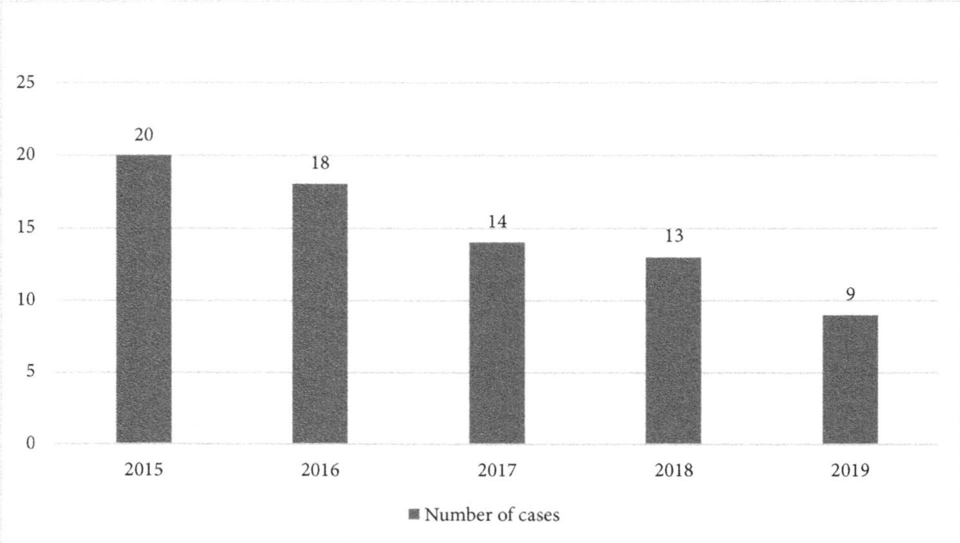

Since 2017, with a view to achieving a breakthrough to increase cases, revitalise international arbitration and promote and develop Japan as a regional hub for international dispute resolution services, the Japanese government has been carrying out several projects.[16] They include the establishment of JIDRC, the amendment of the Act on Special Measures concerning the Handling of Legal Services by Foreign Lawyers,[17] and the amendment of AA and other relevant statutes to reflect recent developments in international arbitration. Judging from a preliminary report,[18] the Japanese Legislative Committee will contemplate (i) rules on provisional measures taken by arbitral tribunals in Japan or abroad and the enforcement (*exequatur*) of such provisional measures along the lines of the 2006 amendment of the UNCITRAL Model Law on Arbitration, and (ii) rules with necessary safeguards for the enforcement of international settlement agreements resulting from mediation in light of the 2018 Singapore Convention and the 2018 UNCITRAL Model Law on Mediation (see section III.D).[19]

[16] In 2020 the Japanese legislature amended the Act on Foreign Lawyers to extend the competence of foreign attorneys so as to represent Japanese clients in commercial arbitration with foreign elements or taking place abroad, and to enact detailed rules for foreign attorneys involved in international commercial mediation. See: www.cas.go.jp/jp/seisaku/kokusai_chusai/index.html (in Japanese); see also Yuko Nishitani, 'Introductory Note' (2020) 63 *JYIL* 124.

[17] See Junya Naito and Ryo Otobe, 'The Act on Special Measures Concerning the Handling of Legal Services by Foreign Lawyers – Recent Developments towards Internationalization' (2020) 1 *Japan Commercial Arbitration Journal* 34. For the new foreign lawyers' system, see: www.japaneselawtranslation.go.jp/common/data/outline/200116134238_9053108.pdf.

[18] See the report 'Chusai hosei no minaoshi wo chushin to shita kenkyukai hokokusho' (Report of the Working Group on Amendments of the Arbitration Act etc) published by Shoji Homu Kenkyukai (Japan Institute of Business Law) in July 2020: www.shojihomu.or.jp/kenkyuu/tyusaiminaoshi (in Japanese).

[19] Given the report by the research group (ibid, submitted in July 2020), the focus of the amendment project appears to be on an updating of the current arbitration system to reflect the 2006 UNCITRAL Model Law (especially in relation to interim or provisional measures). Following amendment of Japan's arbitration law along the lines discussed, it is likely that Japan would have an arbitration law in line with global standards. But the question

These projects launched by the Japanese government extend to alternative dispute resolution methods in cross-border cases, which also include international sports arbitration. Indeed, the government of Japan has been rushing to build a judicial framework for sports arbitration, aiming to enable the international arbitration community in Japan to provide athletes with sufficient legal service during the 2021 Olympic and Para-Olympic Games in Tokyo.

B. Jurisdiction of the Arbitral Tribunal

i. Arbitration Agreement

The jurisdiction of the arbitral tribunal is grounded in the parties' agreement to refer their disputes to the arbitral tribunal. In other words, arbitral proceedings presuppose the existence of a valid arbitration agreement. The first question to be considered is, therefore, whether such an agreement exists and is legally valid. Pursuant to AA article 23(1), an arbitral tribunal may rule on its authority to conduct arbitral proceedings and render arbitral awards (the 'competence–competence' doctrine). Following an arbitral tribunal's decision that it has jurisdiction, according to AA article 23(5) a party may, within 30 days of receipt of notice of such decision, request the court to rule on whether the tribunal has jurisdiction. While such a request is pending before the court, the arbitral tribunal may continue with the arbitral proceedings and render an award. A typical ground of challenge to the jurisdiction of the arbitral tribunal is the absence or non-validity of an arbitration agreement which will normally have been incorporated as a provision in the parties' contract. AA article 13(6) adopts the principle of separability or severability, whereby the arbitration agreement is considered as an independent agreement for the purpose of determining its validity. Consequently, the validity of an arbitration agreement is examined independently from the validity of the main contract containing such arbitration agreement. The Tokyo District Court has upheld this principle. In a case involving a patent licence agreement, the plaintiff claimed that the arbitration agreement was null and void because the underlying licence agreement containing the arbitration agreement had been terminated. Dismissing the plaintiff's argument, the Court held that 'the arbitration agreement will not retroactively become null and void because of the termination of the license agreement, so the plaintiff's argument in this regard is not reasonable'.[20]

is whether this would enable it to catch up with other popular destinations for international arbitration such as Hong Kong and Singapore in terms of the number of foreign arbitration cases received annually by Japanese arbitral institutions. It is doubtful whether the contemplated amendment would be sufficient to revitalise international arbitration in Japan and attract foreign parties to designate Japan as the seat of any arbitration arising out of their commercial contracts. Given current capacity in Japan in relation to international arbitration (especially, in light of the language barrier posed by the widespread use of English in international dispute resolution), parties would still be likely to select already established destinations (such as Singapore) for the resolution of their disputes, everything else being equal. Thus, if Japan is to compete with Singapore or Hong Kong as an international dispute resolution hub, more drastic amendments to the existing arbitration infrastructure will be required to achieve a real breakthrough in the number of arbitrations brought to Japan. As a seat of arbitration, Japan will need to offer something extra, that neither Singapore nor Hong Kong currently offers. For instance, Japan might consider giving the parties the option to exclude or expand the grounds for setting aside of arbitral awards. Japan might also consider allowing parties to submit documents in English (rather than having them translated into Japanese) for the purpose of arbitration-related proceedings before the Japanese court.

[20] Judgment of Tokyo District Court, 21 October 2005, HJ 1926, 127. The Intellectual Property High Court upheld this position (Judgment, 28 February 2006, 2006WLJPCA02280016).

ii. Arbitrability of Disputes

The subject matter of the arbitral proceedings must be capable of being settled through arbitration (ie, the subject matter must be arbitrable). Under Japanese law, the parties may agree on dispute resolution by arbitration, insofar as civil disputes (excluding divorce or separation) which can be settled between the parties.[21] Although it is not entirely clear what precisely the expression 'civil disputes which can be settled between the parties' means, it has long been understood that all material claims are in principle arbitrable. Therefore, claims seeking private law remedies such as injunctions or damages based on the infringement of a certain law that is wholly or partly of a public law nature (such as intellectual property law, securities law and antitrust law) are essentially arbitrable, as the parties are free to dispose of those claims (for instance, by reaching an amicable settlement agreement). They are not compelled to bring those claims before a national court or authority.

A consumer may enter into an arbitration agreement with a business to submit to arbitration disputes that may arise in the future. Under AA supplemental provisions article 3, however, a consumer may at any time unilaterally cancel such an agreement. In addition, pursuant to AA supplemental provisions article 4, an arbitration agreement is null and void if its subject matter is a labour-related dispute.

iii. Types of Arbitration Agreement

There are many types of arbitration agreement or clauses. For instance, as in a Supreme Court case in 1997, parties sometimes insert a 'finger pointing arbitration clause'. Under this type of clause, procedural matters relating to arbitration such as the place of arbitration, arbitral institution, and applicable rules change depending on who files an application and commences arbitration proceedings.[22] Further, parties may agree on a dispute resolution clause combining several dispute resolution methods (a 'hybrid dispute resolution clause'). This type of agreement can be further broken down into two groups. The first sets out a general dispute resolution clause as well as specific dispute resolution methods for particular issues. The second group provides for a multitiered dispute resolution process (a 'multitiered dispute resolution clause'). For instance, the parties agree: first, to negotiate and attempt to settle their differences amicably over a prescribed number of days; second, if negotiations fail, to attempt mediation within a prescribed period of time; and third, if mediation is likewise unsuccessful, then either party may commence arbitration proceedings.

C. Choice of Law

Choice of law questions arise in relation to an arbitration agreement, the arbitrability of disputes or claims, the arbitration proceedings, and the merits of a case.

[21] AA article 13(1) stipulates: 'Except as otherwise provided for in laws and regulations, an Arbitration Agreement shall be effective only when the subject thereof is a civil dispute (excluding disputes of divorce or dissolution of adoptive relation) which can be settled between the parties'.

[22] A typical example is as follows: 'All disputes controversies or difference which may arise between the parties hereto, out of or in relation or in connection with this Agreement shall be finally settled by arbitration in Tokyo pursuant to the Commercial Arbitration Rules of the Japan Commercial Arbitration Association if X requests the arbitration or in New York pursuant to Arbitration Rules of the American Arbitration Association if Y requests the arbitration'.

i. Validity of an Arbitration Agreement

First, to determine the validity of an arbitration agreement (including its substantive and personal scope), the governing law of the latter must be identified. There are three scenarios in which the governing law can come into question before a national court: (a) where one party seeks to set aside an arbitral award; (b) where one party objects to the recognition and enforcement of an arbitral award; and (c) where one party invokes an arbitration agreement as a defence to civil litigation commenced before the Japanese courts.

(a) At the stage of setting aside an arbitral award, pursuant to AA article 44(1)(ii), the applicable law of an arbitration agreement is the law that the parties have explicitly or implicitly chosen or, in the absence of such choice, Japanese law.
(b) At the stage of recognition and enforcement, pursuant to article 45(2)(ii) and NYC article 5(1)(a), the applicable law of an arbitration agreement is the law that the parties have explicitly or implicitly chosen or, in the absence of such choice, the law of the seat of arbitration (*lex arbitri*).
(c) On the other hand, there exists no choice of law rule for situations in which the existence of an arbitration agreement is raised by a party as a defence to civil litigation before a Japanese court. In this regard, although under *Horei* and before the enactment of AA, the Supreme Court in 1997 held:

> Arbitration is a procedure in which the parties agree to delegate the settlement of a dispute between themselves to the arbitral award of a third-party, an arbitrator, and based upon this agreement, the parties are bound by the arbitral award and the dispute is settled without recourse to court. In the light of the nature of arbitration which is a means of dispute settlement based upon the agreement of the parties, it is appropriate to understand that concerning the existence and effect of arbitration agreement in international arbitration, in accordance with *Horei* article 7(1), the governing law should be determined primarily by the intention of the parties. Even in cases where there is no explicit agreement on the governing law in the arbitration agreement, if it can be discerned that there is a tacit agreement by the parties on the governing law in the light of the existence of the agreement on the place of arbitration and its content, the content of the main contract, and other circumstances, this law should be applied.[23]

After the enactment of AA in 2003, some lower courts followed the Supreme Court approach,[24] while other courts respected the parties' choice of law pursuant to *Horei* article 7(1), referring the matters though, in the absence of that choice by the parties, to the law of the seat of arbitration instead of the *lex loci actus* under *Horei* article 7(2).[25]

To be formally valid in Japan, an arbitration agreement must satisfy the formal requirements under AA article 13. By AA article 13(2) and (4), an arbitration agreement must be in writing (including in the form of an electromagnetic record). In addition, if one party

[23] Judgment of Supreme Court, 4 September 1997, *Minshu* 51(8), 3657 ((1998) 41 *JAIL* 109). For details, Yuko Nishitani, 'Zur Bestimmung des Schiedsvertragsstatuts und dessen sachlichen und persönlichen Reichweite – Urteil des OGH vom 4.9.1997' in (1998) 6 *JJL* 185; Keiichiro Nakabayashi, 'Applicable Law of International Arbitration Agreement' (2009) 52 *JYIL* 598.

[24] Judgment of Tokyo District Court, 10 March 2011, HT 1358, 236.

[25] Judgment of Tokyo High Court, 21 December 2012, HJ 2112, 36 ((2012) 55 *JAIL* 566).

submits written statements contending the existence of an arbitration agreement to the arbitral tribunal and the other party does not contest it in a written response, the arbitration agreement is treated as evidence in writing by such exchange (article 13(5)). The legal capacity and ability of the parties to conclude an arbitration agreement is subject to a party's national law in the case of a natural person and, in the case of a judicial person, the law of the place of incorporation.[26]

ii. *Effects of an Arbitration Agreement*

The procedural effects of an arbitration agreement concern questions, for instance, of (a) whether such an agreement excludes court proceedings (AA article 14(1)) or suspends them (when such an agreement is submitted as a defence in court proceedings), or (b) whether the court seised can issue an order to suspend arbitral proceedings. The procedural effects of an arbitration agreement are governed by the law of the forum (*lex fori*) in accordance with the maxim *forum regit processum*. Pursuant to AA article 28, the place of arbitration shall be specified by the parties' agreement and, in the absence of such agreement, the arbitral tribunal must determine the place of arbitration by considering the circumstances of the dispute including the convenience of the parties.

iii. *Arbitrability of Disputes*

The law governing the admissibility of an arbitration agreement (ie, arbitrability) varies, depending on the stage of the arbitration proceedings. There are three scenarios in which the arbitrability of subject matters comes into question before a Japanese court: (a) where one party seeks to set aside an arbitral award; (b) where one party objects to the recognition and enforcement of a foreign arbitral award; and (c) where one party invokes an arbitration agreement as a defence to civil litigation before a national court.

(a) At the stage of setting aside an arbitral award, pursuant to AA article 44(1), arbitrability is subject to the law of the seat of arbitration (ie, Japanese law).
(b) At the stage of recognition and enforcement of a foreign arbitral award in Japan, pursuant to AA article 45(2)(viii) and NYC article 5(2)(a), it is subject to the law of the state where recognition is sought (ie, Japanese law).

With regard to (c), special consideration is required. NYC article 2(1) requires each contracting state to recognise an arbitration agreement. However, NYC article 2(3) does not clarify the applicable law as to arbitrability at this stage and simply stipulates that:

> The court of a Contracting State, when seized of an action in a matter in respect of which the parties have made an agreement within the meaning of this article, shall, at the request of one of the parties, refer the parties to arbitration, unless it finds that the said agreement is null and void, inoperative or incapable of being performed.

[26] Judgment of Supreme Court, 15 July 1975, *Minshu* 29(6), 1061; Nakano (n 3) 107; Yoshiaki Sakurada, *Kokusai Shiho* (*Private International Law*), 7th edn (Yuhikaku, 2020) 405.

Where the place of arbitration is Japan, arbitrability ought to be governed by Japanese law because, pursuant to AA article 3(1),[27] the application of AA article 13 on the standard for determining the arbitrability of a dispute is mandatory. On the other hand, it is unclear what law determines arbitrability, when the place of arbitration is somewhere else. The arbitral tribunal initially has exclusive competence to decide the merits of the case, where the parties agree to resolve a dispute through arbitration. A national court can only decide the merits of the case, if arbitration cannot proceed. Accordingly, the issue to be resolved is whether the dispute is arbitrable under the *lex arbitri*. In view of this principle of arbitration, it is submitted that arbitrability at the stage of the recognition of an arbitration agreement should also be governed by the *lex arbitri*, namely, the place where the arbitration is supposed to take place.[28]

iv. Arbitration Proceedings

The law applicable to arbitration proceedings had been hotly debated before AA was enacted.[29] Some authors maintained that it was subject to the law chosen by the parties because arbitral proceedings are a private dispute resolution method and not necessarily related to the judiciary of the state of arbitration.[30] To the contrary, a minority opinion stated that it was always to be governed by the law of the seat of arbitration because it was closely linked with the place of arbitration and party autonomy would lead to inadmissible proceedings from the perspective of that place.[31] The legislature eventually adopted the latter approach. AA article 3 stipulates that the procedural rules in AA apply when the seat of arbitration is Japan. The law governing arbitral proceedings covers the commencement of arbitration proceedings, the appointment of arbitrators, the constitution of arbitral tribunals, arbitrators' competence and formation, and the form of arbitral awards.

v. Merits of the Case

Insofar as the merits of a case are concerned, by AA article 36(1), parties are free to choose a law of a given state or 'rules of law', that is, non-state law (eg, UNIDROIT Principles or Uniform Customs and Practice for Documentary Credits, UCP 600), as the law governing the merits of the case.[32] Such choice of law by the parties is deemed to refer to the

[27] AA article 3 reads:

> '(1) The provisions of Chapters II through VII and Chapters IX and X, except the provisions specified in the following paragraph and article 8, apply only if the place of arbitration is in the territory of Japan.
> (2) The provisions of article 14(1) and article 15 apply when the place of arbitration is in or outside the territory of Japan, or when the place of arbitration is not designated.
> (3) The provisions of Chapter VIII apply when the place of arbitration is in or outside the territory of Japan'.

[28] Also, Nakano (n 3) 108.

[29] See, eg, Akira Takakuwa, 'Chusai Tetsuzuki no Junkyoho' in Akira Takakuwa and Masato Dogauchi (eds), *Shin Saiban Jitsumu Taikei (3): Kokusai Minji Soshoho (Zaisanho Kankei) (International Civil Litigation Law (Proprietary Matters))* (Seirinshoin, 2002) 431–39.

[30] Also, Judgment of Tokyo District Court 10 April 1953, *Kaminshu* 4(4), 502.

[31] Even though before AA (when arbitration was governed by CCP), the Court of Cassation adopted this approach based on the territoriality of CCP. Judgment of Court of Cassation, 15 April 1918, *Minroku* 24, 865.

[32] Nevertheless, party autonomy under AA article 36(1) is subject to certain limitations. According to the prevailing view, even if the parties have chosen the law of a given state as the governing law of their dispute, the

substantive law of the state to the exclusion of its conflict of laws rules, unless the parties agree otherwise. In the absence of a choice of law by the parties, the law of the state which is most closely connected to the legal relationship applies (AA article 36(2)).[33]

Further, pursuant to AA article 36(3), an arbitral tribunal is entitled to decide the merits of the case *ex aequo et bono*, if the parties have expressly requested it. In that case, the tribunal can determine the case by applying any norms which are formally not part of state law or non-state law formulated by private institutions.[34]

In any event, pursuant to AA article 36(4), when there is a contract relating to a civil dispute that is subject to arbitral proceedings, the arbitral tribunal 'shall' decide in accordance with the terms of such contract and shall take into consideration the usages, if any, that may apply to the case.

An arbitral tribunal may issue interim protective measures when the parities to the arbitration proceedings have conferred such power on the tribunal by agreement. Even in the absence of agreement, an arbitral tribunal in a Japan-seated arbitration may grant interim measures pursuant to AA article 24 (ie, the law governing the arbitration proceedings), unless the parties have agreed otherwise. To enforce any measures ordered by a tribunal, however, a party would need to resort to the Japanese courts.

D. Setting Aside of Arbitral Awards

i. *Grounds for Setting Aside*

Under AA article 3(1), the provisions on setting aside of an arbitral award only apply if the seat of arbitration lies in Japan. Accordingly, Japanese courts can only deal with a claim for the setting aside of an arbitral award rendered by an arbitral tribunal seated in Japan. A party may apply to a Japanese court to set aside an arbitral award in accordance with AA article 44(1), if any of the following grounds is provided:

(i) The arbitration agreement is not valid due to the limited capacity of a party.
(ii) The arbitration agreement is not valid on grounds other than the limited capacity of a party pursuant to the laws and regulations designated by the parties to govern the arbitration agreement (or absent a choice of law, under the law of Japan).
(iii) The claimant did not receive the notice required under the laws and regulations of Japan (or where the parties made an agreement on matters not regulated by mandatory rules, such agreement) in the proceedings of appointing arbitrators or in the arbitral proceedings.

arbitral tribunal is required to apply the law designated by the parties only to contractual claims, while the designated law does not extend to certain issues such as the capacity of the parties and rights *in rem* under a mortgage. Nakano (n 3) 111.

[33] *cf* Model Law article 28(2). Pursuant to this provision, 'the arbitral tribunal shall apply the law determined by the conflict of laws rules which it considers applicable'.

[34] It seems that there have been in actuality a few cases in which the parties agreed on arbitration based on *ex aequo et bono*. Some commentators have urged the international arbitration community to consider deciding the merits of cases based on *ex aequo et bono* without adherence to technical rules of law. See, eg, Nobumichi Teramura, *Ex Aequo et Bono as a Response to the 'OverJudicialisation' of International Commercial Arbitration* (Wolters Kluwer, 2020).

(iv) The claimant was unable to submit a defence in the arbitral proceedings.
(v) The arbitral award contains a decision on matters beyond the scope of the arbitration agreement or of the claims brought to the arbitral proceedings.
(vi) The composition of the arbitral tribunal or the arbitral proceedings violated laws and regulations of Japan (or where the parties made an agreement on matters not regulated by mandatory rules, such agreement).
(vii) The claims brought to the arbitral proceedings relate to a dispute that cannot be the subject matter of an arbitration agreement pursuant to laws and regulations of Japan.
(viii) The content of the arbitral award runs counter to public policy or good morals of Japan.

AA article 44 essentially follows and adopts the grounds of the Model Law. However, there are some notable structural and substantive differences. For instance, AA article 44(1) simply lists the grounds for refusal without mentioning whether a challenging party must prove the existence of any ground, as opposed to Model Law article 34(2). On the other hand, AA article 44(6)[35] categorises those grounds described above into two groups. As is evident from their wording, with regard to the grounds in items (i)–(vi), a court seised can only set aside an arbitral award if *the party challenging the award* proves the existence of such ground, while when it comes to the grounds in items (vii) and (viii), a court seised can set aside when *the court* finds any of those grounds is present. Further, AA does not contain an equivalent rule to Model Law article 34(4)[36] that allows a court seised to suspend the setting aside proceedings.

ii. Procedural Issues

There have been some reported cases in which Japanese courts have dealt with some of the grounds for refusal.[37] With regard to item (iv), one may argue that, if the challenging party was unable to submit a defence in the arbitral proceedings, the arbitral award will always be set aside. However, the Tokyo District Court has held that the arbitral award can only be set aside if there has been a serious violation of due process as, for instance, where the arbitral tribunal unreasonably prevented the challenging party from presenting its case or where the tribunal decided an issue based on evidence which the challenging party had no reasonable opportunity to refute.[38] Further, according to item (v), the arbitral award can be set aside, when it contains decisions on matters beyond the scope of the arbitration agreement or the claims in the arbitral proceedings. In a case involving claims for damages due

[35] AA article 44(6) reads: 'Where an application is made under paragraph (1), an arbitral award may be set aside by the court in the event that it finds any of the grounds described in each of the items under the same paragraph to be present (*with respect to the grounds described in items (i) through (vi) of the same paragraph, this shall be limited to where the party making the application has proved the existence of such grounds*)' (emphasis added).

[36] Model Law article 34(4) reads: 'The court, when asked to set aside an award, may, where appropriate and so requested by a party, suspend the setting aside proceedings for a period of time determined by it in order to give the arbitral tribunal an opportunity to resume the arbitral proceedings or to take such other action as in the arbitral tribunal's opinion will eliminate the grounds for setting aside'.

[37] For recent decisions, see Naoshi Takasugi, 'Setting Aside of Arbitral Awards under the Japan Arbitration Act – Recent Decisions by the Japanese Courts' (2020) 1 *Japan Commercial Arbitration Journal* 50.

[38] Decision of Tokyo District Court, 28 July 2009, HT 1304, 292.

to breach of contract, the arbitral tribunal changed the legal characterisation of the claim to one of unjust enrichment, the Tokyo High Court held that, even if the original claim was transformed by the arbitral tribunal into a claim of different nature, such transformed claim still came under the scope of the original claim, insofar as the transformation of claim was reasonably foreseeable from the circumstances of the dispute in the arbitral proceedings.[39] As for item (vi), the arbitral award can be set aside, when the arbitral proceeding did not follow the parties' agreement or the *lex arbitri*.

iii. Conflict of Interests

In order for the arbitral award to be set aside, a contravention must be serious. In this regard, there is a notable series of cases involving the arbitrator's obligation to disclose conflicts of interests.[40] Pursuant to AA article 18(4):

> An arbitrator, during the course of arbitral proceedings, shall without delay disclose any circumstances likely to give rise to justifiable doubts as to its impartiality or independence (unless the parties have already been informed of them by the arbitrator).

In the underlying arbitration case, the presiding arbitrator's law firm (albeit a different branch office) had represented a sister company of the opposing party in a lawsuit in the US, but the arbitrator had failed to disclose this fact to the parties to the arbitration prior to the rendering of the award. The question was whether the failure to disclose amounted to a violation of item (iv). The Osaka District Court held that, even if an arbitrator failed to disclose to the parties those circumstances likely to give rise to justifiable doubts as to his or her impartiality or independence and there was a violation of item (iv), such violation, insofar as a minor one, would not lead to a setting aside of the arbitral award.[41] Notably, the Osaka High Court at second instance ruled that the circumstances were 'likely to give rise to justifiable doubts as to [the tribunal's] impartiality or independence'. It set aside the arbitral award on two grounds. First, a general statement of the possibility of a future conflict of interests did not suffice as a proper disclosure.[42] Second, whether or not an investigation into potential conflicts had been conducted, the arbitrator could have discovered the existence of the conflict of interests without difficulty.[43]

The Supreme Court, however, overturned the Osaka High Court's decision and remanded the case back to the Osaka High Court for further investigation into whether the

[39] Decision of Tokyo High Court, 1 August 2018, HJ 2415, 24 ((2019) 62 *JYIL* 462).

[40] Decision of Osaka District Court, 17 March 2015, HJ 2270, 74; Decision of Osaka High Court, 28 June 2016, HJ 2319, 32; Decision of Supreme Court, 12 December 2017, *Minshu* 71(10), 2106 ((2018) 61 *JYIL* 395). For an analysis of this case, Yoichiro Hamabe, 'Four Court Decisions After an Arbitral Award' (2020) 1 *Japan Commercial Arbitration Journal* 42.

[41] Decision of Osaka District Court, 17 March 2015, HJ 2270, 74.

[42] The arbitrator had submitted to the JCAA a written declaration stating: 'Attorneys at the law firm [A] may in the future give advice to, or represent, clients in cases which are not related to the present Arbitration Case but in which the clients' interests conflict with those of any of the parties to the present Arbitration Case and/or any of its/their affiliated companies. Attorneys at [A] may also in the future give advice to, or represent, any of the parties to the present arbitration case and/or any of its/their affiliated companies in cases not related to the present arbitration case'.

[43] Decision of Osaka High Court, 28 June 2016, HJ 2319, 32.

arbitrator knowingly withheld the facts in question and whether the arbitrator could have discovered the facts through a reasonable investigation.[44] In fact, as for the first ground, the Supreme Court agreed with the High Court and upheld its reasoning. Yet, as for the second ground, the Supreme Court ruled that, in order for an arbitrator to have breached his or her obligation to disclose a potential conflict under AA article 18, the arbitrator must have either been aware of the conflict in question or ordinarily could have discovered such conflict on the grounds of a reasonable investigation by the time the arbitration proceedings were completed.

iv. Public Policy

Since AA article 44(1)(viii) simply refers to the term 'public policy', it is not entirely clear from its wording whether it only covers substantive public policy, or extends to procedural public policy. Focusing attention on the term 'content', some commentators have argued that it only refers to substantive public policy. The Tokyo District Court, however, has clarified that it extends to procedural public policy as well.[45] The Court held that it ran counter to procedural public policy that the arbitral tribunal regarded the disputed facts between the parties as undisputed, insofar as those facts were important circumstances that affected the resulting award. In another case, the Tokyo District Court ruled that unreasonable findings of fact or erroneous legal determinations on the part of an arbitral tribunal were not sufficient grounds to justify setting aside an arbitral award.[46]

As to substantive public policy under AA article 44(1)(viii), a much-debated question is whether public policy intervenes when an arbitral award does not abide by the applicable mandatory rules or when the tribunal fails to apply the relevant applicable law correctly. The Tokyo High Court held that, in order to assess the conformity of an award with public policy, the court ought to examine whether the result of the law application by the tribunal runs counter to public policy (not whether the arbitral tribunal applied laws that are deemed contrary to public policy).[47] The Court observed that the mere fact that an arbitral tribunal fails to apply substantive law or any mandatory law, or makes an incorrect application of them, will not necessarily lead to setting aside an award.[48] It is clear from the judgment that, at the stage of setting aside an award, the relevant public policy is only that of Japan, while mandatory rules (especially the mandatory rules of another country) do not necessarily form part of public policy in Japan.

[44] After the Supreme Court decision, the Osaka High Court rejected the petition for the setting aside of the award, reasoning that before the award was rendered, the arbitrator had not been aware of and could not have discovered the facts through a reasonable investigation. Decision of Osaka High Court, 11 March 2019, HT 1468, 65.

[45] Decision of Tokyo District Court, 13 June 2011, HJ 2128, 58. Higher courts have upheld this decision: Decision of Tokyo High Court, 13 March 2012 and Decision of Supreme Court, 25 July 2012 (unpublished).

[46] Decision of Tokyo District Court, 28 July 2009, HT 1304, 292.

[47] Decision of Tokyo High Court, 19 August 2016, 2016WLJPCA08196002.

[48] The Tokyo High Court held that mandatory rules of EU competition law did not necessarily form part of public policy in Japan and, even if the tribunal had issued an award based on a misinterpretation of contractual obligations and had wrongly applied applicable mandatory rules, such mistake was simply an error of interpretation that did not warrant setting aside the award as contrary to public policy.

When it comes to the interpretation of procedural public policy within the meaning of AA article 44(1)(viii), lower courts have recently rendered some notable judgments. In a case involving disputes arising out of cross-licensing agreements, the Tokyo District Court held that the fact that the arbitral tribunal did not deal with important facts, which could have affected the resulting award, amounted to a ground for retrial under the Code of Civil Procedure (CCP) article 338(1)(ix)[49] and, therefore, ran counter to procedural public policy under AA article 44(1)(viii).[50] The Tokyo High Court at second instance, however, overturned this judgment and held that there was no violation of procedural public policy.[51] The High Court stated that in light of the legislative process of AA and the underlying purpose of AA, its provisions on grounds for setting aside and the recognition and enforcement of arbitral awards should not be interpreted along the lines of 'the elaborate theories of interpretation of CCP, but by reference to basic international standards that should be used in the resolution of civil disputes'. The Court continued:

> In the end, it must be examined whether those basic international standards found in AA article 25[52] ... are in fact followed. The decision as to whether AA article 25 is abided by is entrusted to the wisdom and sensibilities of lawyers, and not to the domestic civil procedure law of the seat of arbitration.

E. Recognition and Enforcement of Arbitral Awards

i. Legal Sources

There are, besides AA, several legal instruments covering the recognition and enforcement of foreign arbitral awards (see section I.A). The most important instrument is NYC.[53] As regards the recognition and enforcement of foreign arbitral awards, the first question is which legal instrument is applicable to the case at hand. Since Japan is a party to several international treaties in this field, the priority among relevant treaties is questioned.

[49] CCP article 338(1)(ix) reads as follows:

> '(1) If any of the following circumstances are present, a party may protest a final judgment that has become final and binding through a demand for a retrial; provided, however, that this does not apply if a party, when filing the appeal to the court of second instance or the final appeal, alleged those circumstances or knew of them but did not allege them: ...
>
> (ix) there has been an omission involving a determination with regard to a matter of material import that would have influenced the judgment'.

[50] Decision of Tokyo District Court, 28 March 2018, HJ 2415, 33.

[51] Decision of Tokyo High Court, 1 August 2018, HJ 2415, 24 ((2019) 62 *JYIL* 462).

[52] AA Article 25 provides:

> '(1) The parties shall be treated with equality in the arbitral proceedings. (2) Each party shall be given a full opportunity of presenting its case in the arbitral proceedings'.

[53] For recognition and enforcement of foreign arbitral awards under NYC in Japan, see Hisashi Harata, 'Interpretation and Application of the New York Convention in Japan' in George Bermann (ed), *Recognition and Enforcement of Foreign Arbitral Awards: The Interpretation and Application of the New York Convention by National Courts* (Springer, 2017).

As for the relationship between NYC, GC[54] and GP, NYC basically prevails over the other two instruments in light of NYC article 7(2)[55] and article 30 of the Vienna Convention on the Law of Treaties.[56] As for the relationship between NYC and bilateral treaties Japan entered into (with, for instance, the US, Argentina,[57] the UK,[58] the PRC,[59] the former Soviet Union,[60] the former Yugoslavia,[61] the former Czechoslovakia,[62] Romania,[63] Bulgaria,[64] Hungary,[65] Poland,[66] the former East Germany,[67] Pakistan,[68] Peru[69] and El Salvador[70]),[71]

[54] GC deals with recognition and enforcement of arbitral awards rendered by an arbitral tribunal in accordance with relevant provisions of GP. Since Japan has made the reciprocal reservation pursuant to NYC article 1(3), GC will only apply when an arbitral award for which enforcement is sought originates from a non-contracting state to NYC. There have been judgments in which Japanese courts have recognised and enforced foreign arbitral awards under GC (Judgment of Tokyo District Court, 20 August 1959, *Kaminshu* 10(8), 1711; Judgment of Osaka District Court, 11 May 1959, *Kaminshu* 10(5), 970).

[55] NYC article 7 stipulates:

'(1) The provisions of the present Convention shall not affect the validity of multilateral or bilateral agreements concerning the recognition and enforcement of arbitral awards entered into by the Contracting States nor deprive any interested party of any right he may have to avail himself of an arbitral award in the manner and to the extent allowed by the law or the treaties of the country where such award is sought to be relied upon.

(2) The Geneva Protocol on Arbitration Clauses of 1923 and the Geneva Convention on the Execution of Foreign Arbitral Awards of 1927 shall cease to have effect between Contracting States on their becoming bound and to the extent that they become bound, by this Convention'.

[56] Articles 30(3) and (4) provide:

'(3) When all the parties to the earlier treaty are parties also to the later treaty but the earlier treaty is not terminated or suspended in operation under article 59, the earlier treaty applies only to the extent that its provisions are compatible with those of the later treaty.

(4) When the parties to the later treaty do not include all the parties to the earlier one:

(a) As between States parties to both treaties the same rule applies as in paragraph 3;

(b) As between a State party to both treaties and a State party to only one of the treaties, the treaty to which both States are parties governs their mutual rights and obligations'.

[57] Treaty of Friendship, Commerce and Navigation between Japan and the Argentine Republic (Treaty No 16 of 20 September 1967).

[58] Treaty of Commerce, Establishment and Navigation between the United Kingdom of Great Britain and Northern Ireland and Japan (Treaty No 17 of 22 April 1963).

[59] Trade Agreement between Japan and PRC (Treaty No 4 of 15 June 1974).

[60] Treaty of Commerce between Japan and the Soviet Union (Treaty No 7 of 9 May 1958).

[61] Treaty of Commerce and Navigation between Japan and the Federal People's Republic of Yugoslavia (Treaty No 17 of 20 July 1959).

[62] Treaty on Commerce between Japan and the Czechoslovak Republic (Treaty No 10 of 26 September 1960).

[63] Treaty of Commerce and Navigation between Japan and the Socialist Republic of Romania (Treaty No 17 of 19 July 1970).

[64] Treaty of Commerce and Navigation between Japan and the People's Republic of Bulgaria (Treaty No 18 of 1 August 1970).

[65] Treaty of Commerce and Navigation between Japan and the Hungarian People's Republic (Treaty No 14 of 25 August 1976).

[66] Treaty on Commerce and Navigation between Japan and the Polish People's Republic (Treaty No 32 of 20 October 1980).

[67] Treaty on Commerce and Navigation between Japan and the German Democratic Republic (Treaty No 14 of 4 September 1982).

[68] Treaty of Friendship and Commerce between Japan and Pakistan (Treaty No 16 of 18 August 1961).

[69] Trade Agreement between Japan and Republic of Peru (Treaty No 18 of 18 December 1961).

[70] Agreement on Commerce between Japan and the Republic of El Salvador (Treaty No 13 of 19 June 1964).

[71] The scheme for recognition and enforcement of these treaties is roughly categorised into four groups: (a) group 1 requires recognition and enforcement of arbitral awards, subject only to public policy (b) group 2 requires recognition and enforcement, subject to specified grounds; (c) group 3 refers recognition and enforcement to a common multilateral treaty; and (d) group 4 refers recognition and enforcement to the laws of the state

as a matter of principle, the later treaty should prevail over an earlier one. However, if some provisions set out explicitly how an instrument relates to existing international treaties (including, for instance, which instrument ought to prevail in the event of conflict), those provisions need to be respected.

Notably, NYC article 7(1) does not specify which treaty prevails over another and thereby does not deny the recognition and enforcement of foreign arbitral awards pursuant to other treaties. This raised an issue in relation to the Sino–Japanese Trade Agreement. Pursuant to article 8(4) of this Trade Agreement, both states are supposed to enforce an award in accordance with the requirements stipulated by the laws of the state where enforcement is sought. The question is whether NYC is regarded as part of the laws of Japan, namely, whether AA or NYC applies. Although Japanese court practice remains divided,[72] it is submitted that NYC should apply in light of the principle described above and Japanese Constitution article 98(2).[73] Nevertheless, AA would still be applicable to the extent that is consistent with NYC article 7(1). On the other hand, the relationship among national law, AA and relevant treaties is clear under Japanese law. Pursuant to Constitution article 98(2), Japan is obliged to abide by the treaties which it has concluded, as well as the established law of nations. Accordingly, relevant treaties should ordinarily prevail over AA in the event of conflict. Where there is no conflict, the matter may still be referred to AA by reason of treaty-based regulation, as NYC article 7 and the Sino–Japan Trade Agreement article 8(4) state.

ii. Grounds for Refusal

The grounds for refusal of recognition under AA and NYC are almost identical.[74] This is because AA essentially follows the requirements of the Model Law that effectively incorporate those of NYC. Accordingly, it is hard to conceive of a situation in which the priority among treaties would lead to significantly different results with regard to the recognition of awards. Although Japan has made a reciprocity reservation under NYC article 1(3), in practical terms it has 'withdrawn' the reservation by the enactment of AA article 45.[75] Nevertheless, there are some differences to be noted between the AA and NYC.

where enforcement is sought. The treaties all require that the parties belong to contracting states. The grounds for refusal of recognition and enforcement may differ from one treaty to another. For details, see Kazushige Ogawa, 'Chusai Handan no Shonin Shikko' in Yasuhei Taniguchi and Isomi Suzuki (eds), *Kokusai Shoji Chusai no Ho to Jitsumu* (Yushodo, 2016).

[72] Some lower courts have applied national law (Judgment of Tokyo District Court, 20 July 1993, HJ 1494, 126 (prior to the enactment of AA); Decision of Osaka District Court, 25 March 2011, HJ 2122, 106), one district court applied NYC (Judgment of Yokohama District Court, 25 August 1999, HJ 1707, 146 (prior to the enactment of AA)). In addition, there is a judgment which dealt with the question but did not clarify its position (Judgment of Okayama District Court, 14 July 1993, HJ 1492, 125).

[73] Japanese Constitution article 98 reads:

> '(1) This Constitution shall be the supreme law of the nation and no law, ordinance, imperial rescript or other act of government, or part thereof, contrary to the provisions hereof, shall have legal force or validity.
> (2) The treaties concluded by Japan and established laws of nations shall be faithfully observed'.

[74] There are some differences to be noted in terms of what types of award can be recognised or enforced. For instance, the scope of AA is not limited to arbitral awards in commercial matters unlike NYC.

[75] Nakano (n 3) 114.

The paragraphs below outline the AA's scheme for the recognition and enforcement of foreign arbitral awards and touch on those differences.

By AA article 45(1), arbitral awards rendered in Japan and those from other states have the same effect as final and binding judgments. In order to enforce such arbitral awards in Japan, a party seeking it is required to obtain an enforcement order (*Shikko-Kettei*) pursuant to AA article 46. An enforcement order follows summary proceedings, which are simpler than the adversarial proceedings for the enforcement of foreign judgments under the Civil Execution Act article 24. Japanese courts may dismiss an application for the enforcement order of an arbitral award, if any of the grounds for refusal in AA article 45(2)(i)–(ix) is present:

(i) The award is not valid due to the limited capacity of a party.
(ii) The award is not valid on grounds other than the limited capacity of a party pursuant to the laws and regulations designated by the parties to govern the arbitration agreement (or absent a choice of law, the laws and regulations of the country to which the place of arbitration falls).
(iii) The party did not receive the notice required under the laws and regulations of the country to which the place of arbitration belongs (or where the parties made an agreement on matters not regulated by mandatory rules, such agreement) in the proceedings of appointing arbitrators or in the arbitral proceedings.
(iv) The party was unable to submit a defence in the arbitral proceedings.
(v) The arbitral award contains a decision on matters beyond the scope of the arbitration agreement or of the claims brought to the arbitration proceedings.
(vi) The composition of the arbitral tribunal or the arbitration proceedings violated laws and regulations of the country to which the place of arbitration belongs (or where the parties have made an agreement on matters not regulated by mandatory rules, such agreement).
(vii) The arbitral award is not final and binding pursuant to the laws and regulations of the country to which the place of arbitration belongs (or where laws and regulations applied to the arbitration proceedings are of a country other than the country to which the place of arbitration belongs, such other country), or the arbitral award has been set aside or its effects have been suspended by a judicial body of that country.
(viii) The claims brought to the arbitral proceedings relate to a dispute that cannot be the subject matter of an arbitration agreement pursuant to the laws and regulations of Japan.
(ix) The content of the arbitral award runs counter to the public policy or good morals of Japan.

There are structural and textual differences between the grounds of AA and those of NYC.[76] For instance: (a) AA article 45(2)(i) does not refer to the law governing a party's capacity to enter into an arbitration agreement.[77] (b) AA article 45(2)(vi) gives priority to the law of

[76] See Harata, 'Interpretation and Application of the New York Convention in Japan' (n 53) 587–88.
[77] NYC article V(1)(b) provides: 'The party against whom the award is invoked was not given proper notice of the appointment of the arbitrator or of the arbitration proceedings or was otherwise unable to present his case'.

the country to which the place of arbitration belongs;[78] (c) Article 45(2)(iii) explicitly refers to the law governing the notice. Furthermore, by AA article 45(2), recognition needs to be refused where any of the grounds in items (i)–(ix) are present. In other words, the judge is not given any discretion in deciding on the recognition of an arbitral award.[79] When it comes to the grounds in items (i)–(vii), the party challenging recognition and enforcement bears the burden of proof, while the court is supposed to examine *ex officio* whether the grounds in items (viii) or (ix) are fulfilled.

Japanese courts have been liberal in recognising foreign arbitral awards.[80] So far, there has been no reported court decision refusing recognition under NYC, nor under any of other multilateral or bilateral agreements, or AA.

II. Investment Treaty Arbitration

A. Overview

Foreign investors and a host state can refer investment disputes to an arbitral tribunal for determination (often referred to as 'investor–state dispute settlement' (ISDS)). As opposed to international commercial arbitration, investment treaty arbitration is not based on the parties' agreement, but on bilateral or multilateral investment treaties (BITs or MITs), economic partnerships or free trade agreements (EPAs or FTAs) between the host state and the investor state. Examples are the Energy Charter Treaty and the Comprehensive and Progressive Agreement for Trans-Pacific Partnership (CPTPP).[81] Typically, BITs, MITs, EPAs and FTAs will include a provision on dispute resolution, including arbitration pursuant to the International Centre for Settlement of Investment Disputes Convention (ICSID Centre) or the UNCITRAL Arbitration Rules.

Japan is a contracting state to the ICSID Convention.[82] It has also entered into BITs or MITs containing provisions on ISDS.[83] More specifically, Japan has concluded BITs or MITs as follows:[84]

[78] NYC article V(1)(d) stipulates: 'The composition of the arbitral authority or the arbitral procedure was not in accordance with the agreement of the parties, or, failing such agreement, was not in accordance with the law of the country where the arbitration took place'.

[79] NYC article V(1) states: 'Recognition and enforcement of the award may be refused, at the request of the party against whom it is invoked, only if that party furnishes to the competent authority where the recognition and enforcement is sought'.

[80] Yasuhei Taniguchi and Tatsuya Nakamura, 'Japanese Court Decisions on article V of the New York Convention' (2008) 25 *Journal of International Arbitration* 857.

[81] For recent developments in Japan's policy towards international investment agreements, see Tomoko Ishikawa, 'A Japanese Perspective on International Investment Agreements: Recent Developments' in Julien Chaisse and Luke Nottage (eds), *International Investment Treaties and Arbitration Across Asia* (Brill/Nijhoff, 2017).

[82] Convention on the Settlement of Investment Disputes between States and Nationals of Other States, which entered into force on 18 March 1965 (Treaty No 10 of 25 August 1967).

[83] For details, see Ohara and Yanase (n 7) 42–51.

[84] See: investmentpolicy.unctad.org/international-investment-agreements/countries/105/japan.

Table 5.1

Short Title	Date (Entry into force)
Egypt–Japan BIT (1977)[85]	14 January 1978
Japan–Sri Lanka BIT (1982)[86]	7 August 1982
China–Japan BIT (1988)[87]	14 May 1989
Japan–Turkey BIT (1992)[88]	12 March 1993
Hong Kong, China SAR–Japan BIT (1997)[89]	18 June 1997
Bangladesh–Japan BIT (1998)[90]	25 August 1999
Japan–Russian Federation BIT (1998)[91]	27 May 2000
Japan–Pakistan BIT (1998)[92]	29 May 2002
Japan–Republic of Korea BIT (2002)[93]	1 January 2003
Japan–Viet Nam BIT (2003)[94]	19 December 2004
Cambodia–Japan BIT (2007)[95]	31 July 2008
Japan–Lao People's Democratic Republic BIT (2008)[96]	3 August 2008
Japan–Uzbekistan BIT (2008)[97]	24 September 2009
Japan–Peru BIT (2008)[98]	10 December 2009
Japan–Papua New Guinea BIT (2011)[99]	17 January 2014

(continued)

[85] Agreement between Japan and the Arab Republic of Egypt concerning the Encouragement and Reciprocal Protection of Investment (Treaty No 1 of 10 January 1978).

[86] Agreement between Japan and the Democratic Socialist Republic of Sri Lanka concerning the Promotion and Protection of Investment (Treaty No 10 of 20 July 1982).

[87] Agreement between Japan and the People's Republic of China concerning the Encouragement and Reciprocal Protection of Investment (Treaty No 3 of 12 May 1989).

[88] Agreement between Japan and Turkey concerning the Encouragement and Reciprocal Protection of Investment (Treaty No 2 of 23 February 1993).

[89] Agreement between the Government of Japan and the Government of Hong Kong for the Promotion and Protection of Investment (Treaty No 7 of 18 June 1997).

[90] Agreement between Japan and the People's Republic of Bangladesh concerning the Promotion and Protection of Investment (Treaty No 8 of 28 July 1998).

[91] Agreement between the Government of Japan and the Government of the Russian Federation concerning the Promotion and Protection of Investment (Treaty No 3 of 1 May 2000).

[92] Agreement between Japan and the Islamic Republic of Pakistan concerning the Promotion and Protection of Investment (Treaty No 3 of 10 May 2002).

[93] Agreement between the Government of the Republic of Korea and the Government of Japan for the Liberalisation, Promotion and Protection of Investment (Treaty No 17 of 12 December 2002).

[94] Agreement between Japan and the Socialist Republic of Viet Nam for the Liberalization, Promotion and Protection of Investment (Treaty No 15 of 25 November 2004).

[95] Agreement between Japan and the Kingdom of Cambodia for the Liberalization, Promotion and Protection of Investment (Treaty No 7 of 7 July 2008).

[96] Agreement between Japan and the Lao People's Democratic Republic for the Liberalisation, Promotion and Protection of Investment (Treaty No 9 of 9 July 2008).

[97] Agreement between Japan and the Republic of Uzbekistan for the Liberalization, Promotion and Protection of Investment (Treaty No 7 of 28 August 2009).

[98] Agreement between Japan and the Republic of Peru for the Promotion, Protection and Liberalisation of Investment (Treaty No 11 of 13 November 2009).

[99] Agreement between the Government of Japan and the Government of the Independent State of Papua New Guinea for the Promotion and Protection of Investment (Treaty No 12 of 20 December 2013).

Table 5.1 ***(Continued)***

Short Title	Date (Entry into force)
Japan–Kuwait BIT (2012)[100]	24 January 2014
China–Japan–Republic of Korea Trilateral Investment Agreement (2012)[101]	17 May 2014
Iraq–Japan BIT (2012)[102]	25 February 2014
Japan–Myanmar BIT (2013)[103]	7 August 2014
Japan–Mozambique BIT (2013)[104]	29 August 2014
Colombia–Japan BIT (2011)[105]	11 September 2015
Japan–Kazakhstan BIT (2014)[106]	25 October 2015
Japan–Ukraine BIT (2015)[107]	26 November 2015
Japan–Uruguay BIT (2015)[108]	14 April 2017
Japan–Oman BIT (2015)[109]	21 July 2017
Islamic Republic of Iran–Japan BIT (2016)[110]	26 April 2017
Israel–Japan BIT (2017)[111]	5 October 2017
Japan–Kenya BIT (2016)[112]	14 September 2017
Japan–Jordan BIT (2018)[113]	Not in force

(continued)

[100] Agreement between Japan and the State of Kuwait for the Promotion and Protection of Investment (Treaty No 17 of 27 December 2013).

[101] Agreement among the Government of Japan, the Government of the Republic of Korea and the Government of the People's Republic of China for the Promotion, Facilitation and Protection of Investment (Treaty No 5 of 14 May 2014).

[102] Agreement between Japan and the Republic of Iraq for the Promotion and Protection of Investment (Treaty No 3 of 29 January 2014).

[103] Agreement between the Government of Japan and the Government of the Republic of the Union of Myanmar for the Liberalisation, Promotion and Protection of Investment (Treaty No 11 of 11 July 2014).

[104] Agreement between the Government of Japan and the Government of the Republic of the Mozambique on the Reciprocal Liberalisation, Promotion and Protection of Investment (Treaty No 13 of 5 August 2014).

[105] Agreement between Japan and the Republic of Colombia for the Liberalization, Promotion and Protection of Investment (Treaty No 5 of 2 September 2015).

[106] Agreement between Japan and the Republic of Kazakhstan for the Promotion and Protection of Investment (Treaty No 6 of 30 September 2015).

[107] Agreement between Japan and Ukraine for the Promotion and Protection of Investment (Treaty No 7 of 30 October 2015).

[108] Agreement between Japan and the Oriental Republic of Uruguay for the Liberalization, Promotion and Protection of Investment (Treaty No 5 of 17 March 2017).

[109] Agreement between Japan and the Sultanate of Oman for the Reciprocal Promotion and Protection of Investment (Treaty No 19 of 23 June 2017).

[110] Agreement between Japan and the Islamic Republic of Iran on Reciprocal Promotion and Protection of Investment (Treaty No 6 of 14 April 2017).

[111] Agreement between the State of Israel and Japan for the Liberalization, Promotion and Protection of Investment (Treaty No 30 of 15 September 2017).

[112] Agreement between the Government of Japan and the Government of the Republic of Kenya for the Promotion and Protection of Investment (Treaty No 27 of 18 August 2017).

[113] Agreement between Japan and the Hashemite Kingdom of Jordan for the Promotion and Protection of Investment.

Table 5.1 ***(Continued)***

Short Title	**Date (Entry into force)**
Armenia–Japan BIT (2018)[114]	15 May 2019
Argentina–Japan BIT (2018)[115]	Not in force
Japan–UAE BIT (2018)[116]	Not in force
Japan–Morocco BIT (2020)[117]	Not in force
Japan–Côte D'Ivoire BIT (2020)[118]	Not in force

As of March 2021, Japan has been negotiating BITs with Paraguay, Turkmenistan, Tajikistan, Republic of Georgia, Kyrgyzstan, Azerbaijan, Bahrain, Qatar, Nigeria, Tanzania, Senegal, Zambia, Ghana, Ethiopia, Angola, and Algeria.

In addition, Japan has concluded EPAs as follows:

Table 5.2

Name	**Date (Entry into force)**
Japan–Singapore EPA (2002)[119]	30 November 2002 (amended in 2007)
Japan–Mexico EPA (2004)[120]	1 April 2005 (amended in 2012)
Japan–Malaysia EPA (2005)[121]	13 July 2006
Chile–Japan EPA (2007)[122]	3 September 2007
Japan–Thailand EPA (2007)[123]	1 November 2007
Brunei–Japan EPA (2007)[124]	31 July 2008
Indonesia–Japan EPA (2007)[125]	1 July 2008

(continued)

[114] Agreement between Japan and the Republic of Armenia for the Liberalisation, Promotion and Protection of Investment (Treaty No 2 of 26 April 2019).
[115] Agreement between Japan and the Argentine Republic for the Promotion and Protection of Investment.
[116] Agreement between Japan and the United Arab Emirates for the Promotion and Protection of Investment.
[117] Agreement between the Kingdom of Morocco and Japan for the Promotion and Protection of Investment.
[118] Agreement between the Government of Japan and the Government of the Republic of Côte D'Ivoire for the Reciprocal Promotion and Protection of Investment.
[119] Agreement between Japan and the Republic of Singapore for a New-age Economic Partnership (Treaty No 16 of 12 November 2002).
[120] Agreement between Japan and the United Mexican States for the Strengthening of the Economic Partnership (Treaty No 8 of 4 March 2005).
[121] Agreement between the Government of Japan and the Government of Malaysia for An Economic Partnership (Treaty No 7 of 15 June 2006).
[122] Agreement between Japan and the Republic of Chile for A Strategic Economic Partnership (Treaty No 8, 2007 of 14 August 2007).
[123] Agreement between Japan and the Kingdom of Thailand for An Economic Partnership (Treaty No 14 of 12 October 2007).
[124] Agreement between Japan and Brunei Darussalam for An Economic Partnership (Treaty No 6 of 4 July 2008).
[125] Agreement between Japan and the Republic of Indonesia for An Economic Partnership (Treaty No 2 of 5 June 2008).

Table 5.2 ***(Continued)***

Name	Date (Entry into force)
Japan–Viet Nam EPA (2008)[126]	1 October 2009
ASEAN–Japan EPA (2008)[127]	1 December 2008
Japan–Philippines EPA (2008)[128]	11 December 2008
Japan–Switzerland EPA (2009)[129]	1 September 2009
India–Japan EPA (2011)[130]	1 August 2011
Japan–Peru EPA (2011)[131]	1 March 2012
Australia–Japan EPA (2014)[132]	15 January 2015
Japan–Mongolia EPA (2015)[133]	7 June 2016
TPP (2016)[134]	Not in force
CPTTP (2018)[135]	30 December 2018
EU–Japan EPA (2018)[136]	1 February 2019
US–Japan Trade Agreement (2019)[137]	1 January 2020
UK–Japan EPA (2020)[138]	1 January 2021

These EPAs contain provisions on ISDS. As of March 2021, Japan is in negotiations for EPAs (or FTAs) with Turkey, Columbia, the Republic of Korea and the PRC. In November 2020, Japan signed the Regional Comprehensive Economic Partnership with ASEAN, Australia, the PRC, the Republic of Korea and New Zealand.

As a matter of national law, Japan has no statute to protect foreign investments. Foreign investment is, therefore, protected under the relevant national laws applicable to all categories of investments (whether domestic or foreign) in Japan. Although the number of Japan's

[126] Agreement between Japan and the Socialist Republic of Viet Nam for An Economic Partnership (Treaty No 8 of 28 August 2009).

[127] Agreement on Comprehensive Economic Partnership among Japan and Member States of the Association of Southeast Asian Nations (Treaty No 12 of 31 October 2008).

[128] Agreement between Japan and the Republic of the Philippines for An Economic Partnership (Treaty No 16 of 14 November 2008).

[129] Agreement on Free Trade and Economic Partnership between Japan and the Swiss Confederation (Treaty No 5 of 6 August 2009).

[130] Comprehensive Economic Partnership Agreement between Japan and the Republic of India (Treaty No 7 of 1 July 2011).

[131] Agreement between Japan and the Republic of Peru for An Economic Partnership (Treaty No 2 of 25 January 2012).

[132] Agreement between Australia and Japan for An Economic Partnership (Treaty No 19 of 19 December 2014).

[133] Agreement between Japan and Mongolia for An Economic Partnership (Treaty No 8 of 9 May 2016).

[134] Trans-Pacific Partnership Agreement, superseded by the CPTPP.

[135] Comprehensive and Progressive Agreement for Trans-Pacific Partnership (Treaty No 16 of 27 December 2018).

[136] Agreement between the European Union and Japan for An Economic Partnership (Treaty No 15 of 27 December 2018).

[137] Trade Agreement between Japan and the United States of America (Treaty No 10 of 13 December 2019).

[138] Agreement between the United Kingdom of Great Britain and Northern Ireland and Japan for a Comprehensive Economic Partnership (Treaty No 2 of 23 December 2020).

investment agreements has been increasing, the number of ISDS cases involving Japan or Japanese entities remains low.[139]

B. Jurisdiction of the Arbitral Tribunal

The jurisdiction of an arbitral tribunal in ISDS is based on the arbitration agreement contained in the BIT, MIT, EPA or FTA between the host state and the investor state. Foreign investors invoke that agreement to seek protection against the host state. Therefore, at the outset, to establish jurisdiction one must examine the terms of the relevant arbitration agreement. Procedural rules to be followed in the arbitral proceedings are normally indicated by the respective agreement, for instance ICSID rules, the rules of some other arbitral institution, the UNCITRAL Arbitration Rules, or some other set of rules for ad hoc administration. Most of Japan's investment treaties and EPAs adopt ICSID arbitration rules.

C. Choice of Law

The law governing the merits of a case depends on provisions in the relevant treaty. Some treaties contain provisions on applicable law. For instance, under article 16(8) of the BIT between Japan and Papua New Guinea, '[a]n arbitral tribunal … shall decide the issues in dispute in accordance with this Agreement and applicable rules of international law'. On the other hand, pursuant to ICSID Convention article 42, the choice of law by the parties first comes into play and, in the absence of such agreement, the arbitral tribunal shall apply the law of the contracting state that is party to the dispute (ie, the host state) (including its choice of law rules) and any rules of international law that may be applicable. Further, when an arbitration proceeding is conducted in accordance with procedural rules other than the ICSID rules, the arbitral tribunal may apply such law (including international law) as it finds appropriate. In any event, the rules of international law (ie, public international law) come into play most of the time.

International investment treaties will normally incorporate certain standard provisions: (a) a clause prohibiting expropriation without fair compensation; (b) a clause requiring the host state to accord 'fair and equitable treatment' (FET) and 'full protection and security' (FPS) to investors; (c) a clause requiring the host state to accord 'no less favourable treatment' to foreign investors than the treatment of domestic investors; and (d) a 'most favoured nation' (MFN) clause. The issues that often arise in investment treaty arbitrations are typically focused on the meaning and scope of such standard clauses. Examples are: (a) whether the claimant is an 'investor' and (if so) whether the claimant has made an 'investment' within the terms of an investment treaty or agreement; (b) whether there has

[139] See Shotaro Hamamoto and Luke Nottage, 'Foreign Investment in and out of Japan: Economic Backdrop, Domestic Law, and International Treaty-Based Investor–State Dispute Resolution' (2010) Sydney Law School Research Paper No10/145. Among decided cases, *Saluka Investments BV v Czech Republic* (PCA 2001–04) is a well-known example. There are some pending cases, for instance, *ITOCHU Corporation v Kingdom of Spain*; *JGC Corporation v Kingdom of Spain*; *Eurus Energy Holdings Corporation and Eurus Energy Europe BV v Kingdom of Spain*; *Nissan Motor Co Ltd v Republic of India*.

been a breach of any of the FRT, FPS, MFN and no less favourable treatment clauses in a treaty or agreement; (c) whether there has been an 'expropriation' by the host state without payment of adequate compensation to the investor; and (d) insofar as there has been any breach by the host state, what should be the remedies for the investor's compensation or damages claims.

D. Recognition and Enforcement of Arbitral Awards

With regard to recognition and enforcement of arbitral awards, the ICSID Convention plays an important role. ICSID Convention article 54 stipulates:

> Each Contracting State shall recognise an award rendered pursuant to this Convention as binding and enforce the pecuniary obligations imposed by that award within its territories as if it were a final judgment of a court in that State. A Contracting State with a federal constitution may enforce such an award in or through its federal courts and may provide that such courts shall treat the award as if it were a final judgment of the courts of a constituent state.

The ICSID Convention does not provide any grounds for refusal of the recognition and enforcement of arbitral awards. If non-ICSID arbitration is concerned, NYC may be available for the purpose of the recognition and enforcement of an arbitral award. For instance, article 18(13) of the BIT between Japan and Myanmar presupposes the applicability of NYC and provides that:

> Unless the disputing parties agree otherwise, the arbitration shall be held in a country that is a party to the United Nations Convention on the Recognition and Enforcement of Foreign Arbitral Awards, done at New York, June 10, 1958.

Further, its article 18(14) stipulates that:

> The award rendered by the arbitral tribunal shall be final and binding upon the disputing parties. This award shall be executed in accordance with the applicable laws and regulations, as well as relevant international law including the ICSID Convention and the New York Convention, concerning the execution of award in force in the country where such execution is sought.

In such case, NYC will have application insofar as the recognition and enforcement of an award between the parties is concerned, in light of article 41(1)(b) of the Vienna Convention on the Law of Treaties.[140] When it comes to the recognition and enforcement under the ICSID Convention and NYC, state immunity comes into question with regard to the enforcement of an arbitral award. For instance, ICSID Convention article 55 stipulates: 'Nothing in article 54 shall be construed as derogation from the law in force in any Contracting State relating to immunity of that State or of any foreign State from execution'. Nevertheless, it may be possible to waive state immunity in an investment treaty. For instance, Japan and Switzerland did so in the EPA between them. The Japan–Switzerland EPA article 94(11) provides that '[t]he disputing Party may not assert as a defence its immunity'.

[140] Shotaro Hamamoto, 'Toshi Joyaku Chusai' in Yasuhei Taniguchi and Isomi Suzuki (eds), *Kokusai Shoji Chusai no Ho to Jitsumu* (Yushodo, 2016).

III. Mediation

A. Overview

As in other jurisdictions, more attention has recently been paid to mediation as an alternative dispute resolution method in addition to arbitration. As opposed to litigation and arbitration, mediation is a non-adjudicative dispute resolution method which will not normally require strict adherence to rules of law. It instead aims to settle disputes through discussion and negotiation between the parties, with the assistance of a third neutral party, or mediator. Geared towards amicable solutions, mediation has the advantages of being flexible, cost-efficient and time-efficient, and supportive of maintaining commercial relationships.

There are two types of mediation. The first type is mediation run by the courts, which is conducted and supervised by the courts in accordance with relevant statutes, such as the Civil Mediation Act (CMA) (dealing with civil disputes)[141] or the Domestic Relations Case Procedure Act (DRCPA) (dealing with family law disputes).[142] In mediation by a court under CMA and DRCPA, the court will initially set up a mediation committee (*Chotei Iinkai*) to carry out the mediation. The mediation committee will consist of a judge (or mediator by appointed the Supreme Court (*Choteikan*) and/or two mediation commissioners (*Chotei Iin*).[143] The Supreme Court appoints mediators from among attorneys of not less than five years' experience to serve as part-time officers.[144] The judge or mediator chairs the committee. The role and function of a commissioner in a mediation is to express an opinion based on the commissioner's expert knowledge and experience, to listen to the views of the parties, and to undertake any other necessary steps to resolve disputes. Notably, there exists no statute prohibiting out-of-court mediations.[145] Parties may, therefore, also agree to settle their disputes through out-of-court mediation. This is the second type of mediation. There are institutions that provide mediation services to parties. Examples are JCAA and the Japan Intellectual Property Arbitration Center. To develop as a regional hub for international dispute resolution, Japan recently established the first mediation centre in Kyoto, the Japan International Mediation Centre – Kyoto (JIMC-Kyoto).[146]

Mediation can broadly be categorised into two styles: facilitative mediation and evaluative mediation. Under the former style, a mediator assists the parties to reach an amicable

[141] There is a special mediation proceeding for expediting arrangements for specified debts. A debtor who is likely to become insolvent may file a petition for such proceeding. See Act on Special Conciliation for Expediting Arrangement of Specified Debts (Act No 158 of 17 December 1999).

[142] For an overview of mediation by courts in Japan see: www.choutei.jp/english/index.html.

[143] CMA article 6 and DRCPA article 247.

[144] CMA article 23-2 and DRCPA article 250.

[145] Japan has not enacted any statute applying the UNCITRAL Model Law on International Commercial Conciliation (2002) or the UNCITRAL Model Law on International Commercial Mediation and International Settlement Agreements Resulting from Mediation (2018).

[146] For details on the centre, see: www.jimc-kyoto.jp; Haruo Okada, 'JIMC-Kyoto – An Attractive Option for International Mediation' (2020) 1 *Japan Commercial Arbitration Journal* 67. Also see, eg, James Claxton and Luke Nottage, '*Wa and the Japan International Mediation Center – Kyoto*', available at: mediationblog.kluwerarbitration.com/2018/02/01/wa-and-the-japanese-international-mediation-centre/; James Claxton and Luke Nottage, 'Getting Into Gear: The Japan International Mediation Centre – Kyoto', available at: mediationblog.kluwerarbitration.com/2018/09/17/getting-gear-japan-international-mediation-centre-kyoto/; James Claxton, Luke Nottage and Nobumichi Teramura, 'Developing Japan as a Regional Hub for International Dispute Resolution: Dream Come True or Daydream?' (2019) 24 *JJL* 109.

resolution but refrains from assessing the parties' arguments and expressing a personal view on the merits of their dispute. Under evaluative mediation, a mediator actively engages in the parties' negotiations, including by expressing a view on the merits of their disputes and putting forward settlement proposals.[147] In mediation by Japanese courts, mediators normally follow the latter style.

In December 2018, the UN General Assembly adopted in unanimity the UN Convention on International Settlement Agreements Resulting from Mediation (often referred to as the 'Singapore Mediation Convention' or 'Singapore Convention on Mediation').[148] At the same time, UNCITRAL also adopted Model Law on Mediation as a soft law instrument to help states to implement comparable rules in their domestic law.[149] The Singapore Convention and the Model Law on Mediation are intended to facilitate international trade and commerce by enabling disputing parties to readily enforce mediated settlement agreements across borders. With ratifications by Singapore, Fiji and Qatar, the Singapore Convention entered into force on 12 September 2020, and has so far attracted six contracting states and 47 signatories (as of March 2021). Japan has not yet signed or ratified this instrument, so mediation is regulated under its domestic law.

B. Jurisdiction of the Mediators

Insofar as mediations by courts in accordance with DRCPA or CMA are concerned, a party may file a petition for mediation with a court based on the parties' agreement or unilaterally (DRCPA article 245 and CMA article 3).[150] Out-of-court mediations, however, can only take place on the basis of the parties' agreement.

C. Choice of Law

As CMA article 1 states, mediation intends to achieve the amicable resolution of disputes 'based on compromise between the parties and in accordance with the reason and the circumstances of the disputes'. Accordingly, in mediation, applicable law or even choice of law is just one of the factors to be taken into consideration in the course of mediation proceedings. It does not necessarily impact the result of the mediation proceedings, unlike in litigation and arbitration.

D. Legal Effects of Mediated Settlement Agreements

i. Settlement Agreements under Domestic Law

As a matter of domestic law, concerning the legal effects of mediated settlement agreements, there are notable differences depending on whether the court was engaged in the mediation

[147] This type of mediation is often referred to as 'conciliation' and the third-party neutral as a 'conciliator'.
[148] Adopted on 20 December 2018. CN.154.2019 TREATIES-XXII.4.
[149] UNCITRAL, Model Law on International Commercial Mediation and International Settlement Agreements Resulting from Mediation (adopted on 20 December 2018).
[150] For Japan's jurisdiction in family law disputes, see ch 2, section III.

proceedings. Pursuant to CMA article 16, where a settlement agreement in a civil dispute was reached by the parties through in-court mediation proceedings and has been entered into the court record, such agreement shall have the same effect as a judicial settlement. A judicial settlement has the same effect as a final and conclusive judgment under CCP article 267 and is enforceable, even though it does not have *res judicata* effect. Similarly, a settlement agreement in family and status disputes (eg, payment of maintenance or return of the child) reached through in-court mediation and entered into the court record, has the same effect as a final and conclusive judgment and is therefore enforceable (DRCPA article 268).

On the other hand, a settlement agreement reached by the parties through out-of-court mediation is simply regarded as a contract, which is not legally binding or enforceable like a judicial settlement. Accordingly, to have a settlement agreement enforced by the court, a party must either claim for a court order that incorporates the settlement agreement or obtain an authentic instrument attesting to the settlement agreement. As a matter of domestic law, such court order and authentic instrument become legally binding and constitute an enforcement title (*samu meigi*).

ii. Recognition and Enforcement of Foreign Settlement Agreements

When it comes to the recognition and enforcement of settlement agreements resulting from a mediation abroad, there exist no explicit rules yet. Notably, according to the prevailing view, neither foreign judicial settlements, nor settlement agreements resulting from a foreign in-court or out-of-court mediation, nor authentic instruments drawn up abroad qualify as a 'foreign judgment' under CCP article 118 for lack of authoritative judicial decision-making. Thus, they cannot be recognised or enforced under current private international law in Japan (see chapter four, section I.C.i). Nor can relevant provisions of AA or NYC apply, since mediated settlement agreements do not fall under the definition of 'arbitral awards'.

To make a foreign mediated settlement agreement enforceable in Japan, a party will have to either (a) bring a claim to the Japanese courts based on that settlement agreement to obtain a judgment or judicial settlement, or (b) have that settlement agreement incorporated into a court order in the foreign state of origin. In the first scenario (a), a party seeking enforcement in Japan will submit that settlement agreement as evidence of the other party's obligation, and the existence and effect of that settlement agreement will be determined by the law applicable to contracts under AGRAL articles 7–9. In the second scenario (b), when the foreign court renders a judgment or (consent) order incorporating that settlement agreement, and not a judicial settlement, it can be recognised and enforced pursuant to CCP article 118.

Since these avenues are cumbersome and time-consuming, it would be desirable to amend the domestic law of Japan. Currently, the Japanese legislature is considering rules with necessary safeguards for the enforcement of international settlement agreements resulting from mediation, in light of the Singapore Convention and the UNCITRAL Model Law on Mediation.[151] It may also be time for Japan to consider joining the Singapore Convention, with a view to meeting international standards and ensuring cross-border enforcement of mediated settlement agreements through international cooperation.

[151] See section I.A.

6

The Harmonisation of Private International Law

I. Japan's Role in the Work of the HCCH, UNCITRAL, UNIDROIT and Other Organisations

Since the late nineteenth century, efforts towards the harmonisation of private international law, especially transnational commercial law such as the law relating to the sale and carriage of goods by sea, air and land, have been driven by intergovernmental organisations such as the Hague Conference on Private International Law (HCCH), the UN Commission on International Trade Law (UNCITRAL), the International Institution for the Unification of Private Law (UNIDROIT), and the International Civil Aviation Organisation. These organisations have produced a number of instruments (both hard and soft law), most of which (particularly, the New York Convention and the United Nations Convention on Contracts for the International Sales of Goods of 11 April 1980 (CISG)) have played an important role in international business and influenced the development of national laws worldwide. Japan has become party to several conventions promulgated by such organisations and enacted or amended its national laws by reference to them.[1]

From the outset, Japan has been actively engaged in the work of international organisations towards the harmonisation of laws relating to cross-border activities. Japan has done this through government representatives and delegations and has developed solid links with the relevant organisations. In particular, insofar as private international law is concerned, Japan has built a long and fruitful relationship with HCCH. Japan attended the 1904 Hague Conference as the first non-European country to do so and officially joined HCCH in 1957.[2] Japan's membership in HCCH is based on the Act on Assumption of Obligations for the Payment of Allocated Charges Incidental to Admission to an International Academic Society, etc.[3] Since joining, Japan has been involved in many projects. An example of a Japanese contribution is the *Explanatory Report on the 2005 HCCH Choice of Court Agreements Convention* by Professor Trevor Hartley and Professor Masato Dogauchi as rapporteurs. In addition, Japan has been engaged in the implementation, promotion and

[1] On conventions that Japan has joined, see ch 1, section II.B. A recent instance of the influence of such conventions or soft law instruments relates to the amendment of the law of obligations. Japan's legislators considered CISG and the UNIDROIT Principles of International Commercial Contracts in determining what reforms to implement.

[2] On Japan's role in the HCCH, see Masato Dogauchi and Keisuke Takeshita, 'Wagakuni no Haag Kokusai Shiho Kaigi heno Kamei ni kansuru Shiryo ni tsuite' (2005) 7 *JYPIL* 140, available at: www.pilaj.jp/ind08_j.html.

[3] Act No 48 of 1957.

revision of Hague Conventions. Among other matters, Japan has publicised judicial decisions on the application of the Convention of 25 October 1980 on the Civil Aspects of International Child Abduction (HCAC) in Japan through HCCH's INCADAT database and Japanese practitioners often speak at domestic and international conferences on the current status of Hague Conventions in Japan and the problems encountered in implementing the same. But the number of instruments promulgated by international organisations that Japan has ratified or to which it has acceded remains relatively small.[4] Consequently, while Japan seems to have played an important role at the preparation and drafting stages of conventions, it does not actually become a party to their promulgation. Nonetheless, scholars and government authorities in Japan (such as the Ministry of Justice and the Ministry of Foreign Affairs) closely monitor the operation and future development of those instruments abroad. Aside from its contributions at the international level, Japan has assisted in the work of HCCH's Regional Office Asia Pacific (ROAP) which is based in Hong Kong. ROAP and Japan held HCCH Asia Pacific Week 2016 in Tokyo to promote HCCH and its instruments in the Asia Pacific region. At the educational level, Japanese universities have forged close ties with HCCH, with a number such as the University of Tokyo, Kyushu University, Osaka University, Doshisha University and Chuo University concluding memorandums of understanding with HCCH or ROAP to enable students to undertake internships at HCCH's Permanent Bureau in the Hague or at ROAP in Hong Kong. In 2016, as a culmination to the HCCH Asia Pacific Week events, Japanese law students who had served as ROAP interns presented an unofficial Japanese translation of the 2015 Principles on Choice of Law in International Commercial Contracts to the Secretary-General of HCCH at a dinner in Tokyo.[5]

As for its relationship with UNCITRAL, Japan has been an UNCITRAL member state since 1968. In over five decades, Japan has been involved in the legislative work in various areas. Currently, Japan has been engaged in projects relating to MSMEs (micro, small and medium-sized enterprises) (Working Group 1 (WG1)); arbitration and conciliation/dispute settlement (WG2), investor-state dispute settlement reform (WG3), electronic commerce (WG4), insolvency law (WG5), and the judicial sale of ships (WG6).

On UNIDROIT, Japan became a member on 1 January 1954. It has been involved in the work of UNIDROIT through government representatives at the organisation's regular meetings. Normally, there will also be a Japanese scholar on UNIDROIT's governing council.

Although not an official government project, a group of Japanese scholars with financial support from several government bodies, has hosted a number of regular conferences with a view to identifying and codifying general principles of private international law (to be known as ('Asian Principles of Private International Law' (APPIL)) to facilitate their

[4] For an analysis of Japan's attitude and strategy to uniform substantive law, see Hiroo Sono, 'Going Forward with Uniform Private Law Treaties: A Study in Japan's Behavioral Pattern' (2017) 60 *JYIL* 10; Tomotaka Fujita, 'When Does Japan Not Conclude Uniform Private Law Conventions?' (2017) 60 *JYIL* 59.

[5] See Anselmo Reyes, 'The Hague Conference on Private International Law in the Asia Pacific (Special Issue: Emergence and Developments of Asian Private International Law)' (2015) 114 *Journal of International Law and Diplomacy* 27; for possible future developments in Asia and the role of the HCCH, see Yuko Nishitani, 'The HCCH's Development in the Asia-Pacific Region' in Rishi Gulati, Thomas John and Ben Köhler (eds), *Elgar Companion to the Hague Conference on Private International Law* (Elgar Publishing, 2020).

eventual acceptance and uniform adoption among Asian jurisdictions.[6] A large number of academics from various jurisdiction in Asia, including Japan, South Korea, Mainland China, Hong Kong, Taiwan, Singapore, Thailand, Viet Nam, Indonesia, Cambodia, the Philippines and Mongolia, have attended APPIL meetings. In the field of private law, Japanese scholars from various universities have formed a Global Private Law Forum to exchange information on the ongoing projects of HCCH, UNCITRAL and UNIDROIT, which helps to conduct empirical research on the unification of private law at the international and regional dimensions with support from governmental bodies.

Since the Meiji Restoration in 1868, Japanese law has developed by importing or referring to legal theory and practice in jurisdictions such as the UK, the US, Germany, France, Italy and Belgium. It remains the tasks of scholars to conduct research in and introduce recent theoretical and practical developments in foreign major jurisdictions into Japan as appropriate. Consequently, comparative law research is important. But such research must be bi-directional. Japan should not merely import foreign developments, but it ought also to contribute to the development of private law elsewhere in the world by frankly discussing what has worked and what has been problematic in Japan's efforts to reform its private laws (including private international law) for the benefit of its citizens. That would be a key element in the harmonisation of law at the international and regional level. Japan, as a leading country in Asia and a global economic power should take the initiative to lead discussions at an international level on how laws can be improved.[7]

II. The Future of Private International Law

Japanese private international law covers four areas: (a) international jurisdiction; (b) applicable law; (c) recognition and enforcement of foreign judgments; and (d) international arbitration and mediation. In each of these fields, Japan has enacted several statutes such as the Act on General Rules for Application of Laws (AGRAL), the Code of Civil Procedure (CCP), the Personal Status Litigation Act, the Domestic Relations Case Procedure Act, the Civil Execution Act (CEA) and the Arbitration Act (AA). In this sense, it might be suggested that Japan's legal infrastructure in the field of private international law has been sufficiently well arranged and is robust enough to deal comfortably with most legal issues likely to arise in daily life. Nonetheless, Japanese law does not have rules for fundamental issues such as characterisation, the incidental question, ascertaining the content of foreign law (see chapter one, sections IV.C, IV.F and VII). Although case law and scholarly writing

[6] For an overview of the APPIL project, see Weizuo Chen and Gerald Goldstein, 'The Asian Principles of Private International Law: Objectives, Contents, Structure and Selected Topics on Choice of Law' (2017) 13 *JPIL* 411; Naoshi Takasugi, 'Asian Principles of Private International Law (APPIL)' (2018) 69 *Doshisha Hohaku* 2305. On Asian principles of international jurisdiction, see Mao Uematasu, 'APPIL (Asian Principles of Private International Law) and its Perspective Regarding International Jurisdiction' (2019) 37 *Ritsumeikan Law Review* 35. It is expected that a comprehensive report will be published in the near future.

[7] In areas other than private international law, Japan through the Japan International Cooperation Agency (JICA), a governmental agency, has provided legal technical assistance in various Asian jurisdictions, including Viet Nam, Cambodia, Laos, Indonesia, Uzbekistan, Mongolia, Mainland China, East Timor, Kirghiz, Tajikistan, Nepal, Myanmar and Bangladesh. For details, see: www.moj.go.jp/EN/housouken/houso_kyouryoc_index.html.

can show how the treatment of these fundamental issues by Japanese courts has evolved over time, it would be desirable to have explicit provisions from the viewpoint of promoting certainty and predictability. For example, due to a lack of explicit provisions, Japanese private international law needs to rely on *jori* to deal with matters such as the law applicable to corporations and legal persons; the law applicable to specific torts such as unfair competition, competition law and intellectual property infringement; *lis pendens*; and the criteria for indirect jurisdiction. While the broad rationale for *jori* may be clear and understandable, how precisely Japanese courts determine what *jori* may be applicable in individual cases, there has been no attempt to identify the principles of *jori* and the circumstances in which a particular principle may be applied in a given case. This brings about legal uncertainty and impairs predictability. Therefore, it is hoped that the future development of Japanese private international law will address such lacunae.[8]

Another possible development is to secure and enhance predictability by acceding to international conventions. For instance, foreign judgments are already readily recognised and enforced under the current Japanese system. In practical terms, there is no real necessity to accede to the 2005 or the 2019 Hague Conventions.[9] But, by becoming a party to the 2005 or 2019 Hague Conventions, Japan can reassure parties that foreign and Japanese judgments will be recognised and enforced under a unified legal framework among member states worldwide. More specifically, there are at least three areas which might be developed insofar as judgments are concerned: (1) overcoming the reciprocity requirement by joining the 2005 and 2019 Hague Conventions; (2) clarifying the grounds of indirect jurisdiction through the 2019 Hague Convention; and (3) recognising and enforcing judicial settlements.

First, if a more liberal regime to the reciprocity requirement in CCP article 118 can be worked out pursuant to the 2019 Hague Convention, judgments from what are currently regarded as non-reciprocating states (such as Mainland China) may be recognised and enforced, provided that such states are also member states of the Convention. Second, grounds for indirect jurisdiction will be clarified. Under the current system, there are no provisions dealing with indirect jurisdiction and therefore the question whether a foreign rendering court has indirect jurisdiction over a case has to be examined in light of *jori* (presently largely based on the rules of direct jurisdiction in the CCP). The 2019 Hague Convention clearly stipulates grounds for recognition and enforcement, with the result that a party seeking recognition and enforcement can readily assess whether the indirect jurisdiction of the rendering court will be upheld. In addition to identifying grounds of indirect jurisdiction, the 2019 Hague Convention will also specify grounds for refusal of recognition. It will be more transparent when recognition of a foreign judgment may be refused, especially in the context of *lis pendens* and inconsistency with a domestic judgment.

[8] That said, it may be disputable whether we should have choice of law rules as to each specific tort. One may argue that only one choice of law rule in tort reflecting the general principle as to tort should cover all types of tort, and choice of law should not be differentiated that much. In light of the fact that cross-border legal relationships are becoming complex and differentiated, however, it is submitted that choice of law rules should also be 'adjusted' to the development to pursue justice at private international law level, namely, quest for the law of the state that has the closest connection to the legal relationship at hand. It would secure and enhance legal certainty and parties' predictability and enable judges to avoid a cumbersome burden of charactering modern-day complicated legal issues.

[9] That is, the 2005 Hague Convention on Choice of Court Agreements, and the 2019 Hague Convention on the Recognition and Enforcement of Foreign Judgments in Civil or Commercial Matters.

Third, judicial settlements will be recognised and enforced in Japan. Under current domestic rules, judicial settlements do not fall within the notion of a 'judgment' under CCP article 118 and therefore are not recognisable. The 2019 Hague Convention will open the door to the recognition of judicial settlements. There seems to be no obvious difficulty in acceding to the 2019 Hague Convention. But, in acceding to such instrument, Japan may need to modify principles and rules on jurisdiction for certain matters (such as jurisdiction relating to rights *in rem* in immovable property in Japan) to secure consistency between the instrument and domestic rules.

Another desirable development would be to facilitate the implementation of HCAC in Japan to ensure prompt return of the abducted child and access to the child by the left behind parent. The most crucial issue concerns the domestic enforcement system. Given the criticisms of Japan's implementation from foreign jurisdictions[10] and concerned parties in Japan, it is desirable to improve the situation in Japan immediately, following the necessary statutory amendments enacted in 2018.[11]

Finally, Japan is keen to promote and develop itself as a regional hub for international dispute resolution services (including arbitration and mediation, see chapter five, section I.A). With regard to international arbitration, an update of AA to bring it in line with the 2006 UNCITRAL Model Law and other foreign laws is currently being examined. In addition, it may make Japan more attractive as an arbitration centre to provide parties with options for excluding or expanding the grounds for recourse against an arbitral award and adopting concepts such as 'supranational' or 'universal' public policy for the setting aside of arbitral awards. Those measures would enable Japan to cater for the needs of different parties, especially those desirous of more expeditious forms of dispute resolution. It would enable Japan to burnish its credentials as a neutral but dependable forum for alternative dispute resolution.

[10] For instance, European Parliament Resolution on the International and Domestic Abduction of EU Children in Japan, adopted on 8 July 2020 (www.europarl.europa.eu/doceo/document/B-9-2020-0205_EN.html).

[11] A recent measure to improve the situation was the 2019 amendment of CEA and AIHCAC. See ch 3, section III.D.v.

SELECTED BIBLIOGRAPHY

The following selected bibliography follows the alphabetical order of the last name.

Books

Moritz Bälz, Marc Dernauer, Christopher Heath and Anja Petersen-Padberg (eds), *Business Law in Japan: Cases and Comments. Intellectual Property, Civil, Commercial and International Private Law* (Alphen aan den Rijn, Kluwer Law International, 2012)

Jürgen Basedow, Harald Baum and Yuko Nishitani (eds), *Japanese and European Private International Law in Comparative Perspective* (Tübingen, Mohr Siebeck, 2008)

Jürgen Basedow, Toshiyuki Kono and Axel Metzger (eds), *Intellectual Property in the Global Arena* (Tübingen, Mohr Siebeck, 2010)

Harald Baum and Moritz Bälz (eds), *Handbuch Japanisches Handels- und Wirtschaftsrecht (Handbook on Japanese Commercial Law and Economic Law)* (Köln, Carl Heymanns Verlag, 2011)

Bessatsu NBL Hensyubu (ed), *Ho no Tekiyo ni kansuru Tsusokuho Kankei Shiryo to Kaisetsu* (*Explanation and Materials on AGRAL*) (Tokyo, Shojihomu, 2002)

Masaaki Haga, *Gaikoku Hanketsu no Shounin* (*Recognition of Foreign Judgments*) (Tokyo, Keio University Press, 2018)

Yasunori Honma, Shun'ichiro Nakano and Hajime Sakai, *Kokusai Minji Tetsuzuki-ho* (*International Procedure Law*), 2nd edn (Tokyo, Yuhikaku, 2012)

Ayako Ikeda (ed), *Kokusai Kaji Jiken no Saiban Kankatsu* (*International Jurisdiction in Cross-border Family Law Matters*) (Tokyo, Nihon Kajo Syuppan, 2019)

Sueo Ikehara, *Kokusai Shiho: Soron* (*Private International Law: General Part*) (Tokyo, Yuhikaku, 1973)

Kazunori Ishiguro, *Gendai Kokusai Shiho: Jou* (*Modern Conflict of Laws in Japan: Volume One*) (Tokyo, University of Tokyo Press, 1986)

Makoto Ito, Masaaki Oka, Mutsuo Tahara, Michiharu Hayashi, Jun'ichi Matasushita, Koji Mori, *Jokai Hasan Ho* (*Commentary on Bankruptcy Act*), 2nd edn (Tokyo, Kobundo, 2014)

Tadashi Kanzaki, *Kaisetsu Ho no Tekiyou ni kansuru Tsuusokuho* (*Commentary on the Act on General Rules for Application of Law*) (Tokyo, Kobundo, 2006)

Kunio Koide (ed), *Chikujo Kaisetsu Ho no Tekiyo ni kansuru Tsusokuho* (*Commentary on the Act on General Rules for Application of Law*) (Tokyo, Shojihomu, expanded edn, 2015)

Toshiyuki Kono (ed), *Intellectual Property and Private International Law* (Oxford, Hart Publishing, 2012)

Toshio Minami, *Kaisei Horei no Kaisetsu (Commentary on the Amended Horei)* (Tokyo, Hosokai, 1992)

Satoshi Minamikata, *Family and Succession Law in Japan*, 2nd edn (Alphen aan den Rijn, Kluwer Law International, 2017)

Yasushi Nakanishi, Aki Kitazawa, Dai Yokomizo and Takami Hayashi, *Kokusai Shiho* (*Private International Law*), 2nd edn (Tokyo, Yuhikaku, 2018)

Yuko Nishitani, *Mancini und die Parteiautonomie im Internationalen Privatrecht – Eine Untersuchung auf der Grundlage der neu zutage gekommenen kollisionsrechtlichen Vorlesungen Mancinis* (Heidelberg, Universitätsverlag Winter, 2000)

Yoshiyuki Noda, *Introduction to Japanese Law* (Tokyo, University of Tokyo Press, 1976)

Yasuhiro Okuda, *Kokusai Kazokuho* (*International Family Law*) (Tokyo, Akashi Shoten, 2015)

—— *Kokusai Zaisanho* (*Private International Law in Business*) (Tokyo, Akashi Shoten, 2019)

Yutaka Orimo, *Kokusai Shiho: Kakuron* (*Private International Law: Special Part*) (Tokyo, Yuuhikaku, 1972)

Karl Riesenhuber and Kanako Takayama, *Rechtsangleichung: Grundlagen, Methoden und Inhalte – Deutsch-Japanische Perspektiven* (Berlin, De Gruyter, 2006)

Karl Riesenhuber and Yuko Nishitani (eds), *Wandlungen oder Erosion der Privatautonomie? - Deusch-japanische Perspektiven des Vertragsrechts* (Berlin, De Gruyter, 2007)

Saiko Saibansho Jimu Sokyoku Minjikyoku (ed), *Kokusai Minji Jiken Tetsuzuki Handbook* (*Handbook in International Civil Procedure*) (Tokyo, Hosokai, 2013)

Yoshiaki Sakurada, *Kokusai Shiho* (*Private International Law*), 7th edn (Tokyo, Yuhikaku, 2020)

Yoshiaki Sakurada and Masato Dogauchi (eds), *Chushaku Kokusai Shio: Dai 1 kan* (*Commentary on Private International Law: Volume 1*) (Tokyo, Yuhikaku, 2011)

—— *Chushaku Kokusai Shio: Dai 2 kan* (*Commentary on Private International Law: Volume 2*) (Tokyo, Yuhikaku, 2011)

Tatsufumi Sato and Yasuhiko Kobayashi, *Ichimon Itto Heisei 23 Nen Minji Soshoho to Kaisei: Kokusai Saiban Kankatsu Hosei no Seibi* (*Explanatory Note on the 2011 Reform of the Code of Civil Procedure and Others: Improvement of the Institution on International Adjudicative Jurisdiction*) (Tokyo, Shojihomu, 2012)

Takao Sawaki and Jun'ichi Akiba, *Kokusai Shiho no Ronten Shinban* (*Points on Private International Law, New Edition*) (Tokyo, Yuhikaku, 1996)

Takao Sawaki and Masato Dogauchi, *Kokusai Shiho Nyumon* (*Introduction to Private International Law*), 8th edn (Tokyo, Yuhikaku, 2018)

Chu'uichi Suzuki and Akira Mikazuki (eds), *Chu'ukai Minji Shikko-ho (1)* (*Annotation on Civil Execution Act*) (Tokyo, Daiichi Hoki Shuppan, 1984)

Masahiro Suzuki and Yoshimitsu Aoyama (eds), *Chu'u Shaku Minji Soshoho (4)* (Tokyo, Yuuhikaku, 1997)

Akira Takakuwa and Masato Dogauchi (eds), *Shin Saiban Jitsumu Taikei (3): Kokusai Minji Soshoho (Zaisanho Kankei)* (*International Civil Litigation Law (Proprietary Matters)*) (Tokyo, Seirinshoin, 2002)

Akira Takakuwa, *Shinban - Kokusai Shotorihiki Ho* (*Law of Cross-border Business Transactions [New Edition]*) (Tokyo, Toshindo, 2019)

Yoshio Tameike, *Kokusai Shiho Kogi* (*Private International Law Course*), 3rd edn (Tokyo, Yuhikaku, 2005)

Muneki Uchino (ed), *Ichimon Itto Heisei 30 Nen Jinji Soshoho Kaji Jiken Tetsuzukiho to Kaisei: Kokusai Saiban Kankatsu Hosei no Seibi* (*Explanatory Note on the 2018 Reform of the Personal Status Litigation Act, Domestic Relations Case Procedure Act: Improvement of the institution on International Adjudicative Jurisdiction*) (Tokyo, Shojihomu, 2019)

Ryoichi Yamada, *Kokusai Shiho*, 3rd edn (*Private International Law*) (Tokyo, Yuhikaku, 2014)

Jun Yokoyama, *Kokusai Shiho* (*Private International Law*) (Tokyo, Sanseido, 2012)

—— *Private International Law in Japan*, 2nd edn (Alphen aan den Rijn, Kluwer Law International, 2019)

Book Chapters

Masato Dogauchi, 'Kokusai Sosho Kyogo' in Akira Takakuwa and Masato Dogauchi (eds), *Shin Saiban Jitsumu Taikei (3): Kokusai Minji Soshoho (Zaisanho Kankei)* (*International Civil Litigation Law (Proprietary Matters)*) (Tokyo, Seirinshoin, 2002)

Hidebumi Egawa, 'Progress or Revision of the Private International Law of Japan' (1962) 6 *JAIL* 1

—— 'International Divorce Jurisdiction in Japan' (1964) 8 *JAIL* 1

Hidebumi Egawa and Sueo Ikehara, 'Divorce in Japanese Private International Law' (1957) 1 *JAIL* 6

Yoshimasa Furuta, 'Sosho Sashitome Meirei' in Akira Takakuwa and Masato Dogauchi (eds), *Shin Saiban Jitsumu Taikei (3): Kokusai Minji Soshoho (Zaisanho Kankei)* (*International Civil Litigation Law (Proprietary Matters)*) (Tokyo, Seirinshoin, 2002)

Sueo Ikehara, 'Kokusaiteki Saiban Kankatsuken' in Chu'ichi Suzuki and Akira Mikazuki (eds), *Shin Jitsumu Minji-Soshoho Koza* (*New Series on Practice of Civil Procedure Law*) (Tokyo, Nihon Hyoronsha, 1982)

Yuji Iwasawa, 'Gaikoku Kokka oyobi Kokusai Kikan no Saibanken Menjo' in Akira Takakuwa and Masato Dogauchi (eds), *Shin Saiban Jitsumu Taikei (3): Kokusai Minji Soshoho (Zaisanho Kankei)* (*International Civil Litigation Law (Proprietary Matters)*) (Tokyo, Seirinshoin, 2002)

Shiho Kato, 'Recent Developments in Rules on Choice of Court Agreements in Japan: New Codification and Remaining Problems' in A Bruns and M Suzuki, *Preventive Instruments of Social Governance* (Tübingen, Mohr Siebeck, 2017)

Toshiyuki Kono, 'Japan' in Adeline Chong (ed), *Recognition and Enforcement of Foreign Judgments in Asia* (Singapore, Asian Business Law Institute, 2017)

—— 'Japan' in Jürgen Basedow, Giesela Rühl, Franco Ferrari and Pedro De Miguel Asensio (eds), *Encyclopedia of Private International Law* (Cheltenham, Elgar Publishing, 2017)
Takeo Kosugi, 'Gaikoku deno Shoko Shirabe' in Akira Takakuwa and Masato Dogauchi (eds), *Shin Saiban Jitsumu Taikei (3): Kokusai Minji Soshoho (Zaisanho Kankei) (International Civil Litigation Law (Proprietary Matters))* (Tokyo, Seirinshoin, 2002)
Yasushi Nakanishi, 'Mass media niyoru Meiyokison, cyberspace deno Chosakuken Shingai tono Kankatsuken' in Akira Takakuwa and Masato Dogauchi (eds), *Shin Saiban Jitsumu Taikei (3): Kokusai Minji Soshoho (Zaisanho Kankei) (International Civil Litigation Law (Proprietary Matters))* (Tokyo, Seirinshoin, 2002)
Kazuaki Nishioka, 'Japan' in Anselmo Reyes, *Recognition and Enforcement of Foreign Judgments in Civil and Commercial Matters* (Studies in Private International Law – Asia) (Oxford, Hart Publishing, 2019)
Yuko Nishitani, 'Party Autonomy and its Restrictions by Mandatory Rules in Japanese Private International Law' in Jürgen Basedow, Harald Baum and Yuko Nishitani (eds), *Japanese and European Private International Law in Comparative Perspective* (Tübingen, Mohr Siebeck, 2008)

Journal Articles

Jun'ichi Akiba, 'The Beginning and Development of Japanese Doctrines on the Private International Law – Koichi Yamaguchi (1866–1945) and Iwataro Kubo (1897–1980)' (2013) 56 *JYIL* 196
Ronald A Brand and Tabitha Fish, 'An American Perspective on the New Japanese Act of General Rules for Application of Laws' (2008) 51 *JYIL* 298
Masato Dogauchi, 'Concurrent Litigations in Japan and the United States' (1994) 37 *JAIL* 72
—— 'Jurisdiction over Foreign Infringement from a Japanese Perspective in Consideration of the Hague Draft Convention on Jurisdiction and Foreign Judgments in Civil and Commercial Matters as of June 2001' (2001) 44 *JAIL* 35
—— 'New Japanese Rules on International Jurisdiction: General Observation' (2011) 54 *JYIL* 260
—— 'The Aftermath of the Fukushima Dai-Ichi Nuclear Accident: How Japanese Lawyers Have Been Playing Their Roles with Regard to the Nuclear Damage' (2018) 61 *JYIL* 284
Beligh Elbalti, 'The Jurisdiction of Foreign Courts and the Recognition of Foreign Judgments Ordering Injunction: The Supreme Court Judgment of April 24, 2014' (2016) 59 *JYIL* 395
Béligh Elbalti and Dai Yokomizo, 'La compétence internationales des tribunaux japonais en matiére civile et commerciale à la lumière de la nouvelle legislation' (2016) 3 *Revue critique de droit international privé* 417
Naoe Fujisawa, 'Cases and Issues in Japanese Private International Law Conflict of Laws in Matters Concerning Property' 53 (2010) *JYIL* 490
Katsutoshi Fujita, 'A New Trend in the Compensation System for International Air Carrier Accidents, the Establishment of the Montreal Convention of 1999 and Recent Airlines Cases in Japan' (2001) 44 *JAIL* 86
Tomotaka Fujita, 'When Does Japan Not Conclude Uniform Private Law Conventions' (2017) 60 *JYIL* 59
Mizuho Hata, 'Kaji Jiken nikakaru Kokusai Saiban Kankatsu' (2018) 27 *Ronkyu Juristo* 39
Shin'ichiro Hayakawa, 'International Aspects of Family Maintenance Law in Japan' (2009) 52 *JYIL* 413
Yoshihisa Hayakawa, 'Japanese Law in the Era of the Internet – The New and Coming Legislation in Japan' (2002) 45 *JAIL* 61
—— 'New Private International Law of Japan: General Rules on Contracts' (2007) 50 *JAIL* 25
—— 'Lis Pendens' (2011) 54 *JYIL* 324
Takami Hayashi, 'International Succession in Japan' (2009) 52 *JYIL* 433
—— 'Cases and Issues in Japanese Private International Law Choice-of-Law Rules to Answer an Incidental Question' (2013) 56 *JYIL* 357
—— 'International Jurisdiction in Cases Related to Succession: New Rules in Japan' (2019) 62 *JYIL* 209
Kiyoshi Hosokawa, 'Ratification of the Hague Convention on the Law Applicable to Maintenance Obligations towards Children' (1977) 21 *JAIL* 115
Sueo Ikehara, 'Nationality in the Private International Law of Japan' (1963) 7 *JAIL* 8
Sueo Ikehara, Akira Takakuwa and Masato Dogauchi, 'Conflict of Laws on Admiralty and Shipping Laws in Japan' (1987) 30 *JAIL* 1
Sueo Ikehara, Ryoichi Yamada and Takao Sawaki, 'Post-War Studies in Private International Law in Japan' (1962) 6 *JAIL* 95

Teruhisa Ishii, 'Carriers' Liability with Particular Reference to the International Carriage of Goods by Sea Act' (1958) 2 *JAIL* 66

Yasuo Ishimoto, 'International Arbitration in the Meiji Era' (1963) 7 *JAIL* 30

Manabu Iwamoto, 'Recognition and Enforcement of Foreign Decisions on Personal Status Litigation and Family Relations Cases' (2019) 62 *JYIL* 226

Tadashi Kanzaki, 'Persons' (2007) 50 *JAIL* 15

—— 'Jurisdiction over Consumer Contracts and Individual Labor-Related Civil Disputes' 55 (2012) *JYIL* 306

Shoichi Kidana, 'Private International Law Principles on Intellectual Property: Recent Development of Court Precedents in Japan and Current Characteristics' (2009) 52 *JYIL* 454

Yoichi Kikuchi, 'Japan's Acceptance of the Hague Convention on the Law Applicable to Maintenance Obligations' (1987) 30 *JAIL* 36

Tokusuke Kitagawa, 'Commercial Arbitration Law and Practice in Japan' (1968) 12 *JAIL* 59

Aki Kitazawa, 'Assignment of Receivables and Set-off' (2007) 50 *JAIL* 77

—— 'Nobushige Hozumi and Saburo Yamada – The Enactment of the Horei of 1898' (2013) 56 *JYIL* 181

—— 'New Legislation on the International Jurisdiction of Japanese Courts on Personal Status Litigations and Domestic Relations Cases: Introductory Note' (2019) 62 *JYIL* 118

Naoki Koizumi, 'Parallel Imports and Intellectual Property Rights in Japan' (2002) 45 *JAIL* 53

Toshiyuki Kono, 'Renvoi in Japan – Doctrine, Precedent and Some Critical Comments' (1992) 35 *JAIL* 62

—— 'Comparative Analysis of Recent Developments in Private International Law in Japan and Europe from a Japanese Perspective' (2008) 51 *JYIL* 217

—— 'The Transparency Project, Its Achievements, and Some Cross-Cutting Issues' (2010) 53 *JYIL* 306

Ryu Kojima, 'Contemporary Problems in Japanese Intellectual Property Law: Copyright Limitations and Exceptions, Indirect Copyright Infringement, and Selected Issues Related to Private International Law' (2010) 53 *JYIL* 358

Souichirou Kozuka, 'The Selective Reception of Uniform Law in Asia' (2017) 60 *JYIL* 86

Takashi Kubota, 'Financial Stability Concern of the Extraterritorial Impacts Caused by the Recent US Financial Sanctions on Foreign Banks' (2016) 59 *JYIL* 229

Peter Mankowski, 'The New Japanese Private International Law Act from a European Perspective' (2008) 51 *JYIL* 241

Junichi Matsushita, 'Transparency of the Japanese Law Project: From the Viewpoint of International Civil Procedure Law' (2010) 53 *JYIL* 377

Hiroshi Mitoma, 'Cross-Border M&As – Japanese Companies and Foreign Investors' (2007) 50 *JAIL* 124

Tetsuo Mitsui, 'Ratification of Convention Relating to Civil Procedure and Convention on the Service Abroad of Judicial and Extrajudicial Documents in Civil and Commercial Matters, and Enactments of Domestic Laws of Japan concerning Enforcement Thereof' (1972) 16 *JAIL* 7

Noriko Mizuno, 'Parent–Child Relationship in the Japanese Civil Code – Regarding Medical Technology for Reproductive Treatment' (2009) 52 *JYIL* 387

Tomonori Mizushima, 'Foreign State Immunity in Japanese Courts at the Beginning of the Twenty-First Century' (2007) 50 *JAIL* 99

Tetsuo Morishita, 'Successes and Failure of Harmonization of Commercial Laws' (2017) 60 *JYIL* 113

Ai Murakami, 'International Adjudicatory Jurisdiction For Divorce Cases' (2009) 52 *JYIL* 583

Masako Murakami, 'Case Proceedings for the Return of An Abducted Child and the Compulsory Execution in Japan' (2014) 57 *JYIL* 33

—— 'Gaikoku Saiban no Shounin, Shikko' (2018) 27 *Ronkyu Juristo* 47

—— 'International Jurisdiction of Child-Related Cases in Japan' (2019) 62 *JYIL* 189

Jiro Muraoka, 'Japan's Participation in the Hague Convention Relating to the Form of Testamentary Dispositions' (1964) 8 *JAIL* 60

Mari Nagata, 'Kokusai Saibankankatsu Kitei no Rippo to Kokusai Torihiki he no Eikyo' (2011) 13 *Kokusai Shotorihiki Gakkai Nenpo* 205

Yasushi Nakanishi, 'Torts' (2007) 50 *JAIL* 60

Shunichiro Nakano, 'International Commercial Arbitration under the New Arbitration Law of Japan' (2004) 47 *JAIL* 96

—— 'Agreement on Jurisdiction' (2011) 54 *JYIL* 278

Tatsushi Nishioka and Takako Tsujisaka, 'Introductory Note: Japan's Conclusion of the Hague Convention on the Civil Aspect of International Child Abduction' (2014) 57 *JYIL* 7

Yuko Nishitani, 'Protection of Weaker Parties and Mandatory Rules' (2007) 50 JAIL 40
—— 'International Jurisdiction of Japanese Courts in a Comparative Perspective' (2013) 60 *Netherlands International Law Review* 251
—— 'Party Autonomy in Contemporary Private International Law: The Hague Principles on Choice of Law and East Asia' (2016) 59 *JYIL* 300
—— 'Treatment of and Access to Foreign Law in Japan' (2018) 46 *Zeitschrift für Japanisches Recht/Journal of Japanese Law* 69
—— 'International Adjudicatory Jurisdiction in Matrimonial Matters in Japan' (2019) 62 *JYIL* 151
—— 'Jinji Sosho Jiken oyobi Kaji Jiken no Kokusai Saibankankatsu tou ni kansuru Shin Hosei (1)' (2019) 71 *Hoso Jiho* 489
—— 'Jinji Sosho Jiken oyobi Kaji Jiken no Kokusai Saibankankatsu tou ni kansuru Shin Hosei (2)' (2019) 71 *Hoso Jiho* 715
—— 'New International Civil Procedure Law of Japan in Status and Family Matters' (2019) 62 *JYIL* 119
Yoshiaki Nomura, 'Activity-Based Jurisdiction of Japanese Courts – A Bold But Unnecessary Departure' (2012) 55 *JYIL* 263
—— 'The Law Applicable to the Assignment of Receivables – Japanese Conflict-of-Law Rules in the Age of Securitization' (1998) 41 *JAIL* 44
—— 'Harmonization and Diversification of Contract Conflicts' (2008) 51 *JYIL* 341
—— 'Fall of Extraterritoriality and Resurgence of Choice of Law in Global Securities Litigation' (2017) 60 *JYIL* 314
Yukiko Oda, 'Japanese Jurisdiction of International Child Custody Cases and Other Parent–Child Matters' (2014) 57 *JYIL* 429
Yuko Okano, 'Japanese Court Cases Involving East Asian Citizens and Corporations – Law Applicable to International Transactions with Chinese, Taiwanese, and Korean Parties before Japanese Courts' (2014) 57 *JYIL* 243
Yasuhiro Okuda, 'Recognition and Enforcement of Foreign Judgments in Japan' (2013/14) 15 *YPIL* 413
—— 'New Rules on International Jurisdiction over Divorce in Japanese Courts' (2018/19) 20 *YPIL* 66
Huang Renting, 'A Comparative Law Analysis on Some Recent Developments in the Conflict of Law Rules of Contract in Japan and China' (2008) 51 *JYIL* 314
Hajime Sakai, 'Enforcing the Obligation to Return a Child in Japan: With Insight into the Recognition and Enforcement of Foreign Judgments in Cross-Border Child Abduction Cases' (2010) 53 *JYIL* 438
Akira Saito, 'International Civil Jurisdiction Based on the Place of Performance of Obligation Relating to a Contract' (2011) 54 *JYIL* 295
Yoshiaki Sakurada, 'The Origin and Evolution of Private International Law in Japan' (2013) 56 *Japanese Yearbook of International Law* 164
Fumihiko Sato, 'Cases and Issues in Japanese Private International Law Acquiring Japanese Nationality Through Recognition' (2011) 54 *JYIL* 443
Yayohi Satoh, 'Law Applicable to Personal Status of Korean and Chinese Nationals before Japanese Courts' (2012) 55 *JYIL* 323
Takao Sawaki, 'Battle of Lawsuits – *Lis Pendens* in International Relations' (1979–80) 23 *JAIL* 17
Hiroo Sono, 'Japan's Accession to and Implementation of the United Nations Convention on Contracts for the International Sale of Goods (CISG)' (2010) 53 *JYIL* 410
—— 'Going Forward with Uniform Private Law Treaties: A Study in Japan's Behavioral Pattern' (2017) 60 *JYIL* 10
—— 'Uniform Law Treaties: Their Reception, Implementation, Success and Failure: Introductory Note' (2017) 60 *JYIL* 4
Kazuaki Sono, 'A Query into the Supremacy of the Traditional Treaty Approach – Experience of UNCITRAL with New Techniques' (1985) 28 *JAIL* 47
Nozomi Tada, 'Enforcement of Foreign Judgments in Japan regarding Business Activities' (2003) 46 *JAIL* 75
—— 'International Civil Jurisdiction Based on the Place of the Tort' 55 (2012) *JYIL* 287
Koji Takahashi, 'Japan's Newly Enacted Rules on International Jurisdiction: with a Reflection on Some Issues of Interpretation' (2011) 13 *JYPIL* 146
—— 'Law Applicable to Choice-of-Court Agreements' (2015) 58 *JYIL* 384
—— 'The Jurisdiction of Japanese Courts in A Comparative Context' (2015) 11 *JPIL* 103
Yuichi Takano, 'International Mediation and Japan: Resume of the Replies of the International Law Association of Japan to the Questionnaire of the Committee on the Charter of the United Nations' (1968) 12 *JAIL* 78

Hiroshige Takata, Muneki Uchino, Mikiko Otani, Masato Dogauchi and Kazuhiko Yamamoto, 'Shogaitekina Jinji Sosho, Kaji Jiken ni kakaru Tetsuzuki Hosei' (2018) 27 *Ronkyu Juristo* 4
Keisuke Takeshita, 'Sadajiro Atobe and Kotaro Tanaka: The Universal Private International Law School of Thought in Japan' (2013) 56 *JYIL* 217
—— 'Critical Analysis of Party Autonomy: From a Theoretical Perspective' (2015) 58 *JYIL* 196
—— 'Atarashii Jinji Sosho Jiken no Kokusai Saiban Kankatsu Kitei' (2018) 27 *Ronkyu Juristo* 31
Morio Takeshita, 'The Recognition of Foreign Judgments by the Japanese Courts' (1996) 39 *JAIL* 55
Yoshio Tameike, 'Nationality of Formosans and Koreans' (1958) 2 *JAIL* 55
—— 'Naien in Japanese Private International Law' (1978) 22 *JAIL* 21
Masayuki Tanamura, 'International Child Abduction Cases and the Act for the Implementation of the Hague Convention' (2014) 57 *JYIL* 2
Junko Torii, 'The Husband's Nationality Principle and the Equality of Both Sexes in International Divorce Cases in Japan' (1978) 22 *JAIL* 104
—— 'Revision of Private International Law in Japan' (1990) 33 *JAIL* 54
Satoshi Watanabe, 'A Study of a Series of Cases Called Non-Recognition of a Judicial Judgment between Japan and mainland China – A Cross-border Garnishment Order of the Japanese Court issued to a Chinese Company as a Third-party Debtor' (2014) 57 *JYIL* 287
Ryoichi Yamada, 'Some Problems of Recent Japanese Precedents concerning Foreign Corporations' (1961) 5 *JAIL* 31
—— 'International Domestic Relations Cases in the Family Courts of Japan' (1965) 9 *JAIL* 69
Ryoichi Yamada, Yoshiro Hayata and Takao Sawaki, 'The Acquisition of Japanese Nationality *Jure Sanguinis* and the Constitution' (1981) 24 *JAIL* 12
Kazuhiko Yamamoto, 'New Japanese Legislation on Cross-Border Insolvency – As Compared with the UNCITRAL Model Law' (2000) 43 *JAIL* 83
—— 'International Jurisdiction Based on the Location of Property' (2011) 54 *JYIL* 311
—— 'Special Proceedings for the Collective Redress for Property Damage Incurred by Consumers' (2018) 61 *JYIL* 168
Dai Yokomizo, 'Cases and Issues in Japanese Private International Law State Immunity From Civil Jurisdiction' (2008) 51 *JYIL* 485
—— 'Hidebumi Egawa: Founder of the Internationalist Tradition in the Japanese Conflict of Laws' (2013) 56 *JYIL* 243
—— 'Conflict of Laws in the Era of Globalization' (2014) 57 *JYIL* 179
—— 'Consumer Collective Redress and Japanese Conflict of Laws' (2018) 61 *JYIL* 189
—— 'International Development of Consumer Collective Redress: Introductory Note' (2018) 61 *JYIL* 167
Jun Yokoyama, 'Cultural Property in Private International Law' (1994) 37 *JAIL* 95

Materials

Legislative Materials

Hosei Shingikai Kokusai Saibankankatsu Hosei (Jinji Sosho Jiken oyobi Kaji Jiken kankei) Bukai Nos 1–18 (Minutes of 1st–18th Meetings (PSLA and DRCPA))
Hosei Shingikai Kokusai Saibankankatsu Hosei Bukai Nos 1–16 (Minutes of 1st–16th Meetings (CCP))
Jinji Sosho Jiken oyobi Kaji Jiken no Kokusai Saibankankatsu Hosei ni kansuru Chukan Shian (Interim Draft (PSLA and DRCPA))
Jinji Sosho Jiken oyobi Kaji Jiken no Kokusai Saibankankatsu Hosei ni kansuru Chukan Shian no Hosoku Setsumei (Hosoku Setsumei (PSLA and DRCPA))
Jinji Sosho Jiken to ni tsuite no Kokusai Saibankankatsu Hosei Kenkyukai Hokokusho (Hokokusho (PSLA and DRCPA))
Kokusai Saibankankatsu Hosei ni kansuru Chukan Shian of 28 July 2009 (Interim Draft (CCP))
Kokusai Saibankankatsu Hosei ni kansuru Chukan Shian Hosoku Setsumei (Hosoku Setsumei (CCP))
Kokusai Saibankankatsu ni kansuru Chosa Kenkyu Hokokusho (Hokokusho (CCP))
Kokusai Shiho no Gendaika ni kansuru Yoko Chukan Shian (Interim Draft (AGRAL))
Kokusai Shiho no Gendaika ni kanausru Yoko Chukan Shian Hosoku Setsumei (Hosoku Setsumei (AGRAL))

Circular Notices and Notifications

Notification No 1722 from Vice-Minister of Justice on 22 September 1953

Circular Notice of Director General of the Civil Affairs Bureau (No 280 of the Civil Affairs Second Division on 14 January 1976)

Circular Notice of Director General of the Civil Affairs Bureau (No.3900 of the Civil Affairs Second Division on 10 July 1989)

Circular Notice of Director General of the Civil Affairs Bureau (No 3900 of the Civil Affairs Second Division on 2 October 1989)

Circular Notice of the Secretary General of the Supreme Court addressed to the presidents of the high courts, district courts and family courts (No 89 of the Civil Affairs Second Division of the Supreme Court on 10 April 1991)

Circular Notification of Director General of the Civil Affairs Bureau (No 2986 of the Civil Affairs Second Division on 5 April 1993)

GLOSSARY OF BASIC TECHNICAL TERMS

Japanese (Roman letter, Kanji character)	**English**
Bukken（物権）	property right
Bunkatsu Shitei（分割指定）	*dépeçage*
Chiteki Zaisan（知的財産）	intellectual property
Chokusetsu Kankatsu（直接管轄）	direct jurisdiction
Chotei（調停）	mediation
Chusai（仲裁）	arbitration
Dairi（代理）	agency
Dai'i（代位）	subrogation
Dosan（動産）	movable property
Doseikon（同性婚）	same-sex marriage/civil union
Forum Non Conveniens（フォーラム・ノン・コンビニエンス）	forum non conveniens
Fudosan（不動産）	immovable property
Fuho Koui（不法行為）	tort
Futo Ritoku（不当利得）	unjust enrichment
Fuyo（扶養）	maintenance/support
Fu'fu Zaisansei（夫婦財産制）	matrimonial property regimes
Giji Gaikoku Gaisha（擬似外国会社）	pseudo-foreign company
Hanchi（反致）	*renvoi*
Ho-iki（法域）	jurisdiction
Horitsu Kaihi（法律回避）	evasion of law/*fraus legis* (*fraude à la loi*)
Hosei Kettei（法性決定）	characterisation
Hoteichi Asari（法廷地漁り）	forum shopping
Igon（遺言）	wills
Jimu Kanri（事務管理）	*negotiorum gestio*

Jisshitsu-ho（実質法）	substantive law
Jittai-ho（実体法）	substantive law
Jokyosho（常居所）	habitual residence
Jori（条理）	rule of reasons, rule of justice
Junkyo-ho Sentaku Kisoku（準拠法選択規則）	choice of law rules
Junkyo-ho Sentaku（準拠法選択）	choice of law
Junkyo-ho（準拠法）/ Tekiyo-ho（適用法）	applicable (governing) law
Jusho（住所）	domicile
Kaihi Joko（回避条項）	escape clause
Kangoken（監護権）	custody rights
Kankatsu Goui（管轄合意）	choice of courts agreements
Kansetsu Kankatsu（間接管轄）	indirect jurisdiction
Keiyaku（契約）	contract
Kojo（公序）	public policy/*ordre public*
Kokusai Saiban Kankatsu（国際裁判管轄）	international (adjudicatory/judicial) jurisdiction
Kokusai Shiho（国際私法）	private international law
Kokuseki（国籍）	nationality
Kon'in（婚姻）	marriage
Koui Noryoku（行為能力）	capacity to act
Kyoko Kitei（強行規定）	mandatory rules
Kyosho（居所）	residence
Meiyo/Shinyo Kison（名誉／信用毀損）	defamation
Mutai Zaisan（無体財産）	intangible property
Ouso（応訴）	submission
Reijo（礼譲）	comity
Renketsu Ten（連結点）	connecting factor
Renketsu（連結）	connection
Rikon（離婚）	divorce
Sai Missetsu Kankeichi（最密接関係地）	the place with the closest connection
Saiken Joto（債権譲渡）	assignment of receivables

Saimu Hikiuke（債務引受）	debt assumption
Seisanbutsu Sekinin（生産物責任）	product liability
Senketsu Mondai（先決問題）	incidental/preliminary question
Senzoku Kankatsu（専属管轄）	exclusive jurisdiction
Shikko（執行）	enforcement/execution
Shinken（親権）	parental responsibility/authority
Shintaku（信託）	trust
Shinyo Jo（信用状）	letter of credit
Shoko（証拠）	evidence
Shonin（承認）	recognition
Sogo no Hosho（相互の保証）	reciprocity
Sosai（相殺）	set-off
Sosho Kyogo（訴訟競合）	*lis (alibi) pendens*
Sosho Sashitome Meirei（訴訟差止め命令）	anti-suit injunction
Sotatsu（送達）	service of process
Souzoku（相続）	succession/inheritance
Syuken Menjo（主権免除）	sovereign immunity
Syuyo（収用）	expropriation
Tanpo Bukken（担保物権）	security rights
Teishoku-ho（抵触法）	conflict of laws
Tekio Mondai（適応問題）	adaptation/adjustment
Tenchi（転致）	transmission
Tetsuzuki-ho（手続法）	procedural law
Tosan（倒産）	insolvency/bankruptcy
Yoshi Engumi（養子縁組）	adoption
Zettaiteki Kyoko Kitei（絶対的強行規定）/ Kyokoteki Tekiyo Hoki（強行的適用法規）	overriding mandatory rules

INDEX